USING THE
IBM PERSONAL COMPUTER

USING THE
IBM PERSONAL COMPUTER

Kenniston W. Lord, Jr., CDP

VNR VAN NOSTRAND REINHOLD COMPANY
NEW YORK   CINCINNATI   TORONTO   LONDON   MELBOURNE

Copyright © 1983 by Van Nostrand Reinhold Company Inc.

Library of Congress Catalog Card Number: 82–15999
ISBN: 0-442-25815-1
ISBN: 0-442-26078-4 pbk.

Manufactured in the United States of America

Published by Van Nostrand Reinhold Company Inc.
135 West 50th Street, New York, N.Y. 10020

Van Nostrand Reinhold Publishing
1410 Birchmount Road
Scarborough, Ontario M1P 2E7, Canada

Van Nostrand Reinhold
480 Latrobe Street
Melbourne, Victoria 3000, Australia

Van Nostrand Reinhold Company Limited
Molly Millars Lane
Wokingham, Berkshire, England

15 14 13 12 11 10 9 8 7 6 5 4 3 2 1

Library of Congress Cataloging in Publication Data

Lord, Kenniston W.
  Using the IBM Personal Computer.

  Includes index.
  1. IBM Personal Computer. I. Title.
QA76.8.I2594L67 1983   001.64   82-15999
ISBN 0-442-25815-1
ISBN 0-442-26078-4 pbk.

Preface

I encountered my first IBM computer 20 years ago. By that time I had all of two months of computer programming under my belt (on another manufacturer's mainframe), and I was off to show the IBM instructor that I knew what programming was all about. It was there at the U.S. Agricultural Department's night school in Washington, DC, that I fell in love with the IBM 1401. It would be another two years before I actually got to *see* one, but I dutifully learned the language with which I would one day communicate with it — the Symbolic Programming System (SPS). I was in the Air Force at the time, involved with computers from UNIVAC, Honeywell, and Burroughs. The 1401 would have to wait until I got out of the service.

By 1965 I was doing software support on the 1401 and loving every minute of it. What magic we seemed to wring out of fewer than 16,000 positions of memory — we called it "core" in those days. We wondered how we would *ever* be able to use all that memory. But alas, it wasn't long before the integrated circuit was upon us, and the 1401 became obsolete. It refused to die, however, and there are still a few around, working as hard as they ever did. In 1975, a couple of years or so before the first commercially produced microcomputer hit the market, I tried, and nearly succeeded, to purchase a 1401 from a power company in Pennsylvania. I simply wanted a computer for my very own — and I was still in love with the IBM 1401.

The PC wasn't my first microcomputer. It simply wasn't the first to become available on the market. Being a very conservative company, IBM waited to determine if a market would develop for the micro, whether it would be profitable, and how it might be serviced. All the while, the micro was drastically changing the shape of the market — particularly for minicomputers — about which IBM had also adopted a wait-and-see attitude before entering. Among the things IBM learned was that the market for microcomputers continued to grow while all the economic indicators indicated that the economy was headed in the opposite direction. More to the point, it was finding that small businesses continued to regard microcomputers strictly as hobby computers and toys, despite evidences to the contrary.

IBM, therefore, chose the month of August 1981 to unveil its own micro-computer — the Personal Computer (PC) — and while it decided to label it *personal,* it is nonetheless hoping that the retail stores that it sets up, its market in the Sears and Computerland outlets, and its direct sales will appeal to the very small (and perhaps not so very small) business that would not otherwise be able to justify a computer system from IBM or any other mainframe vendor.

The PC is much more than just a personal computer. Some will find their way into homes, to be certain. But it is this writer's impression that five years down the road will tell us that the majority of them will be used — at least most of the time — in support of business activities. This book will sample several of the more common uses and show you how the PC can be used in nearly any environment. It is not slated strictly for business — or for school — or for the home. It is not a book of programs, per se. There will be plenty of books of programs available on the market. No, instead, this book presents some applications that may be useful to your use of the PC and details on how this machine is constructed so that you might have a better understanding of it, how it works, how a program is constructed for it, and how you can pay yourself back for your investment. You'll probably purchase some prepared software. You'll probably copy some programs out of a book. But sooner or later you'll want to do something for yourself. No book can ever tell you everything you need to know. Perhaps this one can at least start you off in the right direction.

Kenniston W. Lord, Jr., CDP

Contents

1
Is There a Computer in Your Future?

Forty years ago there was no such thing as an electronic computer as we know them today. Forty years ago we were embroiled in World War II, and electronics development was just coming of age. Although the *concept* of computers had been with us for at least 200 years, it was not until 1930 that an American scientist built the first general-purpose *analog* computer. The war spurred progress, however, and the first electronic *digital* computer was to have been a device capable of calculating artillery shell trajectories. In another development, the British produced an electronic device that sucessfully cracked Axis radio codes. But it would rest with a professor named Howard Aiken, in 1944, to develop the first *information-processing* digital computer. The first commercial computer would not hit the market until 1951, founding an industry whose growth limits have yet to be discovered.

The possibility of the modern computer had existed since the eighteenth century, when scientist Joseph Jacquard designed the first automated loom to weave patterns. Another scientist who followed in the next century, Charles Babbage, invented a mechanical calculator that was not only a direct ancestor of today's computing machines but exhibited all their basic concepts. These were the forerunners of the concepts of computer *hardware* — the physical parts of a computing machine, its nuts and bolts. All the while, there were either pioneers who were developing techniques that would ultimately be implemented upon the computer, either in the form of applications *software* — the programs that enable the system to function — or of improvements to the working of the hardware.

For more than 30 years now, we have been improving on both hardware and software at a rapid pace. With each technological change, new and interesting devices emerge. We have often developed devices before finding profitable and useful ways in which to use them. It can safely be said, however, that the computer has touched our lives in many many ways. Often it may seem that we have been reduced to the status of a number of processing through a computer. Often, even though we may be unaware of it, the computer has made our lives a little easier. One thing is certain — like it or not, the computer is here to stay. As of now, there are any number of computers that you can take home, the PC being but one of them. Whereas for years we could claim that we didn't understand them, it is now possible to understand not only how they work, but how best to put them to use in support of your home, your school, or a business.

The first microcomputer offered to the public was the Altair 8800 in 1975. It was a kit and not very successful, but it did open up the market to the hobby computerist. Recognizing a trend in consumer electronics, two more manufacturers became involved, and in 1977 the TRS-80 Model I (Radio Shack) and the Apple II (Apple Computers, Inc.) were introduced and met with phenomenal results. Many manufacturers climbed on the bandwagon; some fell by the wayside, some have been marginally successful, and some have succeeded in targeting a single segment of the market. By 1981 it had become obvious that the market would continue to grow in quantum leaps. At that point, IBM brought forth its Personal Computer (PC).

The PC is not only a good microcomputer but one available at an affordable price. IBM has the distribution and service facilities necessary to bring the microcomputer into the home, school, or office as a consumer item. On the surface, a computer might seem like a luxury, a sophisticated toy. And, of course, it *can* be used as a toy, because there are countless games that can be played on a micro. But the PC has many more important uses than this. Some of them can be accomplished right now. Others, such as its use in electronic mail networks, must await the passage of time.

A GLIMPSE AT THE FUTURE

Towards the end of the twentieth century, or early in the twenty-first, we will begin sending our correspondence by electronic mail. The U.S. Postal Service has already begun to investigate ways to establish an electronic mail system (EMS). To use the EMS, you'll write a letter on your microcomputer, transmit it, and the letter itself will appear on the computer of the recipient at some distant point, having traveled through the telephone or satellite network. The response can appear on your computer within minutes. It is possible that the charge for such a service will be small in comparison to postal or long-distance telephone rates. One advantage among many might be quaranteed delivery at very competitive prices in comparison to other forms of guaranteed delivery. We are beginning to see some evidence of such message-handling procedures now with the appearance of computerized bulletin boards throughout the country. There are also a variety of services that will provide information directly to the computer — agricultural and stock market news and information, time-sharing networks, and the like. By the time this book appears, IBM will have a working network.

People without microcomputers would be able to receive messages through a service similar to that of the current Mailgram. Junk mail could be screened out by blocking it with codes given to a computer program. Although advertisers might have a fit, this feature would allow individuals to exercise some control over incoming mail and manage their time more profitably. They might decide to have the computer produce a list of their correspondents to determine which mail to read first. In fact, it may become possible for a home or business computer to read all correspondence and present only the most important items for viewing. The logical next step would be to have the computer automatically reply to routine correspondence, based upon guidelines prepared by the individual.

Using a micro, you would be able to prepare a single invitation and have the computer distribute it to potential guests via their own home computers. They, in turn, would be able to reply in a matter of minutes. Such conveniences are for the future, of course, but it is a realistic view of the future. Even now, you can use a micro to remind you of birthdays and anniversaries. You can even use it to generate nearly similar letters. One day it will enable you to order that new outfit from Sears, a special tool from Black & Decker, your groceries, or whatever. Coupled to a standard television set, your computer will enable you to view these purchases before you buy them. Think of the possibilities the computer offers to those people who are housebound. In fact, strong evidence indicates that more and more work will done at home with a micro interfaced with a larger computer. Trips to the office will then become the exception, not the rule. The same can be said for specialized education.

The electronics funds transfer system (EFTS) already in existence, will find its full implementation in the home computer. Using EFTS, you'll be able to complete both a purchase and all the financial work at the same time. The sequence of events will work like this: Any purchase will result in the purchased product being sent to your home and the act of the purchase will cause funds to be transferred from your bank account directly into the bank account of the supplying firm. At that point, the firm's computer will take over, keeping its books, accounting for its inventory, etc. Several such "call and pay" services have already sprung up around the country. The home computer will allow you to have more control over the process, providing reports of your purchases, alerting you to the availability of bargains, and so forth. In other words, your computer will be able to do your shopping for you.

Every convenience just mentioned applies to the small businessman as well. The very same activities required by General Motors are also required by Acme Machine Repair; only the scale is different. GM must maintain a payroll. So must Acme. GM must purchase raw materials. So must Acme. GM has an assembly line to schedule. Acme, a large machine repair company, also requires some scheduling. GM must plan its cash flow. Acme has been planning its own with pencil and paper, but it could well use a computer. GM must track its payables. Acme has bills to pay as well. An so on and on. The point is that microcomputers can provide the capabilities of a very large business to the Mom and Pop Store on the corner.

Whole libraries will be placed "on-line" to personal microcomputers. Your Johnny will be able to research his paper at the country's largest libraries. Lawyers tie onto a precedents service, such as Westlaw, saving them hundreds of hours of investigation. The ability to capture the best of what others have already accomplished will be at your fingertips.

For a number of years, computers have been the basis of "word processing systems," used until now exclusively in businesses, and large businesses at that. A microcomputer will put word processing at your own beck and call. You can do form letters, produce manuscripts like this one, maintain mailing lists. Students will love the ability to produce letter-perfect documents. We've advanced so far that there are even automated dictionaries that check each word entered for correctness of spelling and grammar.

What does the proprietor of a small machine shop have in common with Johnny's mother? Both are responsible for someone who needs to learn. For Johnny, a microcomputer can be a tireless tutor to train him in his multiplication tables or his deductive reasoning through scientific analysis. For the machine shop proprietor, a microcomputer can provide a tool for the job education of his employees. Using microcomputers as a teaching device is one of their best applications, and we will live to see the time when it will be possible to check out a tutorial program from a library as easily as it is now possible to check out a book.

Computers will be an integral part of the design of the home of the future and will provide a variety of services for its management. It will be installed much as heating or plumbing systems are installed today. It will take over the kitchen functions of food storage, preparation, and cooking. It will provide security functions, from screening visitors to locking doors at predetermined times. It will be applied for energy conservation, selecting the forms of energy to be used in terms of cost and comfort. Not least, it will become a handy tool for entertainment.

You probably would not want it used for entertainment in a small business environment (or at least to let your employees know it could be), but there will be plenty of work for it to do. This book will discuss in detail some of the things the computer can accomplish at work. If you want to stay at work after hours to play chess against the computer, who would mind? But you should not purchase a microcomputer for home *or* office for the sole purpose of playing games. Less expensive devices are available for that. Just remember that quite a number of things the computer can do for you in a business environment are equally applicable to the home.

MONEY MANAGEMENT

Logging Checks

Needless to say, every check you write will not automatically appear on your computer. You'll have to enter such information as it occurs. The computer *will* keep an accurate balance of your account, however. To be sure, you could do that with an inexpensive calculator, but consider how much time and expense you could save if, at the end of the year, your computer tells you precisely how much sales tax you have paid and how much you have spent for medical expenses, auto repairs, etc. These necessary details for itemizing expenditures on your tax report could result in savings that alone would justify the purchase of the computer. In a small business, your accountant will insist that such costs be itemized because they are part of the cost of doing business.

Balancing the Checkbook

A computer can post returned checks and then compute the balance automatically. We have been moving for some years now toward what has been termed a "checkless society." In time, thanks to the microcomputer, the use of checks to effect transactions may disappear altogether. Although the checkless society will not be with us for some time, in the meanwhile it's nice to have a microcomputer to take over the balancing headaches we face every month. That's certainly one chore a small businessman can do without. Even if he hires a bookkeeper, the latter's task can be greatly simplified by a microcomputer.

Investments

If you have an interest in stocks or bonds, the microcomputer will allow you to manage your own portfolio. Having your own device to compare investments, returns on investments, and potential areas of investment could not only save brokerage fees but allow you to plan your investment programs more thoroughly. If your investments are in the form of property — or if your small business is the purchase and operation of property — a microcomputer can provide the necessary procedures for tracking rents, scheduling repairs, planning escrow accounts, comparing interest rates on available money sources, etc. Computer programs already exist to assist you in such planning.

Cash Management

A computer can advise you when bill payments are due and specify the optimum time for making those payments. Many firms offer terms for early payment, such as a 2 percent discount if the invoice is paid within 10 days. Since money can be saved by keeping track of when those discounts are available, you can draw interest up until the final day when the invoice must be paid.

Other Business Uses

Anything that can be counted, scheduled, sequenced, or controlled is a likely candidate for the microcomputer. Business accounts receivable, customer files, salesman records, payroll, commissions, raw material planning, bill of materials, job shop tickets, production line scheduling, accounts payable, business forecasting, and general ledger accounting are just a few of the jobs a microcomputer may be applied to in a business setting. So you're not GM — perhaps you're only Acme — but you must still do these things, even if some of them only intuitively.

Other Personal Uses

You can use the microcomputer to keep track of your car's mileage, using this data to determine your operating costs, schedule necessary maintenance, and account for taxes. You can use it to plan trips and give cost-effective alternatives. You can use it to shop for groceries, keep inventory of the pantry or the freezer, prepare the meals, schedule critical tasks like the kids' chores, monitor heat costs, and so on. If you must supply heat to rental property, monitoring the gallon usage can be extremely important.

Education

Don't overlook the tremendous value of microcomputers for education both at home and on the job. As educators become accustomed to their use, entire learning modules similar to those now used by many schools will be developed in a variety of subject areas for home and business applications. The computer has tremendous capabilities for subject exploration and repetitive drill. Unlike human teachers, it never gets angry or tired. And even though many things cannot be computerized — one could never learn how to handle dynamite using a computer, or season a steak, or play a piano — a micro can certainly be used to tutor a child in geography, a young man in auto mechanics, a young lady in pattern-making, an adult in computer programming or systems analysis, and a retiree in tracing his genealogy. It can even help a part-time writer do his thing. I know.

The song is endless, and there will be enough variations on the theme for people to find the microcomputer up to the challenge for decades. Unquestionably, it will become ever more capable. What I can now hold in the palm of my hand, twenty years ago I would have had to walk into. Twenty years from now will hold many more miracles, and our children will find the computer to be as commonplace as television. Some reading this book will remember, as I do, a time when there was no television, when we wondered if our grandparents had had automobiles when they were kids. Read on.

2
How Computers Work

If you look inside the **IBM PC**, you might become convinced that if you can't understand what you see, it might be beyond you. Nothing could be further from the truth. We need not be experts on the internal combustion engine to use the family car; we need not be refrigeration experts to use a refrigerator or air conditioner. There are many devices we use daily whose inner workings are *technically* beyond our understanding but which we know we can use for our benefit. The same is true of the microcomputer.

What *is* important is that we understand how the computer *operates* and how we can cause it to perform functions for us. It's something like the control exercised by pressing on an accelerator, which causes a car to increase speed. Such action activates a lever, which in turn causes certain changes to take place in the car's engine. With a computer, control takes two forms: *external* controls, which cause certain things to happen on the inside of the computer, and *internal* controls, which cause things to happen automatically.

The external controls take the form of switches and keys on the computer's keyboard. The internal controls are customarily embodied in a *program*. A program is a sequence of steps that are defined to the computer in advance in such a way that the computer can perform them automatically. Although there are many ways to program a computer, programming is usually the function of a computer *language*. Many languages are available for the PC, among them *Pascal* (a microcomputer scientific language), *FORTRAN* (an older, more mathematically oriented scientific language, usually implemented on larger machines, *COBOL* (an Englishlike programming language, used primarily for business applications), *FORTH* and *LISP* both list-oriented languages, and the most common of all microcomputer languages, *BASIC* (*B*eginners *A*ll-purpose *S*ymbolic *I*nstruction *C*ode). BASIC, which is distributed with the PC, is a language implementation similar to that of other microcomputers. I say "similar" because the majority of the BASIC implementations on microcomputers are products of the *Microsoft* Corporation; the similarity, however, stops there. PC BASIC has features and requirements that make it unique.

In simple terms, every computer must have a means for accepting the entry of data — a process called *input*. The means available to a PC take several forms, the most common being a *keyboard*. With a keyboard you can develop programs, build data files, respond to program commands, and so on. Another means of entering programs or data to a PC is the cassette tape. Cassette tapes allow purchased programs to be entered or will store programs that you have developed yourself. *General Note:* Although the PC offers many optional features, such as expanded memory, this book has been purposely structured to show what can be done with the minimum configuration (perhaps the first configuration you will be able to purchase). The author will, however, point out at various places in the text where alternative facilities may be used.

Other forms of input available to the PC are diskettes (5 1/4-in. size), digitizers (devices for reducing graphics to digital information), and "joy sticks" (levers that are customarily used for games). For purposes of this text, we will concentrate on the keyboard and cassette tape but will set programs up for diskette where appropriate. The devices are the ones most commonly used. It may be asked why no more coverage is given to the diskette, as you will not doubt have diskette capability ultimately. There are many reasons, but the one most to the point is the following. To use diskettes with a PC, you must first acquire one of two available items of executive software, called an *operating system*. The two available operating systems for the PC are the DOS (*Disk Operating System*) and the CP/M (Control Program/Monitor). The intricacies of a diskette-based operating system are beyond the scope of this book.

Every computer has a place to store programs and information. It is called *memory*. The memory of the PC is a semiconductor device called a *chip*. The amount of memory available for the PC ranges from 16K to 256K, in 16K increments. Since "K" is equal to 1,024 positions of memory, a 64K-machine actually contains 65,536 positions. Similarly, a 128K machine contains 131,072 positions. The memory is used to hold both programs and *variables*, the latter being numeric or alphabetic data for which special positions of memory are designed. The memory is actually contained within the keyboard.

Also enclosed in the system unit, in addition to the memory, is the electronic hardware that controls the *logic*, that is, the sequence of events that takes place within the computer. The logic section is part of the arithmetic/logic unit (ALU), which also contains the electronics for performing calculations.

Finally, every computer has some form of *output*. In the case of the PC output, takes the form of printed output (on a matrix printer), displays on either a monochrome or color display screen, on cassette, or on diskette. The word *monochrome,* by the way, means "one color." The display screen that accompanies the basic computer is one color — green. Interfaces are available to allow you to connect to black-and-white and color television sets. There are a variety of printers on the market, moreover, that can be used to produce paper (hardcopy) output.

Memory positions are technically called *bytes*. Each byte can be used to store a single alphabetic character (letters A to Z), a single *special character* (punctuation marks and symbols), or a numeric value in the range of 0 to 255. Many of these bytes will be used to contain the program you develop or purchase and are *running*. Some will be used to contain the data upon which the program will operate. These data are called *variables*, of which there are a variety of types. For simplicity, we'll refer only to *numeric variables* (the alphabetic letters A to Z) and to *alphabetic variables* (often called *string variables,* and denoted A$ to Z$). There are many other types and configurations of variables, but these two account for the majority of types you will encounter until you begin to use your PC more extensively.

NUMERIC VARIABLES

Let's concentrate first upon the numeric variable. Suppose, for instance, that the numeric variables A to Z represent addresses of houses on a street, addresses that correspond to persons whose last names begin with one of those letters. Your name is Jones, and you live in house *J*. Mrs. Smith customarily lives at house *S* but is currently in the hospital. You have decided to collect money from your neighbors for a get-well present for Mrs. Smith. Other people who live on the street are: Mr. Brown, who lives at house *B*; Mrs. Greene, who lives at house *G*; Mrs. Martin, who lives at house *M*; and Mrs. Rogers, who lives at house *R*. Get the picture? We have labeled each house with a letter that serves as a symbol for its occupant and its address, and we'll treat each address as a repository of funds. For purposes of this example, your house and the total dollars you collect will *both* be given the numeric variable *J*. You decide to kick the fund off with a contribution of $8. At this moment,

$$J = 8$$

In the computer, we would place the number 8 — meaning 8 dollars — in the numeric variable *J*.

Mr. Brown chips in 10 lovely crisp dollar bills. Up to this point, those 10 dollars were located at *B*, that is, *B* = 10. But now, since Mr. Brown has given them over to you, *B* = 0. On the majority of microcomputers, the zero is "slashed" to distinguish it from the letter "O." Depending upon which type of printer you obtain, the zero may or may not be slashed in the printed output. In this book, we will not use the slash.

Up to this point, all that was located at *J* was 8, but because of Mr. Brown there are not $18 at your house. In other words,

$$J = J + 10$$

That equation might seem a little confusing. How can *J* be equal to itself plus 10? Well, the first *J* is known as the *result,* or *sum.* Taking the original value of *J*, 8, and adding to it the 10 that represents Mr. Brown's contribution provides a *new J*, or result, of 18. If we knew for sure that all the money Mr. Brown had was $10, then the equation could have been expressed as *J = J + B*. But we do not know that for certain. In our examples, we will continue to compound the dollars at the single address *J*.

Technically, your original fund contained nothing − 0. Thus, initially,

$$J = 0$$

To that you added $8, as follows:

$$J = J + 8$$

And then, Mr. Brown's $10:

$$J = J + 10$$

J now holds the number 18, which is the representation of the $18 you have acquired for the fund for Mrs. Smith. Next, Mrs. White appears and she offers to double the amount you have already collected − two times $18, or $36. How would that be expressed on the computer? Like this:

$$J = J * 2$$

In the computer language BASIC, the asterisk (∗) signifies multiplication. In this case, we took the value of *J*, 18, multiplied it by 2, and stored it again at *J*. *J* now has a new value of 36, representing $36 for the Smith Fund. The use of the asterisk is required by computer convention to distinguish it from the "X" we use when calculating by hand. Don't forget that *X* is one of the numeric variables.

Mrs. Smith calls from the hospital to say she's just heard about the fund. Although appreciative of your efforts, she tells you that she's quite comfortable and doesn't really need the money. She asks you instead to distribute the money to her three favorite charities: the Heart Fund, the Cancer Fund, and the Home for Little Wanderers. Furthermore, she advises that Mrs. Greene (house *G*), Mrs. Martin (house *M*), and Mrs. Rogers (house *R*) are collecting, respectively, for those funds. How do we indicate that on the computer? Well, we know that Mrs. Greene is going to get one-third of the Smith Fund for the Heart Fund and that she lives at house *G*. We therefore divide our pile of dollars by three, as follows:

$$G = J/3$$

In this instance, we took the value of the dollars at J, 36, divided it by 3 (the slash, $/$, is the computer's division symbol), and stored 12 at G. In other words, we said that G is equal to one-third of J, but just because we said so does not mean that we have taken the 12 away from J to give it to G. We must now tell the computer that the fund (J) is minus \$12. That's done like this:

$$J = J - G$$

Why didn't we just say that J was equal to J minus \$12? We could have done so in *this* instance, because we *know* the value of J. Suppose, however, that there had been other contributors. We needed to take merely a third of the Smith Fund, and that third is presently located at G. Thus, if the dollars at G are removed from the dollars at J, our totals will remain accurate.

Now there are \$24 left at J, half of which is to go to Mrs. Martin for the Cancer Fund and half to Mrs. Rogers for the Home for Little Wanderers. The following instructions will place the funds in the proper place:

$$M = J/2$$
$$R = J/2$$

Of course, since nothing is left in your fund now, once again

$$J = 0$$

There are, of course, many ways to obtain the desired result. We could have repeated the steps taken above and subtracted the variable from J ($J = J - M$ and $J = J - R$), but the result would be just the same.

On first examination, you'll note that we have created a series of very simple formulas, but programming the PC need be no more complicated than this for any problem.

If you have bought this book *after* acquiring your PC, you will already be familiar with the instructions IBM has provided, and no doubt the place you purchased the computer has shown you how to hook it up and get it started. It is not the intention of this book to show you how to operate the PC. The manufacturer's directions and any local instruction you have received should be more than adequate. What we're attempting to do here is to explain some of the thinking that goes into developing a computer program, using BASIC as its language. For want of a better term, we'll call this process *problem solving*.

GETTING STARTED

The PC, as you receive it, will be comprised of at least three parts. There will be the *keyboard*, the *system unit*, and the *display*. The latter you will have obtained either with the system or separately. The keyboard provides the essential means of communication with the system unit, which contains the memory and interfaces necessary to operate the computer. The "Guide to Operations" that accompanies the computer will show you how to hook up the machine. The BASIC language is distributed with the computer, held internally in what is known as *Read Only Memory* (ROM). In actuality, there are three versions of BASIC: Cassette BASIC, Disk BASIC, and Advanced BASIC. Disk BASIC is used with systems configured for a Disk Operating System (DOS). Advanced BASIC is configured for use with a color monitor, requires Disk BASIC, and includes features to handle colors, color graphics, and music. The differences between Disk BASIC and Advanced BASIC will be discussed in a later chapter. We will concentrate primarily upon the use of Cassette BASIC because it is the language distributed with the machine. Doing so will allow the first-time user to get a taste of developing programs at the elementary level before proceeding to more complex workings.

Because there are three separate BASIC configurations, the keyboard reacts differently to each. Before developing the concept of a program, we should therefore concentrate upon some features of the machine and some features of its language, Cassette BASIC. It should be mentioned that even if you purchase a machine with DOS and the other BASICs, you can still operate with Cassette BASIC.

If your computer is off, turn it on. The BASIC start-up screen will be displayed. If your computer is on, press the CTRL and ALT keys simultaneously *and then* press the DEL key. Doing so will show the BASIC start-up screen. This screen will be similar to the one displayed here.

```
The IBM Personal Computer Basic
Version C1.00 Copyright IBM Corp. 1981
xxxx Bytes free
Ok

—

1LIST       2RUN       3LOAD"       4SAVE"       5CONT, etc.
```

Looking at the screen, the "C" of "C1.00" (notice that display zeroes are slashed) stands for Cassette Basic. If a "D" appears, that stands for Disk BASIC. Advanced BASIC shows an "A." Instead of the "xxxxx," you will see some number that indicates how much room the computer memory contains for your programs and data.

"Ok" is the prompt provided by BASIC, telling you that it is looking for something to do. That something may be the entry of a program, the operation of a program, or a calculator mode statement. More about those later. Suffice it to say now that when you see "Ok," you know you're in BASIC mode.

The line that begins with "1LIST" is a reference to what are called *function keys*. At the left side of your keyboard is a double row of keys marked "F1" to "F10" (the latter shown as just 0 on the screen). These keys have predefined functions. Unless changed, they provide keyword commands to the computer and are programmed for Cassette BASIC as follows:

F1   "LIST": This BASIC keyword is used to display upon the screen any program statement you have developed. You can either type the word "LIST" into the machine (followed by "ENTER," as discussed below), or you can press this function key.

F2   "RUN": This BASIC keyword assumes that you have a program present in the computer's memory and causes it to commence execution from the beginning.

F3   "LOAD": This function key causes a program to be read from a cassette and stores it in main memory.

F4   "SAVE": This function key causes a program to be stored on cassette.

F5   "CONT": This BASIC keyword causes the program to be restarted after it has been interrupted by a STOP command from within the program or a CRRL BREAK from outside the program.

F6   "LPTI": This BASIC keyword refers to the line printer (if one is available) and transfers what appears on the screen to the printer.

F7   "TRON": This key, known as "trace on," causes the line numbers of program lines to be displayed on the screen.

F8   "TROFF": This key reverses the function of F7.

F9   "KEY": This key allows you to change the function of the function keys.

F10   "SCREEN": This key returns the program to character mode from graphics mode and turns off the color.

In Cassette BASIC, F10 does not apply. Although F7 and F8 will be useful to trace the execution of a difficult program, they require you to have some knowledge of what you're doing (the manual accompanying the machine will explain their use). Essentially, then, since you will probably not have a line printer at the outset, the first five function keys will be sufficient for your use — and perhaps even a little over your head. Hang in there — we'll get to them in time.

CURSOR CONTROL KEYS

There are several keys that affect the cursor, which indicates the position where data is to be shown on the screen. Also, there are a couple of other keys that affect the operation of the keyboard. Let's look first at those five keys to the left of the standard typewriter keyboard, top to bottom:

ESC   This, the ESCAPE key, removes the list line indicated by the cursor for corrections but does not delete it from memory.

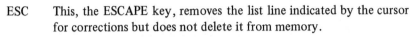   These are the TAB keys, left and right. Tabs are set after every eight characters and work just like those on a regular typewriter.

CRTL   The CONTROL key is always used with a second key for specific commands or functions. These will be identified as necessary.

⇧   This is the shift key that changes lower-case letters to capital letters.

ALT   The ALTERNATE key is used with the alpha keys for the entry of BASIC keywords.

⬅   This is the BACKSPACE key, which moves the cursor to the left and removes one character each time it's pressed.

⬅⏎   This is the ENTER key, which completes the entry of a line and positions the cursor at the beginning of the next line. This may be thought of as a RETURN or Carriage Return key.

USING THE NUMERIC KEYPAD

In the PC, the numeric keyboard is what is called an *enabled pad*. It cannot be used unless the NUM LOCK key is pressed. The NUM LOCK key is called a *toggle key*. Use of the keypad is detailed fully in the "Guide to Operations" book. For the time being, the numbers along the top row of the keyboard are the most useful for program entry. It's safe to say that the numeric keyboard would be better used for entering numeric data to a program.

SMITH FUND ACCOUNTING

Let's now walk through the Smith Fund program we've just discussed to see what the computer will do with it. Type the following into the PC:

J = 8   ENTER

What happened? What you typed is visible on the screen, often called the CRT (*C*athode *R*ay *T*ube), but otherwise nothing much seems to have happened. So try this next:

PRINT J   ENTER

Well, this is different. In addition to the things you've typed, there now appears the number 8. What happened was that with J = 8 you set the variable J equal to 8, and with PRINT J you instructed the computer to display the value of variable J on the screen, which it did. Now type this:

J = J + 10   ENTER

Other than what you just typed, nothing else seems to have happened. So type this:

PRINT J   ENTER

The number 18 comes back. So far the program seems to be working just like the example. Type this:

J = J * 2   ENTER
PRINT J   ENTER

If you did everything correctly, the answer 36 should now be displayed. To proceed, type this:

G = J / 3   ENTER
PRINT G, J   ENTER

Here we've done something slightly different. We've set G equal to a third of the value of J and then displayed the values of both G and J. As you can see, G certainly equals 12, but J still contains 36. In other words, J is unchanged. That's why you should type the next instructions:

J = J – G   ENTER
PRINT G, J   ENTER

The variables should now be shown at their proper values. When you PRINT more than one variable, separated by a comma, the values of the variables will be "printed" (displayed) in different *zones*. There are five zones on the screen. To print the variables closer together, substitute a semicolon (;) for the comma, like this:

PRINT G; J   ENTER

See the difference? Now it's time to divide up the remainder of the Fund between Mrs. Martin and Mrs. Rogers with the following instructions:

```
M = J / 2          ENTER
R = J / 2          ENTER
PRINT G, J, M, R   ENTER
```

If you did this correctly, the screen should show, left to right, the numbers 12, 24, 12, and 12, one to each zone. Now, to "empty" J, type

```
J = 0              ENTER
PRINT G, J, M, R   ENTER
```

The screen should show 12, 0, 12, and 12. Does it?

Now, let's dress the display up a bit by identifying who gets what, as follows:

```
PRINT "MRS. GREENE", G    ENTER
```

What happened? Did Mrs. Greene's name and the value 12 appear on the screen? They should have, because any time you PRINT something that is enclosed in quotation marks, it should appear on the screen. Be very careful about where you type the quote in relation to the comma. "MRS. GREENE," will produce an error because a comma before a quote is used to separate the *operands* of a PRINT instruction. If you used the comma correctly, Mrs. Greene's name will appear in zone 1 and the amount (variable G) in zone 2.

Up to this point, we've operated in what is termed *direct* (often called *calculator*) *mode*; that is, we have used the IBM PC in much the same manner as we might use an inexpensive hand-held calculator. In the calculator mode, things happen more or less immediately. However, the strength of the computer is its *indirect mode,* which causes things to happen *automatically*. A program can therefore be developed to handle specific data even though that data is unknown until the program is operated more on this later.

Before we leave the calculator mode, however, let's try something else with the instructions,

```
J = ( (G * 2) + M) / R    ENTER
PRING J                   ENTER
```

If you typed that into the computer and pressed ENTER at the appropriate place, the computer will tell you how many people contributed to the fund. As you can see, the formula is different from the earlier ones, but, in fact, you have done nothing different from what you've been doing all along. The inserted parentheses group the actions to be taken in a specified sequence. In the computer's order of things, you have to multiply G by 2 *before* you can add M to it, and you have to add M *before* dividing the total by R. The parentheses, in other words, specify the order of operation of an instruction within the computer. The inside parentheses must always be "cleared" first, followed by the next set.

Now try the operation this way:

PRINT ((G * 2) + M) / R   ENTER

It works just the same. To illustrate the importance of the parentheses, try the same formula without them, as follows:

PRINT G * 2 + M / R   ENTER

In the first instance, you came up with 3. In the second, you came up with 25. Do you know why? Here's how to find out. Type

PRINT G * 2   ENTER

and you should get back 24. Type

PRINT M / R   ENTER

and you should get back 1. The sum of them, of course, is 25.

ENOUGH, ALREADY — LET'S PROGRAM

You could continue to operate in the calculator mode and cause the computer to produce answers for you. Suppose, however, that you want to display all the answers at once rather than singly as they occur. Furthermore, suppose that you want a method whereby *any* contributor could contribute to *any* fund, which would then be redistributed to *any* charity of his or her choosing. In other words, the very concept of a program is that it can be operated automatically so long as you provide data for it, presenting the information you choose. Moreover, you want *one* computer to provide all those services.

A program is to a computer what a road map is to a traveler. It is a way to get from here to there, making the necessary stops along the way and making the necessary alterations en route occasioned by changes that can only be determined en route. To the computer, a program is the prespecification (thinking through) of a process you wish it to undertake. Like a note left for a friend, you detail the steps you'd like him to accomplish, advising him of alternatives, and instructing him in methods. And just like the note does, you number the steps. In BASIC, here is the short program that plots the route for the Smith Fund:

```
10    J = 0
20    J = J + 10
30    J = J * 2
40    G = J / 3
50    J = J – G
60    M = J / 2
70    R = J / 2
80    J = 0
```

Before entering the program listed above, clear the computer by hitting the CTRL and BREAK keys together. If you have acquired the system printer, press the Shift and the PRT SC key after the program has been entered to give you a print-out of what appears on the screen. Once you have the entire program entered, run it (type RUN ENTER or press function key 2). What happened? It looks as if nothing has happened, but many things have happened *inside* the PC. All the answers determined by the program now reside in the computer, but the computer hasn't told anyone about it. You didn't tell it to.

As you typed the instructions into the IBM PC, you may have wondered why you didn't number the steps 1, 2, 3, etc. You did; only you did it in multiples of 10. You could have used any number, so long as the next number was larger than its predecessor, but spacing of 10 units between instructions is normal because it allows you to insert instructions later between the ones you've already written. For example, type the following instructions:

```
15    PRINT J
25    PRINT J
35    PRINT J
45    PRINT G, J
55    PRINT G, J
65    PRINT M, J
75    PRINT R, J
85    PRINT J
```

Again, after each statement, press ENTER.

When you have completed the entry of these instructions, type LIST   ENTER (or use function key 1). If you have a printer, type (shift) PRT SC   ENTER. You should now see the entire program arranged in proper sequence on the screen. Now, type RUN   ENTER (or F2). The display should look like this:

8	
18	
36	
12	36
12	24
12	24
0	

Well, you have your answers, but there are other items of information of the screen, and you don't really know, from looking at them, what those numbers really represent. To get rid of the extra information on the screen, insert the following instruction:

5   CLS

CLS stands for *clear screen*, and 5 is the instruction, or statement number.

RUN the program again. Doesn't that look better? Still, since you don't really know what the numbers mean, it's time to modify the instructions to relate something meaningful. Type the following, followed by LIST   ENTER. By the way, we're going to drop the mention of ENTER at this point; just remember that it must be pressed *whenever* you complete an entry.

```
15   PRINT "MRS. SMITH'S FUND:"; J
25   PRINT "MRS. SMITH'S FUND:"; J
35   PRINT "MRS. SMITH'S FUND:"; J
45   PRINT "MRS. GREENE'S FUND:"; G, "MRS. SMITH'S FUND:"; J
55   PRINT "MRS. GREENE'S FUND:"; G, "MRS. SMITH'S FUND:"; J
65   PRINT "MRS. MARTIN'S FUND:"; M, "MRS. SMITH'S FUND:"; J
75   PRINT "MRS. ROGERS' FUND:"; R, "MRS. SMITH'S FUND:"; J
85   PRINT "MRS. SMITH'S FUND:"; J
```

You'll note that these statement numbers have been used before. When you retype them, they replace the old statements. The ability to do so is useful so long as the instructions are improved, as they are in this case, but be careful not to rewrite an instruction you don't intend to rewrite. Note that there is a space after the colon in each of the statements; this space keeps the number contained in the variable separated from the message. Now run the revised program. Doesn't it look better?

What you've done is to trace the progress of the Smith Fund, the Cancer Fund, the Heart Fund, and the Fund for Little Wanderers. Generally speaking, we're interested only in the final results and not in the process and contents as we go along. The exception is when we must use the intermediate results to *debug* (check for errors) the program. So, let's get out the eraser. Since you can delete a line simply by typing its line number, type 5, 15, 25, 35, 45, 55, 65, 75, and 85. Was all that effort wasted? Not really, because you did get to see what was happening, and now you know some of the steps you must take to debug the program.

With that done, add the following instructions

```
 90    PRINT "MRS. SMITH'S FUND:"; J
100    PRINT "MRS. GREENE'S FUND:"; G
110    PRINT "MRS. MARTIN'S FUND:"; M
120    PRINT "MRS. ROGERS' FUND:"; R
```

and run the program again. There should be four lines in the upper left-hand corner of the screen, containing the name and amount of each fund. Add the following termination instruction (merely a branch to itself, to freeze the display), and run the program again:

```
130    GOTO 130
```

You have now written and successfully run a computer program. The GOTO of the last statement is called an *unconditional branch* because it offers a means of change sequence without having to meet conditions. In this instance, the GOTO references the instruction that contains it. It keeps the computer operative but in a "locked" mode.

Let's recap what we've done so far. We have talked about the *calculator* (direct) *mode* and seen what it can do. We have also talked abou the *command* (indirect) *mode*. Recall that the calculator mode functions precisely as a hand-held electronic calculator. The command mode includes all those actions at the keyboard that provide, amongst other things, the means to list a program on the screen, a function key to list that program onto hardcopy, and a combination of keys to break the instruction sequence.

By now you've discovered that your PC can handle both upper- and lower-case letters, but there are other function keys you still need to know about. We've learned that we can use letters to represent numbers or, more specifically, the *value* of numbers. The letters used (J, G, M, R) are called *numeric variables*. Actually, the setting of the numeric variable to a value is an abbreviated form of another BASIC instruction called LET. Statement 10 could have been written like this:

```
10    LET J = 8
```

The designers, in their wisdom, however, decided to let us express the instruction without having to type LET every time.

We've also learned that information can be displayed on the screen by using the PRINT instruction and that anything enclosed in quotation marks appears on the screen just as it has been typed. We've learned, moreover, that semicolons in the PRINT instruction cause numbers to displayed in positions adjacent to other displayed information and that commas present information in zones.

Finally, we've learned that if we want to "short-circuit" the instruction sequence, we have only to instruct the computer to GOTO some statement number. In the preceding example, we had the BASIC instruction 130 GOTO go to itself, thereby causing the computer to seem to stop. In reality, it continues to operate, but the operation is not obvious because it takes place inside the machine and is not apparent on the CRT.

Look at the list you produced on hardcopy, if you did so, and even at the list of your program on the screen. Right now you are fully aware of what you tried to do. Six months down the line, however, you might have difficulty recapturing what you originally tried to accomplish. It would be useful to be able to put comments in the program, right? Right. Comments are entered with REMark statements, such as the following:

```
1    REM * MY FIRST PROGRAM *
```

If you brought a system with a 256K memory, don't worry about the space occupied by comments; comment liberally. If you bought a system with a 16K memory, however, you will have to recognize that each REMark occupies memory space.

When we wrote statement 130, we wrote it as a GOTO to itself, causing the computer to continue to operate and to "hang." If you really do want the computer to come to a halt, replace statement 130 with either the END command or the STOP command, as follows:

```
130    END
```

or

```
130    STOP
```

Try it both ways. You'll see that the only perceptible difference is that with STOP you'll get a "break" message as well as a prompt. Both commands stop the machine, but STOP makes it possible to resume operation using another command instruction, CONT, which is short for CONTinue. CONT is also a function key, as described previously.

ADAPT, ADAPT

Given our fund-raising problem and the values we have been using, the resulting answers will be precisely the same each time the program is run. Suppose, however, that we don't know the initial value of J and want to adapt the program to allow *any* value. Here's what to do:

```
10    INPUT J
```

That's all. Now, instead of giving J an initial value of 8, the computer will ask you what you'd like J to be. It will give a prompt, followed by a question mark, followed by the cursor (the position indicator on the screen). You must then enter the value that you'd like J to be. Note that the INPUT statement caused the computer to stop temporarily to await an answer. If you change statement 130 to GOTO 5, the computer will stop at statement 10 every time. Try doing so, entering different values for J. Note that a long as you enter a number, you will get an answer in return. Now try the same thing again entering an alphabetic letter. You'll see that the computer will not permit you to do so and will indicate an error.

The INPUT instruction is like PRINT because it allows a message to be displayed on the screen. Retype statement 10 as follows:

```
10    INPUT "ENTER AMOUNT CONTRIBUTED TO THE SMITH FUND:"; J
```

and run the program again. You'll see that it takes the value you give it — J in this case — and returns the correct answer.

AN IMPERFECT MACHINE

Computers do not operate perfectly; they are subject to error. They are, however, subject to errors of a predictable nature, and because these are predictable, we can compensate for them. This fact can be demonstrated by multiplying a number by its reciprocal. Type in and run the following:

```
PRINT (1/3) * (3/1)
```

By your own calculation you would get the number 1, but what result did you get from the computer? The computer, unfortunately, is subject to a precision problem because it is a decimal and not a fractional machine. For instance, it writes the fraction 1/3 in decimal form as 0.3333333333 . . . , and the 3's go on forever. Thus, the computer instruction yields a number slightly less than 1. Interestingly enough, the statement PRINT (1/4) * (4/1) would work out the way you'd expect. Note that the preceding operation was performed in calculator mode. One of the fine features of *interpretative BASIC* (which is the technical name for it) is that you can include a STOP command anywhere in the program, display (PRINT) the results of any variable within the program, and then CONTinue with the program.

DETERMINING THE SIZE OF MEMORY

Whatever size of memory you determine to purchase, the system will announce the memory space available when you first start it up. Once you enter programs, however, it is nice to be able to determine the remaining available memory. That's done with the FRE command. You have only to enter the following in command mode:

PRINT FRE (0)

The number now presented on the screen will tell you how much memory remains. Each character on the screen that you have entered occupies one memory position, *except* for the line number. The line number is stored in *binary* and occupies two bytes only. The mandatory space after the line number accounts for a third byte.

For example, the author's system is a 64K system, which means that there are 65,536 positions of memory in the machine. Yet, when the system is turned on, the message indicates that there are only 61,404 bytes available. Did somebody eat the remaining 4,132 bytes? It would seem so, but no, that storage space is merely overhead. To determine the amount of overhead in your system, multiply the memory you purchased (in the author's case, 64K) by 1,024 and subtract from it the free space, as follows:

PRINT (64 * 1024) – FRE (0)

ERROR CONDITIONS

The PC has 49 predetermined error conditions, 29 of which are applicable to the BASIC language itself. The remaining 20 deal with a variety of input/output conditions and other facilities and functions that will be useful for you to know as you become more sophisticated about the machine. In addition, in Advanced BASIC, to which you may later move, it is possible to define your own error conditions and to modify your program's direction accordingly.

Appendix A of the "IBM BASIC Reference" book will give you each message number and its explanation and remedy in detail. Only the number and type of the message will be shown here:

1. NEXT without FOR
2. Syntax error
3. RETURN without GOSUB
4. Out of data
5. Illegal function call
6. Overflow
7. Out of memory
8. Undefined line number
9. Subscript out of range
10. Duplicate definition
11. Division by zero
12. Illegal direct
13. Type mismatch
14. Out of string space
15. String too long
16. String formula too complex
17. Can't continue
18. Undefined user function
19. No RESUME
20. RESUME without error
21. Unprintable error
22. Missing operand
23. Line buffer overflow
24. Device timeout
25. Device fault
26. FOR without NEXT
27. Out of paper
29. WHILE without WEND
30. WEND without WHILE

No mistake was made. There is no message numbered 28. WEND and WHILE, by the way, are BASIC keywords for use in a concept called *structured programming.*

MATH OPERATORS

In our little fund-raising program, we used some *math operators*, the symbols =, +, −, *, and /. Respectively, they indicate equation, addition, subtraction, multiplication, and division [what the PC calls *floating point division*, to distinguish it from *integer division*, denoted by a *backslash* (\)] . The computer is, of course, a number machine, but it is decimally, not fractionally, oriented. When you begin to use or obtain very large or very small numbers, therefore, some strange things happen. The PC uses *standard scientific notation* (also called *exponential notation* or more simply *E-notation*) in the presentation of very large or very small numbers.

To illustrate, let's examine the number 8 in our decimal system. In the decimal system, the number 8 is really 8. (eight followed by a decimal point, or 8.0). What would 8 million look like? It would look like 8000000. (commas are not used to punctuate numerical data within a computer). That's eight followed by six zeros and a decimal point. In mathematical parlance, 8 million is

$$8 * 10 * 10 * 10 * 10 * 10 * 10 \qquad \text{or} \qquad 8 * 10^{+6}$$

The PC, like many computers, would express this number in what is called *E-notation.* Eight million would then look like 8E+6. If the number gets too large, the PC shifts from E mode (also called *single precision*) into D mode (*double precision*). Thus, 8 followed by 17 zeroes would become 8D+17. It's not likely that you'll encounter many numbers like this, but it's helpful to know what you're looking at. The important thing to remember is that counting begins at the decimal point.

RELATIONAL OPERATORS

The computer is also a *logic* machine. It has a mechanical ability, or more specifically, an electronic ability, to reason. By *reason*, we mean the ability to make very simple decisions of the IF ... THEN variety. In reasoning, the computer also uses its numbering abilities to compare numbers or characters to other numbers or characters. It can do so because each number or character has a numerical value or weight. The number 2 is "heavier" — that is, larger — than the number 1. The letter B is "heavier" than the letter A. In the PC, each letter is represented by a number. The number for the capital letter A is 65. The number for the capital letter Z is 90. The rest of the capital letters fall between these two values. In fact, everything within the machine is represented by numbers in the range of 0 to 255, known as the *character set*, and is coded in what is known as the ASCII convention. ASCII stands for the *A*merican *S*tandard *C*ode for *I*nformation *I*nterchange.

Suppose that we have two numeric variables, A and B. Both contain a number, but these numbers are not known. The numbers may be alike, or they may be dissimilar. Variable A may be greater than variable B (correspondingly, variable B is less than variable A). A may not be equal to B. B may be equal to or greater than A (which is, by definition, less than or equal to B). Get the picture? On the PC, we express it by using these *relational operators*:

OPERATOR	RELATION TESTED	EXAMPLE
=	EQUALITY	A = B
<> OR ><	INEQUALITY	A <> B ; A >< B
<	LESS THAN	A < B
>	GREATER THAN	A > B
<= OR =<	LESS THAN OR EQUAL TO	A <= B ; A =< B
>= OR =>	GREATER THAN OR EQUAL TO	A >= B ; A => B

These relational operators are customarily placed into a IF . . . THEN statement, as follows:

```
10 B = 8
20 IF B >= 6 THEN 50
```

In this instance, B contains the value 8, which is definitely greater than or equal to 6. The program sequence will then proceed to statement 50.

The use of the relational operators in an IF . . . THEN statement constitutes a *conditional branching* situation. The first variable (or number) following the IF is compared to the second variable (or number), and a branch is taken to the THEN address if the condition is met. The statement could have been written as follows with the same results:

```
20 IF 6 <= B THEN 50
```

It is important to remember that the branching takes place conditionally upon the relationship of the first variable, or, more specifically, the contents of those variables. If the branching to the THEN statement address is not taken, the computer assumes that the condition has not been met, and the program proceeds with the statement that follows statement 20.

In our funds program at statement 130, we told the computer to GOTO. GOTO is an example of an *unconditional* branch, that is, one that requires no conditional operators. The GOTO is customarily used to return to an instruction at the beginning of a process called *looping*. It's also used for changing direction within a program. Let's try some of these abilities in a program:

```
5 CLS
10 A = 0
20 B = 5
30 C = 10
40 IF A > B THEN 90
50 PRINT "A not greater than B"
60 IF A <> B THEN 120
70 PRINT "A is equal to B"
80 GOTO 140
90 IF A = C THEN 160
100 PRINT "A is greater than B but less than C"
110 GOTO 140
120 IF A > B THEN 90
130 PRINT "A is less than B"
140 A = A + 1
150 GOTO 40
160 PRINT "A is equal to C"
170 END
```

A general thought about this program: As you use the PC, you'll find that it's easier to enter programs in lower-case letters. The BASIC interpreter will change them to upper-case letters, except for data contained between quotation marks.

This little program exercises all but the greater than/less than/equal combinations and thus gives an indication of how conditional branching systems work. Enter the program into your PC and run it. Your display should show the following:

```
A not greater than B
A is less than B
A not greater than B
A is less than B
A not greater than B
A is less than B
A not greater than B
A is less than B
A not greater than B
A is less than B
A not greater than B
A is equal to B
A is greater than B but less than C
A is greater than B but less than C
A is greater than B but less than C
A is greater than B but less than C
A is equal to C
```

Now, just so you may see what has happened, the program will be modified slightly to present the variables as they are treated. Changes have been made in statements 50, 70, 100, 130, and 160, as shown below:

```
5 CLS
10 A = 0
20 B = 5
30 C = 10
```

```
40 IF A > B THEN 90
50 PRINT "A not greater than B",,A;"   ";B;"   ";C
60 IF A <> B THEN 120
70 PRINT "A is equal to B",,A;"   ";B;"   ";C
80 GOTO 140
90 IF A = C THEN 160
100 PRINT "A is greater than B but less than C",A;"   ";B;"   ";C
110 GOTO 140
120 IF A > B THEN 90
130 PRINT "A is less than B",,A;"   ";B;"   ";C
140 A = A + 1
150 GOTO 40
160 PRINT "A is equal to C",,A;"   ";B;"   ";C
170 GOTO 170
```

Run the modified program, and the following will result. Do not be concerned about the alignment of numbers in the final line. Examine the modified statements and you'll note that the first variable was printed on a zone boundary.

```
A not greater than B                              0     5    10
A is less than B                                  0     5    10
A not greater than B                              1     5    10
A is less than B                                  1     5    10
A not greater than B                              2     5    10
A is less than B                                  2     5    10
A not greater than B                              3     5    10
A is less than B                                  3     5    10
A not greater than B                              4     5    10
A is less than B                                  4     5    10
A not greater than B                              5     5    10
A is equal to B                                   5     5    10
A is greater than B but less than C               6     5    10
A is greater than B but less than C               7     5    10
A is greater than B but less than C               8     5    10
A is greater than B but less than C               9     5    10
A is equal to C                                  10     5    10
```

ABOUT THE EDITOR

What if you wish to change a statement? The IBM PC is different from most microcomputers in that its editing features are hardware rather than software oriented. Its editor is enabled by setting the NUM LOCK in the off (or *unlocked*) position. If you follow these steps closely, you will learn just how powerful this editor can be:

1. Press the CTRL key and the numeric pad 7 (marked "Home"). You'll note that the screen is cleared and the cursor is now blinking in its upper left corner. Where did everything go?

2. Press F1. This will display the BASIC keyword LIST on the screen. Now press ENTER. The program just entered shown now be on the screen, followed by the prompt (Ok) and the cursor.

3. Type KEY OFF and press ENTER. The bottom line disappears. It can be returned simply by typing KEY ON. In the off position, nothing is on the screen but your program.

4. What you have now on the screen is a representation of what is in memory. As you work on the program, remember that *any* change that is followed by an ENTER will return that statement (only) to memory. To ensure that all the changes you wish to make are actually made, make *all* necessary changes *in a single statement* and then hit ENTER.

5. You already know what happens when you press the Home key. Now press the "up" arrow (keypad 8) and watch what happens. Press it several times. Then, in succession, press the "down" arrow (keypad 2) and the left and right arrows (keypads 4 and 6). Even run them off the edge of the screen in both directions. Interesting.

6. Now position the cursor on any statement number and change the number by typing over it. Then press ENTER. Repeat Steps 1 and 2, above, and you'll note that you've created a new statement simply by changing the number. Note that the original statement is still displayed.

7. To remove a statement, simply type its number and press ENTER.

8. To add a statement, simply type a new statement (with an unused number) and press ENTER. If you use a statement number that has been used before, the original statement will be replaced.

9. Position the cursor somewhere in the middle of a line. Let's assume that you want to delete the character at that position. Now press the decimal point key on the numeric keyboard, also marked "Del." Note that the character disappears and the others jump to the left to fill in the space.

10. Now let's add a couple of characters. Press the zero key, also marked "Ins." Enter the new characters and then either press the Ins key a second time or press ENTER.

11. Whenever you press keypad 1, "End," the cursor will jump to the end of the current line. You can then use the cursor control keys as described, or you can use the backspace key, which will erase each character as it reaches it.

12. If you wish to access a specific line, just type EDIT n, where n represents the line number. The rest of the program still works the same.

It takes a little getting used to, but the editor is powerful and easy to use.

KEEPING A COPY OF THE PROGRAM

What if your programming is interrupted by such mundane activities as getting a night's sleep or going to work? If you have opted for the cassette version of

BASIC, it will be necessary to supply your own cassette recorder and to purchase a cable connection to the system unit. A note of caution here. There is a jumper that must be set at the store to allow you to use a cassette, and the cable must be fabricated by the store since it's not provided by IBM. The connections are critical, as follows:

1. Block the AUX with a dummy plug. Since the PC is different from other microcomputer systems, be careful to do so.
2. The motor control is the smallest of the three plugs and must be plugged into the REMOTE jack.
3. The connector that will transmit the audio tone *to* the recorder from the system unit must be plugged into the MIC jack, but *when in use only*.
4. The connector that will transmit the audio tone to the system unit *from* the recorder must be plugged into the EAR jack, but *when in use only*.
5. *Do not* plug in the MIC and EAR plugs simultaneously. Be extremely careful to label them (have the store label them) if they are not already so labeled.
6. You'll have to experiment with volume level. IBM says "up full." The author's experience is that it should be set at about 75 percent.
7. Position the recording tape *beyond the leader* before transmitting data to the recorder from the computer.
8. The recording and playing functions are your responsibility since they are *external* to the computer. When you tell the computer to record, it turns on the motor and moves the data towards the recorder. If the recorder is not set up to record, it will not work. Generally speaking, the RECORD button is colored and must be used in conjunction with the PLAY button. When the computer is reading programs or data, it is your responsibility to set the PLAY button.
9. The save command, which must be entered in direct mode, is:

SAVE *filespec*, where *filespec* is *devicename:filename*

In Cassette BASIC, the cassette is assumed, but the devicename can be entered as CAS1: (including the colon). The filename may be as many as eight characters in length and use any combination of letters and numbers as well as the symbols $ and @ . Refer to the section on "Disk Differences," later in the book, for diskette information. There are a couple other options, but let's keep it simple for now.

10. The program can be read back into the computer from the cassette by using the instruction:

LOAD *filespec*

The same rules apply as before. If you want to get cute, you can type:

LOAD filespec, R

and the result will be the same as if you had loaded the cassette and typed RUN ENTER or had hit F2.

That's all there is to it, but it does take some practice.

IF YOU HAVE TROUBLE

Since expertise in saving and loading of tapes comes with practice, experiment on small programs that don't matter until you get the hang of it.

Care for your tapes. Keep them in cases, stored away from dust. Clean the heads of the cassette recorder frequently with a cotton-tipped stick and some rubbing alcohol (they work as well as anything you can purchase). Make several copies of your programs on the tape. Experience has shown that "outside" copies of a program on a magnetic tape are often destroyed by magnetic interference. The interference can come from any source — the display unit used with your computer, the telephone, an electric clock, etc.

Purchase a tape degausser. The package will advise you of the motions to use when "cleaning" a tape. Be very careful to avoid holding the degausser close to other tapes when you use it (the instructions say no closer than 3 ft). The wisest practice is to leave the degausser in another room. Keep everything away from motors and appliances. And then, if the program is really important, put one copy in a safe deposit box at a bank or other secure location.

You can always tell if a program has loaded properly. Just hit F1 and then ENTER.

It's possible to record on both sides of a tape, but, it's not recommended. When the tape is new and the oxide is strong, it's OK. After use is another question. Take into consideration that a C-30 tape is heavier than a C-120 tape and will therefore wear better.

Now let's get back to business.

LOOP CONTROL

You will recall from the previous discussion that when a sequence of instructions is repeated, the process is called *looping*. Occasionally it is necessary to control the number of times we go through the loop. This process is called *iteration*. The instruction to be used is the FOR instruction, which works in conjunction with the NEXT instruction. The pair of instructions surrounds the loop. For example, and to have a little fun, type

```
10 FOR N = 110 TO 3520
20      SOUND N,2
30 NEXT N
```

If this doesn't make your dog howl, nothing will. What happened? Well, we used a nifty little instruction that generates sound, beginning at the musical note A (two octaves below middle C) and sliding upward for six octaves. Make the following change to statement 20 so that you can see what took place:

```
10 FOR N = 110 TO 3520
20      SOUND N,2:PRINT N;
30 NEXT N
```

And then, just to preserve your sanity, change the program to this:

```
10 FOR N = 110 TO 3520 STEP 110
20      SOUND N,2:PRINT N;
30 NEXT N
```

Note that the FOR instruction involves the use of a numeric variable (in this case N) and a range through which the count is to be made (in this case from 110 to 3520). Unless the STEP instruction is used, the incrementation is made by a single unit (1), which you no doubt saw on the screen. The inclusion of STEP 110 merely increments the variable N by that amount (110) with each cycle. Now let's modify the FOR . . . NEXT concept just a bit:

```
10 CLS
20 FOR S = 0 TO 59
30      PRINT S;
40 NEXT S
50 GOTO 10
```

Now run the program. What happened? Oops! That's *movin'*! In fact, it's *still* going, and it will continue forever unless interrupted or the power fails. How could that possibly be useful? Who wants to count from 0 to 59 anyway? Anyone who wants to build a clock. Look over the above, and you'll see that what we've set up is a nifty way to count seconds. Unfortunately, however, it's moving too fast to be accurate, and so we change the program to look like this:

```
10 CLS
20 FOR S = 0 TO 59
30      PRINT S;
35      FOR N = 1 TO 500:NEXT N
40 NEXT S
50 GOTO 10
```

Run the program again. What happened? It slowed down, didn't it? Hold CTRL and BREAK, and run the program again. Time the computer against a wrist watch with a sweep-second hand. A new number should appear on the screen every second. If the hand on the watch runs faster than the computer, decrease the count at statement 35. If the hand on the watch runs slower than the computer, increase the count at statement 35. Note that the extra spacing in statements 30 and 35 are for readability.

How does the program work? The first thing we did was to set up a controlled loop that begins at 0, increments by 1 until variable S reaches 59, resets, and then starts over again. That controlled loop looks like this:

```
20 FOR S = O TO 59
 . . .
 . . .
40 NEXT S
```

In other words, those instructions that fall between statement 20 and statement 40 will be done a total of 60 times (0 to 59). Embedded within the FOR ... NEXT loop just mentioned is another FOR ... NEXT loop that counts from 1 to 500. The PC can perform approximately 500 single-step FOR ... NEXT loops in 1 second. Thus, for every time through the "S" loop, the printing of the variable S will be done at a rate of approximately one per second.

Thus, the "N" loop has been made subordinate to the "S" loop. This procedure is called *nesting*. Loop "S" has a nested loop "N." Can that same principle be extended to the hour and minute hands? Certainly, but we'll have to start over. By the way, the addition of the semicolon to statement 30 merely allows continuous printing on the same line. Delete it, run the program again, and watch it work without it.

Now type the following, observing the spacing given:

```
10 CLS
20 FOR H = O TO 23
30     FOR M = O TO 59
40        FOR S = O TO 59
50           LOCATE 13,32
60              PRINT H; ":";M; ":";S
70              FOR N = 1 TO 500:NEXT N
80           NEXT S
90        NEXT M
100 NEXT H
110 GOTO 110
```

The spacing shown in statements 30 through 90 allows you to determine how the FOR ... NEXT loops are paired. The only thing different from what we have discussed is the LOCATE instruction. LOCATE takes the form *x, y,* where x is the vertical row (range 1 to 25 if KEY OFF; 1 to 24 if KEY ON) and y is the horizontal column (range 1 to 80). LOCATE 13,32 positions the display centrally on the screen. This function is similar to the "PRINT @ " used in other microcomputers, should you be asking.

This set-up is all very nice, but unless you plan to wait until midnight to run it, it won't keep accurate time. (If you take out the timing loop, you'll be able to see the whole thing function under test.) How should the "clock" be set? Enter the following:

```
12 INPUT "ENTER HOUR"; A
14 INPUT "ENTER MINUTE"; B
16 INPUT "ENTER SECOND"; C
```

Now edit statements 20, 30, and 40, substituting "A," "B," and "C" for the zero in each case. Also, let's calibrate the "clock" by changing statement 70 as previously discussed. Run the program and let it go for 5 minutes or so.

At the end of some significant time, look at your watch. Does the time indicated on the screen match your watch? If you made the entry at the beginning of an hour, it's probably pretty close. But if you made your entry at 10 minutes to the hour or 10 seconds to the minute, you'll note that something is not quite right. Let the computer run another 10 or 15 minutes. When you come back, you'll note that things have gone from bad to worse. Why? Probably the hour indicator is still OK, because you haven't been gone that long. But no doubt the minutes indicator is 15 or so more than it should be, and the seconds indicator is liable to be anywhere.

The reason why this has happened is that a FOR . . . NEXT loop increments from the initial value you give it — which in this case was the hour (A), minute (B), and second (C) — continues through until it finds the higher value, and then *resets to the initial value that you gave it.* If you had made your entry at 10 minutes before the hour (50), you'll "burn up" an hour every time you count to 10. Obviously, that's not right. We want that 59 at the second and minute indicators to revert to 0 even though we have entered something else at first. Here's what you should do to make this happen:

```
85 C = 0
95 B = 0
105 A = 0
```

Adjust the horizontal spaces on these instructions to make the symmetry correct. Now run the program again, entering the correct time to begin with, and then check the time again in 5 minutes or so. It should be pretty close. To calibrate the "clock" more closely, all you'll have to do is modify the count in statement 70.

Want to have a little fun? Try these changes:

```
 20 FOR H = 23 TO A STEP -1
 30      FOR M = 59 TO B STEP -1
 40           FOR S = 59 TO C STEP -1
 85           C = 59
 95      B = 59
105 A = 23
```

Make the entries and run the program to see what it does, but first note the changes in the FOR statements. The controlled loop can be incremented (+) or decremented (–) by adding the STEP modifier, as mentioned in the SOUND instruction discussed previously.

Note that the program gets longer than can be LISTed on the screen. There are two ways to see only that portion which is of interest:

1. LIST without a range, pressing CTRL and BREAK at the appropriate moment.
2. LIST a specified range, as follows (using 100 and 200 as examples):

> LIST 100-200 lists an inclusive range.
> LIST -100 lists everything up to and including 100.
> LIST 100- lists everything from 100 to the end.

PRINTING TO THE DISPLAY SCREEN

PRINTing is really another way to say that a computer must have a means to produce output. There are several forms of output available to the PC – print-out (on paper), disk, cassette, and even a communications line. The form we must first study, however, is the display on the output screen. Note that we are still discussing the monochrome screen.

The BASIC command PRINT sends output to the display screen. Its counter-part for hardcopy (paper) output is known as LPRINT (or "line print"). The discussion of LPRINT will be reserved for later.

There are several ways to position information upon the screen. Two of them we have already discussed: normal display (the PRINT instruction merely displays a new character in the next available position) and LOCATE which selects a specific place on the screen). Also, we've talked about PRINTing in contiguous spaces (those immediately adjacent to the previous position) and in zones.

It is important to distinguish between the *physical line* on the screen and the *logical line* that is to be displayed. In simple terms, a physical line is a fixed area of space on the face of the screen. There are 25 physical lines on the face of the PC's monochrome display, numbered 1 to 25. Also, there are horizontal positions on each physical line, and they are numbered, beginning with 1 and ending at either 40 or 80, depending upon the WIDTH option you have selected.

Since you must set the screen to a width of 40 to use it, the default is to a width of 80, and we'll deal with the latter width throughout these discussions. Thus, the physical layout of the screen is a 25 by 80 matrix. The LOCATE instruction used previously placed the cursor at line 13, column (horizontal position) 32.

Suppose that it is desired to print the message "HELLO, SAM" somewhere on the screen. You've developed an application to teach your child Sam how to add; he has entered his name in the PC and now you wish to greet him. For all intents and purposes, the message "HELLO, SAM" may be thought of as the logical line in search of a physical line on which to be placed. If you want to PRINT it next in sequence, then any physical line will do. If it must be located in a specific place, then you must use the LOCATE command to assign that place. As mentioned before, all that LOCATE does is position the cursor.

Management of the screen may be very important to your application. If you fill it up and then go one line beyond, the new line will be added to the bottom and all the lines above it will be shifted up one line. This effect is c lled *scrolling*. For programs developed in BASIC, the scrolling actually takes place at line 24 and not at line 25 since the twenty-fifth line is reserved for the display of the function key designations. If you wish to get rid of the latter, then you must command the PC to KEY OFF. The function keys themselves are not disabled, but they will not be displayed on the screen.

As mentioned, a display line contains 80 spaces. If a message is to be presented on the physical line correctly, the spacing must be planned during the construction of the message. If the message is a single unit of fewer than 80 spaces, then there is no problem provided that the message begins at the left margin. To place it elsewhere, however, requires some knowledge of where you are and how the instruction itself is constructed. Recall the previous discussion of the PRINT instruction. To suppress a linefeed, a semicolon was used within the print instruction itself and therefore the next character was PRINTed on the same line; a comma was used to print in zones. If nothing is placed at the end of the line, the computer inserts the linefeed. Examine, please, the following two instructions. Enter them, run them, and then add a semicolon at the end of statement 10 and run them again.

```
10 PRINT "This statement contains";"an error."
20 PRINT "This statement contains";" no errors."
```

As can be seen, the instruction in statement 10 will create an erroneous message (which will nevertheless be displayed). The means to correct the message is to embed a space before the second part of the message, as in statement 20. The displayed output from these instructions will look like this:

```
This statement containsan error.
This statement contains no errors.
```

The spacing of mixed lines is extremely important. Recall the PRINT line that was used in the clock example: PRINT H;":";M;":";S. If you took a good look at the screen, you may have noted that there were spaces surrounding the numeric variables. This space is customarily reserved for a sign, and positive signs (+) are not displayed. In this instance, the colon is enclosed within the quotation marks, meaning that it is a part of the data to be displayed. If it were between two instructions on the same line, it would function as an *instruction separator*. Insofar as BASIC instructions are concerned, there must be spaces surrounding numbers, but spaces surrounding instruction operands are not necessary, although acceptable.

The completion of a PRINT instruction forces a carriage return. Ordinarily, any PRINT instruction following a PRINT instruction with carriage return will display on the next available line (unless a LOCATE is used). However, if the PRINT instruction is terminated by a semicolon, the carriage return will be suppressed. For example, the instructions

```
10 PRINT "Printing this way ";
20 PRINT "allows you to ";
30 PRINT "break up the ";
40 PRINT "instruction without ";
50 PRINT "breaking up ";
60 PRINT "the line."
```

produce output that looks like this on the screen:

```
Printing this way allows you to break up the instruction without breaking up
the line.
```

Now word of caution. The appending of a printed line to a previously printed line is strictly contingent upon the ability, spacewise, to fit the *entire next message on the same display line*. Observe statements 50 and 60 above and then observe the printed output or display upon the screen. The addition of the two words in statement 60 was too much for a screen whose width has been defined as 80 characters. Although you can enter an instruction with as many as 254 characters and the line "wrap" as needed, the same is not true of printed output. It looks that way, of course, but move the word *the* from statement 60 to statement 50 and you will see the following:

```
Printing this way allows you to break up the instruction without
breaking up the line.
```

If you type PRINT with nothing following, you'll get only a linefeed or a blank line. A question mark can be used as shorthand for the PRINT instruction and gets translated for you. If you follow the PRINT statement with a variable expression (A, B, C, etc.) the values of those variables will be displayed —

contiguously if separated by a semicolon or in one of the zones if separated by a comma. If you wish to use a string expression, you may use either a string variable (A$, B$, C$, etc.) or enclose the string within the print instruction itself, between quotation marks. If spacing for several messages is required and you find that the previously described methods don't work, there are still a couple of ways to accomplish it — embedded spaces or tabulation.

Before we look at tabulation, however, change the PRINT instructions to LPRINT instructions (if you have a printer), and run the program again. You'll find that it works precisely the same way on the printer. There are many things we can do with the IBM matrix printer available with the system. We'll discuss them later on.

TABULATION

One interesting variation of both the PRINT and the LPRINT commands is the ability to structure the screen into columns very easily. It could be structured in zones, of course, but this approach limits you to five zones of 14 positions. That problem is solved by the TAB subsection of the PRINT (and LPRINT) command. Consider the following instructions:

```
10 PRINT TAB(10);"CHECK";TAB(20);"PERSON";
20 PRINT TAB(30);"AMOUNT";TAB(40);"DATE OF"
30 PRINT TAB(9);"NUMBER";TAB(21);"PAID";
40 PRINT TAB(31);"PAID";TAB(41);"CHECK"
```

If you enter these statements and then run them, you'll see headings line up as follows:

```
CHECK       PERSON    AMOUNT    DATE OF
NUMBER      PAID      PAID      CHECK
```

Then, in successive lines, you can align the data to be presented in the same manner. There are two important things to remember about TAB:

1. It is separate operation in the PRINT (or LPRINT) command and *must* be both preceded and followed by a semicolon.
2. It is descriptive of a position on the physical line itself. TAB(85) will not work on a monochrome display, although it will on a printer if given the appropriate set-up.

LOCATE, LOCATE

The LOCATE statement is used to position the cursor on the screen, both on a row (range 1-25) and in a column (range 1-40 or 1-80, depending on WIDTH);

to make it visible or invisible; and to determine its size. The format of the instruction is this:

LOCATE row, column, cursor, start, stop

You'll note that the instruction manual indicates each as an option. The only *mandatory* option is *row*. If nothing else is specified, the specification of row will position the cursor at column 1 on that row. The cursor, start, and stop attributes remain as they are currently specified.

The cursor subcommand entry can be either 0 or 1. A zero (0) will turn the cursor off, making it invisible. A one (1) will turn the cursor on, making it visible. Even though the cursor may be invisible, it still exists. You may later use fixed-formatted screens where the presentation of a cursor could be undesirable.

The vertical size of the cursor can be specified, as well. The guide book says it may range from 0 to 31, but there are limitations for the equipment. The monotone display specifies a range of 0 to 13, with zero being located high on the character position and 13 being located low. The best possible way to demonstrate the cursor subcommands is to run the following little program:

```
10 CLS
20 FOR X = 0 TO 13
30     LOCATE 13,40,1,0,X:PRINT X;" ";
40         FOR Z = 1 TO 500:NEXT Z
50 NEXT X
60 GOTO 60
```

Note that the stop attribute of the locate statement varies from 0 to 13, increasing the size of the cursor. Experiment with the values. There will be times when a pin-thin cursor will not be sufficient.

Cursor placement can also be dynamic. The following is a modification of the previous program. Expect eight cursors to be developed and then the program to fail with an illegal function call.

```
10 CLS
20 Y = 1
30 FOR X = 0 TO 13
40     LOCATE 13,Y,1,0,X:PRINT X;" ";
50         FOR Z = 1 TO 500:NEXT Z
60 NEXT X
70 Y = Y + 10
80 GOTO 30
```

RENUMBERING

Note that the last two programs are *almost* identical. The instructions look the same, but the statement numbers are different. What happened? RENUM happened. Additional instructions were entered between the lines of the first program. Typing RENUM followed by ENTER will resequence your program. Nice!

THIS BLINKING DISPLAY

The message displayed upon the screen can be made to blink in a couple of ways, one of which is software oriented and the other hardware oriented. The software method involves setting the display up in its appropriate place, printing the message, pausing for a period of time so that it can be read, clearing the message, pausing for a similar period of time to provide relief, and repeating the process. A program to do this follows:

```
10 CLS
20 A$ = "THIS MESSAGE WILL BLINK ON AND OFF"
30 B$ = "                                   "
40 LOCATE 13,20,0,0,13
50 PRINT C$
60 FOR Z = 1 TO 200:NEXT Z
70 IF S = 1 THEN C$ = B$:S = 0:GOTO 40
80 IF S = 0 THEN C$ = A$:S = 1:GOTO 40
```

Let's talk a little about the technique used in this routine. Note that statements 20 and 30 are identically sized, one containing the message and the other containing blanks. Statements 70 and 80 comprise a small switching arrangement. In the first, if the switch is *on* (variable S is set to 1), then the message is cleared and the switch is turned off. In the second, if the switch is *off* (Variable S is set to 0), then the message is loaded and the switch is turned on. It's important to note that in each case, the right-hand instructions in their respective three-instruction sets are executed only if the condition of the first instruction is met. In other words, if S = 0 at statement 70, then control would immediately transfer to statement 80.

The LOCATE statement merely places the message in the middle of the screen and sets a full cursor. Note, however, that the cursor has been made invisible. Make it visible (change the third parameter to 1) to see the difference. Statement 60 provides the delay. Otherwise, the message would flash too rapidly.

The second method to blink the display is the COLOR instruction, which not only causes blinking but allows you to change the color intensity of the foreground and background as well. When you look at the monochrome display, you'll note that it is green against a black background. Technically, it's *white on black*. The COLOR instruction is primarily for use with a color monitor, but there are some features that permit its use on the monochrome as well. The general form of the COLOR instruction as it relates to the monochrome display is

COLOR foreground, background

If you use the COLOR instruction, the foreground entry is mandatory but the background entry is optional. Consider, however, that if the foreground and background *are the same color*, they will cancel each other, having the effect of making an entry invisible. Available colors are as follows:

Colors available for foreground: 0 Black
               1 Underline character with
                   white foreground
               7 White
             15 High intensity white

Colors available for background: 0 Black
               7 White

OK, let's experiment. Enter and run the following:

```
10 CLS
20 A$ = "THIS MESSAGE WILL BLINK ON AND OFF"
30 B$ = "                                  "
35 COLOR 1,0
40 LOCATE 13,20,0,0,13
50 PRINT C$
60 FOR Z = 1 TO 200:NEXT Z
70 IF S = 1 THEN C$ = B$:S = 0:GOTO 40
80 IF S = 0 THEN C$ = A$:S = 1:GOTO 40
```

Actually, only line 35 was added. Run the program and you will see the same flashing message as before except that it's underlined. Break and list it and you'll note that the underline spreads all over the screen. That's annoying but easily cleared if you'll just type COLOR 0,0 ENTER, followed by CLS ENTER. If the system gets away from you, hold CTRL and ALT down with your left hand and press BREAK. That will restart the system. Now, make the following change and rerun the program:

```
10 CLS
20 A$ = "THIS MESSAGE WILL BLINK ON AND OFF"
30 B$ = "                                  "
35 COLOR 15,0
40 LOCATE 13,20,0,0,13
50 PRINT C$
60 FOR Z = 1 TO 200:NEXT Z
70 IF S = 1 THEN C$ = B$:S = 0:GOTO 40
80 IF S = 0 THEN C$ = A$:S = 1:GOTO 40
```

Do you see any difference? Probably not. It's time now to modify the program with another perspective:

```
10 CLS
20 A$ = "THIS MESSAGE WILL BLINK ON AND OFF"
30 B$ = "                                  "
40 COLOR 15,0
```

```
50 LOCATE 13,20,0,0,13
60 PRINT C$
70 FOR Z = 1 TO 200:NEXT Z
80 IF S = 1 THEN C$ = B$:S = 0:GOTO 50
90 IF S = 0 THEN C$ = A$:S = 1
100 LOCATE 13,20,0,0,13
110 COLOR 7,0:PRINT "THIS ";
120 COLOR 15,0:PRINT "MESSAGE ";
130 COLOR 7,0:PRINT "WILL ";
140 COLOR 15,0:PRINT "BLINK ";
150 COLOR 7,0:PRINT "ON ";
160 COLOR 15,0:PRINT "AND ";
170 COLOR 7,0:PRINT "OFF"
180 GOTO 70
```

In this case, the entire message still blinks, but alternate words are of differing intensities. If they do not look significantly different on your display, adjust your brightness and contrast controls until they do. They will.

Now, go into program statements 120, 140, and 160, and change each 15 to 31. Watch it. For a while, it will look as if nothing is different, and then gradually you will see that the blinking cycle is changing. When you do, interrupt the program with a CTRL and BREAK. If you happen to catch the program on instruction 70, the display will continue to blink even though the program has been interrupted. You may have to experiment a few times until this happens, but what you will discover is that the hardware blink is assigned to the screen and not to the program itself. Once the display has begun to blink, it will continue to blink until it has been reset. It will look as if it has gone into self-oscillation after you've fiddled with it for a while, with the whole screen gradually becoming affected. To prove this, delete statements 20 through 90, change 180 to GOTO 110, and run the program again. Flashy!

```
20 CLS
30 LOCATE 13,20,0,0,13
40 COLOR 7,0:PRINT "THIS";
50 COLOR 16,7:PRINT " MESSAGE ";
60 COLOR 0,7:PRINT "WILL ";
70 COLOR 31,0:PRINT "BLINK";
80 COLOR 0,7:PRINT " ON ";
90 COLOR 17,0:PRINT "AND";
100 COLOR 0,7:PRINT " OFF"
110 GOTO 110
```

This final version, above, will demonstrate other characteristics of the COLOR instruction. Try it.

PRINTING ON THE PRINTER

Insofar as the presentation of text is concerned, use of a hardcopy (paper) printer is essentially the same as the use of the display itself. Instead of PRINT, however, the instruction used is LPRINT. Rules for tabulation and spacing are the same.

LOCATE and COLOR do not apply to printers, but a whole host of other items do, and before we can begin to study those things that are specific to printers, we will have to introduce a new instruction — CHR$, or string character.

CHR$

As stated before, the PC is designed to operate in ASCII (*A*merican *S*tandard *C*ode for *I*nformation *I*nterchange). Let's examine the character set that can be displayed upon the screen. Enter and run the following:

```
10 CLS
20 LOCATE 22
30 FOR N = 0 TO 11
40     PRINT N;CHR$(N);
50 NEXT N
60 FOR N = 13 TO 255
70     PRINT N;CHR$(N);
80 NEXT N
90 PRINT:PRINT
```

This routine shows you the character set. Because ASCII character 12 causes the cursor to move to the first position on the screen (the "home" position), we have located the first eleven characters beginning at screen line 22 and the characters from 13 to the highest character in the set, 255, at the beginning of the screen. These are, of course, interesting characters, and each is useful —

160	176	192	208
161	177	193	209
162	178	194	210
163	179	195	211
164	180	196	212
165	181	197	213
166	182	198	214
167	183	199	215
168	184	200	216
169	185	201	217
170	186	202	218
171	187	203	219
172	188	204	220
173	189	205	221
174	190	206	222
175	191	207	223

especially the graphics characters — but none of the *screen* characters above ASCII 140 can be dumped onto the printer with PrtSc. In fact, many of the ASCII codes have different meanings to the printer. Some of them are printable graphics characters; some are control codes for spacing. We'll discuss these next. In the meantime, here is a program that will display the graphic codes on the printer. A copy of those codes is shown on the facing page.

```
10 CLS
20 FOR X = 1 TO 16
30     LPRINT X+159;"   ";CHR$(X+159);
40     LPRINT TAB(10);X+159+16;CHR$(X+159+16);
50     LPRINT TAB(20);X+159+32;CHR$(X+159+32);
60     LPRINT TAB(30);X+159+48;CHR$(X+159+48)
65     LPRINT
70 NEXT X
80 END
```

BACK TO THE PRINTER

If you haven't figured it out yet, it's possible to get rid of the program you have in memory simply by typing NEW   ENTER. Do that now.

With the IBM printer supplied with the system there are a few differences that can be made to your printed output through the use of specialized ASCII characters and CHR$ codes. You will wish to refer to the ASCII Control Code Chart in your "Guide to Operations" book, but we'll deal with the important ones here:

CHR$(7)   will sound a horn at the printer when used in an LPRINT statement. It will sound an alarm within the system unit when used in a PRINT statement.

CHR$(14)   will set the print to double size (and therefore take up double the horizontal space on the paper). Note that the vertical spacing does not change.

CHR$(15)   will set the print to smaller than normal size with a compression that allows 132 characters to be printed within the width normally used by 80 characters.

CHR$(18)   turns off the compressed mode.

CHR$(20)   turns off the double size mode.

     These two mode changes must be used when returning from the selected size to the normal size of print, which is 10 characters to the inch.

CHR$(27)   is the code for ESCape. This code must be used preceding those CHR$ codes that follow in this list, as the ESCape code clears the buffer.

CHR$(69)   turns on an emphasized mode of print. Since ASCII 69
                  is also the letter "E," that letter may be used when pre-
                  ceded by CHR$(27).

CHR$(70)   turns off the emphasized mode. Since ASCII 70 is also the
                  letter "F," that letter may be used when preceded by
                  CHR$(27).

CHR$(71)   turns on the double strike mode of print. ASCII 71 is also
                  the letter "G," so that letter may be used when preceded
                  by CHR$(27).

CHR$(72)   turns off the double strike mode. Since ASCII 72 is also
                  the letter "H," that letter may be used when preceded by
                  CHR$(27).

Now enter this program:

```
10 LPRINT CHR$(14);"      TITLE LINE"
20 LPRINT
30 LPRINT "Normal Line"
40 LPRINT
50 LPRINT CHR$(15);"This line is in condensed print"
60 LPRINT
70 LPRINT CHR$(18);"Normal again"
80 LPRINT
90 LPRINT CHR$(27);"E";"This line is emphasized print"
100 LPRINT
110 LPRINT CHR$(27);"F";"Back to normal again"
120 LPRINT
130 LPRINT CHR$(27);"G";"This is double strike print"
140 LPRINT
150 LPRINT CHR$(27);"H";"Back to normal again"
160 END
```

Run it and you will achieve the following:

```
                 TITLE LINE

Normal Line

This line is in condensed print

Normal again

This line is emphasized print

Back to normal again

This is double strike print

Back to normal again
```

WHO WAS THAT MASKED CHARACTER?

Recall when we screen-printed the zones and the two-digit numbers aligned
incorrectly under the one-digit number? The reason was that the numbers had

to begin on a zone boundary. What would be required to have them line up correctly? Glad you asked! We will now introduce PRINT USING.

We shall also introduce what is commonly called the *print mask*. The print mask is a filter through which *editing* of a numeric or alphabetic string can be accomplished. Concentrating first upon numeric strings, by editing we mean the insertion of things like decimal points, commas, dollar signs, algebraic signs, floating asterisks, etc. Consider the following program and its output:

```
10 CLS
20 INPUT "ENTER A NUMBER: ";A
30 PRINT "THE NUMBER YOU ENTERED WAS: ";
40 PRINT USING "$$,###.##";A
50 PRINT
60 INPUT "ENTER TWO NUMBERS, SEPARATED BY A COMMA: ",A,B
70 PRINT "THE NUMBERS YOU ENTERED WERE: ";
80 PRINT USING "$##.##    ";A,B
90 PRINT:PRINT
100 END


ENTER A NUMBER: ? 1234.56
THE NUMBER YOU ENTERED WAS: $1,234.56

ENTER TWO NUMBERS, SEPARATED BY A COMMA: 12.34,56
THE NUMBERS YOU ENTERED WERE: $12.34    $56.00

ENTER A NUMBER: ? .23
THE NUMBER YOU ENTERED WAS:    $0.23

ENTER TWO NUMBERS, SEPARATED BY A COMMA: .14,1234.56
THE NUMBERS YOU ENTERED WERE: $ 0.14    $%1234.56
```

Compare the output to the program. Note specifically the differences in the INPUT statements at 20 and at 60. In the first instance, only one variable is requested (A), whereas in the second, two variables (A and B) are requested. Note the punctuation that precedes variable A. In statement 20 there is a semicolon. In 60 there is a comma. Look at the corresponding messages on the first two elements of output. Where the semicolon was used, a question mark is displayed on the screen.

Now about the mask. The first mask ($$, # # #. # #) is set up to provide a sliding dollar (double) sign, punctuation, and space for six numbers (including one now containing the $). Note that when 1234.56 was entered, it was edited perfectly as $1,234.56. In the second example, two numbers are accepted by the INPUT statement and placed appropriately relative to the decimal point. Note that in the final entry, the number was too large to be edited. It was still placed in the output, but flagged with a % to let you know it could not be edited by the printing mask you had provided.

Finally, look at the edit mask in line 80. The spacing between the numbers on the display is a function of the extra spaces contained in the mask variable. If you were to place a semicolon between A and B in this statement, you would be told that it is erroneous. The comma will display the numbers directly adjacent unless you include the spaces in the mask.

These same functions with LPRINT, and you'll no doubt have to experiment to get them right as there are myriad usable combinations. These are detailed fully under PRINT USING in your BASIC manual.

SO GO, ALREADY

It often happens that you must change direction within a program. You may wish to change direction unconditionally; that's done with GOTO. You may wish to change direction with anticipation of returning; that's done with GOSUB. Or you may wish to do either on the basis of a selection of values; that's done with ON . . . GOTO and ON . . . GOSUB. .

The GOTO is straightforward. You've completed a loop (look back at several of the program examples we've discussed), and you wish to repeat it. The GOTO statement number will *unconditionally branch* to the statement you want.

Often it happens that you might want to develop an amount of instruction coding that can be used over and over again but you don't want to code it each time it is needed. At such times you can resort to a *subroutine*. Subroutines are any routine that is terminated with a RETURN command, as shown in the following program:

```
10 CLS
20 LOCATE 13,32
30 PRINT "PERFORM A SUBROUTINE"
40 FOR N = 1 TO 500:NEXT N
50 GOSUB 1000
60 GOTO 10
1000 '*****************************************
1010 '*                                      *
1020 '*          THIS IS A SUBROUTINE        *
1030 '*                                      *
1040 '*****************************************
1050 CLS
1060 LOCATE 13,34
1070 PRINT "DISPLAY A MESSAGE"
1080 FOR N = 1 TO 500:NEXT N
1090 RETURN
```

Although this routine simply exchanges messages in the middle of the screen, it clearly demonstrates the use of the subroutine. To get into a subroutine, you need a GOSUB. To get back to the next sequential instruction, there must be a RETURN at the end of the subroutine.

When your responses are in a defined order, it's possible to place a multiple branch within the same statement. For instance, suppose that you had begun your program with a *menu*. A menu is, as the word denotes, a selection of options. Enter the following program and run it:

```
10 CLS
20 LOCATE 10,30
30 PRINT "1.     MENU OPTION ONE"
40 LOCATE 12,30
50 PRINT "2.     MENU OPTION TWO"
60 LOCATE 14,30
70 PRINT "3.     MENU OPTION THREE"
80 LOCATE 16,30
90 PRINT "4.     MENU OPTION FOUR"
100 LOCATE 20
110 INPUT "SELECT: ",A
120 ON A GOTO 140,160,180,200
130 GOTO 10
140 PRINT:PRINT "YOU SELECTED MENU OPTION ONE"
150 END
160 PRINT:PRINT "YOU SELECTED MENU OPTION TWO"
170 END
180 PRINT:PRINT "YOU SELECTED MENU OPTION THREE"
190 END
200 PRINT:PRINT "YOU SELECTED MENU OPTION FOUR"
210 END
```

As you can see, if you select one of the offered options (follow your entry with the ENTER key), this option will be displayed. Try one that is not offered, and you'll see that the program doesn't work. This is called *error trapping*.

The same result can be achieved with GOSUB. Modify the preceding program as follows:

```
10 CLS
20 LOCATE 10,30
30 PRINT "1.     MENU OPTION ONE"
40 LOCATE 12,30
50 PRINT "2.     MENU OPTION TWO"
60 LOCATE 14,30
70 PRINT "3.     MENU OPTION THREE"
80 LOCATE 16,30
90 PRINT "4.     MENU OPTION FOUR"
100 LOCATE 20
110 INPUT "SELECT: ",A
120 ON A GOSUB 140,170,200,230
130 GOTO 10
140 PRINT:PRINT "YOU SELECTED MENU OPTION ONE"
150 GOSUB 260
160 RETURN
170 PRINT:PRINT "YOU SELECTED MENU OPTION TWO"
180 GOSUB 260
190 RETURN
200 PRINT:PRINT "YOU SELECTED MENU OPTION THREE"
210 GOSUB 260
220 RETURN
230 PRINT:PRINT "YOU SELECTED MENU OPTION FOUR"
240 GOSUB 260
250 RETURN
260 FOR N = 1 TO 1000:NEXT N:RETURN
```

One minor twist occurs here. Note that within each separate subroutine, a common subroutine is executed — a subroutine within a subroutine. The latter subroutine is known as a *nested subroutine.*

INKEY$

There is a way to enter data without having to press the ENTER key; it is called INKEY$. INKEY$ is the computer's method of strobing the keyboard for the entry of a single *alphabetic* character. Since the ON ... GOTO and ON ... GOSUB statements require a *numeric* quantity, it's necessary to convert the alphabetic value being received from the keyboard to a numeric value that is useful to the ON. There is a more sophisticated way to do this, but the following method works and is more easily understood:

```
10 CLS
20 LOCATE 10,30
30 PRINT "1.     MENU OPTION ONE"
40 LOCATE 12,30
50 PRINT "2.     MENU OPTION TWO"
60 LOCATE 14,30
70 PRINT "3.     MENU OPTION THREE"
80 LOCATE 16,30
90 PRINT "4.     MENU OPTION FOUR"
100 LOCATE 20
110 PRINT "SELECT: ";
120 Z$ = INKEY$
130 IF Z$ = "" THEN 120
140 IF Z$ = "1" THEN A = 1:GOTO 200
150 IF Z$ = "2" THEN A = 2:GOTO 200
160 IF Z$ = "3" THEN A = 3:GOTO 200
170 IF Z$ = "4" THEN A = 4:GOTO 200
180 GOSUB 350
190 GOTO 20
200 PRINT A
210 ON A GOSUB 230,260,290,320
220 GOTO 10
230 PRINT:PRINT "YOU SELECTED MENU OPTION ONE"
240 GOSUB 420
250 RETURN
260 PRINT:PRINT "YOU SELECTED MENU OPTION TWO"
270 GOSUB 420
280 RETURN
290 PRINT:PRINT "YOU SELECTED MENU OPTION THREE"
300 GOSUB 420
310 RETURN
320 PRINT:PRINT "YOU SELECTED MENU OPTION FOUR"
330 GOSUB 420
340 RETURN
350 PRINT
360 LOCATE 22
370 PRINT "INVALID SELECTION -- RE-ENTER"
380 GOSUB 420
390 LOCATE 22
400 PRINT "                              "
410 RETURN
420 FOR N = 1 TO 1000:NEXT N:RETURN
```

Most of this program should be straightforward. About the only thing we haven't discussed is the double quote (" ") at statement 130. Known as a *null string*, it merely redirects the program back to the keyboard strobe (INKEY$) when no entry has been made.

As previously remarked, there is a more sophisticated way of doing this, and that is to find the numeric value of the alphabetic variable. This is accomplished, appropriately, with a VAL instruction. Study the following:

```
10 CLS
20 LOCATE 10,30
30 PRINT "1.     MENU OPTION ONE"
40 LOCATE 12,30
50 PRINT "2.     MENU OPTION TWO"
60 LOCATE 14,30
70 PRINT "3.     MENU OPTION THREE"
80 LOCATE 16,30
90 PRINT "4.     MENU OPTION FOUR"
100 LOCATE 20
110 PRINT "SELECT: ";
120 Z$ = INKEY$
130 IF Z$ = "" THEN 120
140 IF VAL(Z$) < 1 OR VAL(Z$) > 4 THEN GOSUB 300:GOTO 20
150 PRINT VAL(Z$)
160 ON VAL(Z$) GOSUB 180,210,240,270
170 GOTO 10
180 PRINT:PRINT "YOU SELECTED MENU OPTION ONE"
190 GOSUB 370
200 RETURN
210 PRINT:PRINT "YOU SELECTED MENU OPTION TWO"
220 GOSUB 370
230 RETURN
240 PRINT:PRINT "YOU SELECTED MENU OPTION THREE"
250 GOSUB 370
260 RETURN
270 PRINT:PRINT "YOU SELECTED MENU OPTION FOUR"
280 GOSUB 370
290 RETURN
300 PRINT
310 LOCATE 22
320 PRINT "INVALID SELECTION -- RE-ENTER"
330 GOSUB 370
340 LOCATE 22
350 PRINT "                           "
360 RETURN
370 FOR N = 1 TO 1000:NEXT N:RETURN
```

SUMMARY

As this chapter closes, let's take stock of how far we have come. We'll do so by reviewing the commands, statements, and functions we have already learned to use. You may then be assured that you are acquainted with all the pertinent ones to which reference has been made, with the added advantage that the explanations are concentrated for easy reference.

Commands

These commands include all those you have already been introduced to, plus a few others useful to know:

AUTO(n, m)   This will help you to generate line numbers automatically, beginning with the first desired line (n) incremented by the desire increment (m). AUTO by itself begins at 10,

	incrementing by 10. Press ALT and "A" as well to get this result.
DELETE (n-m)	This will allow you to remove blocks of instructions beginning with the first desired line (n) and ending with the last desired line (m) inclusive. The interesting thing about DELETE is that it can be included in a program as an instruction to wipe out program instructions that are no longer needed.
EDIT n	As explained before, you have only to LIST a program on the screen, modify it as detailed in the section on the Editor, and press ENTER to return it to memory. The EDIT command allows you to isolate a single instruction for the purpose of editing.
LIST (n-m)	LIST by itself — without the (n-m) — will display a program on the screen, a function that can also be generated by Function Key 1. Once begun, the program, if it is too long for the screen, with scroll. The scroll can be arrested by pressing on CTRL and NUM LOCK and begun again by pressing any key. If only part of a program is required, the inclusive lines can be specified with LIST (n-m). Also n or m can be separately specified (using the hyphen) to select only a portion of the program for display.
LLIST (n-m)	Same as LIST but targeted to the line printer; the same rules apply.
LOAD filespec	Is used to LOAD a program from the media — cassette or diskette.
NEW	Wipes out the program in memory and clears all variables.
RENUM i, j, k	Resequences a program. RENUM by itself will resequence the entire program in increments of 10. If that is not suitable, the new number (i), old number (j), and increment (k) can be specified.
RUN	Causes the program in memory to be executed, a function also performed by Function Key 2. If the program is entered as RUN filespec, the computer will read the program from the appropriate media and begin execution.
SAVE filespec	Is used to record a copy of the program located in memory onto an output media, cassette or diskette.
TRON, TROFF	Turns (on/off) the trace function, which displays the sequence numbers on the display unit.

Statements

END	Returns the program to the command level. The "Ok" prompt will appear again.
FOR	Repeats program lines a specified number of times. The ellipsis can consist of a variable, expression, target expression, or incremental step. For ... is used with NEXT.
GOSUB	Transfers control to a subroutine, which must include a RETURN statement.
GOTO	Unconditionally branches to a specified line.
IF	Is used to test logical conditions, allowing branches at logical differences.
KEY ON/OFF	Can be used to illuminate or darken the specification of the function keys on line 25 of the monochrome display screen.
LET	Assigns the value of an expression to a variable not necessary to use.
NEXT	The closure for a FOR ... NEXT loop.
ON ... GOSUB	Performs a subroutine selected on the basis of the value of a variable.
ON ... GOTO	Unconditionally branches to a selected subroutine on the basis of the value of a variable.
REM	Includes REMarks within a program. This function can also be generated by an apostrophe.
RETURN	Is used to return from a subroutine. It enables a return to a particular location given the specification of a line number.
STOP/CONT	Stops the program execution, prints the break message, and returns a program to command level. The program can be restarted with a CONTinue command.
WIDTH	Is used to establish a 40-character or 80-character width to a monochrome display screen. The 80-character width is the default.

Input/Output Statements

CLS	Clears the screen and puts the cursor in home position.

COLOR	Sets foreground and background colors. It is far more applicable to a color monitor but has some uses with a monochrome display.
INPUT	Reads data (either alphabetic or numeric) from the keyboard.
LPRINT LPRINT USING	Prints data on the printer. If editing is desired, a print mask can be developed for punctuation, dollar signs, and the like.
PRINT PRINT USING	Displays data on the display screen. If editing is desired, a print mask can be developed for punctuation, dollar signs, and the like.
SOUND	Is used to generate a musical note within six octaves, establishing the frequency, and to hold that note for a specified duration.

String Functions

CHR$(n)	Displays, on the screen or the line printer, any ASCII character within the range of 0-255. The same ASCII character may generate entirely different display characters on the monochrome display and the printer.
TAB(n)	Is used for horizontal spacing on display or printer.
VAL(x$)	Is used to determine the value of a number that has been developed in alphabetic form.

There are others, of course, and we'll get to most of them, but these are the ones we've dealt with already.

3
Developing and Manipulating Data

Already having a solid idea of how the PC functions, we can now turn our attention to the development of programs, routines, and methods of handling data. Data, of course, is the raison d'etre for possessing a computer. Even if you devote your PC solely to playing Space Invaders, which you probably will not, the program within the computer must work upon data that is (1) either already contained within the computer, (2) entered from outside the computer, or (3) developed as a result of previous manipulations on either or both (1) and (2).

Thus far, we have used certain types of data — namely numeric variables and alphabetic variables — the latter being signified by the terminating dollar sign on the name (label) of the data. In the majority of the microcomputers on the market, data variables can be identified by one, two, or three characters. Some can have longer names, but only the first three characters are relevant. The PC also has a limitation — 40 characters, that is, the first 40 characters are the significant characters. Anything beyond that limit is not treated as relevant. You should certainly have no trouble being sufficiently descriptive within 40 characters.

There are three types of numeric variables and one type of string (alphabetic) variable. The types of variables are shown this way:

%   Integer (whole number) variable (two bytes).

!   Single precision variable (four bytes). This is the default classification. Thus A and A! would appear the same to the machine.

Double-precision variable (eight bytes). It is used for mathematical operations where the answer derived would be too large (or too small to fit within the four bytes allocated to the single-precision number.

$ String variable, with a range of 0-255 characters, defined between quotation marks. Exceptions will be discussed later.

RULES FOR VARIABLE NAMES

As stated, variable names can have any size, but only the first 40 characters are relevant. They must begin with an alphabetic character, but characters thereafter may be letters, numbers, or decimal points. Numeric variables without a trailing ! are assumed to be single-precision variables. Other forms of variables must be declared as integer (%), double-precision (#), or string ($). A class of variables may be defined according to the name of the variable. For instance, consider the following:

```
10 DEFINT A-G
20 DEFSNG H-K
30 DEFDBL L-R
40 DEFSTR S-Z
```

All variables here that begin with the letters A through G are defined as *integer variables*. Variables beginning with the letters H through K are *single-precision variables*. Those beginning with the letters L through R are *double-precision variables*. Those beginning with letters S through Z are *string variables*. Once it has been defined by the DEF- method (see Summary at end of Chapter), it is no longer necessary to add the type designator to the variable name.

The only real restriction to the use of the variable names is confined to the use of *reserved words* (BASIC commands, actually) alone. In other words, *END* by itself is not allowed, whereas END.ROUTINE would be perfectly permissible.

The following are the reserved words that cannot be used alone as variable names:

ABS	AND	ASC	ATN	AUTO
BEEP	BLOAD	BSAVE	CALL	CDBL
CHAIN	CHR$	CINT	CIRCLE	CLEAR
CLOSE	CLS	COLOR	COM	COMMON
CONT	COS	CSNG	CSRLIN	CVD
CVI	CVS	DATA	DATE$	DEF
DEFDBL	DEFINT	DEFSNG	DEFSTR	DELETE
DIM	DRAW	EDIT	ELSE	END
EOF	EQV	ERASE	ERL	ERR
ERROR	EXP	FIELD	FILES	FIX
FNxxxxxxxx	FOR	FRE	GET	GOSUB

GOTO	HEX$	IF	IMP	INKEY$
INP	INPUT	INPUT#	INPUT$	INSTR
INT	KEY	KILL	LEFT$	LEN
LET	LINE	LIST	LLIST	LOAD
LOC	LOCATE	LOF	LOG	LPOS
LPRINT	LSET	MERGE	MID$	MKD$
MKI$	MKS$	MOD	MOTOR	NAME
NEW	NEXT	NOT	OCT$	OFF
ON	OPEN	OPTION	OR	OUT
PAINT	PEEK	PEN	PLAY	POINT
POKE	POS	PRESET	PRINT	PRINT#
PSET	PUT	RANDOMIZE	READ	REM
RENUM	RESET	RESTORE	RESUME	RETURN
RIGHT	RND	RSET	RUN	SAVE
SCREEN	SGN	SIN	SOUND	SPACE$
SPC(	SQR	STEP	STICK	STOP
STR$	STRIG	STRING$	SWAP	SYSTEM
TAB(	TAN	THEN	TIME$	TO
TROFF	TRON	USING	USR	VAL
VARPTR	WAIT	WEND	WHILE	WIDTH
WRITE	WRITE#	XOR		

Avoid using these words or use them only in combination with other words, and there should be no difficulty.

A PLACE FOR EVERYTHING

A variable is a place to *put something*. It may be a *constant* (A$ = "STRING CONSTANT"). It may be a *literal* (PRINT "HELLO"). It may be a value used by an instruction (FOR N = 1 to 10). The point is that variables are places to store data. The names you assign to variables must, of necessity, occupy space. If you make a habit of using 40-character labels, the available memory will be quickly consumed. Thereafter, each time you define or develop variables, they will utilize the size defined. At some point you will have memory restriction, irrespective of the amount of memory purchased. It's called *Parkinson's Law*, and it will eventually force you to condense your variables.

    BASIC reserves the lesser of 512 bytes or one-eighth of the available memory in your system as a default. The system will let you know when you've used that quota up. When it does, it will be necessary for you to reserve additional storage for data by using a CLEAR command within the program you're running. CLEAR frees all memory used for data without erasing the program itself in memory. After CLEAR, arrays (to be discussed shortly) will be no longer defined, numeric variables will contain a value of zero, string variables will contain a null value, and any DEFinitions established will be lost. Let us repeat that the system will *tell you* when it needs more space for data. The necessary amount of data to be added can be determined only by counting. General practice reveals that a fixed increment, such as 1,000 bytes, is customarily added and is reduced only if that is necessary to contain the program. Recall our discussion of FRE(0).

Other places data may reside are as follows:

1. They may reside as a DATA statement (stored within the program itself), which is accessed by a READ instruction. The DATA statement is a *permanent constant* that can store both alphabetic and numeric data. Once set, these are not modifiable by the BASIC program using them. As with every rule, there is an exception. BASIC DATA statements can be modified by a machine-language knowledgeable person.
2. They may reside as an element of an array. Arrays will be discussed later on. They are used as the place to store data arriving from magnetic media or to develop data targeted for magnetic media.
3. They may reside in magnetic media — cassette tape or diskette. Data can be read from the media or written to the media and are moved into variables or, more usually into an array when staged.

IT'S CALLED CONCATENATION

It's possible to add two alphabetic fields together; at least it seems that way. In one method, it's called *appending*. In another, it's called *concatenation*. Note the definitions of the variables A$ and B$ in statements 10 and 20 below. Statement 30 *appends* the two variables to itself into a permanent variable, C$. That combination is displayed in statement 50. In statement 40, however, the two variables are joined temporarily (*concatenated*) for purposes of the display. Both ways work, but concatenation occupies less memory.

```
10 A$ = "BELL"
20 B$ = "WEATHER"
30 C$ = A$ + B$
40 PRINT A$ + B$
50 PRINT C$
```

THE DATA STATEMENT

Consider the following:

```
1000 DATA 42377,KEN,LORD,007328933,9,3,36
1010 DATA 27365,NANCY,LORD,024372122,10,19,36
1020 DATA 34582,KAREN,LORD,073327344,12,12,59
1030 DATA 57263,TIMOTHY,LORD,008328814,9,11,61
1040 DATA 23649,SANDRA,SCOFIELD,012663429,12,5,65
```

Here is structured data about five people, data that will be used by a program to perform some function — perhaps for display in a report. From left to right, each DATA statement contains a number (perhaps an employee number), a first name, a last name, a social security number, and the month, day, and year of birth. Note that each line is structured in precisely the same manner. Note also that the first item is numeric, the next two are alphabetic, and the remaining four are numeric. Thus, in sequence, they can be described as

EMPLOYEE.NUMBER

FIRST.NAME$

LAST.NAME$

SOCIAL.SECURITY.NUMBER$

MONTH.OF.BIRTH

DAY.OF.BIRTH

YEAR.OF.BIRTH

Following is a routine to READ the DATA lines and to present them on both the display screen and on the printer. Each is presented twice for comparison of the treatment of the birthdate as numeric or alphabetic. The social security number has been defined as a string variable to preclude suppression of leading zeroes and the presentation of the numbers in mathematical notation.

```
10 CLS
20 LPRINT CHR$(14);"Date Of Birth (Numeric)":LPRINT
30 FOR N = 1 TO 5
40     READ EMPLOYEE.NUMBER,FIRST.NAME$,LAST.NAME$
50     READ SOCIAL.SECURITY.NUMBER$
60     READ MONTH.OF.BIRTH,DAY.OF.BIRTH,YEAR.OF.BIRTH
70     PRINT EMPLOYEE.NUMBER,FIRST.NAME$,LAST.NAME$,;
80     PRINT SOCIAL.SECURITY.NUMBER$,;
90     PRINT MONTH.OF.BIRTH;"/";DAY.OF.BIRTH;"/";YEAR.OF.BIRTH
100    LPRINT EMPLOYEE.NUMBER,FIRST.NAME$,LAST.NAME$,;
110    LPRINT SOCIAL.SECURITY.NUMBER$,;
120    LPRINT MONTH.OF.BIRTH;"/";DAY.OF.BIRTH;"/";YEAR.OF.BIRTH
130 NEXT N
140 PRINT:PRINT:LPRINT:LPRINT
```

```
150 RESTORE
160 LPRINT CHR$(14);"Date Of Birth (Alphabetic)":LPRINT
170 FOR N = 1 TO 5
180     READ EMPLOYEE.NUMBER,FIRST.NAME$,LAST.NAME$
190     READ SOCIAL.SECURITY.NUMBER$
200     READ MONTH.OF.BIRTH$,DAY.OF.BIRTH$,YEAR.OF.BIRTH$
210     PRINT EMPLOYEE.NUMBER,FIRST.NAME$,LAST.NAME$,;
220     PRINT SOCIAL.SECURITY.NUMBER$,;
230     PRINT MONTH.OF.BIRTH$;"/";DAY.OF.BIRTH$;"/";YEAR.OF.BIRTH$
240     LPRINT EMPLOYEE.NUMBER,FIRST.NAME$,LAST.NAME$,;
250     LPRINT SOCIAL.SECURITY.NUMBER$,;
260     LPRINT MONTH.OF.BIRTH$;"/";DAY.OF.BIRTH$;"/";YEAR.OF.BIRTH$
270 NEXT N
280 LPRINT:LPRINT:LPRINT
290 END
1000 DATA 42377,KEN,LORD,007328933,9,3,36
1010 DATA 27365,NANCY,LORD,024372122,10,19,36
1020 DATA 34582,KAREN,LORD,073327344,12,12,59
1030 DATA 57263,TIMOTHY,LORD,008328814,9,11,61
1040 DATA 23649,SANDRA,SCOFIELD,012663429,12,5,65
```

Date Of Birth (Alphabetic)

42377	KEN	LORD	007328933	9/3/36
27365	NANCY	LORD	024372122	10/19/36
34582	KAREN	LORD	073327344	12/12/59
57263	TIMOTHY	LORD	008328814	9/11/61
23649	SANDRA	SCOFIELD	012663429	12/5/65

Date Of Birth (Numeric)

42377	KEN	LORD	007328933	9 / 3 / 36
27365	NANCY	LORD	024372122	10 / 19 / 36
34582	KAREN	LORD	073327344	12 / 12 / 59
57263	TIMOTHY	LORD	008328814	9 / 11 / 61
23649	SANDRA	SCOFIELD	012663429	12 / 5 / 65

As you examine this program, some questions are certain to arise. What's a RESTORE? Why are the PRINT and LPRINT statements broken down? Isn't this the kind of data that would normally reside in some sort of media?

The pattern of the READ instruction is that DATA line elements are read one at a time in the sequence in which they are called. However, you'd better be very certain they you call for what you need. READs can be single or multiple-variable types, with no punctuation specifications. The PRINT and LPRINT statements are broken down simple because the limited page size of this book doesn't permit full-width instructions *or* data. Recall that so long as linefeeds are suppressed (with the semicolon), the printing will be contiguous.

Finally, of course, this sort of data customarily resides in magnetic media. What is ordinarily kept in DATA lines is the sort of information that is basically unchanging, such as rate tables.

ALL RIGHT, POST A SENTINEL

We know that precisely five DATA lines were required to do the above program. And we will now (because we will program it) what the count will be at any time. Suppose, however, that the table is constantly changing and that we must make additions to and deletions from the table. Every change in the table will require a corresponding change in the count of the FOR ... NEXT loops used to control the READ instructions. That's too much like work.

To get around that hassle, we can add a sentinel line as the *last* DATA line in the given sequence (DATA lines can be located *anywhere* within a program and are treated as if they were contiguous. RESTORE resets the pointer to the first DATA record. As a matter of convenience, however, DATA lines are customarily located en masse at the end of a program). This sentinel line is something uniquely distinguishable and unlikely to occur of natural causes. The most commonly used sentinels are 9's for numeric fields and Z's for alphabetic fields. As a result, the FOR ... NEXT loop must be structured toward an impossible-to-reach number, and a test for the sentinel must be contained within the FOR ... NEXT loop, as follows:

```
10 CLS
20 FOR N = 1 TO 1000
30      READ EMPLOYEE.NUMBER,FIRST.NAME$,LAST.NAME$
40      READ SOCIAL.SECURITY.NUMBER$
50      READ MONTH.OF.BIRTH$,DAY.OF.BIRTH$,YEAR.OF.BIRTH$
60      IF EMPLOYEE.NUMBER = 99999! THEN 160
70      PRINT EMPLOYEE.NUMBER,FIRST.NAME$,LAST.NAME$,;
80      PRINT SOCIAL.SECURITY.NUMBER$,;
90      PRINT MONTH.OF.BIRTH$;"/";DAY.OF.BIRTH$;"/";YEAR.OF.BIRTH$
100     LPRINT EMPLOYEE.NUMBER,FIRST.NAME$,LAST.NAME$,;
110     LPRINT SOCIAL.SECURITY.NUMBER$,;
120     LPRINT MONTH.OF.BIRTH$;"/";DAY.OF.BIRTH$;"/";YEAR.OF.BIRTH$
130 NEXT N
140 LPRINT:LPRINT:LPRINT
150 END
160     PRINT:PRINT "SENTINEL LOCATED"
170     LPRINT:LPRINT "SENTINEL LOCATED"
180 LPRINT:LPRINT:LPRINT
190 END
1000 DATA 42377,KEN,LORD,007328933,9,3,36
1010 DATA 27365,NANCY,LORD,024372122,10,19,36
1020 DATA 34582,KAREN,LORD,073327344,12,12,59
1030 DATA 57263,TIMOTHY,LORD,008328814,9,11,61
1040 DATA 23649,SANDRA,SCOFIELD,012663429,12,5,65
5000 DATA 99999,ZZZZZ,ZZZZZ,ZZZZZ,ZZZZZ,ZZZZZ,ZZZZZ
```

Note the specification of a single-precision number in statement 60. That is entered to the BASIC interpreter strictly as 99999, and the interpreter changes it to 99999!. Note also the location and magnitude of the line numbers for the data and the sentinel.

The following will show that the sentinel was located:

42377	KEN	LORD	007328933	9/3/36
27365	NANCY	LORD	024372122	10/19/36
34582	KAREN	LORD	073327344	12/12/59
57263	TIMOTHY	LORD	008328814	9/11/61
23649	SANDRA	SCOFIELD	012663429	12/5/65

SENTINEL LOCATED

ARRAY (OF SUNSHINE?)

Although the DATA statement is a good way to provide temporary input to a program, it is by no means the only way to introduce data to the system. Another is the use of an array. As previously stated, it is into the array that data retrieved from a magnetic media is placed.

An array can be thought of as a series of mailboxes or pigeon holes into which items of data can be sorted. There are essentially two types of arrays: undimensional and multidimensional.

The undimensional array is merely a sequential list, just as if we had used separate variables. The following is an example of a xix-element array (ARRAY.A$) with locations (mailboxes) 0 through 5 (yes, 0 is a number):

```
. . . . . . . . . . . . . . . . . . . . . . . .
.         ARRAY.A$(0)           .
. . . . . . . . . . . . . . . . . . . . . . . .
.         ARRAY.A$(1)           .
. . . . . . . . . . . . . . . . . . . . . . . .
.         ARRAY.A$(2)           .
. . . . . . . . . . . . . . . . . . . . . . . .
.         ARRAY.A$(3)           .
. . . . . . . . . . . . . . . . . . . . . . . .
.         ARRAY.A$(4)           .
. . . . . . . . . . . . . . . . . . . . . . . .
.         ARRAY.A$(5)           .
. . . . . . . . . . . . . . . . . . . . . . . .
```

The multidimensional array is comprised of rows and columns. There are boxes across the horizontal span, and there are boxes along the vertical span. The following is an example of an array consisting of four rows of four elements (mailboxes):

```
                          Columns
         . . . . . . . . . . . . . . . . . . . . . . . . . . . . . . . . . . .
         . B(0,0) . B(0,1) . B(0,2) . B(0,3) .
         . . . . . . . . . . . . . . . . . . . . . . . . . . . . . . . . . . .
         . B(1,0) . B(1,1) . B(1,2) . B(1,3) .
  Rows   . . . . . . . . . . . . . . . . . . . . . . . . . . . . . . . . . . .
         . B(2,0) . B(2,1) . B(2,2) . B(2,3) .
         . . . . . . . . . . . . . . . . . . . . . . . . . . . . . . . . . . .
         . B(3,0) . B(3,1) . B(3,2) . B(3,3) .
         . . . . . . . . . . . . . . . . . . . . . . . . . . . . . . . . . . .
```

TAKING A DIM VIEW

In order to use an array, it is necessary to specify its characteristics to the PC. The process is called *DIMensioning*. It requires an instruction within the program (*after* any CLEAR statement). The DIM statements for the previously illustrated arrays look like this:

```
10   DIM ARRAY.A$(5)
20   DIM B(2,3)
```

If you're sharp, something doesn't look quite right. The illustration of ARRAY.A$ had *six* elements, not five. The illustration of Array B had 12 little mailboxes, not the six it would seem that you asked for. There, however, is a common thread to the quandry. Of the six boxes, one of them had a zero reference. Of the 12 boxes, six of them had a zero reference. Therefore, what the DIMension statement does for you is to identify the *top* position relative to zero. You can use the zero referenced places. What will happen in practice is that you'll use them for work space.

Go back to the multidimensional array and darken the outline of boxes B(1,1), B(1,2), B(1,3), B(2,1), B(2,2), and B(2,3). For all intents and purposes, these are the working elements of the array. The first position to be referenced, therefore, is B(0,0) plus one. The "plus one" is commonly called a *subscript*. To illustrate it, consider the following:

```
10 DIM ARRAY.A$(5)
20 CLS
30 FOR N = 1 TO 5
40     ARRAY.A$(N) = "ELEMENT " + STR$(N)
50 NEXT N
60 FOR N = 1 TO 5
70     PRINT ARRAY.A$(N)
80 NEXT N
90 END
```

In this program, we have dimensioned the single-dimensioned array and have loaded a value into it. The program loads the word "ELEMENT" into the array followed by the number. There is a new instruction in statement 40: STR$. Because of it, Statement 40 concatenates and stores two values in the array. Since it is impossible to concatenate an alphabetic value and a numeric value and since the FOR ... NEXT loop is controlled by the numeric variable, it is necessary to convert the numeric value to an alphabetic value. STR$ is the precise opposite of the VAL function (see the Summary at the end of this chapter).

Here's a similar program to load a multidimensioned array:

```
10 DIM B(2,3)
20 CONSTANT = 111
30 CLS
40 FOR N = 1 TO 2
50      FOR X = 1 TO 3
60            B(N,X) = CONSTANT
70            CONSTANT = CONSTANT + 111
80      NEXT X
90 NEXT N
100 FOR N = 1 TO 2
110     FOR X = 1 TO 3
120           LPRINT "ELEMENT B(";N;",";X;") = " B(N,X)
130     NEXT X
140 NEXT N
150 FOR N = 1 TO 3:LPRINT:NEXT N
160 END
```

Enter and run the program and you'll see that the several elements of the array have indeed been filled — with an incremental constant. In case you're wondering about the spacing of the printed output (between the parentheses, as shown below), recall that all numbers are signed and the positive sign (+) does not print. To avoid this spacing you would have to complicate the LPRINT instruction to insert a backspace, ASCII 008.

```
ELEMENT B( 1 , 1 ) =   111
ELEMENT B( 1 , 2 ) =   222
ELEMENT B( 1 , 3 ) =   333
ELEMENT B( 2 , 1 ) =   444
ELEMENT B( 2 , 2 ) =   555
ELEMENT B( 2 , 3 ) =   666
```

DATA ON CASSETTE TAPE

Recall that earlier in the book LOAD and SAVE were discussed in relation to loading and saving the *program* on tape. When you have used DATA lines for the storage of data in your program, you *must* take the SAVE/LOAD approach. For data developed and stored in an array, however, there are further considerations because the array is *not* stored on tape with the program. The differences involved in using diskette will be discussed later.

As with the use of SAVE and LOAD, you must be very careful about the mechanical controls of a tape recorder. To record on tape you must ensure that you are past any leader before you begin to "write" on tape, and you must also ensure that both the PLAY and RECORD levers are depressed. When it is time to read the data from the tape, you must ensure that the tape is rewound and the PLAY lever depressed.

It is important to know how much data is to be written to the tape (and therefore to be read from the tape). You can find out in one of two ways:

1. The array can be scanned for the sentinel line, counting the lines until it is found. This count can then be written into the first record to be stored on tape (a *header record*). The count can also be placed into a FOR ... NEXT loop into which the writing instruction or the reading instruction has been placed.
2. The array can be written to tape including the sentinel line, or, assuming that the count is known, only the array need be written, recalling precisely the same amount of data when the data is read back into the computer.

Perhaps a couple of definitions would be useful here. A *record* is a collection of data elements about a data subject. All information about you, for instance, comprises your record. A *file* is a collection of similarly organized records. A file of data residing on cassette is known as a *sequential file*, in respect of the fact that each record *immediately* follows its predecessor. For it to be effective, the file should be organized in an ascending sequence — for example, on employee number. We will discuss methods to sort the array into a prescribed sequence later on.

AN OPEN AND SHUT CASE

At this point, the proper perspective is important. In a later chapter we will discuss the Disk Operating System (DOS) and Disk BASIC. It is vital to know, however, in which BASIC you are operating so that you can identify your default options.

PC BASIC supports general-device input/output (I/O). This means that I/O for diskette or communications looks the same to the computer as I/O for cassette. For this reason, files in PC BASIC must meet the following conditions:

1. They must have a file number. The file number is a unique number that is "tagged" to a file when it is OPENed.
2. They must have a device name. Default device names exist. In Cassette BASIC, the default is CAS1:. For Diskette BASIC, it is A: or B:. Thus, if you wish to access the cassette recorder in Cassette BASIC, you need not specify CAS1:. It is, however, a good habit to get into, and is defined as part of the file specification.
3. Whereas the device name tells BASIC *where* to find a file, the filename tells BASIC *which* file to look for. In Cassette BASIC, this name may not exceed eight characters (the limit is different for Diskette BASIC, as we shall learn. Permitted characters are A-Z, 0-9, $, and @ .
4. All files must be OPENed before use and CLOSEd after use. There are some methods of automatic file closing in the event of problems.

ANOTHER OPENING . . .

The general form of the OPEN statement that applies here is

OPEN "O", #1, "DATA"

or

OPEN "I", #1, "DATA"

The first operand of the statement — "O" (for sequential Output) or "I" (for sequential Input) — will be used. The second operand, #1, indicates the file number (buffer) in use for this file. It will be associated with an input/output accomplished throughout the program. "DATA" is the filespec. The filespec could also be coded "CAS1:DATA". Either way will work.

READIN' AND WRITIN'

The terms "read" and "write" have been used, for those are the functions to be performed. However, the computer statements "read" and "write" are reserved for Disk BASIC. To write to a cassette recorder and to read from it, forms of the PRINT (write) and INPUT (read) instructions are used. This is the format:

PRINT #1, list of expressions

or

INPUT #1, list of expressions

The number, of course, corresponds to the buffer number specified in the OPEN statement. The list of expressions is another matter. Let's go back to the example in which we introduced DATA lines and write these instructions to cassette file:

```
10 CLS
20 PRINT "OPENING THE CASSETTE FILE":PRINT
30 OPEN "O",#1,"CAS1:DATA"
40 FOR N = 1 TO 1000
50      PRINT "READING RECORD: ";N
60      READ EMPLOYEE.NUMBER,FIRST.NAME$,LAST.NAME$
70      READ SOCIAL.SECURITY.NUMBER$
80      READ MONTH.OF.BIRTH$,DAY.OF.BIRTH$,YEAR.OF.BIRTH$
90      PRINT#1,EMPLOYEE.NUMBER;FIRST.NAME$;LAST.NAME$;
100     PRINT#1,SOCIAL.SECURITY.NUMBER$;
110     PRINT#1,MONTH.OF.BIRTH$;DAY.OF.BIRTH$;YEAR.OF.BIRTH$
```

```
120    PRINT "     WRITING RECORD:  ";N
130    IF EMPLOYEE.NUMBER = 99999! THEN 160
140 NEXT N
150 END
160 PRINT:PRINT "SENTINEL LOCATED"
170 PRINT:PRINT "TAPE FILE WRITTEN"
180 PRINT:PRINT "CLOSING THE CASSETTE FILE"
190 CLOSE #1
200 END
1000 DATA 42377,KEN,LORD,007328933,9,3,36
1010 DATA 27365,NANCY,LORD,024372122,10,19,36
1020 DATA 34582,KAREN,LORD,073327344,12,12,59
1030 DATA 57263,TIMOTHY,LORD,008328814,9,11,61
1040 DATA 23649,SANDRA,SCOFIELD,012663429,12,5,65
1050 DATA 99999,ZZZZZ,ZZZZZ,ZZZZZ,ZZZZZ,ZZZZZ,ZZZZZ
```

Note as you examine this program that the test for the sentinel was moved to the bottom of the FOR . . . NEXT loop to allow the sentinel to be written onto tape. The messages about opening and closing the cassette files are placed where they are to give you some indication of the time required to perform the process. Your display should look like this:

```
OPENING THE CASSETTE FILE

READING RECORD:   1
          WRITING RECORD:   1
READING RECORD:   2
          WRITING RECORD:   2
READING RECORD:   3
          WRITING RECORD:   3
READING RECORD:   4
          WRITING RECORD:   4
READING RECORD:   5
          WRITING RECORD:   5
READING RECORD:   6
          WRITING RECORD:   6

SENTINEL LOCATED

TAPE FILE WRITTEN

CLOSING THE CASSETTE FILE
```

THE ARRAY, THE ARRAY

All of the foregoing is well and good so long as you desire to write the DATA lines to the magnetic media. It would be impossible, however, to read those data items back into the machine and return them to the DATA lines. It will therefore be necessary to put them somewhere, and that somewhere is an array.

Examine the DATA lines and you will see that there are six rows of seven elements. It follows, therefore, that the DIMension must be 6 or 7. Let's call the array something spiffy like PERSONNEL.FILE$. It is an attribute of an array that it must be either numeric or alphabetic but never both. Since we have a mixture of data types, let's treat them all as alphabetic, because we know that with the STR$ and VAL functions we can change them at will. Just so we are clear as to what goes where, the following will define the first record in detail:

PERSONNEL.FILE$(1,1) = 42377
PERSONNEL.FILE$(1,2) = KEN
PERSONNEL.FILE$(1,3) = LORD
PERSONNEL.FILE$(1,4) = 007328933
PERSONNEL.FILE$(1,5) = 9
PERSONNEL.FILE$(1,6) = 3
PERSONNEL.FILE$(1,7) = 36

Nancy's record would then begin at 2,1; Karen's at 3,1; and so forth.

Before we code the routine to read the data from the tape, let's merely load the DATA lines into the array and print them off to ensure that we understand what is where:

```
10 CLS
20 FOR N = 1 TO 1000
30         PRINT "READING RECORD: ";N
40     FOR X = 1 TO 7
50         READ PERSONNEL.FILE$(N,X)
60         PRINT "   ";PERSONNEL.FILE$(N,X);
70         IF PERSONNEL.FILE$(N,X) = "99999" THEN 120
80     NEXT X
90     PRINT
100 NEXT N
110 END
120 PRINT:PRINT "SENTINEL LOCATED"
130 END
1000 DATA 42377,KEN,LORD,007328933,9,3,36
1010 DATA 27365,NANCY,LORD,024372122,10,19,36
1020 DATA 34582,KAREN,LORD,073327344,12,12,59
1030 DATA 57263,TIMOTHY,LORD,008328814,9,11,61
1040 DATA 23649,SANDRA,SCOFIELD,012663429,12,5,65
1050 DATA 99999,ZZZZZ,ZZZZZ,ZZZZZ,ZZZZZ,ZZZZZ,ZZZZZ
```

Note as you examine this program that it was not necessary to identify as target the original names assigned to the data fields and then transfer them to the array. It was necessary only to identify the array parts. We used variable X to scan the columns and variable N to scan the rows, producing this output:

```
READING RECORD:   1
   42377   KEN  LORD   007328933   9   3   36
READING RECORD:   2
   27365   NANCY  LORD   024372122   10   19   36
READING RECORD:   3
   34582   KAREN  LORD   073327344   12   12   59
READING RECORD:   4
   57263   TIMOTHY  LORD   008328814   9   11   61
READING RECORD:   5
   23649   SANDRA  SCOFIELD   012663429   12   5   65
READING RECORD:   6
   99999
SENTINEL LOCATED
```

Finally, the routines necessary to load the array from the tape are as follows:

```
10 CLS
20 PRINT "OPENING THE CASSETTE FILE":PRINT
30 OPEN "I",#1,"CAS1:DATA"
40 FOR N = 1 TO 1000
50    FOR X = 1 TO 7
60        PRINT "READING RECORD: ";N
70        INPUT#1,PERSONNEL.FILE$(N,X)
80        IF PERSONNEL.FILE$(N,X) = "99999" THEN 120
90    NEXT X
100 NEXT N
110 END
120 PRINT:PRINT "SENTINEL LOCATED"
130 PRINT:PRINT "TAPE FILE READ"
140 PRINT:PRINT "CLOSING THE CASSETTE FILE"
150 CLOSE #1
160 END
```

OK, the array is loaded, you've used the data, and now you need the storage. What next? Simple: When you've finished with an array and find that you need space (usually the case in a very large program), you can ERASE the array. You ERASE it in the same manner as you DIMensioned it, as follows:

DIM PERSONNEL.FILE$(1000,7)
ERASE PERSONNEL.FILE$

Look carefully at the previous two programs that used an array and you'll note that neither contains a DIMension statement. Why? The reason is that the PC will automatically define a minimum 10 by 10 matrix for you without this statement. For any larger matrix, however, the PC will give you an error message requiring one.

STRINGs and Things

In business applications you will find yourself manipulating more nonnumeric data than you will numeric data. The specification of "nonnumeric" should not be arbitrarily assumed to be alphabetic, for as we have seen, it's possible to treat numeric data (from DATA lines or from tape) as if it were alphabetic (nonnumeric) data. It would therefore behoove us to become more acquainted with how the PC handles string data.

The first three instructions required are those that can be used to "break down" an alphabetic string. They are LEFT$, MID$, and RIGHT$. With LEFT$ and RIGHT$, you can specify the number of characters you wish to extract (copy) from the left or right side of the string. With MID$ you can extract from the center of the string; the only difference here is that you must specify the beginning position of the extraction. Enter the following program and run it, and you will achieve the results shown in the output below it:

```
10 CLS
20 TEST.STRING$ = "ABCDEFGHI"
30 LOCATE 8,20
40 PRINT "TEST STRING POSITION:   123456789"
50 LOCATE 10,20
60 PRINT "TEST STRING CHARACTER: ";TEST.STRING$
70 LOCATE 14,1
80 PRINT "LEFT THREE CHARACTERS:"
90 LOCATE 14,30
100 PRINT LEFT$(TEST.STRING$,3)
110 LOCATE 16,1
120 PRINT "CENTER THREE CHARACTERS:"
130 LOCATE 16,30
140 PRINT MID$(TEST.STRING$,4,3)
150 LOCATE 18,1
160 PRINT "RIGHT THREE CHARACTERS:"
170 LOCATE 18,30
180 PRINT RIGHT$(TEST.STRING$,3)
190 FOR X = 11 TO 14
200     LOCATE X,44
210     PRINT "!"
220 NEXT X
230 FOR Y = 35 TO 43
240     LOCATE X-1,Y
250     PRINT "."
260 NEXT Y
270 FOR X = 11 TO 16
280     LOCATE X,47
290     PRINT "!"
300 NEXT X
310 FOR Y = 35 TO 46
320     LOCATE X-1,Y
330     PRINT "."
340 NEXT Y
350 FOR X = 11 TO 18
```

```
360      LOCATE X,50
370      PRINT ":"
380 NEXT X
390 FOR Y = 35 TO 49
400      LOCATE X-1,Y
410      PRINT "."
420 NEXT Y
430 LOCATE 14,55
440 PRINT "LEFT$(TEST.STRING$,3)"
450 LOCATE 16,55
460 PRINT "MID$(TEST.STRING$,4,3)"
470 LOCATE 18,55
480 PRINT "RIGHT$(TEST.STRING$,3)"
490 PRINT
```

```
                TEST STRING POSITION:   123456789

                TEST STRING CHARACTER: ABCDEFGHI
                                       !   !   !
                                       !   !   !
                                       !   !   !
LEFT THREE CHARACTERS:      ABC  .........!   !   !     LEFT$(TEST.STRING$,3)
                                             !   !
CENTER THREE CHARACTERS:    DEF  .............!   !     MID$(TEST.STRING$,4,3)
                                                 !
RIGHT THREE CHARACTERS:     GHI  ................!     RIGHT$(TEST.STRING$,3)
```

All this is well and good, and we have extracted from a string whose size is known a specified number of characters. Suppose, however, that we were searching through data for a specified combination of characters, such as could be used, for example, in a keyword. What then? The INSTR function will tell where in the string the specific sequence of characters is located. For instance, if from our brief alphabetic sequence we wished to locate the sub-string EFG, we would assume that the computer would tell us that they are located in the fifth position. Enter and try the following program.

```
10 CLS
20 TEST.STRING$ = "ABCDEFGHI"
30 INPUT "ENTER THE STRING YOU SEEK: ",A$
40 X = INSTR(TEST.STRING$,A$)
50 IF X > 0 THEN PRINT "THE LOCATION OF ";A$;" IS";X:GOTO 70
60 PRINT A$;" IS NOT LOCATED IN THE TARGET STRING"
70 PRINT
80 GOTO 20
```

Occasionally it's important to know the length of a given string of data. Let's say, perhaps, that you can print only the first 10 characters of a field on a page of printed output. To determine the length, the LENgth function is used. Once the length is known, you can determine the size of the data to be presented. For instance, consider the following program:

```
10 CLS
20 TEN$ = "              1         2         3         4"
30 UNIT$ = "1234567890123456789012345678901234567890"
40 LOCATE 6
50 PRINT "SCALE:"
60 LOCATE 5,20
70 PRINT TEN$
80 LOCATE 6,20
90 PRINT UNIT$
100 LOCATE 8
110 PRINT "ENTER STRING:"
120 LOCATE 8,20
130 INPUT "",A$
140 LOCATE 10
150 PRINT "SIZE OF OUTPUT:"
160 LOCATE 10,20
170 INPUT "",SIZE
180 LOCATE 12
190 PRINT "RESULTING STRING:"
200 LOCATE 12,20
210 IF LEN(A$) < SIZE THEN PRINT "IMPOSSIBLE!":GOTO 230
220 PRINT LEFT$(A$,SIZE)
230 LOCATE 14
240 PRINT "PRESS ANY KEY TO CONTINUE"
250 Z$ = INKEY$
260 IF Z$ = "" THEN 250 ELSE 10
```

Here we see a variable-length field entered and are presented with an opportunity to specify the output length. This approach would work as surely as if we were to trim all variables down to a common size. In this particular example, the coding advises you if it is impossible to specify a length for a field to be entered. In actuality, you would accept any length up to and including the length specified. The output should look as follows:

```
                          1         2         3         4
SCALE:            1234567890123456789012345678901234567890

ENTER STRING:     ABCDEFGHINKLMNOPQRSTUVWXYZ

SIZE OF OUTPUT:   15

RESULTING STRING: ABCDEFGHINKLMNO

PRESS ANY KEY TO CONTINUE
```

The last two string functions to be discussed in this section are SPACE$ and STRING$. The former will allow you to insert a specified number of spaces. Thus, PRINT SPACE$ (5) would put five spaces wherever you need them. STRING$ allows you to move a prescribed number of ASCII or string characters. PRINT STRING$(80,223), for instance, will light up one line of the screen. Try it. It will have some value when we try to use the line graphics of the monochrome display. Both these instructions will be discussed in greater detail when we get to our discussion of graphics.

YOU TAKE THE HIGH ROAD . . . .

One of the better techniques in common use in computer applications is the "binary search." Binary means "two" and the principle of the binary search assumes the following:

1. That whatever you're searching for is in some predetermined sequence, usually ascending.
2. That the field of search can be narrowed merely by using the "rule of halves," that is, by dividing the object of the search into equal parts, determining the relationship of the item for which you're searching to the midpoint, selecting the proper half, dividing it into two equal parts, and then continuing in the same fashion until the required item is found. In other words, a computerized twenty-questions-type game.

That's how it works, but what is it? Suppose that there is a very long list, such as a list of names, perhaps of a thousand names. If the list were compiled in just any random sequence, it would be very difficult to find the name of any one person, say John Smith. What is needed is a list arranged in alphabetical sequence, beginning with A and ascending through the alphabet to Z. Now, when you wish to search the list for Smith, your eyes fall to the S's, you look at them one by one until you find the Smiths, and then, you look for John. The computer works in the same way except that it cannot "see" the S's. What happens is that after the list has been put into alphabetic sequence, it must be divided right down the middle, between M and N. The name Smith(s) is checked against N and found to be larger since it is known that S falls somewhere between N and Z. The "bottom half" of the alphabet (A to M) is therefore not searched. The next step is to split the upper half of the alphabet so that the midpoint is now T. Since S is smaller than T, the upper quarter of the alphabet is no longer searched. It is known then that S falls somewhere between N and T, and so on.

Although the development of games is a topic for later consideration, there is one game we can now develop to illustrate this search. Known by the general title of "guess the number," it can be programmed as follows:

```
10 CLS
20 DEFINT A,C,R
30 PRINT "PICK A NUMBER FROM 1 TO 100":PRINT
40 PRINT "PRESS ANY KEY WHEN YOU HAVE DECIDED ON THE NUMBER."
50 Z$ = INKEY$
60 IF Z$ = "" THEN 50
```

The purpose of these instructions is merely to give you time to select a number in the range of 1 to 100. You do not need to tell that number to the computer. Simply write it down or keep it in mind. The integer definitions in statement 20 will ensure our dealing with whole numbers. Numeric variable A is used as part of an ON ... GOTO statement; C is used to keep track of your guesses; and each of three data variables begins with R. Statements 50 and 60 form a tight loop that waits for the keyboard entry.

The computer doesn't know the number you have in mind, of course, but it does know the *range* it has offered you and the extremes and midpoint of that range because of the additional following statements:

```
70 RANGE.MIDPOINT = 50:RANGE.TOP = 100:RANGE.BOTTOM = 0
80 CLS
90 GOSUB 210
```

These statements define the midpoint, clear the screen, and establish the linkage to a subroutine. In the subroutine, the following alternatives will be displayed:

```
210 '**************************************
220 '*         DISPLAY SUBROUTINE         *
230 '**************************************
240 PRINT TAB(30);"1.   GREATER THAN ";RANGE.MIDPOINT
250 PRINT
260 PRINT "IS IT:";TAB(30);"2.   EQUAL TO ";RANGE.MIDPOINT
270 PRINT
280 PRINT TAB(30);"3.   LESS THAN ";RANGE.MIDPOINT
290 PRINT
300 PRINT "WHICH";
310 Z$ = INKEY$
320 IF Z$ = "" THEN 310
330 IF VAL(Z$) > 3 OR VAL(Z$) < 1 THEN 310
340 A = VAL(Z$)
350 C = C + 1
360 RETURN
```

Here we have a simple menu arrangement with three options. Presentation of the menu is straightforward enough, right down to statement 330. What happens there? Recall that INKEY$ accepts an *alphabetic* input. Because we will wish to use numeric variable A for an ON ... GOTO, the input value must be changed to a numeric type. Simultaneously, the *validity* of the entry is error-trapped, and if you enter a value greater than 3, it will be rejected. The same is true if you try a value less than 1 (0, –1, etc.). Try it. The integer variable A is established in statement 340, the "guess" counter is incremented in 350, and the computer leaves the subroutine at 360.

In the subroutine, you are asked to compare the number in your head to the current midpoint. "Greater than" is option No. 1; "equal to" is option No. 2; and "less than" is option No. 3. These values correspond to the ON ... GOTO in statement 100, shown below with four new statements. In this program, only the "equal to" has been coded, recognizing that at some point you must (if you're honest) respond to this condition.

```
100 ON A GOTO ___, 120, ___
110 GOTO 70
120 PRINT:PRINT:PRINT "HA! HA!  I GUESSED YOUR NUMBER IN ONLY ";
130 PRINT C;" TRIES"
140 END
```

Back to statement 100, amplified as shown below, along with four new statements:

```
100 ON A GOTO 150, 120, ___
150 RANGE.BOTTOM = RANGE.MIDPOINT
160 GOSUB 370
170 GOTO 80
```

Now we can concentrate upon the "greater than" side of the option. In the "greater than" situation, the range is 50 to 100. The first thing to do, therefore, is to establish that range. Recall that the program is being developed to make the routines useful no matter what the numbers may be. What is now known, however, is that there is a new midpoint (RANGE.MIDPOINT). Before the old midpoint value is destroyed, however, the variable used for the bottom of the range (RANGE.BOTTOM) must be established with the *current* value of variable RANGE.MIDPOINT. That occurs in statement 150. Now a new midpoint must be established (the subroutine at 370), although the upper limit (RANGE.TOP) does not need adjustment. Here is that subroutine:

```
370 '**********************************
380 '*        UPPER HALF SUBROUTINE     *
390 '**********************************
400 RANGE.MIDPOINT = (RANGE.MIDPOINT + RANGE.TOP)/2
410 RETURN
```

This sends us back again to statement 100 and an additional set of statements:

```
100 ON A GOTO 150, 120, 180
180 RANGE.TOP = RANGE.MIDPOINT
190 GOSUB 420
200 GOTO 80
420 '**********************************
430 '*        LOWER HALF SUBROUTINE     *
440 '**********************************
450 RANGE.MIDPOINT = (RANGE.MIDPOINT + RANGE.BOTTOM)/2
460 RETURN
```

On the "less than" side, the range is now 0 to 50, although those values cannot be used directly. The upper limit must be adjusted, and that is done in statement 180. The lower limit remains as it is. It is now necessary to find a new midpoint, a job done by the subroutine at 420.

If the variables had not been defined as integers, there would have been one minor problem. When the ranges are such that the midpoint develops a decimal (for example, half of 25 is 12.5), a specific position cannot be determined, and therefore a number cannot be selected from the list. To ensure that that does not happen (if the variable has not been defined as an integer), a new instruction is required — the INTeger instruction. The INTeger instruction selects only the whole number portion of a number, disregarding the decimal fraction. It may not be absolutely precise, but it suits the problem. The general format of the instruction is A = INT(B). In this particular program, you will become aware of the problem if you continue to answer the menu on the high side. After it reaches 99, it will go to 100 and stay there. The same is true on the low side, where it rests at zero.

Here is the program in its entirety:

```
10 CLS
20 DEFINT A,C,R
30 PRINT "PICK A NUMBER FROM 1 TO 100":PRINT
40 PRINT "PRESS ANY KEY WHEN YOU HAVE DECIDED ON THE NUMBER."
50 Z$ = INKEY$
60 IF Z$ = "" THEN 50
70 RANGE.MIDPOINT = 50:RANGE.TOP = 100:RANGE.BOTTOM = 0
80 CLS
90 GOSUB 210
100 ON A GOTO 150, 120, 180
110 GOTO 70120
120 PRINT:PRINT:PRINT "HA! HA!  I GUESSED YOUR NUMBER IN ONLY ";
130 PRINT C;" TRIES"
140 END
150 RANGE.BOTTOM = RANGE.MIDPOINT
160 GOSUB 370
170 GOTO 80
180 RANGE.TOP = RANGE.MIDPOINT
190 GOSUB 420
200 GOTO 80
210 '**************************************
220 '*         DISPLAY SUBROUTINE         *
230 '**************************************
240 PRINT TAB(30);"1.   GREATER THAN ";RANGE.MIDPOINT
250 PRINT
260 PRINT "IS IT:";TAB(30);"2.   EQUAL TO ";RANGE.MIDPOINT
270 PRINT
280 PRINT TAB(30);"3.   LESS THAN ";RANGE.MIDPOINT
290 PRINT
300 PRINT "WHICH";
310 Z$ = INKEY$
320 IF Z$ = "" THEN 310
```

```
330 IF VAL(Z$) > 3 OR VAL(Z$) < 1 THEN 310
340 A = VAL(Z$)
350 C = C + 1
360 RETURN
370 '*************************************
380 '*        UPPER HALF SUBROUTINE      *
390 '*************************************
400 RANGE.MIDPOINT = (RANGE.MIDPOINT + RANGE.TOP)/2
410 RETURN
420 '*************************************
430 '*        LOWER HALF SUBROUTINE      *
440 '*************************************
450 RANGE.MIDPOINT = (RANGE.MIDPOINT + RANGE.BOTTOM)/2
460 RETURN
```

Spend some time tracing the program through, using data of your own choice. You'll find that it works not only for the upper half and the lower half, but also for the upper quarter of the lower half and the lower quarter of the upper half. Isn't that great? Teriffic! Once that is accomplished, finding the number that you "dreamed up" is not difficult; in fact, you should find it within 18 tries. There are more sophisticated routines for "guessing the number," but this example illustrates the binary search principle. *You* might have been able to figure from 1 to 100, but suppose that the range had been from 10,000 to 10,000,000. Things might have been a little more difficult.

HANDS ON THE TABLE . . .

Taking the process a step further, this technique might be applied to searching a table for the presence of a number. Up to this point, an absolute match has been the goal. To search a number table, we must remember that the number may *or may not* be in the table and that it is our responsibility to determine the matter.

The first step, naturally, is to build a table. It is possible to take one from a data file (cassette, diskette, or DATA lines), but even that would have to be built first. To illustrate the principle, we'll do a little simple construction. We'll *generate* our own table. Assume that the table consists of three elements — a stock number (in the range of 1 to 10,000), a description (which will be generated merely for illustrative purposes), and a quantity on hand in the range of 1 to 10,000). Enter and run the following little program:

```
10 CLS
20 RANDOMIZE 10000
30 FOR X = 1 TO 100
40     PRINT INT(RND(X) * 10000);" ";
50 NEXT X
60 END
```

After clearing the screen, reseed the number table (statement 20), which merely keeps you from getting the same sequence of random numbers for subsequent use. It then generates 100 random numbers. What is actually generated is the *integer* of a random number (RND(X)) – between 0 and 1 – multiplied by 10,000 so that it falls into the 1 to 1000 range. PC does not generate random whole numbers, as some other microcomputers do. But, as you can see, it's no loss. Our program generated this list of random numbers:

4196	4715	7926	5867	3701	2104	557	6083	1231	7485	3003
5486	5299	947	8116	6146	7824	2358	9422	8109	6790	3391
5027	7682	1403	2056	4024	8213	9743	9734	5397	3373	8925
705	9431	2934	7755	4180	1614	1055	1881	8836	9047	7060
1456	9840	9347	8721	1289	8388	2056	8038	3507	3730	2546
9521	2703	7705	8424	970	3601	1773	8441	6760	1205	6540
3898	3616	3462	3798	2547	8900	6410	1049	5006	1390	1843
8540	3657	4560	7462	8795	4058	2364	9533	8641	8846	7514
8040	3748	4145	2265	4346	5650	8470	1692	1349	1284	4138
9477										

You'll note that since they do not appear in any specific sequence, it will be difficult to do a binary search. To be usable, they will have to be arranged within an ascending sequence. Before we do that, however, we need to develop an array (DIM INVENTORY.TABLE$(100,3) into which we can store the item number, the description, and the quantity on hand. Because no calculation is done on these figures, the table is a string variable table, which means that the numbers generated by our table program must be changed somehow. The following program is sufficient to generate and display the array and for us to build upon:

```
10 CLS
20 CLEAR 1000
30 DIM INVENTORY.TABLE$(100,3)
40 '*************************************************
50 '*       THIS ROUTINE GENERATES THE TABLE        *
60 '*************************************************
70 FOR X = 1 TO 10
80      RANDOMIZE 10000
90      STOCK.NUMBER = INT(RND(X) * 10000):IF STOCK.NUMBER <1000 THEN 90
100     INVENTORY.TABLE$(X,1) = STR$(STOCK.NUMBER)
110     INVENTORY.TABLE$(X,2) = "ITEM DESCRIPTION"
120     RANDOMIZE 20000
130     QUANTITY.ON.HAND = INT(RND(X) * 10000)
140     INVENTORY.TABLE$(X,3) = STR$(QUANTITY.ON.HAND)
150 NEXT X
160 '*************************************************
170 '*    THIS ROUTINE DISPLAYS THE GENERATED TABLE  *
180 '*************************************************
190 FOR X = 1 TO 10
200     PRINT INVENTORY.TABLE$(X,1);TAB(20);
210     PRINT INVENTORY.TABLE$(X,2);TAB(50);
220     PRINT INVENTORY.TABLE$(X,3)
230 NEXT X
```

At this point, the really interesting things begin to happen. Recall that the premise of a binary search is that a table may or may not contain a stock number. As the table is presently constructed, such a search is impossible, since the table must be in *ascending order* on the *key field*. The key field is that field on which sequencing is to be accomplished. In this case, it's the first of the three array elements: item number. Consequently, the table must be sorted.

Of the many ways to perform a sort, the easiest to construct and explain is called the *exchange sort*. The exchange sort examines an array in pairs, changing the positions of each pair within the table such that the longest constituent of the pair is in the higher position within the array. In this manner, array element 1 (corresponding to array elements 1,2, and 3, which contain a complete record) is compared with array element 4 (corresponding to elements 4,5, and 6 — the next record). In a multidimensioned array, we're really talking about (1,Y) being compared to (2,Y), and so on. If the second record is larger than the first record (a higher inventory number), or if it is equal, then nothing changes except that you are now able to compare the second and third pairs, and the process continues. In this instance, we'll not worry about eliminating duplicate table entries. If, on the other hand, the first record is larger than the second, the first record must be removed from the table and placed in a temporary work area, the second record must take over the space formerly occupied by the first record, and the first record must then be removed from the temporary work area and take over the space formerly occupied by the second record. Got that?

Just one more thing, and then we'll take the plunge. When you're sorting *and an exchange is made*, it is necessary to identify that it has, in fact, occurred. It is possible to exchange two numbers that are not only out of sequence *between themselves* but also out of sequence *within the entire set of numbers*. Thus, if a flag is turned on (set to "ON" or 1) when an exchange is made (a flag is essentially a switch), the program can then be told to continue through the list of data until the flag is not set (no exchange has been made). When the program goes entirely through a table without making an exchange, then the table is in sequence. This procedure requires additional program statements, as follows:

```
240 ' ***********************************************
250 ' * TERMINATE THE ARRAY WITH A SENTINEL; SET FLAG *
260 ' ***********************************************
270 FOR Y = 1 TO 3
280     INVENTORY.TABLE$(X,Y) = "ZZZZZ"
290 NEXT Y
300 FLAG$ = "OFF"
310 ' ***********************************************
320 ' *          EXCHANGE SORT THE ARRAY ROUTINE       *
330 ' ***********************************************
340 FOR X = 1 TO 100
350     IF INVENTORY.TABLE$(X,1) = "ZZZZZ" THEN 480
```

```
360      IF INVENTORY.TABLE$(X + 1,1) > = INVENTORY.TABLE$(X,1) THEN 47
370      TEMP.ITEM$ = INVENTORY.TABLE$(X,1)
380      TEMP.DESCRIPTION$ = INVENTORY.TABLE$(X,2)
390      TEMP.QUANTITY$ = INVENTORY.TABLE$(X,3)
400      INVENTORY.TABLE$(X,1) = INVENTORY.TABLE$(X + 1,1)
410      INVENTORY.TABLE$(X,2) = INVENTORY.TABLE$(X + 1,2)
420      INVENTORY.TABLE$(X,3) = INVENTORY.TABLE$(X + 1,3)
430      INVENTORY.TABLE$(X + 1,1) = TEMP.ITEM$
440      INVENTORY.TABLE$(X + 1,2) = TEMP.DESCRIPTION$
450      INVENTORY.TABLE$(X + 1,3) = TEMP.QUANTITY$
460      FLAG$ = "ON"
470 NEXT X
480 IF FLAG$ = "OFF" THEN 540
490 FLAG$ = "OFF"
500 GOTO 340
```

The flag is now set, the table is sealed with sentinels, and the sorting process begins as previously described. We now add the following display routine:

```
510 '****************************************************
520 '*      THIS ROUTINE DISPLAYS THE SORTED TABLE     *
530 '****************************************************
540 PRINT
545 FOR X = 1 TO 10
550     PRINT INVENTORY.TABLE$(X,1);TAB(20);
560     PRINT INVENTORY.TABLE$(X,2);TAB(50);
570     PRINT INVENTORY.TABLE$(X,3)
580 NEXT X
590 END
```

Run it and you'll note something peculiar. There may be a stock number that is smaller than 1000 but nevertheless is left-justified in the number field. That's because we have treated this field as an alphabetic field, and alphabetic fields align to the *high order* (left-justified), whereas numeric fields align to the *low order* (right-justified). There are several ways to solve this problem, but since this is a demonstration program only, change statement 90 to look as follows:

```
90      STOCK.NUMBER = INT(RND(X) * 10000):IF STOCK.NUMBER <1000 THEN 9
```

Here is the program in its entirety:

```
10 CLS
20 CLEAR 1000
30 DIM INVENTORY.TABLE$(100,3)
40 '****************************************************
50 '*      THIS ROUTINE GENERATES THE TABLE           *
60 '****************************************************
70 FOR X = 1 TO 10
80      RANDOMIZE 10000
90      STOCK.NUMBER = INT(RND(X) * 10000):IF STOCK.NUMBER <1000 THEN 9
100     INVENTORY.TABLE$(X,1) = STR$(STOCK.NUMBER)
110     INVENTORY.TABLE$(X,2) = "ITEM DESCRIPTION"
120     RANDOMIZE 20000
130     QUANTITY.ON.HAND = INT(RND(X) * 10000)
```

```
140       INVENTORY.TABLE$(X,3) = STR$(QUANTITY.ON.HAND)
150 NEXT X
160 '*************************************************
170 '*    THIS ROUTINE DISPLAYS THE GENERATED TABLE   *
180 '*************************************************
190 FOR X = 1 TO 10
200       PRINT INVENTORY.TABLE$(X,1);TAB(20);
210       PRINT INVENTORY.TABLE$(X,2);TAB(50);
220       PRINT INVENTORY.TABLE$(X,3)
230 NEXT X
240 '*************************************************
250 '* TERMINATE THE ARRAY WITH A SENTINEL; SET FLAG *
260 '*************************************************
270 FOR Y = 1 TO 3
280       INVENTORY.TABLE$(X,Y) = "ZZZZZ"
290 NEXT Y
300 FLAG$ = "OFF"
310 '*************************************************
320 '*          EXCHANGE SORT THE ARRAY ROUTINE        *
330 '*************************************************
340 FOR X = 1 TO 100
350       IF INVENTORY.TABLE$(X,1) = "ZZZZZ" THEN 480
360       IF INVENTORY.TABLE$(X + 1,1) > = INVENTORY.TABLE$(X,1) THEN 470
370       TEMP.ITEM$ = INVENTORY.TABLE$(X,1)
380       TEMP.DESCRIPTION$ = INVENTORY.TABLE$(X,2)
390       TEMP.QUANTITY$ = INVENTORY.TABLE$(X,3)
400       INVENTORY.TABLE$(X,1) = INVENTORY.TABLE$(X + 1,1)
410       INVENTORY.TABLE$(X,2) = INVENTORY.TABLE$(X + 1,2)
420       INVENTORY.TABLE$(X,3) = INVENTORY.TABLE$(X + 1,3)
430       INVENTORY.TABLE$(X + 1,1) = TEMP.ITEM$
440       INVENTORY.TABLE$(X + 1,2) = TEMP.DESCRIPTION$
450       INVENTORY.TABLE$(X + 1,3) = TEMP.QUANTITY$
460       FLAG$ = "ON"
470 NEXT X
480 IF FLAG$ = "OFF" THEN 540
490 FLAG$ = "OFF"
500 GOTO 340
510 '*************************************************
520 '*     THIS ROUTINE DISPLAYS THE SORTED TABLE      *
530 '*************************************************
540 PRINT
545 FOR X = 1 TO 10
550       PRINT INVENTORY.TABLE$(X,1);TAB(20);
560       PRINT INVENTORY.TABLE$(X,2);TAB(50);
570       PRINT INVENTORY.TABLE$(X,3)
580 NEXT X
590 END
```

The exchange sort is not the fastest type of sort, but it is very effective and easily implemented. This particular example has been structured on a base of 100 numbers. If the amount to be sorted is sufficiently large, it would be wise to add instructions to display the items sorted as they are being sorted.

TABLE MAINTENANCE

The actual input/output with cassette and diskette is not complicated. We've briefly talked about cassette and will concentrate later on diskette. We've generated data for a table and have sorted it. At this stage, the ability to write a table on diskette or to the printer in the form of a report is simply an interface step.

We will now concentrate, therefore, upon building a table directly from input entered at the keyboard and upon the routines needed to add to the table, delete from the table, change a table entry, sort it upon any data element (using the exchange method), and report from it. Let's make a decision up front: Our inventory table will never exceed 100 items.

While we're at it, let's consider *all* the features that are necessary to table handling:

1. We must be able to add to the table and in any sequence.
2. We must be able to change an entry already made to the table.
3. We must also be able to delete a table entry.
4. Simple inquiry facilities are needed. We might not want to make a second entry under the same control element.
5. A facility is needed to display and (upon selection of the option) to produce a hardcopy output of the table.
6. A facility is needed to sort the table in preparation for its storage on magnetic media.
7. Interfaces are needed to load the table *from* magnetic media and dump *to* magnetic media.

As you might surmise, these requirements will produce a program of considerable size. The program now to be discussed has been developed in *modules*. If memory is a limiting factor for you, these modules must be selected and combined as necessity demands.

INVENTORY DATA ENTRY PROGRAM

The general heading for this program is INVENTORY DATA ENTRY. The block diagram shown on the opposite page (and the program that produced it) will be the subject of a later discussion in the area of monochrome text-mode screen graphics.

The opening menu of the program looks like this:

```
I N V E N T O R Y    D A T A    E N T R Y

     A.   ADD DATA TO THE TABLE

     C.   CHANGE DATA ON THE TABLE

     D.   DELETE DATA FROM THE TABLE

     L.   LOCATE DATA (ITEM NUMBER)
```

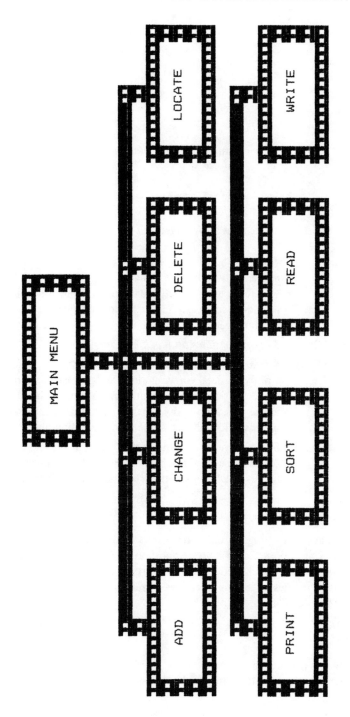

```
P.   PRINT (DISPLAY OR PAPER)

S.   SORT THE TABLE

R.   READ THE TABLE FROM MEDIA

W.   WRITE THE TABLE TO MEDIA

SELECT:


PRESS 'X' TO TERMINATE THE PROGRAM
```

The Table

The table is a 100 X 3 element array, organized as follows:

Element 1	*4-position item code, alphanumeric:* If the number is to be numeric, it should be converted and tested before storage. This feature is not included in the program. Since the program provides acceptance features and modification capabilities, it was not necessary to do so.
Element 2	*35-position description, alphanumeric.*
Element 3	*4-position quantity-on-hand, alphanumeric:* Since this is strictly a data entry module and no calculation is to be made on this field, alphanumeric is used to simplify storing in the same array. Any enhancements that require calculations on this field will necessitate conversion to numeric.
Sentinel	Five Z's are loaded into each element at the end of the table. As the size of the table increases, the sentinels are moved forward. Displays of the table include the first sentinel.

Narrative of the Program

This is a data entry program only. It permits loading of a data array from the keyboard. Correction of data is offered both at entry and after the array has been loaded. Data may be deleted from the array. The program includes printing and sorting facilities as well as interfaces to read and write any media modules that may be added later.

Add Option

The program permits the addition of up to 10 three-element entries at a time. After each 10 elements, it returns to the main menu to permit sorting or printing and correction or deletion before it resumes acceptance of additional entries. No rejection is made of duplicate item numbers.

Change Option

The program permits display of a single array entry by key (item number). The operator is asked if the code is known. If the code is not known and the operator responds accordingly, the program returns to the main menu where the operator can obtain a display or list of the entire array. Once the key is known, the entry can be called out again and corrected.

Delete Option

As with the delete option, and by the same procedure, once the key is known, an entry can be called out and deleted. The operator must confirm the deletion. Deletions are not actually removed from the array; they are merely changed to "/" for removal in the sort module.

Locate Option

This is the inquiry module. The operator enters the key (item number), and the item is displayed if it is in the table. If it is not in the table, the program says so and returns to the main menu.

Print Option

This is simple output of data on the screen and (by screen option) on hardcopy that is not formatted. It is accomplished 10 units at a time with "go forward" and "abort" mechanisms.

Sort Option

This sort is an exchange sort on item number. Deleted entires are dropped since the array is copied to a work array without them. Sort completion invokes the print module's display option.

Read/Write Options

At this stage only the interfaces have been installed. The modules will not be completed until after our discussion of diskette input/output, later on. The intent is to offer two read options (LOAD and APPEND) and one write option (DUMP). More on these at that time.

Discussion

As the program is discussed, bear in mind that the statement numbers correspond to the location of the instruction in the completed program. The parts will be presented, not in sequence, but in terms of their logical relationship to the whole. We will first discuss the overheads.

Overheads

The functions of statements 10 to 160 are to make room for a large number of alphanumeric items (statement 20) and to establish the screen coordinates for display of the data. These statements are as follows:

```
10 CLS
20 CLEAR 10000
30 KEY OFF
40 DIM SCREEN.LOCATOR(30,3)
50 FOR N = 1 TO 30
60      READ SCREEN.LOCATOR(N,1)
70      READ SCREEN.LOCATOR(N,2)
80      READ SCREEN.LOCATOR(N,3)
90 NEXT N
100 RESTORE
110 DIM INVENTORY.TABLE$(101,3)
120 FOR N = 1 TO 3                         'LOAD SENTINEL
130     INVENTORY.TABLE$(1,N) = "ZZZZZ"    'AT HEAD OF TABLE
140 NEXT N
150 DIM WORK.TABLE$(101,3)
160 ITEMS.LOADED = 1
```

In statement 20, the size of the CLEAR will be a function of your available memory. The table, as structured in this program, consists of 101 records of three elements each, including the sentinel. Since each record will occupy 43 bytes, 4300 bytes are required for the inventory table alone. An equal number is required for the work table. The remaining bytes will be a function of the messages used. This program uses the 10,000 reserved. Note that prior to use, the sentinel is set into the first record and its existence noted (statements 120-140 and 160).

The instructions from statement 50 through 90 load the DATA lines into an array. Because it is necessary to "back up" to make a correction, and because BASIC does not allow reverse reads on DATA statements, it is necessary to load them into an array where reverse addressing can be accomplished. Here are the required DATA lines:

```
5150 '*******************************************************
5160 '*      SCREEN COORDINATES FOR LOAD AND CHANGE       *
5170 '*******************************************************
5180 DATA 10,8,4,10,23,35,10,65,4
5190 DATA 11,8,4,11,23,35,11,65,4
5200 DATA 12,8,4,12,23,35,12,65,4
```

```
5210 DATA 13,8,4,13,23,35,13,65,4
5220 DATA 14,8,4,14,23,35,14,65,4
5230 DATA 15,8,4,15,23,35,15,65,4
5240 DATA 16,8,4,16,23,35,16,65,4
5250 DATA 17,8,4,17,23,35,17,65,4
5260 DATA 18,8,4,18,23,35,18,65,4
5270 DATA 19,8,4,19,23,35,19,65,4
5280 DATA 99999,99999,99999
```

These happen not to be at the very end of the program, but they are near the
end and all in a group. They correspond to the thirty data elements that are
presented on the screen (three to each record, with ten records). The numbers
are ordered in sets of three: screen line, screen column, and length of data.
You'll note that each record has a 4,35,4 data length.

Some line graphics — simple and straightforward — are performed by this
program. Included are the following:

1. *Screen frame subroutine:* This subroutine displays an overall heading
   and draws the horizontal and vertical lines needed to frame the screen
   work:

```
610 '**********************************************
620 '*          SCREEN FRAME SUBROUTINE          *
630 '**********************************************
640 FOR Y = 1 TO 24
650     LOCATE Y,1
660     PRINT CHR$(223);TAB(20);CHR$(223);
670     PRINT TAB(60);CHR$(223);TAB(79);CHR$(223)
680 NEXT Y
690 LOCATE 1
700 PRINT STRING$(79,223)
710 LOCATE 2,20
720 PRINT "I N V E N T O R Y   D A T A   E N T R Y
730 LOCATE 3,20
740 PRINT "
750 LOCATE 4
760 PRINT STRING$(79,223)
770 LOCATE 24
780 PRINT STRING$(79,223);
790 RETURN
```

There is one thing worth noting here. Statement 740 clears out the
vertical lines that clutter the heading. In actuality, such a large constant
of spaces is not necessary. The same thing can be accomplished with the
SPACE$ command, as can other such operations in the program.

2. *Screen heading subroutine:* This subroutine superimposes a heading
   upon the frame with the following statements:

```
920 '**********************************************
930 '*          SCREEN HEADING SUBROUTINE        *
940 '**********************************************
950 LOCATE 6
```

```
960 PRINT STRING$(79,223)
970 LOCATE 7,5
980 PRINT "ITEM NUMBER"
990 LOCATE 7,35
1000 PRINT "DESCRIPTION"
1010 LOCATE 7,68
1020 PRINT "QUANTITY"
1030 LOCATE 8
1040 PRINT STRING$(79,223)
1050 RETURN
```

3. *Clear screen frame subroutine:* This subroutine clears out the center of the screen. Like the previous subroutine, it is not complex.

```
800 '********************************************************
810 '*         CLEAR SCREEN FRAME SUBROUTINE              *
820 '********************************************************
830 FOR SCREEN.LINE = 6 TO 22
840     LOCATE SCREEN.LINE,2
850     PRINT SPACES$(5);
860     LOCATE SCREEN.LINE,22
870     PRINT SPACE$(35);
880     LOCATE SCREEN.LINE,62
890     PRINT SPACES$(6)
900 NEXT SCREEN.LINE
910 RETURN
```

4. *Error message subroutine:* The message subroutine uses line 25 of the screen, that portion which has been cleared as a result of the KEY OFF instruction at 30. Since the majority of the messages are error messages, that is the name of the variable used, as follows:

```
5060 RETURN
5070 '********************************************************
5080 '*              ERROR MESSAGE SUBROUTINE              *
5090 '********************************************************
5100 BEEP
5110 LINEFILL = 60 - LEN(ERROR.MESSAGE$)
5120 LOCATE 25,1
5130 PRINT ERROR.MESSAGE$ + SPACE$(LINEFILL);
5140 RETURN
```

5. *Screen line numbers and blank lines subroutine:* The final overhead routine is that which draws the internal screen lines upon which data will be entered and displayed, including the line numbers:

```
5290 '********************************************************
5300 '*    SCREEN LINE NUMBERS AND BLANK LINES            *
5310 '********************************************************
5320 LOCATE 10,4:PRINT " 1.";
5330 LOCATE 11,4:PRINT " 2.";
5340 LOCATE 12,4:PRINT " 3.";
5350 LOCATE 13,4:PRINT " 4.";
```

```
5360 LOCATE 14,4:PRINT " 5.";
5370 LOCATE 15,4:PRINT " 6.";
5380 LOCATE 16,4:PRINT " 7.";
5390 LOCATE 17,4:PRINT " 8.";
5400 LOCATE 18,4:PRINT " 9.";
5410 LOCATE 19,4:PRINT "10.";
5420 RESTORE
5430 FOR N = 1 TO 30
5440     READ LINE.NUMBER,COLUMN.NUMBER,SHADE.LENGTH
5450     LOCATE LINE.NUMBER,COLUMN.NUMBER
5460     FOR Z = 1 TO SHADE.LENGTH
5470         PRINT CHR$(22);
5480     NEXT Z
5490 NEXT N
5500 BEEP
5510 RESTORE
5520 RETURN
```

Menu Module

The menu selection module is usually a presentation of the options followed by a change in direction on the basis of the option selected. It begins by clearing the message line and storing the exit option (statements 210-260) and is followed by the presentation of letter-specified options. Each letter is converted to a relative number (480-560) to allow the ON . . . GOSUB to be used in statement 590.

The menu module is as follows:

```
180 '********************************************
190 '*              OPTION SELECTION MENU        *
200 '********************************************
210 ERROR.MESSAGE$ = SPACE$(60)
220 GOSUB 5070             'ERROR MESSAGE SUBROUTINE
230 ERROR.MESSAGE$ = "PRESS 'X' TO TERMINATE THE PROGRAM"
240 GOSUB 5070             'ERROR MESSAGE SUBROUTINE
250 SCREEN.LINE = 6
260 SCREEN.COLUMN = 25
270 LOCATE SCREEN.LINE,SCREEN.COLUMN
280 PRINT "A.   ADD DATA TO THE TABLE"
290 LOCATE SCREEN.LINE + 2,SCREEN.COLUMN
300 PRINT "C.   CHANGE DATA ON THE TABLE"
310 LOCATE SCREEN.LINE + 4,SCREEN.COLUMN
320 PRINT "D.   DELETE DATA FROM THE TABLE"
330 LOCATE SCREEN.LINE + 6,SCREEN.COLUMN
340 PRINT "L.   LOCATE DATA (ITEM NUMBER)"
350 LOCATE SCREEN.LINE + 8,SCREEN.COLUMN
360 PRINT "P.   PRINT (DISPLAY OR PAPER)"
370 LOCATE SCREEN.LINE + 10,SCREEN.COLUMN
380 PRINT "S.   SORT THE TABLE"
390 LOCATE SCREEN.LINE + 12,SCREEN.COLUMN
400 PRINT "R.   READ THE TABLE FROM MEDIA"
410 LOCATE SCREEN.LINE + 14,SCREEN.COLUMN
420 PRINT "W.   WRITE THE TABLE TO MEDIA"
430 LOCATE SCREEN.LINE + 16,SCREEN.COLUMN
440 PRINT "SELECT: ";
450 Z$ = INKEY$
460 IF Z$ = "" THEN 450
```

```
470 IF Z$ = " " THEN 450
480 IF Z$ = "X" THEN PRINT Z$:END
490 IF Z$ = "A" THEN MENU.SELECTION = 1
500 IF Z$ = "C" THEN MENU.SELECTION = 2
510 IF Z$ = "D" THEN MENU.SELECTION = 3
520 IF Z$ = "L" THEN MENU.SELECTION = 4
530 IF Z$ = "P" THEN MENU.SELECTION = 5
540 IF Z$ = "S" THEN MENU.SELECTION = 6
550 IF Z$ = "R" THEN MENU.SELECTION = 7
560 IF Z$ = "W" THEN MENU.SELECTION = 8
570 IF (MENU.SELECTION < 1) OR (MENU.SELECTION > 8) THEN 450
580 PRINT Z$
590 ON MENU.SELECTION GOSUB 1060,1920,2890,3510,4070,4510,5530,5590
600 GOTO 170
```

Add Module

The add module and the change module are the two largest modules of the program. The reason is that each must have the ability to revise data. The add module must first determine whether the data to be added is new data or merely being appended to existing data. It does so – and the headings, lines, and clearing all take place – in statement 1210. The FIELDS.RECEIVED variable is used to determine whether the entire record has in fact been received, once it has been incremented to three.

Statements 1230-1840 constitute the routine for accepting data. Note that there are 30 cycles through the FOR . . . NEXT loop, three fields per record times ten records per screen.

An interesting thing can be learned as this program is put together – something that is not in the machine manuals. Whatever variable is used to identify the position on the screen is *incremented* as the printing is done. Of particular interest to us here is that once a variable is identified for column, expect that variable to be incremented to the next sequential position on the screen line for each character displayed. For that reason, you will find places where the screen locator is saved in a location that is not incremented (1270-1280) and is restored from the array that was discussed when the "back-up" requirement was mentioned (statements 1610-1690). The fields are loaded in threes, and the sentinel is placed immediately following the last data item loaded into the array (1410-1430). Each entry must be confirmed. If it cannot be confirmed, then the backup process must be undertaken. This is significant because the routines to put a backspace option into the program are not only extensive, but not included. An unacceptable entry is simply repeated. All fields must have something placed within them, moreover; otherwise, the operator is advised that the entry is mandatory (1860-1890).

Finally, note the assemblage of the data on a character-by-character basis in statement 1350. At 1340 the character is printed at the next sequential location. Not until either the field size restriction (4,35,4) has been reached or a carriage return (CHR$(13) has been entered is the field considered to be complete.

Cessation of data entry is accomplished by the entry of "STOP" in the item field. As the program is written, the STOP entry will be interpreted at any of the three elements on the line and may result in an incomplete entry. A more sophisticated program would either preclude that possibility or clear the entire entry. That level of sophistication is not necessary at this point.

The table addition subroutine is as follows:

```
1060 '********************************************
1070 '*            TABLE ADDITION SUBROUTINE            *
1080 '********************************************
1090 IF INVENTORY.TABLE$(1,1) = "ZZZZZ" THEN 1150
1100 FOR X = 1 TO 101
1110     IF INVENTORY.TABLE$(X,1) = "ZZZZZ" THEN 1140
1120 NEXT X
1130 GOTO 1150
1140 ITEMS.LOADED = X
1150 GOSUB 800            'CLEAR OUT INSIDE OF FRAME
1160 GOSUB 920            'ADDITION HEADING
1170 LOCATE 5,20
1180 PRINT "TYPE 'STOP' UNDER ITEM TO TERMINATE ENTRY          "
1190 ERROR.MESSAGE$ = "TABLE ADDITION"
1200 GOSUB 5070           'ERROR MESSAGE SUBROUTINE
1210 GOSUB 5290           'CLEAR AND NUMBER LINES
1220 FIELDS.RECEIVED = 0
1230 FOR N = 1 TO 30
1240     LINE.NUMBER = SCREEN.LOCATOR(N,1)
1250     COLUMN.NUMBER = SCREEN.LOCATOR(N,2)
1260     DATA.LENGTH = SCREEN.LOCATOR(N,3)
1270     HOLD.LINE.NUMBER = LINE.NUMBER
1280     HOLD.COLUMN.NUMBER = COLUMN.NUMBER
1290     LOCATE LINE.NUMBER,COLUMN.NUMBER
1300     A$ = ""
1310     Z$ = INKEY$
1320     IF Z$ = "" THEN 1310
1330     HOLD.COLUMN.NUMBER = COLUMN.NUMBER
1340     PRINT Z$;
1350     A$ = A$ + Z$
1360     IF A$ = "STOP" THEN 1850
1370     IF LEN(A$) = DATA.LENGTH THEN 1400
1380     IF (Z$ = CHR$(13)) AND (LEN(A$) = 1) THEN GOSUB 1860:GOTO 1310
1390     IF (Z$ = CHR$(13)) AND (LEN(A$) > 1) THEN 1400 ELSE 1310
1400     FIELDS.RECEIVED = FIELDS.RECEIVED + 1
1410     IF FIELDS.RECEIVED = 1 THEN INVENTORY.TABLE$(ITEMS.LOADED,1) = A$
1420     IF FIELDS.RECEIVED = 2 THEN INVENTORY.TABLE$(ITEMS.LOADED,2) = A$
1430     IF FIELDS.RECEIVED = 3 THEN INVENTORY.TABLE$(ITEMS.LOADED,3) = A$
1440     INVENTORY.TABLE$(ITEMS.LOADED + 1,1) = "ZZZZZ"
1450     INVENTORY.TABLE$(ITEMS.LOADED + 1,2) = "ZZZZZ"
1460     INVENTORY.TABLE$(ITEMS.LOADED + 1,3) = "ZZZZZ"
1470     IF FIELDS.RECEIVED <> 3 THEN 1840
1480     FIELDS.RECEIVED = 0
1490     ERROR.MESSAGE$ = "ACCEPTABLE (Y/N)?"
1500     GOSUB 5070      'ERROR MESSAGE SUBROUTINE
1510     Z$ = INKEY$:IF Z$ = "" THEN 1510
1520     IF Z$ = "N" THEN 1580
1530     IF Z$ < > "Y" THEN 1510
1540     ITEMS.LOADED = ITEMS.LOADED + 1
1550     ERROR.MESSAGE$ = SPACE$(60)
1560     GOSUB 5070      'ERROR MESSAGE SUBROUTINE
1570     GOTO 1840
1580     ERROR.MESSAGE$ = "ENTRY REJECTED"
1590     GOSUB 5070      'ERROR MESSAGE SUBROUTINE
1600     N = N - 2
1610     A1 = SCREEN.LOCATOR(N,1)
1620     A2 = SCREEN.LOCATOR(N,2)
1630     A3 = SCREEN.LOCATOR(N,3)
1640     B1 = SCREEN.LOCATOR(N + 1,1)
```

```
1650      B2 = SCREEN.LOCATOR(N + 1,2)
1660      B3 = SCREEN.LOCATOR(N + 1,3)
1670      C1 = SCREEN.LOCATOR(N + 2,1)
1680      C2 = SCREEN.LOCATOR(N + 2,2)
1690      C3 = SCREEN.LOCATOR(N + 2,3)
1700      LOCATE A1,A2
1710      FOR Z = 1 TO A3
1720          PRINT CHR$(22);
1730      NEXT Z
1740      LOCATE B1,B2
1750      FOR Z = 1 TO B3
1760          PRINT CHR$(22);
1770      NEXT Z
1780      LOCATE C1,C2
1790      FOR Z = 1 TO C3
1800          PRINT CHR$(22);
1810      NEXT Z
1820      FIELDS.RECEIVED = 0
1830      N = N - 1
1840 NEXT N
1850 RETURN
1860 ERROR.MESSAGE$ = "MANDATORY ENTRY"
1870 GOSUB 5070              'ERROR MESSAGE SUBROUTINE
1880 COLUMN.NUMBER = HOLD.COLUMN.NUMBER
1890 LOCATE LINE.NUMBER,COLUMN.NUMBER
1900 A$ = ""
1910 RETURN
```

Change Module

The change routine, like the add routine, is lengthy. Much of that length is taken up with internal messages, the reason being that you are asked for the key (item number) and if you do not know it, you are directed back to the main menu so that you can review the entire contents of the array. If you know the key, the array is searched for it. If the key is not located within the array, you are so notified at statement 2330. If the item is present, it is displayed (statements 2380-2430).

Once you have had the opportunity to verify visually the record (2440-2470), a second, blank line is presented beneath the record, and you must retype the entire entry. After the entry has been retyped, it must be confirmed. If it is confirmed, the revised entry is refiled in the location from which it was extracted.

Again, there is an assemblage — actually, three of them (2610, 2680, and 2750). The same methods for entry and termination of data apply as before.

The table change subroutine is as follows:

```
1920 '***********************************************
1930 '*            TABLE CHANGE SUBROUTINE          *
1940 '***********************************************
1950 A$ = "":B$ = "":C$ = ""
1960 IF ITEMS.LOADED > 1 THEN 2000
1970 ERROR.MESSAGE$ = "NO TABLE TO CHANGE"
1980 GOSUB 5070              'ERROR MESSAGE SUBROUTINE
1990 RETURN
2000 GOSUB 800              'CLEAR OUT INSIDE OF FRAME
2010 GOSUB 920              'HEADING SUBROUTINE
2020 ERROR.MESSAGE$ = "TABLE CHANGE"
```

```
2030 GOSUB 5070              'ERROR MESSAGE SUBROUTINE
2040 FOR Z = 1 TO 500:NEXT Z
2050 LOCATE 10,23
2060 PRINT "CHANGE WORKS ON ONE ELEMENT ONLY.";
2070 LOCATE 12,23
2080 PRINT "IF YOU KNOW THE ITEM NUMBER, THEN";
2090 LOCATE 13,23
2100 PRINT "ANSWER YES TO THE QUESTION.  IF";
2110 LOCATE 14,23
2120 PRINT "YOU DO NOT KNOW IT, ENTER PRINT";
2130 LOCATE 15,23
2140 PRINT "AT THE MAIN MENU, LOCATE THE ITEM";
2150 LOCATE 16,23
2160 PRINT "NUMBER AND COME BACK TO HERE."
2170 ERROR.MESSAGE$ = "DO YOU KNOW THE ITEM NUMBER (Y/N)?"
2180 GOSUB 5070              'ERROR MESSAGE SUBROUTINE
2190 Z$ = INKEY$:IF Z$ = "" THEN 2190
2200 IF Z$ < > "Y" THEN RETURN
2210 ERROR.MESSAGE$ = "ENTER THE ITEM NUMBER: "
2220 GOSUB 5070              'ERROR MESSAGE SUBROUTINE
2230 Z$ = INKEY$:IF Z$ = "" THEN 2230
2240 IF Z$ = CHR$(13) THEN 2290
2250 A$ = A$ + Z$
2260 ERROR.MESSAGE$ = "ITEM NUMBER: " + A$
2270 GOSUB 5070              'ERROR MESSAGE SUBROUTINE
2280 GOTO 2230
2290 FOR X = 1 TO 101
2300     IF INVENTORY.TABLE$(X,1) = A$ THEN 2360
2310     IF INVENTORY.TABLE$(X,1) = "ZZZZZ" THEN 2330
2320 NEXT X
2330 ERROR.MESSAGE$ = "ITEM NOT ON TABLE"
2340 GOSUB 5070              'ERROR MESSAGE SUBROUTINE
2350 RETURN
2360 GOSUB 800               'CLEAR INSIDE OF FRAME
2370 GOSUB 920               'HEADING SUBROUTINE
2380 LOCATE 10,8
2390 PRINT INVENTORY.TABLE$(X,1);
2400 LOCATE 10,23
2410 PRINT INVENTORY.TABLE$(X,2);
2420 LOCATE 10,65
2430 PRINT INVENTORY.TABLE$(X,3);
2440 ERROR.MESSAGE$ = "CORRECT RECORD (Y/N)?"
2450 GOSUB 5070
2460 Z$ = INKEY$:IF Z$ = "" THEN 2460
2470 IF Z$ < > "Y" THEN RETURN
2480 LOCATE 12,8
2490 PRINT STRING$(4,CHR$(22));
2500 LOCATE 12,23
2510 PRINT STRING$(35,CHR$(22));
2520 LOCATE 12,65
2530 PRINT STRING$(4,CHR$(22));
2540 A$ = "":B$ = "":C$ = ""
2550 ERROR.MESSAGE$ = "ENTER THE CORRECTED ITEM - ALL ELEMENTS"
2560 GOSUB 5070              'ERROR MESSAGE SUBROUTINE
2570 LOCATE 12,8
2580 Z$ = INKEY$:IF Z$ = "" THEN 2580
2590 IF Z$ = CHR$(13) THEN 2640
2600 PRINT Z$;
2610 A$ = A$ + Z$
2620 IF LEN(A$) = 4 THEN 2640
2630 GOTO 2580
```

```
2640 LOCATE 12,23
2650 Z$ = INKEY$:IF Z$ = "" THEN 2650
2660 PRINT Z$;
2670 IF Z$ = CHR$(13) THEN 2710
2680 B$ = B$ + Z$
2690 IF LEN(B$) = 35 THEN 2710
2700 GOTO 2650
2710 LOCATE 12,65
2720 Z$ = INKEY$:IF Z$ = "" THEN 2720
2730 IF Z$ = CHR$(13) THEN 2780
2740 PRINT Z$;
2750 C$ = C$ + Z$
2760 IF LEN(C$) = 4 THEN 2780
2770 GOTO 2720
2780 ERROR.MESSAGE$ = "IS THE CORRECTION CORRECT (Y/N)?"
2790 GOSUB 5070              'ERROR MESSAGE SUBROUTINE
2800 Z$ = INKEY$:IF Z$ = "" THEN 2800
2810 IF Z$ = "N" THEN 2480
2820 IF Z$ < > "Y" THEN 2800
2830 INVENTORY.TABLE$(X,1) = A$
2840 INVENTORY.TABLE$(X,2) = B$
2850 INVENTORY.TABLE$(X,3) = C$
2860 ERROR.MESSAGE$ = "CORRECTED RECORD RE-FILED INTO THE ARRAY"
2870 GOSUB 5070              'ERROR MESSAGE SUBROUTINE
2880 RETURN
```

Deletion Module

There are two schools of thought about designing a deletion module. The first involves total removal of the record and compression of the table at the same time the record is removed. The second involves "flagging" that record for removal at some more convenient time. The latter alternative has been chosen for this example.

Within that choice lie two schools of thought as well. Either the record can be flagged in a special flagging position, leaving it identifiable, or the record can be totally destroyed by the flagging. Again, the second approach has been selected. We're trying to acquaint you with the process and how the machine works — *not* make supersophisticated programmers of you.

As in the change routine, the operator is asked if the key of the record is known. If the key is not known, the program returns to the main menu so that you can choose whether to display or print the table. If the item number is known, the record is presented for confirmation of the deletion. If the confirmation is not forthcoming, the process is repeated. If the deletion is confirmed, each element of the record is overlaid with five slashes (/////), and the operator is alerted that the record has been deleted. The actual removal of the deleted record does not take place until the sort module.

The deletion module is as follows:

```
2890 '*****************************************************
2900 '*          TABLE DELETION SUBROUTINE              *
2910 '*****************************************************
```

```
2920 A$ = ""
2930 IF ITEMS.LOADED > 1 THEN 2970
2940 ERROR.MESSAGE$ = "NO TABLE TO DELETE"
2950 GOSUB 5070          'ERROR MESSAGE SUBROUTINE
2960 RETURN
2970 GOSUB 800           'CLEAR OUT INSIDE OF FRAME
2980 GOSUB 920           'HEADING SUBROUTINE
2990 ERROR.MESSAGE$ = "TABLE DELETE"
3000 GOSUB 5070          'ERROR MESSAGE SUBROUTINE
3010 FOR Z = 1 TO 500:NEXT Z
3020 LOCATE 10,23
3030 PRINT "DELETE WORKS ON ONE ELEMENT ONLY.";
3040 LOCATE 12,23
3050 PRINT "IF YOU KNOW THE ITEM NUMBER, THEN";
3060 LOCATE 13,23
3070 PRINT "ANSWER YES TO THE QUESTION.  IF";
3080 LOCATE 14,23
3090 PRINT "YOU DO NOT KNOW IT, ENTER PRINT";
3100 LOCATE 15,23
3110 PRINT "AT THE MAIN MENU, LOCATE THE ITEM";
3120 LOCATE 16,23
3130 PRINT "NUMBER AND COME BACK TO HERE."
3140 ERROR.MESSAGE$ = "DO YOU KNOW THE ITEM NUMBER (Y/N)?"
3150 GOSUB 5070          'ERROR MESSAGE SUBROUTINE
3160 Z$ = INKEY$:IF Z$ = "" THEN 3160
3170 IF Z$ < > "Y" THEN RETURN
3180 ERROR.MESSAGE$ = "ENTER THE ITEM NUMBER: "
3190 GOSUB 5070          'ERROR MESSAGE SUBROUTINE
3200 Z$ = INKEY$:IF Z$ = "" THEN 3200
3210 IF Z$ = CHR$(13) THEN 3260
3220 A$ = A$ + Z$
3230 ERROR.MESSAGE$ = "ITEM NUMBER: " + A$
3240 GOSUB 5070          'ERROR MESSAGE SUBROUTINE
3250 GOTO 3200
3260 FOR X = 1 TO 1001
3270     IF INVENTORY.TABLE$(X,1) = A$ THEN 3330
3280     IF INVENTORY.TABLE$(X,1) = "ZZZZZ" THEN 3300
3290 NEXT X
3300 ERROR.MESSAGE$ = "ITEM NOT ON TABLE"
3310 GOSUB 5070          'ERROR MESSAGE SUBROUTINE
3320 RETURN
3330 GOSUB 800           'CLEAR INSIDE OF FRAME
3340 GOSUB 920           'HEADING SUBROUTINE
3350 LOCATE 10,8
3360 PRINT INVENTORY.TABLE$(X,1);
3370 LOCATE 10,23
3380 PRINT INVENTORY.TABLE$(X,2);
3390 LOCATE 10,65
3400 PRINT INVENTORY.TABLE$(X,3);
3410 ERROR.MESSAGE$ = "CORRECT RECORD (Y/N)?"
3420 GOSUB 5070          'ERROR MESSAGE SUBROUTINE
3430 Z$ = INKEY$:IF Z$ = "" THEN 3430
3440 IF Z$ < > "Y" THEN 2970
3450 INVENTORY.TABLE$(X,1) = "/////"
3460 INVENTORY.TABLE$(X,2) = "/////"
3470 INVENTORY.TABLE$(X,3) = "/////"
3480 ERROR.MESSAGE$ = "RECORD DELETED FROM THE ARRAY"
3490 GOSUB 5070          'ERROR MESSAGE SUBROUTINE
3500 RETURN
```

Inquiry Module

The inquiry module — or table location module as it's called in the program — is a simple sequential key search. The operator is asked for the key, as before, and the table is searched on the assumption that the operator is merely trying to determine whether the key is located in the table so that he can enter it.

If the key is on file, the entry is displayed. If the key is not on file, the operator is notified of that fact as well. If the record is displayed, the program is set up to freeze the display until the operator releases it.

The inquiry module is as follows:

```
3510 '*************************************************
3520 '*            TABLE LOCATION SUBROUTINE          *
3530 '*************************************************
3540 A$ = ""
3550 IF ITEMS.LOADED > 1 THEN 3590
3560 ERROR.MESSAGE$ = "NO TABLE TO QUERY"
3570 GOSUB 5070              'ERROR MESSAGE SUBROUTINE
3580 RETURN
3590 GOSUB 800               'CLEAR OUT INSIDE OF FRAME
3600 GOSUB 920               'HEADING SUBROUTINE
3610 ERROR.MESSAGE$ = "TABLE INQUIRY"
3620 GOSUB 5070              'ERROR MESSAGE SUBROUTINE
3630 FOR Z = 1 TO 500:NEXT Z
3640 LOCATE 10,23
3650 PRINT "LOCATE WORKS ON ONE ELEMENT ONLY.";
3660 LOCATE 12,23
3670 PRINT "IF YOU KNOW THE ITEM NUMBER, THEN";
3680 LOCATE 13,23
3690 PRINT "ANSWER YES TO THE QUESTION.  IF";
3700 LOCATE 14,23
3710 PRINT "YOU DO NOT KNOW IT, ENTER PRINT";
3720 LOCATE 15,23
3730 PRINT "AT THE MAIN MENU, LOCATE THE ITEM";
3740 LOCATE 16,23
3750 PRINT "NUMBER AND COME BACK TO HERE."
3760 ERROR.MESSAGE$ = "DO YOU KNOW THE ITEM NUMBER(Y/N)?"
3770 GOSUB 5070              'ERROR MESSAGE SUBROUTINE
3780 Z$ = INKEY$:IF Z$ = "" THEN 3780
3790 IF Z$ < > "Y" THEN RETURN
3800 ERROR.MESSAGE$ =  "ENTER THE ITEM NUMBER: "
3810 GOSUB 5070              'ERROR MESSAGE SUBROUTINE
3820 Z$ = INKEY$:IF Z$ = "" THEN 3820
3830 IF Z$ = CHR$(13) THEN 3880
3840 A$ = A$ + Z$
3850 ERROR.MESSAGE$ = "ITEM NUMBER: " + A$
3860 GOSUB 5070              'ERROR MESSAGE SUBROUTINE
3870 GOTO 3820
3880 FOR X = 1 TO 1001
3890     IF INVENTORY.TABLE$(X,1) = A$ THEN 3950
3900     IF INVENTORY.TABLE$(X,1) = "ZZZZZ" THEN 3920
3910 NEXT X
3920 ERROR.MESSAGE$ = "ITEM NOT ON TABLE"
3930 GOSUB 5070              'ERROR MESSAGE SUBROUTINE
3940 RETURN
```

```
3950 GOSUB 800          'CLEAR INSIDE OF FRAME
3960 GOSUB 920          'HEADING SUBROUTINE
3970 LOCATE 10,8
3980 PRINT INVENTORY.TABLE$(X,1);
3990 LOCATE 10,23
4000 PRINT INVENTORY.TABLE$(X,2);
4010 LOCATE 10,65
4020 PRINT INVENTORY.TABLE$(X,3);
4030 ERROR.MESSAGE$ = "PRESS ANY KEY TO CONTINUE"
4040 GOSUB 5070         'ERROR MESSAGE SUBROUTINE
4050 Z$ = INKEY$:IF Z$ = "" THEN 4050
4060 RETURN
```

Printing Module

The printing module *always* displays the array contents and will also, at your option, produce a hardcopy print-out of the array. The screen display is produced on the same 10 three-element lines that were used for the add module and thus has a line count of 30. In the routine that fills the screen statements 4270-4430, the records are indexed by variable X; the screen location is separately accounted for statements 4260, 4280, 4370, and 4400; and the display takes place 10 items at a time. The operator is given the opportunity to scan the display, to move forward by hitting any key (other than "X"), or to abort the process (by hitting "X").

The production of the hardcopy is a function of the question of statement 4170, and the function of the switch in 4330 is based on the yes or no response in statements 4190-4210. Note that the hard copy is not formatted. You'll see that for yourself when you try to print descriptions of different sizes. You can change that situation merely by inserting TAB commands in the LPRINT lines, but there is a problem in doing so. Because the printing is set up as a printing of the current array element (three elements per printed line) and since not all three elements are printed as a part of the same LPRINT command, it will be necessary to establish the TAB as a variable (TAB(T)) and then substitute the appropriate tabulation for the variable.

There are several things looping in this routine. There is the movement through the array (INVENTORY.TABLE$) of up to 101 places (including the sentinel). That means 101 *three-element* data items. This is accomplished by the FOR ... NEXT loop utilizing variable X. Then there is the movement through each of the elements of *one* data item. This is accomplished by using variable Y, counting 1, 2, 3, ... 1, 2, 3, etc. Then, there is the movement from the upper part of the display area downward. This is accomplished by using variable N to move through the array SCREEN.LOCATOR to obtain the proper line and column coordinates. The whole process is limited to 30 data elements by the testing of LINECOUNT in statement 4360.

The printing module is as follows:

```
4070 '************************************************
4080 '*            TABLE PRINT SUBROUTINE            *
4090 '************************************************
4100 LINECOUNT = 0
4110 IF ITEMS.LOADED > 1 THEN 4150
4120 ERROR.MESSAGE$ = "NO TABLE TO PRINT"
4130 GOSUB 5070            'ERROR MESSAGE SUBROUTINE
4140 GOTO 4440
4150 GOSUB 800             'CLEAR OUT INSIDE OF FRAME
4160 GOSUB 920             'HEADING SUBROUTINE
4170 ERROR.MESSAGE$ = "TABLE PRINT - HARDCOPY (Y/N)?"
4180 GOSUB 5070            'ERROR MESSAGE SUBROUTINE
4190 Z$ = INKEY$:IF Z$ = "" THEN 4190
4200 IF Z$ = "Y" THEN HARDCOPY = 1:GOTO 4220
4210 IF Z$ = "N" THEN HARDCOPY = 0:GOTO 4230
4220 ERROR.MESSAGE$ = "HARDCOPY REQUESTED":GOTO 4240
4230 ERROR.MESSAGE$ = "HARDCOPY NOT REQUESTED"
4240 GOSUB 5070            'ERROR MESSAGE SUBROUTINE
4250 GOSUB 5290            'LOAD NUMBERS AND LINES
4260 N = 1
4270 FOR X = 1 TO 101
4280     Y = 1
4290     LINE.NUMBER = SCREEN.LOCATOR(N,1)
4300     COLUMN.NUMBER = SCREEN.LOCATOR(N,2)
4310     LOCATE LINE.NUMBER,COLUMN.NUMBER
4320     PRINT INVENTORY.TABLE$(X,Y);
4330     IF HARDCOPY = 1 THEN LPRINT INVENTORY.TABLE$(X,Y),
4340     IF INVENTORY.TABLE$(X,Y) = "ZZZZZ" THEN GOTO 4450
4350     LINECOUNT = LINECOUNT + 1
4360     IF LINECOUNT = 30 THEN LINECOUNT = 0:GOTO 4450
4370     N = N + 1
4380     IF N = 31 THEN N = 1
4390     IF Y = 3 THEN Y = 0:GOTO 4420
4400     Y = Y + 1
4410     GOTO 4290
4420 IF HARDCOPY = 1 THEN LPRINT
4430 NEXT X
4440 RETURN
4450 ERROR.MESSAGE$ = "PRESS ANY KEY TO CONTINUE - PRESS 'X' TO ABORT"
4460 GOSUB 5070            'ERROR MESSAGE SUBROUTINE
4470 IF Z$ = "X" THEN 4440
4480 Z$ = INKEY$:IF Z$ = "" THEN 4480
4490 IF INVENTORY.TABLE$(X,Y) = "ZZZZZ" THEN 4440
4500 GOTO 4370
```

Sort Module

The final module to be discussed is the sort module, which employs the exchange method of sorting previously discussed.

In the sort module, the deleted records are dropped by copying INVENTORY.TABLE$ (which contains the deleted records) to a temporary array (WORK.TABLE$), thereby losing the slash (deleted) records. The purged array is then copied back to the original array, and the sorting process continues. As before, the items are examined in pairs (statements 4900-4920). If the second item of the pair is the same or larger than the first, the counters are updated and the process continues. If the second is smaller than the first, they are exchanged by moving the first group to a temporary area (statements 4870-4900), moving the second group to the original position of the first (statements 4900-4920), and then removing the first group from the temporary area (4930-4950) to the position formerly occupied by the second group. As stated before, each time an exchange is made, the flag is set to ON. When the program can go completely through the array without turning the flag on, the table is in sequence.

The sort module is as follows:

```
4510 '**************************************************
4520 '*              TABLE SORT SUBROUTINE            *
4530 '**************************************************
4540 IF ITEMS.LOADED > 1 THEN 4590
4550 A$ = ""
4560 ERROR.MESSAGE$ = "NO TABLE TO SORT"
4570 GOSUB 5070          'ERROR MESSAGE SUBROUTINE
4580 RETURN
4590 GOSUB 800           'CLEAR OUT INSIDE OF FRAME
4600 GOSUB 920           'HEADING SUBROUTINE
4610 ERROR.MESSAGE$ = "TABLE SORT"
4620 GOSUB 5070          'ERROR MESSAGE SUBROUTINE
4630 BUMP = 1
4640 FOR X = 1 TO 101
4650     IF INVENTORY.TABLE$(X,1) = "/////" THEN 4730
4660     WORK.TABLE$(BUMP,1) = INVENTORY.TABLE$(X,1)
4670     WORK.TABLE$(BUMP,2) = INVENTORY.TABLE$(X,2)
4680     WORK.TABLE$(BUMP,3) = INVENTORY.TABLE$(X,3)
4690     IF INVENTORY.TABLE$(X,1) = "ZZZZZ" THEN 4740
4700     BUMP = BUMP + 1
4710     LOCATE 10,23
4720     PRINT "COMPRESSING THE TABLE";
4730 NEXT X
4740 FOR X = 1 TO 101
4750     INVENTORY.TABLE$(X,1) = WORK.TABLE$(X,1)
4760     INVENTORY.TABLE$(X,2) = WORK.TABLE$(X,2)
4770     INVENTORY.TABLE$(X,3) = WORK.TABLE$(X,3)
4780     IF WORK.TABLE$(X,1) = "ZZZZZ" THEN 4820
4790     LOCATE 10,23
4800     PRINT "COPYING THE TABLE";SPACE$(10);
4810 NEXT X
4820 FOR X = 1 TO 101
4830     LOCATE 10,23
4840     PRINT "SORTING: ";INVENTORY.TABLE$(X,1);SPACE$(10);
4850     IF INVENTORY.TABLE$(X,1) = "ZZZZZ" THEN 5000
4860     IF INVENTORY.TABLE$(X + 1,1) > = INVENTORY.TABLE$(X,1) THEN 4990
4870     TEMP.ITEM$ = INVENTORY.TABLE$(X,1)
4880     TEMP.DESCRIPTION$ = INVENTORY.TABLE$(X,2)
4890     TEMP.QUANTITY$ = INVENTORY.TABLE$(X,3)
4900     INVENTORY.TABLE$(X,1) = INVENTORY.TABLE$(X + 1,1)
4910     INVENTORY.TABLE$(X,2) = INVENTORY.TABLE$(X + 1,2)
4920     INVENTORY.TABLE$(X,3) = INVENTORY.TABLE$(X + 1,3)
4930     INVENTORY.TABLE$(X + 1,1) = TEMP.ITEM$
4940     INVENTORY.TABLE$(X + 1,2) = TEMP.DESCRIPTION$
4950     INVENTORY.TABLE$(X + 1,3) = TEMP.QUANTITY$
4960     FLAG$ = "ON"
4970     LOCATE 10,23
4980     PRINT SPACE$(10);
4990 NEXT X
5000 IF FLAG$ = "OFF" THEN 5030
5010 FLAG$ = "OFF"
5020 GOTO 4820
5030 ERROR.MESSAGE$ = "SORT COMPLETE"
5040 GOSUB 5070          'ERROR MESSAGE SUBROUTINE
5050 GOSUB 4240          'JUMP INTO MIDDLE OF PRINT ROUTINE
5060 RETURN
```

Media Modules

As mentioned before, we will delay discussion of the media options until we have had the opportunity to discuss diskette usage at length. That discussion would be a bit much at this stage.

Final Program (Minus Media Modules)

Here is the program in its entirety, minus the media modules that will be added in a later chapter.

```
10 CLS
20 CLEAR 10000
30 KEY OFF
40 DIM SCREEN.LOCATOR(30,3)
50 FOR N = 1 TO 30
60      READ SCREEN.LOCATOR(N,1)
70      READ SCREEN.LOCATOR(N,2)
80      READ SCREEN.LOCATOR(N,3)
90 NEXT N
100 RESTORE
110 DIM INVENTORY.TABLE$(101,3)
120 FOR N = 1 TO 3                            'LOAD SENTINEL
130      INVENTORY.TABLE$(1,N) = "ZZZZZ"      'AT HEAD OF TABLE
140 NEXT N
150 DIM WORK.TABLE$(101,3)
160 ITEMS.LOADED = 1
170 GOSUB 610          'SCREEN FRAMING SUBROUTINE
180 '***********************************************
190 '*            OPTION SELECTION MENU           *
200 '***********************************************
210 ERROR.MESSAGE$ = SPACE$(60)
220 GOSUB 5070          'ERROR MESSAGE SUBROUTINE
230 ERROR.MESSAGE$ = "PRESS 'X' TO TERMINATE THE PROGRAM"
240 GOSUB 5070          'ERROR MESSAGE SUBROUTINE
250 SCREEN.LINE = 6
260 SCREEN.COLUMN = 25
270 LOCATE SCREEN.LINE,SCREEN.COLUMN
280 PRINT "A.   ADD DATA TO THE TABLE"
290 LOCATE SCREEN.LINE + 2,SCREEN.COLUMN
300 PRINT "C.   CHANGE DATA ON THE TABLE"
310 LOCATE SCREEN.LINE + 4,SCREEN.COLUMN
320 PRINT "D.   DELETE DATA FROM THE TABLE"
330 LOCATE SCREEN.LINE + 6,SCREEN.COLUMN
340 PRINT "L.   LOCATE DATA (ITEM NUMBER)"
350 LOCATE SCREEN.LINE + 8,SCREEN.COLUMN
360 PRINT "P.   PRINT (DISPLAY OR PAPER)"
370 LOCATE SCREEN.LINE + 10,SCREEN.COLUMN
380 PRINT "S.   SORT THE TABLE"
390 LOCATE SCREEN.LINE + 12,SCREEN.COLUMN
400 PRINT "R.   READ THE TABLE FROM MEDIA"
410 LOCATE SCREEN.LINE + 14,SCREEN.COLUMN
420 PRINT "W.   WRITE THE TABLE TO MEDIA"
430 LOCATE SCREEN.LINE + 16,SCREEN.COLUMN
440 PRINT "SELECT: ";
450 Z$ = INKEY$
460 IF Z$ = "" THEN 450
470 IF Z$ = " " THEN 450
480 IF Z$ = "X" THEN PRINT Z$:END
490 IF Z$ = "A" THEN MENU.SELECTION = 1
500 IF Z$ = "C" THEN MENU.SELECTION = 2
510 IF Z$ = "D" THEN MENU.SELECTION = 3
520 IF Z$ = "L" THEN MENU.SELECTION = 4
530 IF Z$ = "P" THEN MENU.SELECTION = 5
540 IF Z$ = "S" THEN MENU.SELECTION = 6
```

```
550 IF Z$ = "R" THEN MENU.SELECTION = 7
560 IF Z$ = "W" THEN MENU.SELECTION = 8
570 IF (MENU.SELECTION < 1) OR (MENU.SELECTION > 8) THEN 450
580 PRINT Z$
590 ON MENU.SELECTION GOSUB 1060,1920,2890,3510,4070,4510,5530,5590
600 GOTO 170
610 '************************************************
620 '*              SCREEN FRAME SUBROUTINE          *
630 '************************************************
640 FOR Y = 1 TO 24
650     LOCATE Y,1
660     PRINT CHR$(223);TAB(20);CHR$(223);
670     PRINT TAB(60);CHR$(223);TAB(79);CHR$(223)
680 NEXT Y
690 LOCATE 1
700 PRINT STRING$(79,223)
710 LOCATE 2,20
720 PRINT "I N V E N T O R Y    D A T A    E N T R Y
730 LOCATE 3,20
740 PRINT "
750 LOCATE 4
760 PRINT STRING$(79,223)
770 LOCATE 24
780 PRINT STRING$(79,223);
790 RETURN
800 '************************************************
810 '*           CLEAR SCREEN FRAME SUBROUTINE       *
820 '************************************************
830 FOR SCREEN.LINE = 6 TO 22
840     LOCATE SCREEN.LINE,2
850     PRINT SPACES$(5);
860     LOCATE SCREEN.LINE,22
870     PRINT SPACE$(35);
880     LOCATE SCREEN.LINE,62
890     PRINT SPACES$(6)
900 NEXT SCREEN.LINE
910 RETURN
920 '************************************************
930 '*           SCREEN HEADING SUBROUTINE           *
940 '************************************************
950 LOCATE 6
960 PRINT STRING$(79,223)
970 LOCATE 7,5
980 PRINT "ITEM NUMBER"
990 LOCATE 7,35
1000 PRINT "DESCRIPTION"
1010 LOCATE 7,68
1020 PRINT "QUANTITY"
1030 LOCATE 8
1040 PRINT STRING$(79,223)
1050 RETURN
1060 '************************************************
1070 '*           TABLE ADDITION SUBROUTINE           *
1080 '************************************************
1090 IF INVENTORY.TABLE$(1,1) = "ZZZZZ" THEN 1150
1100 FOR X = 1 TO 101
1110     IF INVENTORY.TABLE$(X,1) = "ZZZZZ" THEN 1140
1120 NEXT X
1130 GOTO 1150
1140 ITEMS.LOADED = X
1150 GOSUB 800            'CLEAR OUT INSIDE OF FRAME
1160 GOSUB 920            'ADDITION HEADING
1170 LOCATE 5,20
1180 PRINT "TYPE 'STOP' UNDER ITEM TO TERMINATE ENTRY
1190 ERROR.MESSAGE$ = "TABLE ADDITION"
1200 GOSUB 5070           'ERROR MESSAGE SUBROUTINE
1210 GOSUB 5290           'CLEAR AND NUMBER LINES
1220 FIELDS.RECEIVED = 0
1230 FOR N = 1 TO 30
1240     LINE.NUMBER = SCREEN.LOCATOR(N,1)
1250     COLUMN.NUMBER = SCREEN.LOCATOR(N,2)
```

```
1260        DATA.LENGTH = SCREEN.LOCATOR(N,3)
1270        HOLD.LINE.NUMBER = LINE.NUMBER
1280        HOLD.COLUMN.NUMBER = COLUMN.NUMBER
1290        LOCATE LINE.NUMBER,COLUMN.NUMBER
1300        A$ = ""
1310        Z$ = INKEY$
1320        IF Z$ = "" THEN 1310
1330        HOLD.COLUMN.NUMBER = COLUMN.NUMBER
1340        PRINT Z$;
1350        A$ = A$ + Z$
1360        IF A$ = "STOP" THEN 1850
1370        IF LEN(A$) = DATA.LENGTH THEN 1400
1380        IF (Z$ = CHR$(13)) AND (LEN(A$) = 1) THEN GOSUB 1860:GOTO 1310
1390        IF (Z$ = CHR$(13)) AND (LEN(A$) > 1) THEN 1400 ELSE 1310
1400        FIELDS.RECEIVED = FIELDS.RECEIVED + 1
1410        IF FIELDS.RECEIVED = 1 THEN INVENTORY.TABLE$(ITEMS.LOADED,1) = A$
1420        IF FIELDS.RECEIVED = 2 THEN INVENTORY.TABLE$(ITEMS.LOADED,2) = A$
1430        IF FIELDS.RECEIVED = 3 THEN INVENTORY.TABLE$(ITEMS.LOADED,3) = A$
1440        INVENTORY.TABLE$(ITEMS.LOADED + 1,1) = "ZZZZZ"
1450        INVENTORY.TABLE$(ITEMS.LOADED + 1,2) = "ZZZZZ"
1460        INVENTORY.TABLE$(ITEMS.LOADED + 1,3) = "ZZZZZ"
1470        IF FIELDS.RECEIVED <> 3 THEN 1840
1480        FIELDS.RECEIVED = 0
1490        ERROR.MESSAGE$ = "ACCEPTABLE (Y/N)?"
1500        GOSUB 5070        'ERROR MESSAGE SUBROUTINE
1510        Z$ = INKEY$:IF Z$ = "" THEN 1510
1520        IF Z$ = "N" THEN 1580
1530        IF Z$ < > "Y" THEN 1510
1540        ITEMS.LOADED = ITEMS.LOADED + 1
1550        ERROR.MESSAGE$ = SPACE$(60)
1560        GOSUB 5070        'ERROR MESSAGE SUBROUTINE
1570        GOTO 1840
1580        ERROR.MESSAGE$ = "ENTRY REJECTED"
1590        GOSUB 5070        'ERROR MESSAGE SUBROUTINE
1600        N = N - 2
1610        A1 = SCREEN.LOCATOR(N,1)
1620        A2 = SCREEN.LOCATOR(N,2)
1630        A3 = SCREEN.LOCATOR(N,3)
1640        B1 = SCREEN.LOCATOR(N + 1,1)
1650        B2 = SCREEN.LOCATOR(N + 1,2)
1660        B3 = SCREEN.LOCATOR(N + 1,3)
1670        C1 = SCREEN.LOCATOR(N + 2,1)
1680        C2 = SCREEN.LOCATOR(N + 2,2)
1690        C3 = SCREEN.LOCATOR(N + 2,3)
1700        LOCATE A1,A2
1710        FOR Z = 1 TO A3
1720            PRINT CHR$(22);
1730        NEXT Z
1740        LOCATE B1,B2
1750        FOR Z = 1 TO B3
1760            PRINT CHR$(22);
1770        NEXT Z
1780        LOCATE C1,C2
1790        FOR Z = 1 TO C3
1800            PRINT CHR$(22);
1810        NEXT Z
1820        FIELDS.RECEIVED = 0
1830        N = N - 1
1840 NEXT N
1850 RETURN
1860 ERROR.MESSAGE$ = "MANDATORY ENTRY"
1870 GOSUB 5070        'ERROR MESSAGE SUBROUTINE
1880 COLUMN.NUMBER = HOLD.COLUMN.NUMBER
1890 LOCATE LINE.NUMBER,COLUMN.NUMBER
1900 A$ = ""
1910 RETURN
1920 '*************************************************
1930 '*            TABLE CHANGE SUBROUTINE            *
1940 '*************************************************
```

```
1950 A$ = "":B$ = "":C$ = ""
1960 IF ITEMS.LOADED > 1 THEN 2000
1970 ERROR.MESSAGE$ = "NO TABLE TO CHANGE"
1980 GOSUB 5070              'ERROR MESSAGE SUBROUTINE
1990 RETURN
2000 GOSUB 800              'CLEAR OUT INSIDE OF FRAME
2010 GOSUB 920              'HEADING SUBROUTINE
2020 ERROR.MESSAGE$ = "TABLE CHANGE"
2030 GOSUB 5070              'ERROR MESSAGE SUBROUTINE
2040 FOR Z = 1 TO 500:NEXT Z
2050 LOCATE 10,23
2060 PRINT "CHANGE WORKS ON ONE ELEMENT ONLY.";
2070 LOCATE 12,23
2080 PRINT "IF YOU KNOW THE ITEM NUMBER, THEN";
2090 LOCATE 13,23
2100 PRINT "ANSWER YES TO THE QUESTION.  IF";
2110 LOCATE 14,23
2120 PRINT "YOU DO NOT KNOW IT, ENTER PRINT";
2130 LOCATE 15,23
2140 PRINT "AT THE MAIN MENU, LOCATE THE ITEM";
2150 LOCATE 16,23
2160 PRINT "NUMBER AND COME BACK TO HERE."
2170 ERROR.MESSAGE$ = "DO YOU KNOW THE ITEM NUMBER (Y/N)?"
2180 GOSUB 5070              'ERROR MESSAGE SUBROUTINE
2190 Z$ = INKEY$:IF Z$ = "" THEN 2190
2200 IF Z$ < > "Y" THEN 2210
2210 ERROR.MESSAGE$ = "ENTER THE ITEM NUMBER: "
2220 GOSUB 5070              'ERROR MESSAGE SUBROUTINE
2230 Z$ = INKEY$:IF Z$ = "" THEN 2230
2240 IF Z$ = CHR$(13) THEN 2290
2250 A$ = A$ + Z$
2260 ERROR.MESSAGE$ = "ITEM NUMBER: " + A$
2270 GOSUB 5070              'ERROR MESSAGE SUBROUTINE
2280 GOTO 2230
2290 FOR X = 1 TO 101
2300      IF INVENTORY.TABLE$(X,1) = A$ THEN 2360
2310      IF INVENTORY.TABLE$(X,1) = "ZZZZZ" THEN 2330
2320 NEXT X
2330 ERROR.MESSAGE$ = "ITEM NOT ON TABLE"
2340 GOSUB 5070              'ERROR MESSAGE SUBROUTINE
2350 RETURN
2360 GOSUB 800              'CLEAR INSIDE OF FRAME
2370 GOSUB 920              'HEADING SUBROUTINE
2380 LOCATE 10,8
2390 PRINT INVENTORY.TABLE$(X,1);
2400 LOCATE 10,23
2410 PRINT INVENTORY.TABLE$(X,2);
2420 LOCATE 10,65
2430 PRINT INVENTORY.TABLE$(X,3);
2440 ERROR.MESSAGE$ = "CORRECT RECORD (Y/N)?"
2450 GOSUB 5070
2460 Z$ = INKEY$:IF Z$ = "" THEN 2460
2470 IF Z$ < > "Y" THEN RETURN
2480 LOCATE 12,8
2490 PRINT STRING$(4,CHR$(22));
2500 LOCATE 12,23
2510 PRINT STRING$(35,CHR$(22));
2520 LOCATE 12,65
2530 PRINT STRING$(4,CHR$(22));
2540 A$ = "":B$ = "":C$ = ""
2550 ERROR.MESSAGE$ = "ENTER THE CORRECTED ITEM - ALL ELEMENTS"
2560 GOSUB 5070              'ERROR MESSAGE SUBROUTINE
2570 LOCATE 12,8
2580 Z$ = INKEY$:IF Z$ = "" THEN 2580
2590 IF Z$ = CHR$(13) •THEN 2640
2600 PRINT Z$;
2610 A$ = A$ + Z$
2620 IF LEN(A$) = 4 THEN 2640
2630 GOTO 2580
```

```
2640 LOCATE 12,23
2650 Z$ = INKEY$:IF Z$ = "" THEN 2650
2660 PRINT Z$;
2670 IF Z$ = CHR$(13) THEN 2710
2680 B$ = B$ + Z$
2690 IF LEN(B$) = 35 THEN 2710
2700 GOTO 2650
2710 LOCATE 12,65
2720 Z$ = INKEY$:IF Z$ = "" THEN 2720
2730 IF Z$ = CHR$(13) THEN 2780
2740 PRINT Z$;
2750 C$ = C$ + Z$
2760 IF LEN(C$) = 4 THEN 2780
2770 GOTO 2720
2780 ERROR.MESSAGE$ = "IS THE CORRECTION CORRECT (Y/N)?"
2790 GOSUB 5070          'ERROR MESSAGE SUBROUTINE
2800 Z$ = INKEY$:IF Z$ = "" THEN 2800
2810 IF Z$ = "N" THEN 2480
2820 IF Z$ < > "Y" THEN 2800
2830 INVENTORY.TABLE$(X,1) = A$
2840 INVENTORY.TABLE$(X,2) = B$
2850 INVENTORY.TABLE$(X,3) = C$
2860 ERROR.MESSAGE$ = "CORRECTED RECORD RE-FILED INTO THE ARRAY"
2870 GOSUB 5070          'ERROR MESSAGE SUBROUTINE
2880 RETURN
2890 '**************************************************
2900 '*            TABLE DELETION SUBROUTINE           *
2910 '**************************************************
2920 A$ = ""
2930 IF ITEMS.LOADED > 1 THEN 2970
2940 ERROR.MESSAGE$ = "NO TABLE TO DELETE"
2950 GOSUB 5070          'ERROR MESSAGE SUBROUTINE
2960 RETURN
2970 GOSUB 800           'CLEAR OUT INSIDE OF FRAME
2980 GOSUB 920           'HEADING SUBROUTINE
2990 ERROR.MESSAGE$ = "TABLE DELETE"
3000 GOSUB 5070          'ERROR MESSAGE SUBROUTINE
3010 FOR Z = 1 TO 500:NEXT Z
3020 LOCATE 10,23
3030 PRINT "DELETE WORKS ON ONE ELEMENT ONLY.";
3040 LOCATE 12,23
3050 PRINT "IF YOU KNOW THE ITEM NUMBER, THEN";
3060 LOCATE 13,23
3070 PRINT "ANSWER YES TO THE QUESTION.  IF";
3080 LOCATE 14,23
3090 PRINT "YOU DO NOT KNOW IT, ENTER PRINT";
3100 LOCATE 15,23
3110 PRINT "AT THE MAIN MENU, LOCATE THE ITEM";
3120 LOCATE 16,23
3130 PRINT "NUMBER AND COME BACK TO HERE."
3140 ERROR.MESSAGE$ = "DO YOU KNOW THE ITEM NUMBER (Y/N)?"
3150 GOSUB 5070          'ERROR MESSAGE SUBROUTINE
3160 Z$ = INKEY$:IF Z$ = "" THEN 3160
3170 IF Z$ < > "Y" THEN RETURN
3180 ERROR.MESSAGE$ = "ENTER THE ITEM NUMBER: "
3190 GOSUB 5070          'ERROR MESSAGE SUBROUTINE
3200 Z$ = INKEY$:IF Z$ = "" THEN 3200
3210 IF Z$ = CHR$(13) THEN 3260
3220 A$ = A$ + Z$
3230 ERROR.MESSAGE$ = "ITEM NUMBER: " + A$
3240 GOSUB 5070          'ERROR MESSAGE SUBROUTINE
3250 GOTO 3200
3260 FOR X = 1 TO 1001
3270     IF INVENTORY.TABLE$(X,1) = A$ THEN 3330
3280     IF INVENTORY.TABLE$(X,1) = "ZZZZZ" THEN 3300
3290 NEXT X
3300 ERROR.MESSAGE$ = "ITEM NOT ON TABLE"
3310 GOSUB 5070          'ERROR MESSAGE SUBROUTINE
3320 RETURN
```

```
3330 GOSUB 800              'CLEAR INSIDE OF FRAME
3340 GOSUB 920              'HEADING SUBROUTINE
3350 LOCATE 10,8
3360 PRINT INVENTORY.TABLE$(X,1);
3370 LOCATE 10,23
3380 PRINT INVENTORY.TABLE$(X,2);
3390 LOCATE 10,65
3400 PRINT INVENTORY.TABLE$(X,3);
3410 ERROR.MESSAGE$ = "CORRECT RECORD (Y/N)?"
3420 GOSUB 5070            'ERROR MESSAGE SUBROUTINE
3430 Z$ = INKEY$:IF Z$ = "" THEN 3430
3440 IF Z$ < > "Y" THEN 2970
3450 INVENTORY.TABLE$(X,1) = "/////"
3460 INVENTORY.TABLE$(X,2) = "/////"
3470 INVENTORY.TABLE$(X,3) = "/////"
3480 ERROR.MESSAGE$ = "RECORD DELETED FROM THE ARRAY"
3490 GOSUB 5070            'ERROR MESSAGE SUBROUTINE
3500 RETURN
3510 '**************************************************
3520 '*            TABLE LOCATION SUBROUTINE            *
3530 '**************************************************
3540 A$ = ""
3550 IF ITEMS.LOADED > 1 THEN 3590
3560 ERROR.MESSAGE$ = "NO TABLE TO QUERY"
3570 GOSUB 5070            'ERROR MESSAGE SUBROUTINE
3580 RETURN
3590 GOSUB 800             'CLEAR OUT INSIDE OF FRAME
3600 GOSUB 920             'HEADING SUBROUTINE
3610 ERROR.MESSAGE$ = "TABLE INQUIRY"
3620 GOSUB 5070            'ERROR MESSAGE SUBROUTINE
3630 FOR Z = 1 TO 500:NEXT Z
3640 LOCATE 10,23
3650 PRINT "LOCATE WORKS ON ONE ELEMENT ONLY.";
3660 LOCATE 12,23
3670 PRINT "IF YOU KNOW THE ITEM NUMBER, THEN";
3680 LOCATE 13,23
3690 PRINT "ANSWER YES TO THE QUESTION.  IF";
3700 LOCATE 14,23
3710 PRINT "YOU DO NOT KNOW IT, ENTER PRINT";
3720 LOCATE 15,23
3730 PRINT "AT THE MAIN MENU, LOCATE THE ITEM";
3740 LOCATE 16,23
3750 PRINT "NUMBER AND COME BACK TO HERE."
3760 ERROR.MESSAGE$ = "DO YOU KNOW THE ITEM NUMBER(Y/N)?"
3770 GOSUB 5070            'ERROR MESSAGE SUBROUTINE
3780 Z$ = INKEY$:IF Z$ = "" THEN 3780
3790 IF Z$ < > "Y" THEN RETURN
3800 ERROR.MESSAGE$ =  "ENTER THE ITEM NUMBER: "
3810 GOSUB 5070            'ERROR MESSAGE SUBROUTINE
3820 Z$ = INKEY$:IF Z$ = "" THEN 3820
3830 IF Z$ = CHR$(13) THEN 3880
3840 A$ = A$ + Z$
3850 ERROR.MESSAGE$ = "ITEM NUMBER: " + A$
3860 GOSUB 5070            'ERROR MESSAGE SUBROUTINE
3870 GOTO 3820
3880 FOR X = 1 TO 1001
3890     IF INVENTORY.TABLE$(X,1) = A$ THEN 3950
3900     IF INVENTORY.TABLE$(X,1) = "ZZZZZ" THEN 3920
3910 NEXT X
3920 ERROR.MESSAGE$ = "ITEM NOT ON TABLE"
3930 GOSUB 5070            'ERROR MESSAGE SUBROUTINE
3940 RETURN
3950 GOSUB 800             'CLEAR INSIDE OF FRAME
3960 GOSUB 920             'HEADING SUBROUTINE
3970 LOCATE 10,8
3980 PRINT INVENTORY.TABLE$(X,1);
3990 LOCATE 10,23
4000 PRINT INVENTORY.TABLE$(X,2);
4010 LOCATE 10,65
```

```
4020 PRINT INVENTORY.TABLE$(X,3);
4030 ERROR.MESSAGE$ = "PRESS ANY KEY TO CONTINUE"
4040 GOSUB 5070          'ERROR MESSAGE SUBROUTINE
4050 Z$ = INKEY$:IF Z$ = "" THEN 4050
4060 RETURN
4070 '*************************************************
4080 '*           TABLE PRINT SUBROUTINE             *
4090 '*************************************************
4100 LINECOUNT = 0
4110 IF ITEMS.LOADED > 1 THEN 4150
4120 ERROR.MESSAGE$ = "NO TABLE TO PRINT"
4130 GOSUB 5070          'ERROR MESSAGE SUBROUTINE
4140 GOTO 4440
4150 GOSUB 800           'CLEAR OUT INSIDE OF FRAME
4160 GOSUB 920           'HEADING SUBROUTINE
4170 ERROR.MESSAGE$ = "TABLE PRINT - HARDCOPY (Y/N)?"
4180 GOSUB 5070          'ERROR MESSAGE SUBROUTINE
4190 Z$ = INKEY$:IF Z$ = "" THEN 4190
4200 IF Z$ = "Y" THEN HARDCOPY = 1:GOTO 4220
4210 IF Z$ = "N" THEN HARDCOPY = 0:GOTO 4230
4220 ERROR.MESSAGE$ = "HARDCOPY REQUESTED":GOTO 4240
4230 ERROR.MESSAGE$ = "HARDCOPY NOT REQUESTED"
4240 GOSUB 5070          'ERROR MESSAGE SUBROUTINE
4250 GOSUB 5290          'LOAD NUMBERS AND LINES
4260 N = 1
4270 FOR X = 1 TO 101
4280     Y = 1
4290     LINE.NUMBER = SCREEN.LOCATOR(N,1)
4300     COLUMN.NUMBER = SCREEN.LOCATOR(N,2)
4310     LOCATE LINE.NUMBER,COLUMN.NUMBER
4320     PRINT INVENTORY.TABLE$(X,Y);
4330     IF HARDCOPY = 1 THEN LPRINT INVENTORY.TABLE$(X,Y),
4340     IF INVENTORY.TABLE$(X,Y) = "ZZZZZ" THEN GOTO 4450
4350     LINECOUNT = LINECOUNT + 1
4360     IF LINECOUNT = 30 THEN LINECOUNT = 0:GOTO 4450
4370     N = N + 1
4380     IF N = 31 THEN N = 1
4390     IF Y = 3 THEN Y = 0:GOTO 4420
4400     Y = Y + 1
4410     GOTO 4290
4420 IF HARDCOPY = 1 THEN LPRINT
4430 NEXT X
4440 RETURN
4450 ERROR.MESSAGE$ = "PRESS ANY KEY TO CONTINUE - PRESS 'X' TO AB
4460 GOSUB 5070          'ERROR MESSAGE SUBROUTINE
4470 IF Z$ = "X" THEN 4440
4480 Z$ = INKEY$:IF Z$ = "" THEN 4480
4490 IF INVENTORY.TABLE$(X,Y) = "ZZZZZ" THEN 4440
4500 GOTO 4370
4510 '*************************************************
4520 '*           TABLE SORT SUBROUTINE              *
4530 '*************************************************
4540 IF ITEMS.LOADED > 1 THEN 4590
4550 A$ = ""
4560 ERROR.MESSAGE$ = "NO TABLE TO SORT"
4570 GOSUB 5070          'ERROR MESSAGE SUBROUTINE
4580 RETURN
4590 GOSUB 800           'CLEAR OUT INSIDE OF FRAME
4600 GOSUB 920           'HEADING SUBROUTINE
4610 ERROR.MESSAGE$ = "TABLE SORT"
4620 GOSUB 5070          'ERROR MESSAGE SUBROUTINE
4630 BUMP = 1
4640 FOR X = 1 TO 101
4650     IF INVENTORY.TABLE$(X,1) = "/////" THEN 4730
4660     WORK.TABLE$(BUMP,1) = INVENTORY.TABLE$(X,1)
4670     WORK.TABLE$(BUMP,2) = INVENTORY.TABLE$(X,2)
4680     WORK.TABLE$(BUMP,3) = INVENTORY.TABLE$(X,3)
4690     IF INVENTORY.TABLE$(X,1) = "ZZZZZ" THEN 4740
4700     BUMP = BUMP + 1
```

```
4710      LOCATE 10,23
4720      PRINT "COMPRESSING THE TABLE";
4730 NEXT X
4740 FOR X = 1 TO 101
4750      INVENTORY.TABLE$(X,1) = WORK.TABLE$(X,1)
4760      INVENTORY.TABLE$(X,2) = WORK.TABLE$(X,2)
4770      INVENTORY.TABLE$(X,3) = WORK.TABLE$(X,3)
4780      IF WORK.TABLE$(X,1) = "ZZZZZ" THEN 4820
4790      LOCATE 10,23
4800      PRINT "COPYING THE TABLE";SPACE$(10);
4810 NEXT X
4820 FOR X = 1 TO 101
4830      LOCATE 10,23
4840      PRINT "SORTING: ";INVENTORY.TABLE$(X,1);SPACE$(10);
4850      IF INVENTORY.TABLE$(X,1) = "ZZZZZ" THEN 5000
4860      IF INVENTORY.TABLE$(X + 1,1) > = INVENTORY.TABLE$(X,1) THEN 4990
4870      TEMP.ITEM$ = INVENTORY.TABLE$(X,1)
4880      TEMP.DESCRIPTION$ = INVENTORY.TABLE$(X,2)
4890      TEMP.QUANTITY$ = INVENTORY.TABLE$(X,3)
4900      INVENTORY.TABLE$(X,1) = INVENTORY.TABLE$(X + 1,1)
4910      INVENTORY.TABLE$(X,2) = INVENTORY.TABLE$(X + 1,2)
4920      INVENTORY.TABLE$(X,3) = INVENTORY.TABLE$(X + 1,3)
4930      INVENTORY.TABLE$(X + 1,1) = TEMP.ITEM$
4940      INVENTORY.TABLE$(X + 1,2) = TEMP.DESCRIPTION$
4950      INVENTORY.TABLE$(X + 1,3) = TEMP.QUANTITY$
4960      FLAG$ = "ON"
4970      LOCATE 10,23
4980      PRINT SPACE$(10);
4990 NEXT X
5000 IF FLAG$ = "OFF" THEN 5030
5010 FLAG$ = "OFF"
5020 GOTO 4820
5030 ERROR.MESSAGE$ = "SORT COMPLETE"
5040 GOSUB 5070              'ERROR MESSAGE SUBROUTINE
5050 GOSUB 4240              'JUMP INTO MIDDLE OF PRINT ROUTINE
5060 RETURN
5070 '*************************************************
5080 '*            ERROR MESSAGE SUBROUTINE           *
5090 '*************************************************
5100 BEEP
5110 LINEFILL = 60 - LEN(ERROR.MESSAGE$)
5120 LOCATE 25,1
5130 PRINT ERROR.MESSAGE$ + SPACE$(LINEFILL);
5140 RETURN
5150 '*************************************************
5160 '*    SCREEN COORDINATES FOR LOAD AND CHANGE     *
5170 '*************************************************
5180 DATA 10,8,4,10,23,35,10,65,4
5190 DATA 11,8,4,11,23,35,11,65,4
5200 DATA 12,8,4,12,23,35,12,65,4
5210 DATA 13,8,4,13,23,35,13,65,4
5220 DATA 14,8,4,14,23,35,14,65,4
5230 DATA 15,8,4,15,23,35,15,65,4
5240 DATA 16,8,4,16,23,35,16,65,4
5250 DATA 17,8,4,17,23,35,17,65,4
5260 DATA 18,8,4,18,23,35,18,65,4
5270 DATA 19,8,4,19,23,35,19,65,4
5280 DATA 99999,99999,99999
5290 '*************************************************
5300 '*    SCREEN LINE NUMBERS AND BLANK LINES        *
5310 '*************************************************
5320 LOCATE 10,4:PRINT " 1.";
5330 LOCATE 11,4:PRINT " 2.";
5340 LOCATE 12,4:PRINT " 3.";
5350 LOCATE 13,4:PRINT " 4.";
5360 LOCATE 14,4:PRINT " 5.";
5370 LOCATE 15,4:PRINT " 6.";
5380 LOCATE 16,4:PRINT " 7.";
5390 LOCATE 17,4:PRINT " 8.";
```

```
5400 LOCATE 18,4:PRINT " 9.";
5410 LOCATE 19,4:PRINT "10.";
5420 RESTORE
5430 FOR N = 1 TO 30
5440     READ LINE.NUMBER,COLUMN.NUMBER,SHADE.LENGTH
5450     .LOCATE LINE.NUMBER,COLUMN.NUMBER
5460     .FOR Z = 1 TO SHADE.LENGTH
5470         PRINT CHR$(22);
5480     NEXT Z
5490 NEXT N
5500 BEEP
5510 RESTORE
5520 RETURN
5530 '*************************************************
5540 '*          READ FROM MEDIA SUBROUTINE          *
5550 '*************************************************
5560 ERROR.MESSAGE$ = "MODULE NOT INSTALLED AT THIS TIME"
5570 GOSUB 5070          'ERROR MESSAGE SUBROUTINE
5580 RETURN
5590 '*************************************************
5600 '*          WRITE TO MEDIA SUBROUTINE           *
5610 '*************************************************
5620 ERROR.MESSAGE$ = "MODULE NOT INSTALLED AT THIS TIME"
5630 GOSUB 5070          'ERROR MESSAGE SUBROUTINE
5640 RETURN
```

SUMMARY

As this chapter closes, let's add the commands, instructions, and functions we've used in it to our list at the conclusion of Chapter 2.

Commands

CLEAR	Clears program variables and dimensioned tables. It is required whenever string variables and arrays occupy more than one-eighth of the available memory.

Non-I/O Statements

DEFtype	Defines default variable types where "type" may be INTeger, SiNGle precision, DouBLe precision, or STRing (INT, SNG, DBL, or STR).
DIM	Allows specification of an array in one or two-dimensions. It is required for tables in excess of 10 elements. A zero-relative element exists but must be specifically addressed. This statement declares the maximum subscript values and reserves the space.
ERASE	Removes arrays previously DIMensioned from a program.
MID$	Either extracts a known number of characters from a known position in the midst of a string or replaces characters on one string with characters from a second string.

| RANDOMIZE | Reseeds the random number generator. |
| RESTORE | Resets the pointer to the first DATA line contained in the program and allows DATA lines to be reread. |

I/O Statements

BEEP	Beeps the speaker [a function also performed by CHR$(7)].
DATA	Is a list of constant data created within the program but unadressable by the BASIC program. It must be stored within an array if manipulation is to be performed; the results of the manipulation are not permanent. Data in DATA lines is accessed by a forward moving (only) READ statement.
LOCATE	Is used to position the cursor on the screen. It takes the general format of LOCATE row, col, where "row" must be in the range of 1 to 25 and "col" must be in the range of 1 to 40 or 1 to 80, depending on WIDTH. If variables are used for row or column, and particularly for column, their addresses are incremented as the PRINTing of data at that location proceeds.
READ	Accesses internally stored DATA lines and retrieves the data as designated variables — customarily array elements.

String Functions

LEN	Returns the length of a string variable.
LEFT$	Allows access to characters on the left side of a string.
MID$	Allows access to characters in the middle of a string.
RIGHT$	Allows access to characters on the right side of a string.
SPACE$	An expandable constant that allows specification of a string of blank characters at execution time.
STRING$	Is used for the repetition of characters, such as the generation of graphics lines.
INKEY$	Is used for a one-character strobe of the keyboard.
STR$	Is used to convert a numeric value to a string variable.

4
Graphics

In the last chapter we presented a program that structured a graphics figure on the screen of the monochrome display. Although most of the graphics capabilities of the PC are provided by the color adaptor and color monitor, there are some graphics capabilities that require neither. These include display graphics on the monochrome display and printer graphics. To illustrate that the two are not the same, look back at the "organization chart" of the inventory data entry module, page 85, and note that the boxes, which were printed on the system printer, are reticulated. On the display, however, the lines of the boxes appear to be solid. The particular character CHR$(219) appears on the display as a solid line, but it appears on the printer with a pixel removed. The printer's solid line would be CHR$(223). The complete chart of the available printer graphics appears in Chapter 2, pages 44 and 45.

Pixel! What in the world is a pixel? Look back to the chart of graphics symbols. You'll note that each of the characters has a 2 X 3 configuration — two elements wide by three elements high. Each of these elements is called a *pixel*. On the PC, the monochrome display is known as a *text* display. The color monitor is pixel-oriented and the printer is pixel-oriented, but not the monochrome display.

SCREEN GRAPHICS

The program that produced the organization chart on page 85 follows. This chart was meant to serve as an example of the screen print capabilities of the PC rather than as an output report. The program is presented to demonstrate commonly used graphics techniques:

```
10 CLS
20 KEY OFF
30 RESTORE
40 '*****************************************
50 '*               DRAW THE BOXES          *
60 '*****************************************
```

```
70 FOR X = 1 TO 72
80     READ A,B,C
90     LOCATE A,B
100     FOR Y = 1 TO C
110         PRINT CHR$(219);
120     NEXT Y
130 NEXT X
140 '*****************************************
150 '*        DRAW THE HORIZONTAL LINES        *
160 '*****************************************
170 FOR X = 1 TO 2
180     READ A,B,C
190     LOCATE A,B
200     FOR Y = 1 TO C
210         PRINT CHR$(223);
220   . NEXT Y
230 NEXT X
240 '*****************************************
250 '*        DRAW THE VERTICAL LINES          *
260 '*****************************************
270 FOR X = 1 TO 34
280     READ A,B,C
290     LOCATE A,B
300     FOR Y = 1 TO C
310         PRINT CHR$(219);
320     NEXT Y
330 NEXT X
340 '*****************************************
350 '*            INSERT THE WORDS             *
360 '*****************************************
370 LOCATE 3,36
380 PRINT "MAIN MENU";
390 LOCATE 12,8
400 PRINT "ADD";
410 LOCATE 12,27
420 PRINT "CHANGE";
430 LOCATE 12,49
440 PRINT "DELETE";
450 LOCATE 12,69
460 PRINT "LOCATE";
470 LOCATE 20,7
480 PRINT "PRINT";
490 LOCATE 20,28
500 PRINT "SORT";
510 LOCATE 20,50
520 PRINT "READ";
530 LOCATE 20,70
540 PRINT "WRITE";
550 GOTO 550
560 '*****************************************
570 '*              TOP BOX                    *
580 '*****************************************
590 DATA 1,31,20
600 DATA 2,31,2,2,49,2
610 DATA 3,31,2,3,49,2
620 DATA 4,31,2,4,49,2
630 DATA 5,31,20
640 '*****************************************
650 '*            MIDDLE BOXES                 *
660 '*****************************************
670 DATA 10,2,16,10,22,16,10,44,16,10,64,16
```

```
680 DATA 11,2,2,11,16,2,11,22,2,11,36,2
690 DATA 11,44,2,11,58,2,11,64,2,11,78,2
700 DATA 12,2,2,12,16,2,12,22,2,12,36,2
710 DATA 12,44,2,12,58,2,12,64,2,12,78,2
720 DATA 13,2,2,13,16,2,13,22,2,13,36,2
730 DATA 13,44,2,13,58,2,13,64,2,13,78,2
740 DATA 14,2,16,14,22,16,14,44,16,14,64,16
750 '*****************************************
760 '*              BOTTOM BOXES              *
770 '*****************************************
780 DATA 18,2,16,18,22,16,18,44,16,18,64,16
790 DATA 19,2,2,19,16,2,19,22,2,19,36,2
800 DATA 19,44,2,19,58,2,19,64,2,19,78,2
810 DATA 20,2,2,20,16,2,20,22,2,20,36,2
820 DATA 20,44,2,20,58,2,20,64,2,20,78,2
830 DATA 21,2,2,21,16,2,21,22,2,21,36,2
840 DATA 21,44,2,21,58,2,21,64,2,21,78,2
850 DATA 22,2,16,22,22,16,22,44,16,22,64,16
860 '*****************************************
870 '*            HORIZONTAL LINES            *
880 '*****************************************
890 DATA 8,11,60,16,11,60
900 '*****************************************
910 '*             VERTICAL LINES             *
920 '*****************************************
930 DATA 6,40,2,7,40,2,8,40,2,9,40,2,10,40,2
940 DATA 11,40,2,12,40,2,13,40,2,14,40,2,15,40,2
950 DATA 8,9,2,9,9,2,10,9,2
960 DATA 16,9,2,17,9,2,18,9,2
970 DATA 8,71,2,9,71,2,10,71,2
980 DATA 16,71,2,17,71,2,18,71,2
990 DATA 8,29,2,9,29,2,10,29,2
1000 DATA 16,29,2,17,29,2,18,29,2
1010 DATA 8,51,2,9,51,2,10,51,2
1020 DATA 16,51,2,17,51,2,18,51,2
1030 DATA 8,65,2,9,65,2,10,65,2
1040 DATA 16,65,2,17,65,2,18,65,2
```

This program demonstrates the techniques for locating a graphics figure and establishing its characteristics on the basis of DATA lines. Look at the DATA lines beginning with statement 590. Each DATA line is structured with one or more sets of three numbers. Statement 590, for instance, contains one set of three numbers: 1,31,20. The first number (1) is the line number of the display; the second number (31) is the column number of the display; and the third number (20) is the length of the line to be drawn.

The three characteristics of each set of lines are drawn off into variables A, B, and C, respectively, by the instructions in statements 70-130. This routine asks for 72 sets of numbers by means of which the rectangular organizational boxes (eight of them) will be drawn. There is a known quantity − 72 − because the chart was deliberately planned that way.

In like manner, the horizontal lines, vertical lines, and labeling words are then inserted to complete the picture in a predictable manner. The use of DATA lines to store coordinates and lengths is not at all unusual. Another means of doing so by developing lines as a result of calculation, will be discussed presently. Unfortunately, the screen graphics cannot be perfectly transferred to the printer because there are certain screen characters that cannot be printed.

The PC display has no ability to draw diagonal lines on the screen in text mode, whatsoever, but it does offer a variety of vertical and horizontal line graphics that will suffice for most business purposes; it is possible to develop irregular lines that roughly stimulate the appearance of diagonal lines.

To obtain an idea of the screen graphics that are available for your use, enter and run the following program. The logic of the program merely displays the ASCII values stored in the DATA lines in groups that are terminated either by the completion of 10 lines or by an intermediate sentinel (8888) or a final sentinel (9999).

```
10 CLS
20 PRINT.LINE = 0
30 FOR X = 1 TO 100
40     READ A
50     IF A = 9999 THEN END
60     IF A = 8888 THEN PRINT.LINE = 0:GOTO 150
70     PRINT A;
80     IF A < 10 THEN PRINT "   ";:GOTO 100
90     IF A < 100 THEN PRINT "  ";
100    FOR N = 1 TO 40:PRINT CHR$(A);:NEXT N
110    PRINT:PRINT
120 PRINT.LINE = PRINT.LINE + 1
130 IF PRINT.LINE = 10 THEN PRINT.LINE = 0:GOTO 150
140 NEXT X
150 Z$ = INKEY$:IF Z$ = "" THEN 150
160 CLS
170 GOTO 30
180 DATA 22,45,95,196,15,42,8888,176,177,178,219,220,223
190 DATA 221,222,8888
200 DATA 180,181,182,185,191,183,187,217,189,188,192,193,194
210 DATA 195,197,198,199,200,201,202,203,204,205,206,207,208
220 DATA 209,210,211,212,213,214,215,216,218,184,186,190,8888
230 DATA 9999
```

It isn't always necessary to store data in DATA lines to develop a graphics display. The entry of data may be more dynamic, such as data is retrieved from a file or entered through the keyboard.

The following program develops a sales report histogram on the basis of data entered from the keyboard. It's important to remember that the data so entered could just as easily have been gathered by passing a file representing each of the years. In this particular program, data is requested for a period of 10 years. Currently, the prestored years are 1978 to 1987, and while 1987 hasn't come around yet (and the period between when you read this book and 1987 are but projections), the purpose here is to show you a method of presenting data gathered by any means in a meaningful graphic form.

The program is as follows:

```
10 CLS
20 CLEAR 1000
30 DIM PEG.DOLLAR(20,2)
40 DIM SALES.HISTORY(10)
50 GOSUB 1200
60 FOR SALES.YEAR = 1 TO 10
70      READ YEAR
80      LOCATE 5 + SALES.YEAR,10
90      PRINT "ENTER SALES FOR";YEAR;":",;
100     INPUT "",SALES.HISTORY(SALES.YEAR)
110     IF SALES.HISTORY(SALES.YEAR)<5000
                    THEN SALES.HISTORY(SALES.YEAR)=5000
120 PRINT
130 NEXT SALES.YEAR
140 RESTORE
150 CLS
160 GOSUB 1200:PRINT:PRINT
170 FOR SALES.YEAR = 1 TO 10
180     READ YEAR
190     PRINT ,,YEAR,SALES.HISTORY(SALES.YEAR)
200 NEXT SALES.YEAR
210 RESTORE
220 PRINT:PRINT "DO YOU WISH TO CHANGE A YEAR (Y/N)?";
230 Z$ = INKEY$:IF Z$ = "" THEN 230
240 IF Z$ = "N" THEN 380
250 IF Z$ < > "Y" THEN 230
260 PRINT:PRINT
270 PRINT "ENTER THE YEAR YOU WISH TO CHANGE: ",;
280 INPUT "",CHANGE.YEAR
290 FOR SALES.YEAR = 1 TO 10
300     READ YEAR
310     IF YEAR < > CHANGE.YEAR THEN 360
320     PRINT:PRINT "ENTER NEW FIGURE: ",,;
330     INPUT "",SALES.HISTORY(SALES.YEAR)
340     RESTORE
350     GOTO 150
360 NEXT SALES.YEAR
370 PRINT "INVALID ENTRY":GOTO 210
380 CLS
390 '*******************************************
400 '*      DRAW THE DOLLAR SCALE AT LEFT      *
410 '*******************************************
420 FOR Y.AXIS = 4 TO 23
430     LOCATE Y.AXIS,10
440     PRINT CHR$(176);CHR$(176)
450 NEXT Y.AXIS
460  '*******************************************
470 '*      DRAW THE TIME SCALE AT BOTTOM      *
480 '*******************************************
490 FOR X.AXIS = 11 TO 70
500     LOCATE Y.AXIS-1,X.AXIS
510     PRINT CHR$(176)
520 NEXT X.AXIS
530 '*******************************************
540 '* LOCATE SCALE -- HASH MARKS AT 15, 21, *
550 '* 27, 33, 39, 45, 51, 57, 63, AND 69.   *
560 '*******************************************
570 FOR YEAR.HASH = 15 TO 70 STEP 6
580     LOCATE Y.AXIS,YEAR.HASH
590     PRINT CHR$(179);
600 NEXT YEAR.HASH
```

```
610 '***********************************************
620 '* LOCATE SCALE -- DATE MARKS AT 14, 20, *
630 '* 26, 33, 38, 44, 50, 56, 62, AND 67.   *
640 '***********************************************
650 FOR YEARS = 13 TO 70 STEP 6
660     READ YEAR.DATE
670     LOCATE Y.AXIS+1,YEARS-1
680     PRINT YEAR.DATE;
690 NEXT YEARS
700 '***********************************************
710 '* LOCATE SCALE -- DOLLAR MARKS AT 4, 8, *
720 '* 12, 16, AND 20.                       *
730 '***********************************************
740 FOR DOLLAR.HASH = 4 TO 21 STEP 4
750     READ DOLLAR.SCALE$
760     LOCATE DOLLAR.HASH,5
770     PRINT DOLLAR.SCALE$;CHR$(196);CHR$(196);
780 NEXT DOLLAR.HASH
790 '***********************************************
800 '*    POSITION HEADING AT TOP OF REPORT    *
810 '***********************************************
820 GOSUB 1200
830 '***********************************************
840 '*    LOAD COMPARANDS TO BUILD HISTOGRAM   *
850 '***********************************************
860 FOR LOAD.ARRAY.LOOP = 1 TO 20
870     READ PEG.DOLLAR(LOAD.ARRAY.LOOP,1)
880     READ PEG.DOLLAR(LOAD.ARRAY.LOOP,2)
890 NEXT LOAD.ARRAY.LOOP
900 RESTORE
910 '***********************************************
920 '*    PLOT THE PREVIOUSLY LOADED NUMBERS   *
930 '***********************************************
940 COLUMN.START = 15
950 FOR N = 1 TO 10              'N SCANS SALES.HISTORY
960     GOSUB 1000
970 NEXT N
980 Z$ = INKEY$:IF Z$ = "" THEN 980
990 GOTO 10
1000 FOR X = 1 TO 20
1010     IF SALES.HISTORY(N) > 50000! THEN SALES.HISTORY(N) = 50000!
1020     IF (SALES.HISTORY(N)/1000) < PEG.DOLLAR(X,2) THEN 1100
1030     TEMP = (SALES.HISTORY(N)/1000)
1040     IF TEMP = PEG.DOLLAR(X,2) THEN ROW = (PEG.DOLLAR(X,1)+1)
1050     IF TEMP > PEG.DOLLAR(X,2) THEN ROW = PEG.DOLLAR(X,1)
1060     COLUMN = COLUMN.START
1070     GOSUB 1120
1080     COLUMN.START = COLUMN.START + 6
1090     GOTO 1110
1100 NEXT X
1110 RETURN
1120 FOR Y = ROW TO 23
1130     LOCATE Y,COLUMN
1140     COLUMN = COLUMN.START
1150     PRINT CHR$(219);
1160 NEXT Y
1170 LOCATE ROW-1,COLUMN          'COMPLETES HISTOGRAM TO SCALE MARK
1180 PRINT CHR$(220);
1190 RETURN
1200 '***********************************************
1210 '*    POSITION HEADING AT TOP OF REPORT    *
```

```
1220 '*****************************************
1230 LOCATE 1,30
1240 PRINT "S A L E S    R E P O R T";
1250 LOCATE 2,25
1260 PRINT "G I Z M O    C O R P O R A T I O N";
1270 RETURN
1280 '*****************************************
1290 '*    DATA LINE FOR YEARS OF THE REPORT    *
1300 '*****************************************
1310 DATA 1978,1979,1980,1981,1982,1983,1984,1985,1986,1987
1320 '*****************************************
1330 '*    DATA LINE FOR DOLLAR SCALE REPORT    *
1340 '*****************************************
1350 DATA 50K,40K,30K,20K,10K
1360 '*****************************************
1370 '*    DATA LINES FOR REPORT SCREEN COORD.   *
1380 '*****************************************
1390 DATA 4,50,5,47.5,6,45,7,42.5,8,40
1400 DATA 9,37.5,10,35,11,32.5,12,30,13,27.5
1410 DATA 14,25,15,22.5,16,20,17,17.5
1420 DATA 18,15,19,12.5,20,10,21,7.5,22,5,23,2.5
```

Let's first examine the data lines (statements 1280-1420):

1. The first set is for the years in question. They, obviously, could be changed to any pertinent dates. These dates will be used in displays that ask for data and adjust data and for the final graphics output.
2. The second data line is for the dollar scale that will appear at the left of the graph. In computer talk, "K" stands for 1,024; we'll use 1,000. Thus, 50K is used to denote 50,000 (dollars) on the scale. Again, these figures can be changed, but if they are, some internal logic and the final four data lines will have to be changed. This program assumes also that no sales figure will be below $5,000 or above $50,000 that and if those extremes are exceeded, the data will be reflected to the boundary.
3. The final four data lines are vertical-screen-coordinate/dollar-value position coordinates. For instance, look at the first two numbers of the first data line in this set: 4,50. They mean that if the data is 50,000, it will be plotted at screen row 4. Note that the screen row increments by one (moves down the screen), whereas the dollar figure decrements by $2,500 (5,47.5; 6,45; 7,42.5; etc.).

To go back to statements 30 and 40, the DATA lines with the screen/dollar coordinates will be stored in the numeric array PEG.DOLLAR. The 10 figures you enter for sales figures, as adjusted by either the program or by you, are entered into the 10 array bins of SALES.HISTORY.

The subroutine is 1200 simply places a heading on the screen that is used in several places for cosmetic purposes.

The routine between statements 60 and 130 reads the year from the DATA line, requests the appropriate input for that year, adjusts the minimum, and files it away in the SALES.HISTORY array in the position of SALES.YEAR (the FOR ... NEXT). Once that is done, the screen is cleared, the pointer is reset to the head of the DATA lines, the DATA lines are read again and displayed with the gathered data, and the operator is then asked to confirm. If it is desired to change a year, that year is presented for change, an invalid year is excluded, the list is presented another time, and the process continues until the operator is satisfied that the data entered is accurate.

Once the data has been completed, the graphing takes place. Statements 390 and 780 draw the axes in a faint mesh and then establish has marks to indicate the years and dollar amounts.

The trick is now to compare the sales amount (divided by 1000) against the coordinates in the DATA line and to plot a point closest to one of the stipulated points. This process is accomplished by the routine in statements 940 to 1110. The process involves drawing a histogram line from top to bottom while simultaneously spreading across the chart with each successive year. The actual drawing of the line takes place in statements 1120 to 1160, with some backwards line drawing of a strictly cosmetic nature (to align with the Y-axis has marks).

Once the lines are drawn, the operator may repeat the process merely by pressing any key.

Another way to use graphics on the monochrome display is a process known as *string packing*. The following program presents line graphics drawn in both the traditional FOR ... NEXT manner and by using string packing:

```
10 CLS
20 FOR N = 30 TO 49
30      LOCATE 10,N
40      PRINT CHR$(219);
50 NEXT N
60 FOR N = 30 TO 49
70 LOCATE 15,N
80      PRINT CHR$(219);
90 NEXT N
100 FOR N = 10 TO 15
110      LOCATE N,30
120      PRINT CHR$(219);CHR$(219);
130 NEXT N
140 FOR N = 10 TO 15
150      LOCATE N,49
160      PRINT CHR$(219);CHR$(219);
170 NEXT N
180 X = 30:ROW = 1
190 GOSUB 240
200 X = 30:ROW = 18
210 GOSUB 240
220 Z$ = INKEY$:IF Z$ = "" THEN 220
```

```
230 GOTO 10
240 A$ = SPACE$(X) + STRING$(19,CHR$(219)) + CHR$(31) +
        STRING$(19,CHR$(29)) + STRING$(2,CHR$(219)) +
        SPACE$(15) + STRING$(2,CHR$(219)) + CHR$(31)
250 A$ = A$ + STRING$(19,CHR$(29)) + STRING$(2,CHR$(219)) +
        SPACE$(15) + STRING$(2,CHR$(219)) + CHR$(31) +
        STRING$(19,CHR$(29)) + STRING$(2,CHR$(219)) + SPACE$(15)
260 A$ = A$ + STRING$(2,CHR$(219)) + CHR$(31) + STRING$(19,CHR$(29)) +
        STRING$(2,CHR$(219)) + SPACE$(15) + STRING$(2,CHR$(219)) +
        CHR$(31) + STRING$(19,CHR$(29)) + STRING$(19,CHR$(219))
270 LOCATE ROW
280 PRINT A$
290 RETURN
```

Enter statements 10-170 only and run the program. You'll note that a box is drawn in the center of the screen, one line at a time, top and bottom first and then left and right. Now enter the balance of the program, and run it to see the difference that string packing (the subroutine at 240) makes. Examine statement 240, omitting the SPACE$(X) for the time being. As you will recall, CHR$(219) draws a solid character on the screen. The second part of statement 240 draws 19 consecutive 219s. CHR$(31) moves the cursor down one line on the screen. CHR$(29) moves the cursor left on the screen — in this instance, 19 positions. Continuing, the statement prints two 219s, 15 spaces, two 219s, drop down, drop back, etc. The concept of string packing, then, is to combine all graphics into a single string variable that can then be printed (A$ in statement 280). Three problems immediately emerge:

1. The length of the *instruction* cannot exceed 255 characters. If more than 255 instruction characters are required, the instruction must be broken up and combined by concatenation, as in statement 250.
2. The length of the final string variable itself (A$ here) cannot exceed 255 characters. If it looks like this will be the case, the packed string must be broken up.
3. The traditional LOCATE will not work with the packed variable. The row portion works, but the column won't. The IBM manual fails to tell you that. If you try to locate the character using the LOCATE instruction, the proper row will be selected, but the character will default to position 1. Thus, the horizontal spacing must be included as part of the packed string with a SPACE$ command. Here again there is a problem, however, because this parameter could drive the size of the final string variable beyond 255 characters. Just to prove that to yourself, add statement 265:

265 PRINT (255 – LEN(A$))

This statement lets you know how much room you have to play with.

A NOTE FROM THE AUTHOR

What follows is a lengthy and reasonably complex program that demonstrates the use of graphics in a program. It's called the P.C. Musician. It also introduces the first things we'll see about writing to and reading from diskette. As written, it will take 48K and requires at least one disk. However, a major portion of that memory consists of comments; if these were removed, the program could fit in a smaller space. Also, the input/output routines involving disk are sequential in nature and can be easily converted to cassette tape.

The program is a musical composition program. It begins by displaying a piano keyboard with slightly more than two octaves. Once that it done, the keys are labeled for familiarization because this is an educational program as well. At this point, the following menu of options is presented:

```
660 '**************************
670 '* THIS IS THE MAIN MENU. *
680 '**************************
690 LOCATE 22,1:PRINT "WELCOME TO THE P.C. MUSICIAN";
700 LOCATE 24,1:PRINT "HERE ARE YOUR OPTIONS:";
710 LOCATE 22,32:PRINT "1. HEAR THE NOTES";
720 LOCATE 23,32:PRINT "2. COMPOSE A SONG";
730 LOCATE 24,32:PRINT "3. DISPLAY/REVISE A SONG";
740 LOCATE 22,58:PRINT "4. PLAY A SONG";
750 LOCATE 23,58:PRINT "5. LOAD/SAVE A SONG";
760 LOCATE 24,58:PRINT "6. TERMINATE PROGRAM";
770 Z$ = INKEY$:IF Z$ = "" THEN 770
780 A = VAL(Z$)
790 ON A GOSUB 820,1160,3030,5450,7420,810
800 GOTO 650
810 END
```

Before we get to the menu (which fits neatly at the bottom of the screen), the program draws the piano keyboard and labels the keys, as shown on page 121.

The instructions that develop the illustration of the keyboard are as follows:

```
10 CLEAR 1000
20 COLOR 15
30 KEY OFF
40 DIM SONG(100,2)
50 LOCATE 25,1
60 PRINT "DO YOU WISH TO SEE THE KEYBOARD (Y/N)? "
70 Z$ = INKEY$:IF Z$ = "" THEN 70
80 IF Z$ = "Y" THEN 140
90 IF Z$ = "N" THEN 650
100 GOTO 70
110 '***********************************************************************
120 '* THIS ROUTINE PAINTS THE KEYBOARD PORTION OF THE SCREEN WHITE *
130 '***********************************************************************
140 CLS
150 FOR N = 1 TO 20
160      PRINT STRING$(79,CHR$(219));
```

```
170 NEXT N
180 '*********************************************************************
190 '* THIS ROUTINE SEPARATES KEYS AND REMOVES COLOR FOR BLANK KEYS *
200 '*********************************************************************
210 A = 5
220 FOR N = 1 TO 20
230     LOCATE N,A
240     PRINT CHR$(0);
250 NEXT N
260 A = A + 5
270 IF A = 80 THEN 290
280 GOTO 220
290 A = 4
300 FOR N = 1 TO 13
310     LOCATE N,A
320     PRINT CHR$(0);
330 NEXT N
340 A = A + 1
350 IF A = 7 THEN A = 9
360 IF A = 12 THEN A = 19
370 IF A = 22 THEN A = 24
380 IF A = 27 THEN A = 29
390 IF A = 32 THEN A = 39
400 IF A = 42 THEN A = 44
410 IF A = 47 THEN A = 54
420 IF A = 57 THEN A = 59
430 IF A = 62 THEN A = 64
440 IF A = 67 THEN A = 74
450 IF A = 77 THEN A = 79
460 IF A = 80 THEN 510
470 GOTO 300
480 '**********************************
490 '* THIS ROUTINE LABELS THE KEYS *
500 '**********************************
510 COLOR 15,0
520 GOSUB 3230:GOSUB 3290:GOSUB 3350        'PRINT C
530 GOSUB 3410:GOSUB 3470:GOSUB 3530        'PRINT C#
540 GOSUB 3590:GOSUB 3650:GOSUB 3710        'PRINT Db
550 GOSUB 3770:GOSUB 3830:GOSUB 3890        'PRINT D
560 GOSUB 3950:GOSUB 4010:GOSUB 4070        'PRINT Eb
570 GOSUB 4130:GOSUB 4190                   'PRINT E
580 GOSUB 4250:GOSUB 4310                   'PRINT F
590 GOSUB 4370:GOSUB 4430                   'PRINT F#
600 GOSUB 4490:GOSUB 4550                   'PRINT G
610 GOSUB 4610:GOSUB 4670                   'PRINT Ab
620 GOSUB 4730:GOSUB 4790                   'PRINT A
630 GOSUB 4850:GOSUB 4910                   'PRINT Bb
640 GOSUB 4970:GOSUB 5030                   'PRINT B
650 GOSUB 5350
```

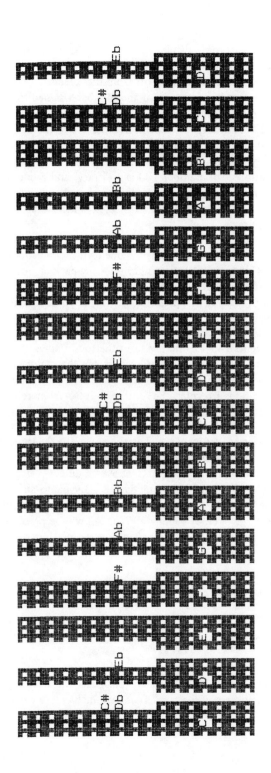

WELCOME TO THE P.C. MUSICIAN   1. HEAR THE NOTES   4. PLAY A SONG

HERE ARE YOUR OPTIONS: 2. COMPOSE A SONG   5. LOAD/SAVE A SONG

                                3. DISPLAY/REVISE A SONG   6. TERMINATE PROGRAM

The fact that the monochrome display is set to brilliant "white" for this program means that COLOR 15 is found in several places and with some variations. Statement 30 turns the function key display off from the screen.

The music in this program is a function of the number assigned to the piano key and its associated musical frequency. The frequency is one parameter of the SOUND command, previously discussed. Because both the key number (and its frequency) and the duration of a note are a function of numbers, the songs are manipulated by an array, SONG(100,2), a 100 by 2 element array that contains note and duration. The number 100 is arbitrary, and a couple of the songs contained in the program come close to that figure when notes and rests are included; in fact, the 100 count would have to be expanded to accommodate an appropriate number of rests.

The message area of the program lies in rows 21-25 of the screen, with 25 being reserved for questions and error messages. One of those questions appears in statements 60-100. This system has no ability to string pack an entire screen, and time is thus required to redraw the piano keyboard. For the first few times, and during composition, the visual presence of the keyboard is necessary. Since the time required to redraw it may come to feel burdensome, the program includes a bypass option.

The routine in statements 140-170 simply turns the top 20 lines of the screen white. Statements 210 to 280 remove the color between the major keys of the keyboard. The "black" keys are then produced by erasing the color in their locations. Since the spacing is irregular, the routine at 290-470 merely specifies the lines to be erased.

The coding from 480 to 650 labels the keys — this time. Examine statement 520, please. Three subroutines are invoked. They happen to be the three routines that correspond to the three occurrences of the note C presented on the keyboard: C below middle C, middle C, and C above middle C. If you aren't certain where middle C is located, find a standard 88-key piano and count up 24 white keys from the left side. Since our screen has only 28 notes, there are 28 subroutines of the sort invoked by statement 520. All will be presented when the program is given in its entirety at the end of this discussion, but we will show the first one (3230) here for examination:

```
3220 '****************************
3230 LOCATE 17,2:PRINT "C";
3240 PK$ = "1"
3250 XX = 15:YY = 3
3260 FREQUENCY = 260
3270 RETURN
3280 '****************************
```

Examine this routine. The LOCATE merely positions the note letter. The PK$ variable receives the number of the note. If you would like to see the numbers assigned to the notes, merely load the program, run it, and select option 2, the composition option. The XX and YY variables are used to store the location of the piano key where CHR$(14) will be printed. CHR$(14) is simply a pair of eighth notes in graphic form. The reason XX and YY are used is that in the actual print routine, both variables are supplied to another pair of variables that are in turn used in a LOCATE instruction. Recall that the LOCATE advances the address of the variable. Later, when we examine the routine that actually prints the CHR$(14), you'll see that the original addresses are used to restore color (or no color) to the position where it had been printed.

Back to the main menu. Option 1 is HEAR THE NOTES. In this routine, the notes are simply played through from bottom to top with a duration of 2 clock beats, which seems about enough for an eighth note. This is the routine that plays the two octave plus three note scale:

```
820  ' ********************************
830  ' *        HEAR THE NOTES         *
840  ' ********************************
850  COLOR 0,7
860  DURATION = 2
870  GOSUB 3230:GOSUB 5080
880  GOSUB 3410:GOSUB 5180    'LOAD AND PLAY C BELOW MIDDLE C
890  GOSUB 3770:GOSUB 5080    'LOAD AND PLAY C# (Db) BELOW MIDDLE C
900  GOSUB 3950:GOSUB 5180    'LOAD AND PLAY D BELOW MIDDLE C
910  GOSUB 4130:GOSUB 5080    'LOAD AND PLAY Eb BELOW MIDDLE C
920  GOSUB 4250:GOSUB 5080    'LOAD AND PLAY E BELOW MIDDLE C
930  GOSUB 4370:GOSUB 5180    'LOAD AND PLAY F BELOW MIDDLE C
940  GOSUB 4490:GOSUB 5080    'LOAD AND PLAY F# BELOW MIDDLE C
950  GOSUB 4610:GOSUB 5180    'LOAD AND PLAY G BELOW MIDDLE C
960  GOSUB 4730:GOSUB 5080    'LOAD AND PLAY Ab BELOW MIDDLE C
970  GOSUB 4850:GOSUB 5180    'LOAD AND PLAY A BELOW MIDDLE C
980  GOSUB 4970:GOSUB 5080    'LOAD AND PLAY Bb BELOW MIDDLE C
990  GOSUB 3290:GOSUB 5080    'LOAD AND PLAY B BELOW MIDDLE C
1000 GOSUB 3470:GOSUB 5180    'LOAD AND PLAY MIDDLE C
1010 GOSUB 3830:GOSUB 5080    'LOAD AND PLAY C# (Db) ABOVE MIDDLE C
1020 GOSUB 4010:GOSUB 5180    'LOAD AND PLAY D ABOVE MIDDLE C
1030 GOSUB 4190:GOSUB 5080    'LOAD AND PLAY Eb ABOVE MIDDLE C
1040 GOSUB 4310:GOSUB 5080    'LOAD AND PLAY E ABOVE MIDDLE C
1050 GOSUB 4430:GOSUB 5180    'LOAD AND PLAY F ABOVE MIDDLE C
1060 GOSUB 4550:GOSUB 5080    'LOAD AND PLAY F# ABOVE MIDDLE C
1070 GOSUB 4670:GOSUB 5180    'LOAD AND PLAY G ABOVE MIDDLE C
1080 GOSUB 4790:GOSUB 5080    'LOAD AND PLAY Ab ABOVE MIDDLE C
1090 GOSUB 4910:GOSUB 5180    'LOAD AND PLAY A ABOVE MIDDLE C
1100 GOSUB 5030:GOSUB 5080    'LOAD AND PLAY Bb ABOVE MIDDLE C
1110 GOSUB 3350:GOSUB 5080    'LOAD AND PLAY B ABOVE MIDDLE C
1120 GOSUB 3530:GOSUB 5180    'LOAD AND PLAY C ABOVE MIDDLE C
1130 GOSUB 3890:GOSUB 5080    'LOAD AND PLAY C# ABOVE C ABOVE MIDDLE C
1140 GOSUB 4070:GOSUB 5180    'LOAD AND PLAY D ABOVE C ABOVE MIDDLE C
1150 RETURN                   'LOAD AND PLAY Eb ABOVE C ABOVE MIDDLE C
```

Examine statement 870. The first subroutine invoked is the same subroutine described above. One subroutine is invoked for each individual note; and is taken from the same set of 28 subroutines previously discussed. The second subroutine invoked will vary from line to line. The subroutine is 5080 is the subroutine used for white keys:

```
5080 ’*******************************************
5090 ’*    BLACK NOTE ON WHITE BACKGROUND    *
5100 ’*******************************************
5110 COLOR 15,0
5120 X = XX:Y = YY
5130 LOCATE X + 1,Y:PRINT CHR$(14);
5140 SOUND FREQUENCY,DURATION
5150 X = XX:Y = YY
5160 LOCATE X + 1,Y:PRINT CHR$(219);
5170 RETURN
```

And there is a corresponding routine used for the black keys:

```
5180 ’*******************************************
5190 ’*    WHITE NOTE ON BLACK BACKGROUND    *
5200 ’*******************************************
5210 COLOR 15,0
5220 X = XX:Y = YY
5230 LOCATE X + 1,Y:PRINT CHR$(14);
5240 SOUND FREQUENCY,DURATION
5250 X = XX:Y = YY
5260 LOCATE X + 1,Y:PRINT CHR$(255);
5270 RETURN
```

The second option is that of composing a song. Perhaps it would be wise at this point to talk about the program's capability in its entirety. The program has the following features:

1. A song can be loaded from the DATA lines, where five songs have already been stored with the program, along with facilities for developing four more songs that will also fit within the program. Recall that DATA lines cannot be changed by the BASIC program itself.
2. A song can be stored on diskette (as written) or on cassette (with minor modification) and can be loaded again.
3. A song can be played.
4. A song can be entered, displayed, modified, printed, and experimented with before being written to media.

The composition routine contains several subphases. First is the "tag" phase, which identifies and numbers each piano key. The composition routine loads and invokes the tag subroutine as follows:

```
1160 ’*******************************
1170 ’*      COMPOSE A SONG         *
1180 ’*******************************
1190 GOSUB 3230:GOSUB 5280      ’LOAD AND TAG C BELOW MIDDLE C
1200 GOSUB 3410:GOSUB 5280      ’LOAD AND TAG C# (Db) BELOW MIDDLE C
```

```
1210 GOSUB 3770:GOSUB 5280    'LOAD AND TAG D BELOW MIDDLE C
1220 GOSUB 3950:GOSUB 5280    'LOAD AND TAG Eb BELOW MIDDLE C
1230 GOSUB 4130:GOSUB 5280    'LOAD AND TAG E BELOW MIDDLE C
1240 GOSUB 4250:GOSUB 5280    'LOAD AND TAG F BELOW MIDDLE C
1250 GOSUB 4370:GOSUB 5280    'LOAD AND TAG F# BELOW MIDDLE C
1260 GOSUB 4490:GOSUB 5280    'LOAD AND TAG G BELOW MIDDLE C
1270 GOSUB 4610:GOSUB 5280    'LOAD AND TAG Ab BELOW MIDDLE C
1280 GOSUB 4730:GOSUB 5280    'LOAD AND TAG A BELOW MIDDLE C
1290 GOSUB 4850:GOSUB 5280    'LOAD AND TAG Bb BELOW MIDDLE C
1300 GOSUB 4970:GOSUB 5280    'LOAD AND TAG B BELOW MIDDLE C
1310 GOSUB 3290:GOSUB 5280    'LOAD AND TAG MIDDLE C
1320 GOSUB 3470:GOSUB 5280    'LOAD AND TAG C# (Db) ABOVE MIDDLE C
1330 GOSUB 3830:GOSUB 5280    'LOAD AND TAG D ABOVE MIDDLE C
1340 GOSUB 4010:GOSUB 5280    'LOAD AND TAG Eb ABOVE MIDDLE C
1350 GOSUB 4190:GOSUB 5280    'LOAD AND TAG E ABOVE MIDDLE C
1360 GOSUB 4310:GOSUB 5280    'LOAD AND TAG F ABOVE MIDDLE C
1370 GOSUB 4430:GOSUB 5280    'LOAD AND TAG F# ABOVE MIDDLE C
1380 GOSUB 4550:GOSUB 5280    'LOAD AND TAG G ABOVE MIDDLE C
1390 GOSUB 4670:GOSUB 5280    'LOAD AND TAG Ab ABOVE MIDDLE C
1400 GOSUB 4790:GOSUB 5280    'LOAD AND TAG A ABOVE MIDDLE C
1410 GOSUB 4910:GOSUB 5280    'LOAD AND TAG Bb ABOVE MIDDLE C
1420 GOSUB 5030:GOSUB 5280    'LOAD AND TAG B ABOVE MIDDLE C
1430 GOSUB 3350:GOSUB 5280    'LOAD AND TAG C ABOVE MIDDLE C
1440 GOSUB 3530:GOSUB 5280    'LOAD AND TAG C# ABOVE C ABOVE MIDDLE C
1450 GOSUB 3890:GOSUB 5280    'LOAD AND TAG D ABOVE C ABOVE MIDDLE C
1460 GOSUB 4070:GOSUB 5280    'LOAD AND TAG Eb ABOVE C ABOVE MIDDLE C
1470 GOSUB 5350
```

And here is the routine that does the tagging:

```
5280 '**************************************
5290 '*      PIANO KEY IDENTIFICATION      *
5300 '**************************************
5310 COLOR 15,0
5320 X = XX:Y = YY - 1
5330 LOCATE X,Y:PRINT PK$;
5340 RETURN
```

The routine at 5350-5440, which clears the lower portion of the screen, is invoked liberally throughout the program:

```
5350 '**************************************
5360 '*  ROUTINE TO CLEAR THE LOWER SCREEN  *
5370 '**************************************
5380 LOCATE 22,1
5390 FOR N = 22 TO 24
5400     PRINT STRING$(79,CHR$(255));
5410 NEXT N
5420 LOCATE 25,1
5430 PRINT SPACE$(60);
5440 RETURN
```

If you decide to compose a song, there will be two phases. The first is the "sound out" phase where you can, as you would at a piano, sit down and strike the notes to see if they sound as they should. You should record these notes on paper at the same time because you'll not be able to sound the during the second phase, which is the entry phase. The first phase of the composition menu, in which two specific exits are provided in statements 1670 and 1680 (88 to return to the main menu and 99 to compose), is as follows:

```
1480 LOCATE 22,1:PRINT "1.   PLAN THE SONG ON. PAPER.   SELECT THE PIANO ";
1490 PRINT "KEY BY NUMBER TO HEAR.";
1500 LOCATE 23,1:PRINT "2.   WHEN YOU HAVE DETERMINED THE APPROPRIATE ";
1510 PRINT "NOTES AND THE NUMBER OF BEATS";
1520 LOCATE 24,1:PRINT "   EACH NOTE GETS, ENTER THE COMPOSE PHASE BY ";
1530 PRINT "TYPING 99.";
1540 LOCATE 25,1
1550 PRINT "ENTER NOTE NUMBER (88 FOR MAIN MENU / 99 TO COMPOSE): ";
1560 A$ = ""
1570 FOR N = 1 TO 3
1580     Z$ = INKEY$:IF Z$ = "" THEN 1580
1590     IF Z$ = CHR$(13) THEN 1640
1600     PRINT Z$;
1610     A$ = A$ + Z$
1620 NEXT N
1630 GOTO 1540
1640 IF LEN(A$) < 1 THEN 1540
1650 NOTE.NUMBER = VAL(A$)
1660 SONG.LOADED = 1
1670 IF NOTE.NUMBER = 88 THEN 650
1680 IF NOTE.NUMBER = 99 THEN 2070
```

Examine the routine from statements 1560 to 1620 first. Note that A$ is set to null (no length). The length of A$ here (and of A$ and other variables later in the program) is important. Because the questions being posed are on screen line 25, the INPUT instruction will require an answer followed by a carriage return (CR). That carriage return would scroll (raise by one line) the contents of the screen, throwing all locations used within the program askew. Therefore, it is necessary to accomplish input as a function of INKEY$ and string concatenation, with numeric answers being converted as in statement 1650.

Statement 1640 ensures that something has been entered, and statement 1650 converts it to numeric form. It's important to note that the program *expects* numbers to be entered. If you enter alphabetic characters, the INKEY$ will accept them, but the program will blow up when it tries to convert them to numerics. Although it is possible to intercept error codes with the PC, it is not necessary in this instance.

Statement 1660 is a switch that is set each time a song is loaded from the keyboard, from the DATA lines, or from the diskette. Granted, this is just a trial phase, but the routines to play the notes will not do so if nothing has been loaded. For the purpose of sounding out notes, the duration has been set at 16 — about the length of a whole note. Since the maximum duration allowed by the program is 16, the note must be repeated if a longer duration is required.

The next procedure in the sounding out phase is the selection of individual notes. Statement 1700 is a range check of the key number. A key number of less than 1 or greater than 28 is not permitted. If such numbers are entered, the message area will be cleared and the process repeated. If you would like to display the words rather than the entry question alone, you may wish to change the GOTO 1540 in statement 1700 to return to the display, changing it to GOTO 1480.

Statement 1710 is a long one and must therefore occupy several lines. Because an instruction can be 255 characters in length, you can "bend the line," and because BASIC compresses spaces at execution, you can insert spaces between operands to make the instruction "look pretty." Even the PRINT instructions that bend to two lines can be left where bent (you can't add spaces to the inside of a string variable), but they can be continued to another PRINT instruction, as they were in statements 1480-1520. In any event, each note is set up as an individual routine that calls for the specific data, prints the CHR$(14) on the appropriate key, and returns. The entire string is kept intact in statements 1760-2030 for explanatory purposes, but GOSUB 5280 could be included in statement 2040 to reduce the memory requirement slightly.

```
1690 DURATION = 16
1700 IF (NOTE.NUMBER < 1) OR (NOTE.NUMBER > 28) THEN GOSUB 5350:GOTO 1540
1710 ON NOTE.NUMBER GOSUB 1760,1770,1780,1790,1800,1810,1820,1830,1840,
     ·1850,1860,1870,1880,1890,1900,1910,1920,1930,1940,1950,1960,1970,
      1980,1990,2000,2010,2020,2030
1720 GOSUB 5350:GOTO 1540
1730 '*****************************************
1740 '* ROUTINES TO SELECT INDIVIDUAL NOTES *
1750 '*****************************************
1760 GOSUB 3230:GOSUB 5080:GOSUB 5280:GOTO 2040  'C BELOW MIDDLE C
1770 GOSUB 3410:GOSUB 5180:GOSUB 5280:GOTO 2040  'C# (Db) BELOW MIDDLE C
1780 GOSUB 3770:GOSUB 5080:GOSUB 5280:GOTO 2040  'D BELOW MIDDLE C
1790 GOSUB 3950:GOSUB 5180:GOSUB 5280:GOTO 2040  'Eb BELOW MIDDLE C
1800 GOSUB 4130:GOSUB 5080:GOSUB 5280:GOTO 2040  'E BELOW MIDDLE C
1810 GOSUB 4250:GOSUB 5080:GOSUB 5280:GOTO 2040  'F BELOW MIDDLE C
1820 GOSUB 4370:GOSUB 5180:GOSUB 5280:GOTO 2040  'F# BELOW MIDDLE C
1830 GOSUB 4490:GOSUB 5080:GOSUB 5280:GOTO 2040  'G BELOW MIDDLE C
1840 GOSUB 4610:GOSUB 5180:GOSUB 5280:GOTO 2040  'Ab BELOW MIDDLE C
1850 GOSUB 4730:GOSUB 5080:GOSUB 5280:GOTO 2040  'A BELOW MIDDLE C
1860 GOSUB 4850:GOSUB 5180:GOSUB 5280:GOTO 2040  'Bb BELOW MIDDLE C
1870 GOSUB 4970:GOSUB 5080:GOSUB 5280:GOTO 2040  'B BELOW MIDDLE C
1880 GOSUB 3290:GOSUB 5080:GOSUB 5280:GOTO 2040  'MIDDLE C
1890 GOSUB 3470:GOSUB 5180:GOSUB 5280:GOTO 2040  'C# (Db) ABOVE MIDDLE C
1900 GOSUB 3830:GOSUB 5080:GOSUB 5280:GOTO 2040  'D ABOVE MIDDLE C
1910 GOSUB 4010:GOSUB 5180:GOSUB 5280:GOTO 2040  'Eb ABOVE MIDDLE C
1920 GOSUB 4190:GOSUB 5080:GOSUB 5280:GOTO 2040  'E ABOVE MIDDLE C
1930 GOSUB 4310:GOSUB 5080:GOSUB 5280:GOTO 2040  'F ABOVE MIDDLE C
1940 GOSUB 4430:GOSUB 5180:GOSUB 5280:GOTO 2040  'F# ABOVE MIDDLE C
1950 GOSUB 4550:GOSUB 5080:GOSUB 5280:GOTO 2040  'G ABOVE MIDDLE C
1960 GOSUB 4670:GOSUB 5180:GOSUB 5280:GOTO 2040  'Ab ABOVE MIDDLE C
1970 GOSUB 4790:GOSUB 5080:GOSUB 5280:GOTO 2040  'A ABOVE MIDDLE C
1980 GOSUB 4910:GOSUB 5180:GOSUB 5280:GOTO 2040  'Bb ABOVE MIDDLE C
1990 GOSUB 5030:GOSUB 5080:GOSUB 5280:GOTO 2040  'B ABOVE MIDDLE C
2000 GOSUB 3350:GOSUB 5080:GOSUB 5280:GOTO 2040  'C ABOVE MIDDLE C
2010 GOSUB 3530:GOSUB 5180:GOSUB 5280:GOTO 2040  'C# ABOVE C ABOVE MIDDLE C
2020 GOSUB 3890:GOSUB 5080:GOSUB 5280:GOTO 2040  'D ABOVE C ABOVE MIDDLE
2030 GOSUB 4070:GOSUB 5180:GOSUB 5280:GOTO 2040  'Eb ABOVE C ABOVE MIDDLE C
2040 IF NOBLANK = 0 THEN GOSUB 5350:RETURN
2050 RETURN
2060 '*******************************************
```

As soon as the song has been sounded out, it's time to enter the compose phase, and entering 99 in response to the question will take you to the data entry phase. Here are the instructions:

```
2070 GOSUB 5350
2080 LOCATE 22,1
2090 PRINT "AT THIS TIME ENTER YOUR SONG IN TWO PARTS.     ";
2100 PRINT "THE FIRST PART IS THE";
2110 LOCATE 23,1
2120 PRINT "NOTE, BY NUMBER.  THE SECOND PART IS TIMING, ";
2130 PRINT "WITH AN EIGHTH NOTE";
2140 LOCATE 24,1
2150 PRINT "RECEIVING TWO BEATS.  PRESS SPACE BAR TO ";
2160 PRINT "CONTINUE DIRECTIONS.";
2170 Z$ = INKEY$:IF Z$ = "" THEN 2170
2180 IF Z$ < > " " THEN 2170
2190 GOSUB 5350
2200 LOCATE 22,1
2210 PRINT "A QUARTER NOTE WOULD RECEIVE FOUR BEATS; A HALF NOTE ";
2220 PRINT "EIGHT BEATS";
2230 LOCATE 23,1
2240 PRINT "ETC.  ENTER A REST MERELY BY ENTERING A NOTE OF 'R' WITH THE";
2250 PRINT "ETC.  ENTER A REST MERELY BY ENTERING A NOTE OF 'R' WITH THE";
2260 LOCATE 24,1
2270 PRINT "APPROPRIATE TIMING.  PRESS SPACE BAR TO CONTINUE DIRECTIONS.";
2280 Z$ = INKEY$:IF Z$ = "" THEN 2280
2290 IF Z$ < > " " THEN 2280
2300 GOSUB 5350
2310 LOCATE 22,1
2320 PRINT "YOU WILL BE ASKED TO ENTER FIRST THE NOTE NUMBER, ";
2330 PRINT "FOLLOWED BY THE TIMING.";
2340 LOCATE 23,1
2350 PRINT "AFTER EACH PAIR, YOU WILL BE ASKED TO CONFIRM.  ";
2360 PRINT "IF REJECTED, YOU SIMPLY";
2370 LOCATE 24,1
2380 PRINT "REPEAT.  YOU CAN CHANGE IT LATER, IF NECESSARY.  ";
2390 PRINT "PRESS SPACE BAR TO BEGIN.";
2400 Z$ = INKEY$:IF Z$ = "" THEN 2400
2410 IF Z$ < > " " THEN 2400
2420 GOSUB 5350
```

As previously stated, a maximum of 100 notes and rests is allowed. You may wish to expand that number — an easy enough thing to do — but since the main point of the program wasn't just to develop a musical tool, the 100-note limitation was deemed reasonable. The numbers assigned to the notes are absolute. If you want a particular tone, you enter its number. The durations are not absolute, however; their flexibility extends from 1 to 16. Rests are entered as a note of 0 and a duration of the extent desired. You will have to experiment with durations until you find the ones that work. No doubt you'll want to change the durations of some of the notes in the songs that are already a part of the program. As the durations get longer, notes begin to run together, making it necessary to separate them by rests. Rests are identified *in the entry phase* as "R," not as "0," since the latter will be rejected as invalid.

The majority of the following routine is screen management, in which you enter the note and the duration, correcting as necessary. Note that you can abort the process by typing 88 or play what you have entered to this point by typing 99, returning to the compose phase afterward. If you abort, what you have entered is still available as option 4 of the main menu, but you cannot add to the song by means of it. As before, data is entered via the INKEY$/concatenation route. The data is then stored in the array (SONG). At the completion of the process (either 100 is reached or 88 is entered), a count is entered to a variable called SENTINEL. SENTINEL is used in several places because it's also set when a song is loaded from DATA lines or from diskette.

Note in the following coding that the array is emptied before it is loaded:

```
2430 LOCATE 25,1
2440 PRINT "ENTER 88 FOR MAIN MENU / 99 TO PLAY TO THIS POINT";
2450 FOR NOTES = 1 TO 100
2460    SONG(NOTES,1) = 0:SONG(NOTES,2) = 0
2470 NEXT NOTES
2480 FOR NOTES = 1 TO 100
2490    LOCATE 22,1
2500    PRINT SPACE$(60);
2510    LOCATE 23,1
2520    PRINT SPACE$(60);
2530    A$ = ""
2540    LOCATE 22,1
2550    PRINT "ENTER THE NOTE NUMBER: ";
2560    FOR Z = 1 TO 3
2570       Z$ = INKEY$:IF Z$ = "" THEN 2570
2580       IF Z$ = "R" THEN PRINT "REST";:A = 0:GOTO 2670
2590       IF Z$ = CHR$(13) THEN 2630
2600       PRINT Z$;
2610       A$ = A$ + Z$
2620    NEXT Z
2630    IF (LEN(A$) < 1) OR (LEN(A$) > 2) THEN 2690
2640    A = VAL(A$)
2650    IF A = 99 THEN GOSUB 5450:GOTO 2490
2660    IF A = 88 THEN SENTINEL = NOTES:GOTO 650
2670    IF (A < 0) OR (A > 28) THEN 2690
2680    GOTO 2760
2690    LOCATE 24,1
2700    PRINT "INVALID ENTRY - PRESS SPACE BAR TO REPEAT";
2710    Z$ = INKEY$:IF Z$ = "" THEN 2710
2720    IF Z$ < > " " THEN 2710
2730    LOCATE 24,1
2740    PRINT SPACE$(50);
2750    GOTO 2490
2760    LOCATE 23,1
2770    PRINT SPACE$(40);
2780    B$ = ""
2790    LOCATE 23,1
2800    PRINT "     ENTER THE TIMING: ";
2810    FOR Z = 1 TO 3
2820       Z$ = INKEY$:IF Z$ = "" THEN 2820
2830       IF Z$ = CHR$(13) THEN 2870
2840       PRINT Z$;
2850       B$ = B$ + Z$
2860    NEXT Z
2870    IF (LEN(B$) < 1) OR (LEN(B$) > 2) THEN 2930
2880    B = VAL(B$)
2890    IF B = 99 THEN GOSUB 5450:GOTO 2490
2900    IF B = 88 THEN SENTINEL = NOTES:GOTO 650
2910    IF (B < 1) OR (B > 16) THEN 2930
2920    GOTO 3000
2930    LOCATE 24,1
2940    PRINT "INVALID ENTRY - PRESS SPACE BAR TO REPEAT";
```

```
2950        Z$ = INKEY$:IF Z$ = "" THEN 2950
2960        IF Z$ < > " " THEN 2950
2970        LOCATE 24,1
2980        PRINT SPACE$(50);
2990        GOTO 2760
3000        SONG(NOTES,1) = A:SONG(NOTES,2) = B
3010 NEXT NOTES
3020 GOTO 650
```

The third option of the main menu is to display and revise the song. The first routine entered under this option is the determination of the hardcopy desired. If hardcopy is not desired, the song is merely displayed on the screen. If hardcopy is desired, then the song is displayed on the screen and is printed on the system printer. The actual production of the hardcopy will be delayed until you have had the opportunity to revise the song to your satisfaction. The routine to turn on the print switch is as follows:

```
3030 '**********************************
3040 '*    DISPLAY HARDCOPY QUESTION    *
3050 '**********************************
3060 IF SONG.LOADED = 1 THEN 3130
3070 GOSUB 5350
3080 LOCATE 25,1
3090 PRINT "NO SONG LOADED";
3100 BEEP
3110 FOR Z = 1 TO 1000:NEXT Z
3120 GOTO 650
3130 GOSUB 5350
3140 LOCATE 22,1
3150 PRINT "DO YOU WISH A PRINTING OF THE NOTES (Y/N)?";
3160 Z$ = INKEY$:IF Z$ = "" THEN 3160
3170 IF Z$ = "Y" THEN HARDCOPY = 1:GOTO 3200
3180 IF Z$ = "N" THEN HARDCOPY = 0:GOTO 3200
3190 GOTO 3130
3200 GOSUB 5760
3210 GOTO 140
```

The actual display involves a bit of interesting technique. Conceptually, it's not difficult to understand if you'll take the time to think the problem through. First, the array containing the song (SONG) must be scanned (think left-to-right) to select the notes and their corresponding durations. Then, in order to display up to 100 notes on the screen, five columns of 20 lines are used, requiring the scanning of the screen to be top-to-bottom, left-to-right. This routine accomplishes the process by using ROW as a variable to control the screen top-to-bottom, COUNT to track the notes within the screen positioning, COL.POSITION to track the screen left-to-right, and NOTES to track the music through the array.

The routine to play the data onto the screen is as follows:

```
5760 '***********************************
5770 '*  DISPLAY AND HARDCOPY ROUTINE  *
5780 '***********************************
5790 CLS
5800 COUNT = 0:NOTES = 0
5810 COL.POSITION = 1:NOTES = 1
5820 FOR ROW = 1 TO 20
5830     COLUMN = COL.POSITION
5840     LOCATE ROW,COLUMN
5850     PRINT NOTES;". ";SONG(NOTES,1);"-";SONG(NOTES,2)
5860     COUNT = COUNT + 1:NOTES = NOTES + 1
5870     IF COUNT = SENTINEL - 1 THEN 5920
5880 NEXT ROW
5890 COL.POSITION = COL.POSITION + 15
5900 IF COL.POSITION = 91 THEN 5920
5910 GOTO 5820
```

The following routine permits you to change notes one by one. The old note and timing is shown on the left side of the screen. As you enter the new note and timing, it will be displayed; once it has been approved, the entire song will be redisplayed:

```
5920 LOCATE 25,1
5930 PRINT "DO YOU WISH TO CHANGE ANY NOTE (Y/N)? ";
5940 Z$ = INKEY$:IF Z$ = "" THEN 5940
5950 A$ = ""
5960 IF Z$ = "Y" THEN PRINT Z$;:GOTO 6040
5970 IF Z$ = "N" THEN PRINT Z$;:GOTO 5990
5980 GOTO 5940
5990 IF HARDCOPY < > 1 THEN GOTO 140
6000 FOR NOTES = 1 TO SENTINEL - 1
6010     LPRINT NOTES;".",SONG(NOTES,1);"-";SONG(NOTES,2)
6020 NEXT NOTES
6030 GOTO 140
6040 LOCATE 25,1
6050 A$ = ""
6060 PRINT "     WHAT NOTE DO YOU WISH TO CHANGE? ";
6070 Z$ = INKEY$:IF Z$ = "" THEN 6070
6080 IF Z$ = CHR$(13) THEN 6120
6090 PRINT Z$;
6100 A$ = A$ + Z$
6110 GOTO 6070
6120 A = VAL(A$)
6130 A$ = ""
6140 LOCATE 22,1
6150 PRINT "PRESENT NOTE:";SONG(A,1)
6160 LOCATE 23,1
6170 PRINT "PRESENT TIME:";SONG(A,2)
6180 LOCATE 22,40
6190 PRINT "ENTER NEW NOTE: ";
6200 Z$ = INKEY$:IF Z$ = "" THEN 6200
6210 IF Z$ = CHR$(13) THEN 6250
6220 PRINT Z$;
6230 A$ = A$ + Z$
6240 GOTO 6200
```

```
6250 SONG(A,1) = VAL(A$)
6260 A$ = ""
6270 LOCATE 23,40
6280 PRINT "ENTER NEW TIME: ";;
6290 Z$ = INKEY$:IF Z$ = "" THEN 6290
6300 IF Z$ = CHR$(13) THEN 6340
6310 PRINT Z$;
6320 A$ = A$ + Z$
6330 GOTO 6290
6340 SONG(A,2) = VAL(A$)
6350 GOTO 5760
```

The following is a copy of part of the screen display for one of the songs within the program (the hardcopy presentation is simply linear):

1 .	17 - 2	21 .	0 - 2	41 .	0 - 2	61 .	20 - 4
2 .	20 - 4	22 .	15 - 2	42 .	20 - 4	62 .	0 - 2
3 .	0 - 2	23 .	13 - 8	43 .	0 - 2	63 .	25 - 2
4 .	20 - 4	24 .	13 - 2	44 .	18 - 3	64 .	24 - 2
5 .	0 - 2	25 .	17 - 2	45 .	0 - 2	65 .	22 - 4
6 .	20 - 4	26 .	20 - 4	46 .	15 - 2	66 .	0 - 2
7 .	0 - 2	27 .	0 - 2	47 .	13 - 8	67 .	18 - 4
8 .	20 - 4	28 .	20 - 4	48 .	25 - 2	68 .	0 - 2
9 .	0 - 2	29 .	0 - 2	49 .	24 - 2	69 .	22 - 4
10 .	20 - 4	30 .	20 - 4	50 .	22 - 4	70 .	0 - 2
11 .	0 - 2	31 .	0 - 2	51 .	0 - 2	71 .	25 - 4
12 .	25 - 2	32 .	20 - 4	52 .	18 - 4	72 .	0 - 2
13 .	20 - 8	33 .	0 - 2	53 .	0 - 2	73 .	20 - 8
14 .	17 - 2	34 .	20 - 4	54 .	22 - 4	74 .	13 - 2
15 .	18 - 2	35 .	0 - 2	55 .	0 - 2	75 .	17 - 2
16 .	20 - 4	36 .	25 - 2	56 .	18 - 4	76 .	20 - 4
17 .	0 - 2	37 .	20 - 8	57 .	0 - 2	77 .	0 - 2
18 .	20 - 4	38 .	17 - 2	58 .	20 - 4	78 .	20 - 4
19 .	0 - 2	39 .	18 - 2	59 .	0 - 2	79 .	0 - 2
20 .	18 - 3	40 .	20 - 4	60 .	22 - 2	80 .	20 - 4

```
DO YOU WISH TO CHANGE ANY NOTE (Y/N)?
```

Following is the routine to play the entered song. Each note routine is entered, the information extracted, and then the note is played. Within the routine, the played notes are shown on the screen, but since they are slightly out of phase with the note itself, you may wish to remove instructions 5580 and 5590:

```
5450 '****************************************
5460 '*   ROUTINE TO PLAY THE ENTERED SONG   *
5470 '****************************************
5480 GOSUB 5350
5490 IF SONG.LOADED = 1 THEN 5550
5500 LOCATE 25,1
5510 PRINT "NO SONG LOADED";
```

```
5520 BEEP
5530 FOR Z = 1 TO 1000:NEXT Z
5540 GOTO 5750
5550 ROW = 22:COLUMN = 1
5560 NOBLANK = 1
5570 FOR Z = 1 TO NOTES - 1
5580     LOCATE ROW,COLUMN
5590     PRINT SONG(Z,1);"-";SONG(Z,2);"   ";
5600     A = SONG(Z,1)
5610     DURATION = SONG(Z,2)
5620     IF A = 0 THEN SOUND 32767,DURATION:GOTO 5640
5630     ON A GOSUB 1760,1770,1780,1790,1800,1810,1820,1830,1840,
               1850,1860,1870,1880,1890,1900,1910,1920,1930,1940.1950,
               1960,1970,1980,1990,2000,2010,2020,2030
5640     COLUMN = COLUMN + 8
5650     IF COLUMN > 72 THEN COLUMN = 1:ROW = ROW + 1
5660     IF ROW = 25 THEN GOSUB 5350:ROW = 22
5670 NEXT Z
5680 LOCATE 25,1
5690 PRINT "PRESS SPACE BAR TO CONTINUE";
5700 Z$ = INKEY$:IF Z$ = "" THEN 5700
5710 IF Z$ < > " " THEN 5700
5720 GOSUB 5350
5730 LOCATE 25,1
5740 PRINT "88 FOR MAIN MENU / 99 TO PLAY TO THIS POINT";
5750 RETURN
```

Finally, the fifth option to the main menu (it's assumed that the sixth option is self-explanatory) is the load/save option. Within the program are notes and timing for five songs: God Bless America, Turkey In the Straw, The Missouri Waltz, Onward Christian Soldiers, and the Marines' Hymn. The notes shown before (located in DATA lines between 6360 and 6930) were from the Marines' Hymn. Four additional DATA structures are available in lines 6940 to 7410. If you use these four, the *precise count* of a song will have to be made and inserted in the appropriate instructions. The DATA line option is part of the following submenu:

```
7460 RESTORE
7470 GOSUB 5350
7480 LOCATE 22,1
7490 PRINT "THESE OPTIONS EXIST FOR";
7500 LOCATE 23,1
7510 PRINT "THE LOAD/SAVE SELECTION:";
7520 LOCATE 22,40
7530 PRINT "1.  LOAD FROM DATA LINES.";
7540 LOCATE 23,40
7550 PRINT "2.  LOAD FROM DISKETTE.";
7560 LOCATE 24,40
7570 PRINT "3.  SAVE TO DISKETTE.";
7580 LOCATE 24,1
7590 PRINT "SELECT :";
7600 Z$ = INKEY$:IF Z$ = "" THEN 7600
7610 A = VAL(Z$)
7620 IF (A < 1) OR (A > 3) THEN 7420
```

```
7630 PRINT A;
7640 ON A GOTO 7660,9130,8820
7650 GOTO 7420
```

Once the DATA lines option has been selected, the following instructions come into play:

```
7660 GOSUB 5350
7670 LOCATE 22,1
7680 PRINT "THESE SONGS";
7690 LOCATE 23,1
7700 PRINT "ARE STORED";
7710 LOCATE 24,1
7720 PRINT "IN PROGRAM.";
7730 LOCATE 22,16
7740 PRINT "1. GOD BLESS AMERICA";
7750 LOCATE 23,16
7760 PRINT "2. TURKEY IN STRAW";
7770 LOCATE 24,16
7780 PRINT "3. MISSOURI WALTZ";
7790 LOCATE 22,38
7800 PRINT "4. CHRISTIAN SOLDIER";
7810 LOCATE 23,38
7820 PRINT "5. THE MARINES' HYMN";
7830 LOCATE 24,38
7840 PRINT "6. XXXXXXXXXXXXXXXXX";
7850 LOCATE 22,60
7860 PRINT "7. XXXXXXXXXXXXXXXXX";
7870 LOCATE 23,60
7880 PRINT "8. XXXXXXXXXXXXXXXXX";
7890 LOCATE 24,60
7900 PRINT "9. XXXXXXXXXXXXXXXXX";
7910 Z$ = INKEY$:IF Z$ = "" THEN 7910
7920 A = VAL(Z$)
7930 IF (A < 1) OR (A > 9) THEN 7420
7940 ON A GOTO 7960,8000,8060,8130,8210,8300,8400,8510,8630
7950 GOTO 7420
```

The routine to load the Marines' Hymn is presented below. It is one of nine routines coded into the program. Now let us repeat something about DATA lines. It is impossible to select in a direct fashion which data elements you wish to read and then read them. To obtain the proper DATA lines, you must RESTORE (7460) and then read through the elements until you find those which apply. In the case of the Marines' Hymn, it's necessary to bypass 224 data element pairs (28 + 54 + 44 + 98) before you can begin to read the specific song you want.

```
8210 FOR NOTES = 1 TO 28:READ Z,Z:NEXT NOTES   'BYPASS GOD BLESS AMERICA
8220 FOR NOTES = 1 TO 54:READ Z,Z:NEXT NOTES   'BYPASS TURKEY IN THE STRAW
8230 FOR NOTES = 1 TO 44:READ Z,Z:NEXT NOTES   'BYPASS MISSOURI WALTZ
8240 FOR NOTES = 1 TO 98:READ Z,Z:NEXT NOTES   'BYPASS CHRISTIAN SOLDIERS
8250 FOR NOTES = 1 TO 97         'MARINES' HYMN
```

```
8260      READ SONG(NOTES,1),SONG(NOTES,2)
8270 NEXT NOTES
8280 SENTINEL = NOTES
8290 GOTO 8760
```

Once you have a song loaded, whether one of your own making or one from the DATA lines, you can store it on diskette using the following routine:

```
8820 '*****************************************
8830 '* ROUTINE FOR WRITING DISKETTE OUTPUT *
8840 '*****************************************
8850 IF SONG.LOADED = 1 THEN 8900
8860 LOCATE 25,1
8870 PRINT "NO SONG LOADED - CANNOT WRITE DISK FILE";
8880 FOR Z = 1 TO 1000:NEXT Z
8890 GOTO 650
8900 A$ = "":B$ = ""
8910 GOSUB 5350
8920 LOCATE 25,1
8930 PRINT "SPECIFY FILE NAME (MAXIMUM 8 CHARACTERS + <CR>: ";
8940 Z$ = INKEY$:IF Z$ = "" THEN 8940
8950 IF Z$ = CHR$(13) THEN 8990
8960 PRINT Z$;
8970 A$ = A$ + Z$
8980 GOTO 8940
8990 B$ = "B:" + A$ + ".SNG"
9000 GOSUB 5350
9010 LOCATE 25,1
9020 PRINT "WRITING DISKETTE FILE";
9030 OPEN B$ FOR OUTPUT AS #1
9040 FOR NOTES = 1 TO SENTINEL
9050     PRINT #1,SONG(NOTES,1);SONG(NOTES,2)
9060 NEXT NOTES
9070 CLOSE #1
9080 GOSUB 5350
9090 LOCATE 25,1
9100 PRINT "DISKETTE WRITE COMPLETE";
9110 RESTORE
9120 FOR Z = 1 TO 1000:NEXT Z:GOTO 650
```

In order to write a file to a diskette, it's necessary to OPEN the file before you do it (9030), to write the file (in this case, PRINT #, 9050), and to CLOSE the file after you've done it. The file opened in line 9030 is a sequential output file associated with buffer No. 1. If you refer to the DOS section of the "*Guide to Operations*," you'll note that you must specify a diskette drive (if omitted, there will be a default to the default drive) and a file name. The file name in this program is a combination name, combining the drive used (B, in this instance) with the name you wish to assign the song (maximum of eight characters, not protected, followed by an assigned suffix, .SNG). Since this is a sequential file with one record — the record in the array SONG — each song is separately named. When the writing to diskette has been completed, you are so informed.

The PRINT #1 instruction can be used in a system with no disks merely by removing the "B:" from statement 8990 (likewise from statement 9280 in the routine that follows). There will be more on disk operations later on.

Once a diskette has been written, a means to read the songs into the program from the diskette is required. That routine is as follows:

```
9130 '****************************************
9140 '* ROUTINE FOR READING DISKETTE INPUT  *
9150 '****************************************
9160 CLS
9170 PRINT "THESE SONGS ARE ON THE DISK":PRINT:PRINT
9180 A$ = "":B$ = ""
9190 FILES "B:*.SNG"
9200 GOSUB 5350
9210 LOCATE 25,1
9220 PRINT "SPECIFY FILE NAME (MAXIMUM 8 CHARACTERS + <CR>: ";
9230 Z$ = INKEY$:IF Z$ = "" THEN 9230
9240 IF Z$ = CHR$(13) THEN 9280
9250 PRINT Z$;
9260 A$ = A$ + Z$
9270 GOTO 9230
9280 B$ = "B:" + A$ + ".SNG"
9290 GOSUB 5350
9300 CLOSE #1
9310 LOCATE 25,1
9320 PRINT "READING DISKETTE FILE";
9330 OPEN B$ FOR INPUT AS #1
9340 FOR NOTES = 1 TO 1000
9350     INPUT #1,SONG(NOTES,1),SONG(NOTES,2)
9360     IF EOF(1) THEN 9380
9370 NEXT NOTES
9380 CLOSE #1
9390 SENTINEL = NOTES
9400 SONG.LOADED = 1
9410 GOSUB 5350
9420 RESTORE
9430 LOCATE 25,1
9440 PRINT "DISKETTE READ COMPLETE";
9450 FOR Z = 1 TO 1000:NEXT Z:GOTO 650
```

Like the write routine, the read routine must have an open, read, and close, but it also has a couple of extra twists. First, since there always is the possibility that you may not recall *exactly which* songs are on this diskette, statement 9190 is a BASIC command known as FILES; its function is to display a diskette directory. For cassette operations, this instruction would have to be removed. To ensure that only songs are extracted, the instruction selects all those (*.) whose suffixes are SNG. The "*." is known as a *wild card*. The second unique feature is the end-of-file command. At the end of each diskette file an end-of-file sentinel is placed. This sentinel is recognized by the EOF command. The same is not true of a cassette file.

And that's it. Have a little fun with the complete program, which immediately follows. Change the notes and timing of the songs. Add new songs to the DATA lines. Try composing directly and then storing the song to diskette. No program ever seems to be perfect, but this one was fun to develop and much is to be learned from it if you take it apart.

```
10 CLEAR 1000
20 COLOR 15
30 KEY OFF
40 DIM SONG(100,2)
50 LOCATE 25,1
60 PRINT "DO YOU WISH TO SEE THE KEYBOARD (Y/N)? "
70 Z$ = INKEY$:IF Z$ = "" THEN 70
80 IF Z$ = "Y" THEN 140
90 IF Z$ =. "N" THEN 650
100 GOTO 70
110 '*********************************************************************
120 '* THIS ROUTINE PAINTS THE KEYBOARD PORTION OF THE SCREEN WHITE *
130 '*********************************************************************
140 CLS
150 FOR N = 1 TO 20
160      PRINT STRING$(79,CHR$(219));
170 NEXT N
180 '*********************************************************************
190 '* THIS ROUTINE SEPARATES KEYS AND REMOVES COLOR FOR BLANK KEYS *
200 '*********************************************************************
210 A = 5
220 FOR N = 1 TO 20
230      LOCATE N,A
240      PRINT CHR$(0);
250 NEXT N
260 A = A + 5
270 IF A = 80 THEN 290
280 GOTO 220
290 A = 4
300 FOR N = 1 TO 13
310      LOCATE N,A
320      PRINT CHR$(0);
330 NEXT N
340 A = A + 1
350 IF A = 7 THEN A = 9
360 IF A = 12 THEN A = 19
370 IF A = 22 THEN A = 24
380 IF A = 27 THEN A = 29
390 IF A = 32 THEN A = 39
400 IF A = 42 THEN A = 44
410 IF A = 47 THEN A = 54
420 IF A = 57 THEN A = 59
430 IF A = 62 THEN A = 64
440 IF A = 67 THEN A = 74
450 IF A = 77 THEN A = 79
460 IF A = 80 THEN 510
470 GOTO 300
480 '********************************
490 '* THIS ROUTINE LABELS THE KEYS *
500 '********************************
510 COLOR 15,0
520 GOSUB 3230:GOSUB 3290:GOSUB 3350         'PRINT C
530 GOSUB 3410:GOSUB 3470:GOSUB 3530         'PRINT C#
540 GOSUB 3590:GOSUB 3650:GOSUB 3710         'PRINT Db
550 GOSUB 3770:GOSUB 3830:GOSUB 3890         'PRINT D
560 GOSUB 3950:GOSUB 4010:GOSUB 4070         'PRINT Eb
570 GOSUB 4130:GOSUB 4190                    'PRINT E
580 GOSUB 4250:GOSUB 4310                    'PRINT F
590 GOSUB 4370:GOSUB 4430                    'PRINT F#
600 GOSUB 4490:GOSUB 4550                    'PRINT G
610 GOSUB 4610:GOSUB 4670                    'PRINT Ab
620 GOSUB 4730:GOSUB 4790                    'PRINT A
```

```
630 GOSUB 4850:GOSUB 4910                'PRINT Bb
640 GOSUB 4970:GOSUB 5030                'PRINT B
650 GOSUB 5350
660 '****************************
670 '* THIS IS THE MAIN MENU. *
680 '****************************
690 LOCATE 22,1:PRINT "WELCOME TO THE P.C. MUSICIAN";
700 LOCATE 24,1:PRINT "HERE ARE YOUR OPTIONS:";
710 LOCATE 22,32:PRINT "1. HEAR THE NOTES";
720 LOCATE 23,32:PRINT "2. COMPOSE A SONG";
730 LOCATE 24,32:PRINT "3. DISPLAY/REVISE A SONG";
740 LOCATE 22,58:PRINT "4. PLAY A SONG";
750 LOCATE 23,58:PRINT "5. LOAD/SAVE A SONG";
760 LOCATE 24,58:PRINT "6. TERMINATE PROGRAM";
770 Z$ = INKEY$:IF Z$ = "" THEN 770
780 A = VAL(Z$)
790 ON A GOSUB 820,1160,3030,5450,7420,810
800 GOTO 650
810 END
820 '********************************
830 '*        HEAR THE NOTES        *
840 '********************************
850 COLOR 0,7
860 DURATION = 2
870 GOSUB 3230:GOSUB 5080              'LOAD AND PLAY C BELOW MIDDLE C
880 GOSUB 3410:GOSUB 5180              'LOAD AND PLAY C# (Db) BELOW MIDDLE C
890 GOSUB 3770:GOSUB 5080              'LOAD AND PLAY D BELOW MIDDLE C
900 GOSUB 3950:GOSUB 5180              'LOAD AND PLAY Eb BELOW MIDDLE C
910 GOSUB 4130:GOSUB 5080              'LOAD AND PLAY E BELOW MIDDLE C
920 GOSUB 4250:GOSUB 5080              'LOAD AND PLAY F BELOW MIDDLE C
930 GOSUB 4370:GOSUB 5180              'LOAD AND PLAY F# BELOW MIDDLE C
940 GOSUB 4490:GOSUB 5080              'LOAD AND PLAY G BELOW MIDDLE C
950 GOSUB 4610:GOSUB 5180              'LOAD AND PLAY Ab BELOW MIDDLE C
960 GOSUB 4730:GOSUB 5080              'LOAD AND PLAY A BELOW MIDDLE C
970 GOSUB 4850:GOSUB 5180              'LOAD AND PLAY Bb BELOW MIDDLE C
980 GOSUB 4970:GOSUB 5080              'LOAD AND PLAY B BELOW MIDDLE C
990 GOSUB 3290:GOSUB 5080              'LOAD AND PLAY MIDDLE C
1000 GOSUB 3470:GOSUB 5180             'LOAD AND PLAY C# (Db) ABOVE MIDDLE C
1010 GOSUB 3830:GOSUB 5080             'LOAD AND PLAY D ABOVE MIDDLE C
1020 GOSUB 4010:GOSUB 5180             'LOAD AND PLAY Eb ABOVE MIDDLE C
1030 GOSUB 4190:GOSUB 5080             'LOAD AND PLAY E ABOVE MIDDLE C
1040 GOSUB 4310:GOSUB 5080             'LOAD AND PLAY F ABOVE MIDDLE C
1050 GOSUB 4430:GOSUB 5180             'LOAD AND PLAY F# ABOVE MIDDLE C
1060 GOSUB 4550:GOSUB 5080             'LOAD AND PLAY G ABOVE MIDDLE C
1070 GOSUB 4670:GOSUB 5180             'LOAD AND PLAY Ab ABOVE MIDDLE C
1080 GOSUB 4790:GOSUB 5080             'LOAD AND PLAY A ABOVE MIDDLE C
1090 GOSUB 4910:GOSUB 5180             'LOAD AND PLAY Bb ABOVE MIDDLE C
1100 GOSUB 5030:GOSUB 5080             'LOAD AND PLAY B ABOVE MIDDLE C
1110 GOSUB 3350:GOSUB 5080             'LOAD AND PLAY C ABOVE MIDDLE C
1120 GOSUB 3530:GOSUB 5180             'LOAD AND PLAY C# ABOVE C ABOVE MIDDLE C
1130 GOSUB 3890:GOSUB 5080             'LOAD AND PLAY D ABOVE C ABOVE MIDDLE C
1140 GOSUB 4070:GOSUB 5180             'LOAD AND PLAY Eb ABOVE C ABOVE MIDDLE C
1150 RETURN
1160 '********************************
1170 '*       COMPOSE A SONG         *
1180 '********************************
1190 GOSUB 3230:GOSUB 5280             'LOAD AND TAG C BELOW MIDDLE C
1200 GOSUB 3410:GOSUB 5280             'LOAD AND TAG C# (Db) BELOW MIDDLE C
1210 GOSUB 3770:GOSUB 5280             'LOAD AND TAG D BELOW MIDDLE C
1220 GOSUB 3950:GOSUB 5280             'LOAD AND TAG Eb BELOW MIDDLE C
1230 GOSUB 4130:GOSUB 5280             'LOAD AND TAG E BELOW MIDDLE C
1240 GOSUB 4250:GOSUB 5280             'LOAD AND TAG F BELOW MIDDLE C
1250 GOSUB 4370:GOSUB 5280             'LOAD AND TAG F# BELOW MIDDLE C
1260 GOSUB 4490:GOSUB 5280             'LOAD AND TAG G BELOW MIDDLE C
1270 GOSUB 4610:GOSUB 5280             'LOAD AND TAG Ab BELOW MIDDLE C
1280 GOSUB 4730:GOSUB 5280             'LOAD AND TAG A BELOW MIDDLE C
1290 GOSUB 4850:GOSUB 5280             'LOAD AND TAG Bb BELOW MIDDLE C
1300 GOSUB 4970:GOSUB 5280             'LOAD AND TAG B BELOW MIDDLE C
1310 GOSUB 3290:GOSUB 5280             'LOAD AND TAG MIDDLE C
```

```
1320 GOSUB 3470:GOSUB 5280        'LOAD AND TAG C# (Db) ABOVE MIDDLE C
1330 GOSUB 3830:GOSUB 5280        'LOAD AND TAG D ABOVE MIDDLE C
1340 GOSUB 4010:GOSUB 5280        'LOAD AND TAG Eb ABOVE MIDDLE C
1350 GOSUB 4190:GOSUB 5280        'LOAD AND TAG E ABOVE MIDDLE C
1360 GOSUB 4310:GOSUB 5280        'LOAD AND TAG F ABOVE MIDDLE C
1370 GOSUB 4430:GOSUB 5280        'LOAD AND TAG F# ABOVE MIDDLE C
1380 GOSUB 4550:GOSUB 5280        'LOAD AND TAG G ABOVE MIDDLE C
1390 GOSUB 4670:GOSUB 5280        'LOAD AND TAG Ab ABOVE MIDDLE C
1400 GOSUB 4790:GOSUB 5280        'LOAD AND TAG A ABOVE MIDDLE C
1410 GOSUB 4910:GOSUB 5280        'LOAD AND TAG Bb ABOVE MIDDLE C
1420 GOSUB 5030:GOSUB 5280        'LOAD AND TAG B ABOVE MIDDLE C
1430 GOSUB 3350:GOSUB 5280        'LOAD AND TAG C ABOVE MIDDLE C
1440 GOSUB 3530:GOSUB 5280        'LOAD AND TAG C# ABOVE C ABOVE MIDDLE C
1450 GOSUB 3890:GOSUB 5280        'LOAD AND TAG D ABOVE C ABOVE MIDDLE C
1460 GOSUB 4070:GOSUB 5280        'LOAD AND TAG Eb ABOVE C ABOVE MIDDLE C
1470 GOSUB 5350
1480 LOCATE 22,1:PRINT "1.  PLAN THE SONG ON PAPER.  SELECT THE PIANO ";
1490 PRINT "KEY BY NUMBER TO HEAR.";
1500 LOCATE 23,1:PRINT "2.  WHEN YOU HAVE DETERMINED THE APPROPRIATE ";
1510 PRINT "NOTES AND THE NUMBER OF BEATS";
1520 LOCATE 24,1:PRINT "  EACH NOTE GETS, ENTER THE COMPOSE PHASE BY ";
1530 PRINT "TYPING 99.";
1540 LOCATE 25,1
1550 PRINT "ENTER NOTE NUMBER (88 FOR MAIN MENU / 99 TO COMPOSE): ";
1560 A$ = ""
1570 FOR N = 1 TO 3
1580    Z$ = INKEY$:IF Z$ = "" THEN 1580
1590    IF Z$ = CHR$(13) THEN 1640
1600    PRINT Z$;
1610    A$ = A$ + Z$
1620 NEXT N
1630 GOTO 1540
1640 IF LEN(A$) < 1 THEN 1540
1650 NOTE.NUMBER = VAL(A$)
1660 SONG.LOADED = 1
1670 IF NOTE.NUMBER = 88 THEN 650
1680 IF NOTE.NUMBER = 99 THEN 2070
1690 DURATION = 16
1700 IF (NOTE.NUMBER < 1) OR (NOTE.NUMBER > 28) THEN GOSUB 5350:GOTO 1540
1710 ON NOTE.NUMBER GOSUB 1760,1770,1780,1790,1800,1810,1820,1830,1840,
        1850,1860,1870,1880,1890,1900,1910,1920,1930,1940,1950,1960,1970,
        1980,1990,2000,2010,2020,2030
1720 GOSUB 5350:GOTO 1540
1730 '****************************************
1740 '* ROUTINES TO SELECT INDIVIDUAL NOTES *
1750 '****************************************
1760 GOSUB 3230:GOSUB 5080:GOSUB 5280:GOTO 2040   'C BELOW MIDDLE C
1770 GOSUB 3410:GOSUB 5180:GOSUB 5280:GOTO 2040   'C# (Db) BELOW MIDDLE C
1780 GOSUB 3770:GOSUB 5080:GOSUB 5280:GOTO 2040   'D BELOW MIDDLE C
1790 GOSUB 3950:GOSUB 5180:GOSUB 5280:GOTO 2040   'Eb BELOW MIDDLE C
1800 GOSUB 4130:GOSUB 5080:GOSUB 5280:GOTO 2040   'E BELOW MIDDLE C
1810 GOSUB 4250:GOSUB 5080:GOSUB 5280:GOTO 2040   'F BELOW MIDDLE C
1820 GOSUB 4370:GOSUB 5180:GOSUB 5280:GOTO 2040   'F# BELOW MIDDLE C
1830 GOSUB 4490:GOSUB 5080:GOSUB 5280:GOTO 2040   'G BELOW MIDDLE C
1840 GOSUB 4610:GOSUB 5180:GOSUB 5280:GOTO 2040   'Ab BELOW MIDDLE C
1850 GOSUB 4730:GOSUB 5080:GOSUB 5280:GOTO 2040   'A BELOW MIDDLE C
1860 GOSUB 4850:GOSUB 5180:GOSUB 5280:GOTO 2040   'Bb BELOW MIDDLE C
1870 GOSUB 4970:GOSUB 5080:GOSUB 5280:GOTO 2040   'B BELOW MIDDLE C
1880 GOSUB 3290:GOSUB 5080:GOSUB 5280:GOTO 2040   'MIDDLE C
1890 GOSUB 3470:GOSUB 5180:GOSUB 5280:GOTO 2040   'C# (Db) ABOVE MIDDLE C
1900 GOSUB 3830:GOSUB 5080:GOSUB 5280:GOTO 2040   'D ABOVE MIDDLE C
1910 GOSUB 4010:GOSUB 5180:GOSUB 5280:GOTO 2040   'Eb ABOVE MIDDLE C
1920 GOSUB 4190:GOSUB 5080:GOSUB 5280:GOTO 2040   'E ABOVE MIDDLE C
1930 GOSUB 4310:GOSUB 5080:GOSUB 5280:GOTO 2040   'F ABOVE MIDDLE C
1940 GOSUB 4430:GOSUB 5180:GOSUB 5280:GOTO 2040   'F# ABOVE MIDDLE C
1950 GOSUB 4550:GOSUB 5080:GOSUB 5280:GOTO 2040   'G ABOVE MIDDLE C
1960 GOSUB 4670:GOSUB 5180:GOSUB 5280:GOTO 2040   'Ab ABOVE MIDDLE C
1970 GOSUB 4790:GOSUB 5080:GOSUB 5280:GOTO 2040   'A ABOVE MIDDLE C
1980 GOSUB 4910:GOSUB 5180:GOSUB 5280:GOTO 2040   'Bb ABOVE MIDDLE C
```

```
1990 GOSUB 5030:GOSUB 5080:GOSUB 5280:GOTO 2040   'B ABOVE MIDDLE C
2000 GOSUB 3350:GOSUB 5080:GOSUB 5280:GOTO 2040   'C ABOVE MIDDLE C
2010 GOSUB 3530:GOSUB 5180:GOSUB 5280:GOTO 2040   'C# ABOVE C ABOVE MIDDLE C
2020 GOSUB 3890:GOSUB 5080:GOSUB 5280:GOTO 2040   'D ABOVE C ABOVE MIDDLE
2030 GOSUB 4070:GOSUB 5180:GOSUB 5280:GOTO 2040   'Eb ABOVE C ABOVE MIDDLE C
2040 IF NOBLANK = 0 THEN GOSUB 5350:RETURN
2050 RETURN
2060 '*****************************************
2070 GOSUB 5350
2080 LOCATE 22,1
2090 PRINT "AT THIS TIME ENTER YOUR SONG IN TWO PARTS.   ";
2100 PRINT "THE FIRST PART IS THE";
2110 LOCATE 23,1
2120 PRINT "NOTE, BY NUMBER.   THE SECOND PART IS TIMING, ";
2130 PRINT "WITH AN EIGHTH NOTE";
2140 LOCATE 24,1
2150 PRINT "RECEIVING TWO BEATS.   PRESS SPACE BAR TO ";
2160 PRINT "CONTINUE DIRECTIONS.";
2170 Z$ = INKEY$:IF Z$ = "" THEN 2170
2180 IF Z$ < > " " THEN 2170
2190 GOSUB 5350
2200 LOCATE 22,1
2210 PRINT "A QUARTER NOTE WOULD RECEIVE FOUR BEATS; A HALF NOTE ";
2220 PRINT "EIGHT BEATS";
2230 LOCATE 23,1
2240 PRINT "ETC.   ENTER A REST MERELY BY ENTERING A NOTE OF 'R' WITH THE";
2250 PRINT "ETC.   ENTER A REST MERELY BY ENTERING A NOTE OF 'R' WITH THE";
2260 LOCATE 24,1
2270 PRINT "APPROPRIATE TIMING.   PRESS SPACE BAR TO CONTINUE DIRECTIONS.";
2280 Z$ = INKEY$:IF Z$ = "" THEN 2280
2290 IF Z$ < > " " THEN 2280
2300 GOSUB 5350
2310 LOCATE 22,1
2320 PRINT "YOU WILL BE ASKED TO ENTER FIRST THE NOTE NUMBER, ";
2330 PRINT "FOLLOWED BY THE TIMING.";
2340 LOCATE 23,1
2350 PRINT "AFTER EACH PAIR, YOU WILL BE ASKED TO CONFIRM.   ";
2360 PRINT "IF REJECTED, YOU SIMPLY";
2370 LOCATE 24,1
2380 PRINT "REPEAT.   YOU CAN CHANGE IT LATER, IF NECESSARY.   ";
2390 PRINT "PRESS SPACE BAR TO BEGIN.";
2400 Z$ = INKEY$:IF Z$ = "" THEN 2400
2410 IF Z$ < > " " THEN 2400
2420 GOSUB 5350
2430 LOCATE 25,1
2440 PRINT "ENTER 88 FOR MAIN MENU / 99 TO PLAY TO THIS POINT";
2450 FOR NOTES = 1 TO 100
2460     SONG(NOTES,1) = 0:SONG(NOTES,2) = 0
2470 NEXT NOTES
2480 FOR NOTES = 1 TO 100
2490     LOCATE 22,1
2500     PRINT SPACE$(60);
2510     LOCATE 23,1
2520     PRINT SPACE$(60);
2530     A$ = ""
2540     LOCATE 22,1
2550     PRINT "ENTER THE NOTE NUMBER: ";
2560     FOR Z = 1 TO 3
2570         Z$ = INKEY$:IF Z$ = "" THEN 2570
2580         IF Z$ = "R" THEN PRINT "REST";:A = 0:GOTO 2670
2590         IF Z$ = CHR$(13) THEN 2630
2600         PRINT Z$;
2610         A$ = A$ + Z$
2620     NEXT Z
2630     IF (LEN(A$) < 1) OR (LEN(A$) > 2) THEN 2690
2640     A = VAL(A$)
2650     IF A = 99 THEN GOSUB 5450:GOTO 2490
2660     IF A = 88 THEN SENTINEL = NOTES:GOTO 650
2670     IF (A < 0) OR (A > 28) THEN 2690
```

```
2680        GOTO 2760
2690        LOCATE 24,1
2700        PRINT "INVALID ENTRY - PRESS SPACE BAR TO REPEAT";
2710        Z$ = INKEY$:IF Z$ = "" THEN 2710
2720        IF Z$ < > " " THEN 2710
2730        LOCATE 24,1
2740        PRINT SPACE$(50);
2750        GOTO 2490
2760        LOCATE 23,1
2770        PRINT SPACE$(40);
2780        B$ = ""
2790        LOCATE 23,1
2800        PRINT "        ENTER THE TIMING: ";
2810        FOR Z = 1 TO 3
2820            Z$ = INKEY$:IF Z$ = "" THEN 2820
2830            IF Z$ = CHR$(13) THEN 2870
2840            PRINT Z$;
2850            B$ = B$ + Z$
2860        NEXT Z
2870        IF (LEN(B$) < 1) OR (LEN(B$) > 2) THEN 2930
2880        B = VAL(B$)
2890        IF B = 99 THEN GOSUB 5450:GOTO 2490
2900        IF B = 88 THEN SENTINEL = NOTES:GOTO 650
2910        IF (B < 1) OR (B > 16) THEN 2930
2920        GOTO 3000
2930        LOCATE 24,1
2940        PRINT "INVALID ENTRY - PRESS SPACE BAR TO REPEAT";
2950        Z$ = INKEY$:IF Z$ = "" THEN 2950
2960        IF Z$ < > " " THEN 2950
2970        LOCATE 24,1
2980        PRINT SPACE$(50);
2990        GOTO 2760
3000        SONG(NOTES,1) = A:SONG(NOTES,2) = B
3010 NEXT NOTES
3020 GOTO 650
3030 '***********************************
3040 '*    DISPLAY HARDCOPY QUESTION    *
3050 '***********************************
3060 IF SONG.LOADED = 1 THEN 3130
3070 GOSUB 5350
3080 LOCATE 25,1
3090 PRINT "NO SONG LOADED";
3100 BEEP
3110 FOR Z = 1 TO 1000:NEXT Z
3120 GOTO 650
3130 GOSUB 5350
3140 LOCATE 22,1
3150 PRINT "DO YOU WISH A PRINTING OF THE NOTES (Y/N)?";
3160 Z$ = INKEY$:IF Z$ = "" THEN 3160
3170 IF Z$ = "Y" THEN HARDCOPY = 1:GOTO 3200
3180 IF Z$ = "N" THEN HARDCOPY = 0:GOTO 3200
3190 GOTO 3130
3200 GOSUB 5760
3210 GOTO 140
3220 '***************************
3230 LOCATE 17,2:PRINT "C";
3240 PK$ = "1"
3250 XX = 15:YY = 3
3260 FREQUENCY = 260
3270 RETURN
3280 '***************************
3290 LOCATE 17,37:PRINT "C";
3300 PK$ = "13"
3310 XX = 15:YY = 38
3320 FREQUENCY = 520
3330 RETURN
3340 '***************************
3350 LOCATE 17,72:PRINT "C";
3360 PK$ = "25"
```

```
3370 XX = 15:YY = 73
3380 FREQUENCY = 1040
3390 RETURN
3400 '***************************
3410 LOCATE 10,4:PRINT "C#";
3420 PK$ = "2"
3430 XX = 8:YY = 5
3440 FREQUENCY = 277
3450 RETURN
3460 '***************************
3470 LOCATE 10,39:PRINT "C#";
3480 PK$ = "14"
3490 XX = 8:YY = 40
3500 FREQUENCY = 554
3510 RETURN
3520 '***************************
3530 LOCATE 10,74:PRINT "C#";
3540 PK$ = "26"
3550 XX = 8:YY = 75
3560 FREQUENCY = 1108
3570 RETURN
3580 '***************************
3590 LOCATE 11,4:PRINT "Db";
3600 PK$ = "2"
3610 XX = 8:YY = 5
3620 FREQUENCY = 277
3630 RETURN
3640 '***************************
3650 LOCATE 11,39:PRINT "Db";
3660 PK$ = "14"
3670 XX = 8:YY = 40
3680 FREQUENCY = 554
3690 RETURN
3700 '***************************
3710 LOCATE 11,74:PRINT "Db";
3720 PK$ = "26"
3730 XX = 8:YY = 75
3740 FREQUENCY = 1108
3750 RETURN
3760 '***************************
3770 LOCATE 17,7:PRINT "D";
3780 PK$ = "3"
3790 XX = 15:YY = 8
3800 FREQUENCY = 294
3810 RETURN
3820 '***************************
3830 LOCATE 17,42:PRINT "D";
3840 PK$ = "15"
3850 XX = 15:YY = 43
3860 FREQUENCY = 588
3870 RETURN
3880 '***************************
3890 LOCATE 17,77:PRINT "D";
3900 PK$ = "27"
3910 XX = 15:YY = 78
3920 FREQUENCY = 1176
3930 RETURN
3940 '***************************
3950 LOCATE 11,9:PRINT "Eb";
3960 PK$ = "4"
3970 XX = 8:YY = 10
3980 FREQUENCY = 311
3990 RETURN
4000 '***************************
4010 LOCATE 11,44:PRINT "Eb";
4020 PK$ = "16"
4030 XX = 8:YY = 45
4040 FREQUENCY = 622
4050 RETURN
```

```
4060 '***************************
4070 LOCATE 11,79:PRINT "Eb";
4080 PK$ = "28"
4090 XX = 8:YY = 80
4100 FREQUENCY = 1244
4110 RETURN
4120 '***************************
4130 LOCATE 17,12:PRINT "E";
4140 PK$ = "5"
4150 XX = 15:YY = 13
4160 FREQUENCY = 330
4170 RETURN
4180 '***************************
4190 LOCATE 17,47:PRINT "E";
4200 PK$ = "17"
4210 XX = 15:YY = 48
4220 FREQUENCY = 660
4230 RETURN
4240 '***************************
4250 LOCATE 17,17:PRINT "F";
4260 PK$ = "6"
4270 XX = 15:YY = 18
4280 FREQUENCY = 349
4290 RETURN
4300 '***************************
4310 LOCATE 17,52:PRINT "F";
4320 PK$ = "18"
4330 XX = 15:YY = 53
4340 FREQUENCY = 698
4350 RETURN
4360 '***************************
4370 LOCATE 11,19:PRINT "F#";
4380 PK$ = "7"
4390 XX = 8:YY = 20
4400 FREQUENCY = 370
4410 RETURN
4420 '***************************
4430 LOCATE 11,54:PRINT "F#";
4440 PK$ = "19"
4450 XX = 8:YY = 55
4460 FREQUENCY = 740
4470 RETURN
4480 '***************************
4490 LOCATE 17,22:PRINT "G";
4500 PK$ = "8"
4510 XX = 15:YY = 23
4520 FREQUENCY = 392
4530 RETURN
4540 '***************************
4550 LOCATE 17,57:PRINT "G";
4560 PK$ = "20"
4570 XX = 15:YY = 58
4580 FREQUENCY = 784
4590 RETURN
4600 '***************************
4610 LOCATE 11,24:PRINT "Ab";
4620 PK$ = "9"
4630 XX = 8:YY = 25
4640 FREQUENCY = 415
4650 RETURN
4660 '***************************
4670 LOCATE 11,59:PRINT "Ab";
4680 PK$ = "21"
4690 XX = 8:YY = 60
4700 FREQUENCY = 830
4710 RETURN
4720 '***************************
4730 LOCATE 17,27:PRINT "A";
4740 PK$ = "10"
```

```
4750 XX = 15:YY = 28
4760 FREQUENCY = 440
4770 RETURN
4780 '****************************
4790 LOCATE 17,62:PRINT "A";
4800 PK$ = "22"
4810 XX = 15:YY = 63
4820 FREQUENCY = 880
4830 RETURN
4840 '****************************
4850 LOCATE 11,29:PRINT "Bb";
4860 PK$ = "11"
4870 XX = 8:YY = 30
4880 FREQUENCY = 466
4890 RETURN
4900 '****************************
4910 LOCATE 11,64:PRINT "Bb";
4920 PK$ = "23"
4930 XX = 8:YY = 65
4940 FREQUENCY = 932
4950 RETURN
4960 '****************************
4970 LOCATE 17,32:PRINT "B";
4980 PK$ = "12"
4990 XX = 15:YY = 33
5000 FREQUENCY = 494
5010 RETURN
5020 '****************************
5030 LOCATE 17,67:PRINT "B";
5040 PK$ = "24"
5050 XX = 15:YY = 68
5060 FREQUENCY = 988
5070 RETURN
5080 '****************************************
5090 '*    BLACK NOTE ON WHITE BACKGROUND   *
5100 '****************************************
5110 COLOR 15,0
5120 X = XX:Y = YY
5130 LOCATE X + 1,Y:PRINT CHR$(14);
5140 SOUND FREQUENCY,DURATION
5150 X = XX:Y = YY
5160 LOCATE X + 1,Y:PRINT CHR$(219);
5170 RETURN
5180 '****************************************
5190 '*    WHITE NOTE ON BLACK BACKGROUND   *
5200 '****************************************
5210 COLOR 15,0
5220 X = XX:Y = YY
5230 LOCATE X + 1,Y:PRINT CHR$(14);
5240 SOUND FREQUENCY,DURATION
5250 X = XX:Y = YY
5260 LOCATE X + 1 Y:PRINT CHR$(255);
5270 RETURN
5280 '****************************************
5290 '*       PIANO KEY IDENTIFICATION       *
5300 '****************************************
5310 COLOR 15,0
5320 X = XX:Y = YY - 1
5330 LOCATE X,Y:PRINT PK$;
5340 RETURN
5350 '****************************************
5360 '*  ROUTINE TO CLEAR THE LOWER SCREEN   *
5370 '****************************************
5380 LOCATE 22,1
5390 FOR N = 22 TO 24
5400     PRINT STRING$(79,CHR$(255));
5410 NEXT N
5420 LOCATE 25,1
5430 PRINT SPACE$(60);
```

```
5440 RETURN
5450 '****************************************
5460 '*   ROUTINE TO PLAY THE ENTERED SONG   *
5470 '****************************************
5480 GOSUB 5350
5490 IF SONG.LOADED = 1 THEN 5550
5500 LOCATE 25,1
5510 PRINT "NO SONG LOADED";
5520 BEEP
5530 FOR Z = 1 TO 1000:NEXT Z
5540 GOTO 5750
5550 ROW = 22:COLUMN = 1
5560 NOBLANK = 1
5570 FOR Z = 1 TO NOTES - 1
5580     LOCATE ROW,COLUMN
5590     PRINT SONG(Z,1);"-";SONG(Z,2);"   ";
5600     A = SONG(Z,1)
5610     DURATION = SONG(Z,2)
5620     IF A = 0 THEN SOUND 32767,DURATION:GOTO 5640
5630     ON A GOSUB 1760,1770,1780,1790,1800,1810,1820,1830,1840,
             1850,1860,1870,1880,1890,1900,1910,1920,1930,1940,1950,
             1960,1970,1980,1990,2000,2010,2020,2030
5640     COLUMN = COLUMN + 8
5650     IF COLUMN > 72 THEN COLUMN = 1:ROW = ROW + 1
5660     IF ROW = 25 THEN GOSUB 5350:ROW = 22
5670 NEXT Z
5680 LOCATE 25,1
5690 PRINT "PRESS SPACE BAR TO CONTINUE";
5700 Z$ = INKEY$:IF Z$ = "" THEN 5700
5710 IF Z$ < > " " THEN 5700
5720 GOSUB 5350
5730 LOCATE 25,1
5740 PRINT "88 FOR MAIN MENU / 99 TO PLAY TO THIS POINT";
5750 RETURN
5760 '**********************************
5770 '*   DISPLAY AND HARDCOPY ROUTINE   *
5780 '**********************************
5790 CLS
5800 COUNT = 0:NOTES = 0
5810 COL.POSITION = 1:NOTES = 1
5820 FOR ROW = 1 TO 20
5830     COLUMN = COL.POSITION
5840     LOCATE ROW,COLUMN
5850     PRINT NOTES;". ";SONG(NOTES,1);"-";SONG(NOTES,2)
5860     COUNT = COUNT + 1:NOTES = NOTES + 1
5870     IF COUNT = SENTINEL - 1 THEN 5920
5880 NEXT ROW
5890 COL.POSITION = COL.POSITION + 15
5900 IF COL.POSITION = 91 THEN 5920
5910 GOTO 5820
5920 LOCATE 25,1
5930 PRINT "DO YOU WISH TO CHANGE ANY NOTE (Y/N)? ";
5940 Z$ = INKEY$:IF Z$ = "" THEN 5940
5950 A$ = ""
5960 IF Z$ = "Y" THEN PRINT Z$;:GOTO 6040
5970 IF Z$ = "N" THEN PRINT Z$;:GOTO 5990
5980 GOTO 5940
5990 IF HARDCOPY < > 1 THEN GOTO 140
6000 FOR NOTES = 1 TO SENTINEL - 1
6010     LPRINT NOTES;".",SONG(NOTES,1);"-";SONG(NOTES,2)
6020 NEXT NOTES
6030 GOTO 140
6040 LOCATE 25,1
6050 A$ = ""
6060 PRINT "       WHAT NOTE DO YOU WISH TO CHANGE? ";
6070 Z$ = INKEY$:IF Z$ = "" THEN 6070
6080 IF Z$ = CHR$(13) THEN 6120
6090 PRINT Z$;
6100 A$ = A$ + Z$
```

```
6110 GOTO 6070
6120 A = VAL(A$)
6130 A$ = ""
6140 LOCATE 22,1
6150 PRINT "PRESENT NOTE:";SONG(A,1)
6160 LOCATE 23,1
6170 PRINT "PRESENT TIME:";SONG(A,2)
6180 LOCATE 22,40
6190 PRINT "ENTER NEW NOTE: ";
6200 Z$ = INKEY$:IF Z$ = "" THEN 6200
6210 IF Z$ = CHR$(13) THEN 6250
6220 PRINT Z$;
6230 A$ = A$ + Z$
6240 GOTO 6200
6250 SONG(A,1) = VAL(A$)
6260 A$ = ""
6270 LOCATE 23,40
6280 PRINT "ENTER NEW TIME: ";;
6290 Z$ = INKEY$:IF Z$ = "" THEN 6290
6300 IF Z$ = CHR$(13) THEN 6340
6310 PRINT Z$;
6320 A$ = A$ + Z$
6330 GOTO 6290
6340 SONG(A,2) = VAL(A$)
6350 GOTO 5760
6360 '*****************************************
6370 '* OPENING STRAINS OF GOD BLESS AMERICA  *
6380 '* CONTAINING 28 PAIRS OF NOTES AND TIME *
6390 '*****************************************
6400 DATA 6,16,5,8,3,8,5,6,3,4,1,16,8,16,6
6410 DATA 8,8,8,10,16,10,8,8,4,10,4,11,8
6420 DATA 3,16,6,4,8,4,10,8,1,16,6,4,8,4
6430 DATA 10,8,8,4,6,4,8,8,6,4,5,4,6,16
6440 '*****************************************
6450 '*          TURKEY IN THE STRAW          *
6460 '* CONTAINING 54 PAIRS OF NOTES AND TIME *
6470 '*****************************************
6480 DATA 22,2,20,2,18,2,17,2,18,2,20,2,18,2,13,2
6490 DATA 10,2,11,2,13,2,15,2,13,2
6500 DATA 10,2,13,8,18,2,20,2,22,4,22,4,22,2,20,2
6510 DATA 18,2,20,2,22,2,20,4
6520 DATA 22,2,20,2,18,2,17,2,18,2,20,2,18,2,13,2
6530 DATA 13,2,10,2,11,2,13,2,15,2,13,2
6540 DATA 10,2,13,4,18,2,20,2,22,2,25,4,27,2,25,2
6550 DATA 22,2,18,2,20,2,22,8,20,8
6560 DATA 18,16
6570 '*****************************************
6580 '*          THE MISSOURI WALTZ           *
6590 '* CONTAINING 44 PAIRS OF NOTES AND TIME *
6600 '*****************************************
6610 DATA 22,8,21,2,22,4,18,2,20,8,19,2,20,4
6620 DATA 21,2,22,8,21,2,22,4,20,2,18,16
6630 DATA 22,8,21,2,22,4,18,2,20,8,19,2,20,4
6640 DATA 21,2,22,8,21,2,22,4,20,2,18,16
6650 DATA 17,4,16,4,15,8,18,4,20,4,18,8,15,4
6660 DATA 14,4,13,8,18,4,20,4,18,8,13,4
6670 DATA 13,2,14,2,15,16,22,16,18,16
6680 '*****************************************
6690 '*        ONWARD CHRISTIAN SOLDIERS      *
6700 '* CONTAINING 98 PAIRS OF NOTES AND TIME *
6710 '*****************************************
6720 DATA 20,4,20,4,20,4,20,4,20,4,22,2,20,8
6730 DATA 15,4,15,4,13,4,15,4,17,8,13,4
6740 DATA 17,4,20,4,25,4,25,8,24,8,22,4,0,2,22,4
6750 DATA 0,2,17,4,0,2,19,4,0,2,20,8,15,4,0,2,15,4,0,2,20,4
6760 DATA 15,4,0,2,17,8,18,2,17,8,20,4,0,2,20,4,0,2,25,4,0,2,20,4
6770 DATA 0,2,22,16,0,2,22,4,0,2,20,4,0,2,18,8,0,2,20,4,0,2
6780 DATA 22,4,0,2,20,4,0,2,18,4,0,2,20,4,0,2,22,4,20,4,0,2,18,4
6790 DATA 0,2,17,4,15,8,13,4,13,4,13,4,13,4
```

```
6800 DATA 13,4,12,2,10,2,12,4,13,4,0,2,15,4,15,4,15,4,13,2,15,2,17,16
6810 DATA 20,4,20,4,25,4,24,4,25,8,20,8,18,4,17,4,15,4,13,2,13,16
6820 '*****************************************
6830 '*              THE MARINE'S HYMN         *
6840 '* CONTAINING 97 PAIRS OF NOTES AND TIME  *
6850 '*****************************************
6860 DATA 13,2,17,2,20,4,0,2,20,4,0,2,20,4,0,2,20,4,0,2,20,4,0,2,25,2
6870 DATA 20,8,17,2,18,2,20,4,0,2,20,4,0,2,18,3,0,2,15,2,13,8
6880 DATA 13,2,17,2,20,4,0,2,20,4,0,2,20,4,0,2,20,4,0,2,20,4,0,2,25,2
6890 DATA 20,8,17,2,18,2,20,4,0,2,20,4,0,2,18,3,0,2,15,2,13,8
6900 DATA 25,2,24,2,22,4,0,2,18,4,0,2,22,4,0,2,18,4,0,2,20,4,0,2,22,2
6910 DATA 20,4,0,2,25,2,24,2,22,4,0,2,18,4,0,2,22,4,0,2,25,4,0,2,20,8
6920 DATA 13,2,17,2,20,4,0,2,20,4,0,2,20,4,0,2,20,4,0,2,20,4,0,2,25,2
6930 DATA 20,8,17,2,18,2,20,4,0,2,20,4,0,2,18,3,0,2,15,2,13,8
6940 '*****************************************
6950 '*           SELECTION NUMBER 6           *
6960 '*CONTAINING 100 PAIRS OF NOTES AND TIME  *
6970 '*****************************************
6980 DATA XXXXXXXXXXXXXXXXXXXXXXXXXXXXXXXXXXXXXX
6990 DATA XXXXXXXXXXXXXXXXXXXXXXXXXXXXXXXXXXXXXX
7000 DATA XXXXXXXXXXXXXXXXXXXXXXXXXXXXXXXXXXXXXX
7010 DATA XXXXXXXXXXXXXXXXXXXXXXXXXXXXXXXXXXXXXX
7020 DATA XXXXXXXXXXXXXXXXXXXXXXXXXXXXXXXXXXXXXX
7030 DATA XXXXXXXXXXXXXXXXXXXXXXXXXXXXXXXXXXXXXX
7040 DATA XXXXXXXXXXXXXXXXXXXXXXXXXXXXXXXXXXXXXX
7050 DATA XXXXXXXXXXXXXXXXXXXXXXXXXXXXXXXXXXXXXX
7060 '*****************************************
7070 '*           SELECTION NUMBER 7           *
7080 '*CONTAINING 100 PAIRS OF NOTES AND TIME  *
7090 '*****************************************
7100 DATA XXXXXXXXXXXXXXXXXXXXXXXXXXXXXXXXXXXXXX
7110 DATA XXXXXXXXXXXXXXXXXXXXXXXXXXXXXXXXXXXXXX
7120 DATA XXXXXXXXXXXXXXXXXXXXXXXXXXXXXXXXXXXXXX
7130 DATA XXXXXXXXXXXXXXXXXXXXXXXXXXXXXXXXXXXXXX
7140 DATA XXXXXXXXXXXXXXXXXXXXXXXXXXXXXXXXXXXXXX
7150 DATA XXXXXXXXXXXXXXXXXXXXXXXXXXXXXXXXXXXXXX
7160 DATA XXXXXXXXXXXXXXXXXXXXXXXXXXXXXXXXXXXXXX
7170 DATA XXXXXXXXXXXXXXXXXXXXXXXXXXXXXXXXXXXXXX
7180 '*****************************************
7190 '*           SELECTION NUMBER 8           *
7200 '*CONTAINING 100 PAIRS OF NOTES AND TIME  *
7210 '*****************************************
7220 DATA XXXXXXXXXXXXXXXXXXXXXXXXXXXXXXXXXXXXXX
7230 DATA XXXXXXXXXXXXXXXXXXXXXXXXXXXXXXXXXXXXXX
7240 DATA XXXXXXXXXXXXXXXXXXXXXXXXXXXXXXXXXXXXXX
7250 DATA XXXXXXXXXXXXXXXXXXXXXXXXXXXXXXXXXXXXXX
7260 DATA XXXXXXXXXXXXXXXXXXXXXXXXXXXXXXXXXXXXXX
7270 DATA XXXXXXXXXXXXXXXXXXXXXXXXXXXXXXXXXXXXXX
7280 DATA XXXXXXXXXXXXXXXXXXXXXXXXXXXXXXXXXXXXXX
7290 DATA XXXXXXXXXXXXXXXXXXXXXXXXXXXXXXXXXXXXXX
7300 '*****************************************
7310 '*           SELECTION NUMBER 9           *
7320 '*CONTAINING 100 PAIRS OF NOTES AND TIME  *
7330 '*****************************************
7340 DATA XXXXXXXXXXXXXXXXXXXXXXXXXXXXXXXXXXXXXX
7350 DATA XXXXXXXXXXXXXXXXXXXXXXXXXXXXXXXXXXXXXX
7360 DATA XXXXXXXXXXXXXXXXXXXXXXXXXXXXXXXXXXXXXX
7370 DATA XXXXXXXXXXXXXXXXXXXXXXXXXXXXXXXXXXXXXX
7380 DATA XXXXXXXXXXXXXXXXXXXXXXXXXXXXXXXXXXXXXX
7390 DATA XXXXXXXXXXXXXXXXXXXXXXXXXXXXXXXXXXXXXX
7400 DATA XXXXXXXXXXXXXXXXXXXXXXXXXXXXXXXXXXXXXX
7410 DATA XXXXXXXXXXXXXXXXXXXXXXXXXXXXXXXXXXXXXX
7420 '*****************************************
7430 '* LOAD/SAVE ROUTINE FOR SONGS CONTAINED  *
7440 '* IN DATA LINES AND ON DISKETTE FILES.   *
7450 '*****************************************
7460 RESTORE
7470 GOSUB 5350
7480 LOCATE 22,1
```

```
7490 PRINT "THESE OPTIONS EXIST FOR";
7500 LOCATE 23,1
7510 PRINT "THE LOAD/SAVE SELECTION:";
7520 LOCATE 22,40
7530 PRINT "1.  LOAD FROM DATA LINES.";
7540 LOCATE 23,40
7550 PRINT "2.  LOAD FROM DISKETTE.";
7560 LOCATE 24,40
7570 PRINT "3.  SAVE TO DISKETTE.";
7580 LOCATE 24,1
7590 PRINT "SELECT :";
7600 Z$ = INKEY$:IF Z$ = "" THEN 7600
7610 A = VAL(Z$)
7620 IF (A < 1) OR (A > 3) THEN 7420
7630 PRINT A;
7640 ON A GOTO 7660,9130,8820
7650 GOTO 7420
7660 GOSUB 5350
7670 LOCATE 22,1
7680 PRINT "THESE SONGS";
7690 LOCATE 23,1
7700 PRINT "ARE STORED";
7710 LOCATE 24,1
7720 PRINT "IN PROGRAM.";
7730 LOCATE 22,16
7740 PRINT "1. GOD BLESS AMERICA";
7750 LOCATE 23,16
7760 PRINT "2. TURKEY IN STRAW";
7770 LOCATE 24,16
7780 PRINT "3. MISSOURI WALTZ";
7790 LOCATE 22,38
7800 PRINT "4. CHRISTIAN SOLDIER";
7810 LOCATE 23,38
7820 PRINT "5. THE MARINES' HYMN";
7830 LOCATE 24,38
7840 PRINT "6. XXXXXXXXXXXXXXXXX";
7850 LOCATE 22,60
7860 PRINT "7. XXXXXXXXXXXXXXXXX";
7870 LOCATE 23,60
7880 PRINT "8. XXXXXXXXXXXXXXXXX";
7890 LOCATE 24,60
7900 PRINT "9. XXXXXXXXXXXXXXXXX";
7910 Z$ = INKEY$:IF Z$ = "" THEN 7910
7920 A = VAL(Z$)
7930 IF (A < 1) OR (A > 9) THEN 7420
7940 ON A GOTO 7960,8000,8060,8130,8210,8300,8400,8510,8630
7950 GOTO 7420
7960 FOR NOTES = 1 TO 28                        'GOD BLESS AMERICA
7970     READ SONG(NOTES,1),SONG(NOTES,2)
7980 NEXT NOTES
7990 GOTO 8760
8000 FOR NOTES = 1 TO 28:READ Z,Z:NEXT NOTES    'BYPASS GOD BLESS AMERICA
8010 FOR NOTES = 1 TO 54                        'TURKEY IN THE STRAW
8020     READ SONG(NOTES,1),SONG(NOTES,2)
8030 NEXT NOTES
8040 SENTINEL = NOTES
8050 GOTO 8760
8060 FOR NOTES = 1 TO 28:READ Z,Z:NEXT NOTES    'BYPASS GOD BLESS AMERICA
8070 FOR NOTES = 1 TO 54:READ Z,Z:NEXT NOTES    'BYPASS TURKEY IN THE STRAW
8080 FOR NOTES = 1 TO 44                        'MISSOURI WALTZ
8090     READ SONG(NOTES,1),SONG(NOTES,2)
8100 NEXT NOTES
8110 SENTINEL = NOTES
8120 GOTO 8760
8130 FOR NOTES = 1 TO 28:READ Z,Z:NEXT NOTES    'BYPASS GOD BLESS AMERICA
8140 FOR NOTES = 1 TO 54:READ Z,Z:NEXT NOTES    'BYPASS TURKEY IN THE STRAW
8150 FOR NOTES = 1 TO 44:READ Z,Z:NEXT NOTES    'BYPASS MISSOURI WALTZ
8160 FOR NOTES = 1 TO 98                        'ONWARD CHRISTIAN SOLDIERS
8170     READ SONG(NOTES,1),SONG(NOTES,2)
```

```
8180 NEXT NOTES
8190 SENTINEL = NOTES
8200 GOTO 8760
8210 FOR NOTES = 1 TO 28:READ Z,Z:NEXT NOTES   'BYPASS GOD BLESS AMERICA
8220 FOR NOTES = 1 TO 54:READ Z,Z:NEXT NOTES   'BYPASS TURKEY IN THE STRAW
8230 FOR NOTES = 1 TO 44:READ Z,Z:NEXT NOTES   'BYPASS MISSOURI WALTZ
8240 FOR NOTES = 1 TO 98:READ Z,Z:NEXT NOTES   'BYPASS CHRISTIAN SOLDIERS
8250 FOR NOTES = 1 TO 97      'MARINES' HYMN
8260     READ SONG(NOTES,1),SONG(NOTES,2)
8270 NEXT NOTES
8280 SENTINEL = NOTES
8290 GOTO 8760
8300 FOR NOTES = 1 TO 28:READ Z,Z:NEXT NOTES   'BYPASS GOD BLESS AMERICA
8310 FOR NOTES = 1 TO 54:READ Z,Z:NEXT NOTES   'BYPASS TURKEY IN THE STRAW
8320 FOR NOTES = 1 TO 44:READ Z,Z:NEXT NOTES   'BYPASS MISSOURI WALTZ
8330 FOR NOTES = 1 TO 98:READ Z,Z:NEXT NOTES   'BYPASS CHRISTIAN SOLDIERS
8340 FOR NOTES = 1 TO 97:READ Z,Z:NEXT NOTES   'BYPASS MARINES' HYMN
8350 FOR NOTES = 1 TO 100     'SELECTION 6
8360     READ SONG(NOTES,1),SONG(NOTES,2)
8370 NEXT NOTES
8380 SENTINEL = NOTES
8390 GOTO 8760
8400 FOR NOTES = 1 TO 28:READ Z,Z:NEXT NOTES   'BYPASS GOD BLESS AMERICA
8410 FOR NOTES = 1 TO 54:READ Z,Z:NEXT NOTES   'BYPASS TURKEY IN THE STRAW
8420 FOR NOTES = 1 TO 44:READ Z,Z:NEXT NOTES   'BYPASS MISSOURI WALTZ
8430 FOR NOTES = 1 TO 98:READ Z,Z:NEXT NOTES   'BYPASS CHRISTIAN SOLDIERS
8440 FOR NOTES = 1 TO 97:READ Z,Z:NEXT NOTES   'BYPASS MARINES' HYMN
8450 FOR NOTES = 1 TO 100:READ Z,Z:NEXT NOTES  'BYPASS SELECTION 6
8460 FOR NOTES = 1 TO 100     'SELECTION 7
8470     READ SONG(NOTES,1),SONG(NOTES,2)
8480 NEXT NOTES
8490 SENTINEL = NOTES
8500 GOTO 8760
8510 FOR NOTES = 1 TO 28:READ Z,Z:NEXT NOTES   'BYPASS GOD BLESS AMERICA
8520 FOR NOTES = 1 TO 54:READ Z,Z:NEXT NOTES   'BYPASS TURKEY IN THE STRAW
8530 FOR NOTES = 1 TO 44:READ Z,Z:NEXT NOTES   'BYPASS MISSOURI WALTZ
8540 FOR NOTES = 1 TO 98:READ Z,Z:NEXT NOTES   'BYPASS CHRISTIAN SOLDIERS
8550 FOR NOTES = 1 TO 97:READ Z,Z:NEXT NOTES   'BYPASS MARINES' HYMN
8560 FOR NOTES = 1 TO 100:READ Z,Z:NEXT NOTES  'BYPASS SELECTION 6
8570 FOR NOTES = 1 TO 100:READ Z,Z:NEXT NOTES  'BYPASS SELECTION 7
8580 FOR NOTES = 1 TO 100     'SELECTION 8
8590     READ SONG(NOTES,1),SONG(NOTES,2)
8600 NEXT NOTES
8610 SENTINEL = NOTES
8620 GOTO 8760
8630 FOR NOTES = 1 TO 28:READ Z,Z:NEXT NOTES   'BYPASS GOD BLESS AMERICA
8640 FOR NOTES = 1 TO 53:READ Z,Z:NEXT NOTES   'BYPASS TURKEY IN THE STRAW
8650 FOR NOTES = 1 TO 44:READ Z,Z:NEXT NOTES   'BYPASS MISSOURI WALTZ
8660 FOR NOTES = 1 TO 98:READ Z,Z:NEXT NOTES   'BYPASS CHRISTIAN SOLDIERS
8670 FOR NOTES = 1 TO 97:READ Z,Z:NEXT NOTES   'BYPASS MARINES' HYMN
8680 FOR NOTES = 1 TO 100:READ Z,Z:NEXT NOTES  'BYPASS SELECTION 6
8690 FOR NOTES = 1 TO 100:READ Z,Z:NEXT NOTES  'BYPASS SELECTION 7
8700 FOR NOTES = 1 TO 100:READ Z,Z:NEXT NOTES  'BYPASS SELECTION 8
8710 FOR NOTES = 1 TO 100     'SELECTION 9
8720     READ SONG(NOTES,1),SONG(NOTES,2)
8730 NEXT NOTES
8740 SENTINEL = NOTES
8750 GOTO 8760
8760 LOCATE 25,1
8770 PRINT "SONG LOADED";
8780 BEEP
8790 FOR Z = 1 TO 1000:NEXT Z
8800 SONG.LOADED = 1
8810 RETURN
8820 '*****************************************
8830 '* ROUTINE FOR WRITING DISKETTE OUTPUT *
8840 '*****************************************
8850 IF SONG.LOADED = 1 THEN 8900
8860 LOCATE 25,1
```

```
8870 PRINT "NO SONG LOADED - CANNOT WRITE DISK FILE";
8880 FOR Z = 1 TO 1000:NEXT Z
8890 GOTO 650
8900 A$ = "":B$ = ""
8910 GOSUB 5350
8920 LOCATE 25,1
8930 PRINT "SPECIFY FILE NAME (MAXIMUM 8 CHARACTERS + <CR>: ";
8940 Z$ = INKEY$:IF Z$ = "" THEN 8940
8950 IF Z$ = CHR$(13) THEN 8990
8960 PRINT Z$;
8970 A$ = A$ + Z$
8980 GOTO 8940
8990 B$ = "B:" + A$ + ".SNG"
9000 GOSUB 5350
9010 LOCATE 25,1
9020 PRINT "WRITING DISKETTE FILE";
9030 OPEN B$ FOR OUTPUT AS #1
9040 FOR NOTES = 1 TO SENTINEL
9050     PRINT #1,SONG(NOTES,1);SONG(NOTES,2)
9060 NEXT NOTES
9070 CLOSE #1
9080 GOSUB 5350
9090 LOCATE 25,1
9100 PRINT "DISKETTE WRITE COMPLETE";
9110 RESTORE
9120 FOR Z = 1 TO 1000:NEXT Z:GOTO 650
9130 '*****************************************
9140 '* ROUTINE FOR READING DISKETTE INPUT   *
9150 '*****************************************
9160 CLS
9170 PRINT "THESE SONGS ARE ON THE DISK":PRINT:PRINT
9180 A$ = "":B$ = ""
9190 FILES "B:*.SNG"
9200 GOSUB 5350
9210 LOCATE 25,1
9220 PRINT "SPECIFY FILE NAME (MAXIMUM 8 CHARACTERS + <CR>: ";
9230 Z$ = INKEY$:IF Z$ = "" THEN 9230
9240 IF Z$ = CHR$(13) THEN 9280
9250 PRINT Z$;
9260 A$ = A$ + Z$
9270 GOTO 9230
9280 B$ = "B:" + A$ + ".SNG"
9290 GOSUB 5350
9300 CLOSE #1
9310 LOCATE 25,1
9320 PRINT "READING DISKETTE FILE";
9330 OPEN B$ FOR INPUT AS #1
9340 FOR NOTES = 1 TO 1000
9350     INPUT #1,SONG(NOTES,1),SONG(NOTES,2)
9360     IF EOF(1) THEN 9380
9370 NEXT NOTES
9380 CLOSE #1
9390 SENTINEL = NOTES
9400 SONG.LOADED = 1
9410 GOSUB 5350
9420 RESTORE
9430 LOCATE 25,1
9440 PRINT "DISKETTE READ COMPLETE";
9450 FOR Z = 1 TO 1000:NEXT Z:GOTO 650
```

PRINTER GRAPHICS

The interesting thing about graphics on a printer is that they are so much more capable than those available to the monochrome display but far less useful. Graphics, in the truest sense, are really useful only on the color display. Those graphics available on a printer are, of course, useful, but most of us have little time for the development of computer pictures and Snoopy calendars.

It follows, then, that to be useful, printer graphics must serve a real purpose. Of the majority of printer graphics codes, most, unfortunately, are decorative. We showed you the individual graphics characters in a previous chapter. But if you will enter and run the following program, enough of them will be shown for you to get a flavor of what they look like in groups:

```
10 CLS
20 LINECOUNT = 0
30 LPRINT CHR$(27) + CHR$(71);
40 FOR N = 160 TO 223
50      LPRINT STR$(N);".";TAB(10);
60      LPRINT STRING$(40,CHR$(N))
70      LPRINT
80      LINECOUNT = LINECOUNT + 2
90      IF LINECOUNT = 44 THEN 140
100 NEXT N
110 PRINT "PRINTOUT IS COMPLETE"
120 LPRINT CHR$(12)
130 END
140 LINECOUNT = 0
150 LPRINT CHR$(12)
160 GOTO 100
```

The program produces a printout like the following:

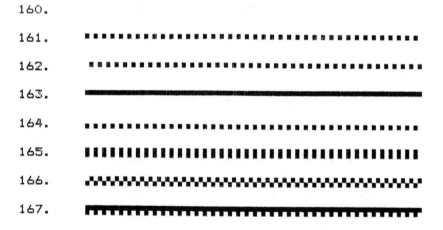

168.

169.

170.

171.

172.

173.

174.

175.

176.

177.

178.

179.

180.

181.

182.

183.

184.

185.

186.

187.

188.

189.

190.

191.

192.

193.

194.

195.

196.

197.

198.

199.

200.

201.

202.

203.

204.

205.

206.

207.

208.

209.

210.

211.

212.

213.

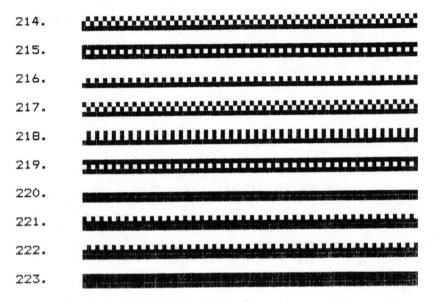

The purpose printer graphics *should* serve is to enhance a report. Perhaps, as we did previously, you might wish to use them to develop an organizational chart. We'll do that again presently. Or, you might wish to use printer graphics to present sales data, much as we did earlier.

When developing graphics on the screen, we can pretty much draw lines at will, top to bottom, left to right, etc. We can intersperse the drawing of lines with the placement of words, content that the final picture will ultimately arrive. Try to do that on the printer, and you will end up with irregularly placed lines on paper. Using the screen graphics approach to the presentation of printer graphics will definitely contain some surprises.

In order to present graphics on the printer, the *entire picture* must be prepared in advance. It follows, then, that the picture must be store somewhere and that somewhere is an array. The following program prepared the previous organizational chart but has now been modified to work with printer graphics. Review it and then we'll discuss it:

```
10 CLS
20 CLEAR 2000
30 OPTION BASE 1
40 DIM REPORT.MATRIX$(25,80)
50 PRINT "CLEARING THE MATRIX"
60 FOR N = 1 TO 25
70     FOR Z = 1 TO 80
80         REPORT.MATRIX$(N,Z) = " "
90     NEXT Z
100 NEXT N
110 KEY OFF
120 RESTORE
```

```
130 '****************************************
140 '*              LOAD THE BOXES          *
150 '****************************************
160 PRINT "LOADING THE BOXES"
170 FOR X = 1 TO 72
180     READ A,B,C
190     FOR Y = 0 TO C - 1
200         REPORT.MATRIX$(A,B + Y) = CHR$(223)
210     NEXT Y
220 NEXT X
230 '****************************************
240 '*       LOAD THE HORIZONTAL LINES      *
250 '****************************************
260 PRINT "LOADING THE HORIZONTAL LINES"
270 FOR X = 1 TO 2
280     READ A,B,C
290     FOR Y = 0 TO C - 1
300         REPORT.MATRIX$(A,B + Y) = CHR$(223)
310     NEXT Y
320 NEXT X
330 '****************************************
340 '*        LOAD THE VERTICAL LINES       *
350 '****************************************
360 PRINT "LOADING THE VERTICAL LINES"
370 FOR X = 1 TO 34
380     READ A,B,C
390     FOR Y = 0 TO C - 1
400         REPORT.MATRIX$(A,B + Y) = CHR$(223)
410     NEXT Y
420 NEXT X
430 '****************************************
440 '*            INSERT THE WORDS          *
450 '****************************************
460 PRINT "LOADING THE WORDS"
470 REPORT.MATRIX$(3,36) = "MAIN MENU"
480 REPORT.MATRIX$(12,8) =  "ADD"
490 REPORT.MATRIX$(12,27) = "CHANGE"
500 REPORT.MATRIX$(12,49) = "DELETE"
510 REPORT.MATRIX$(12,69) = "LOCATE"
520 REPORT.MATRIX$(20,7) = "PRINT"
530 REPORT.MATRIX$(20,28) = "SORT"
540 REPORT.MATRIX$(20,50) = "READ"
550 REPORT.MATRIX$(20,70) = "WRITE"
560 '****************************************
570 '*          PRINT THE REPORT            *
580 '****************************************
590 PRINT "PRINTING THE REPORT"
600 FOR ROW = 1 TO 25
610     FOR COLUMN = 1 TO 80
620         LENGTH.OF.ITEM = LEN(REPORT.MATRIX$(ROW,COLUMN))
630         LPRINT REPORT.MATRIX$(ROW,COLUMN);
640         IF LENGTH.OF.ITEM > 1 THEN COLUMN = COLUMN + LENGTH.OF.ITEM - 1
650     NEXT COLUMN
660 NEXT ROW
670 PRINT "END OF REPORT"
680 LPRINT CHR$(12)
690 END
700 '****************************************
710 '*              TOP BOX                 *
720 '****************************************
730 DATA 1,31,20
740 DATA 2,31,2,2,49,2
750 DATA 3,31,2,3,49,2
760 DATA 4,31,2,4,49,2
770 DATA 5,31,20
780 '****************************************
790 '*            MIDDLE BOXES              *
800 '****************************************
810 DATA 10,2,16,10,22,16,10,44,16,10,64,16
```

```
820 DATA 11,2,2,11,16,2,11,22,2,11,36,2
830 DATA 11,44,2,11,58,2,11,64,2,11,78,2
840 DATA 12,2,2,12,16,2,12,22,2,12,36,2
850 DATA 12,44,2,12,58,2,12,64,2,12,78,2
860 DATA 13,2,2,13,16,2,13,22,2,13,36,2
870 DATA 13,44,2,13,58,2,13,64,2,13,78,2
880 DATA 14,2,16,14,22,16,14,44,16,14,64,16
890 '*****************************************
900 '*              BOTTOM BOXES              *
910 '*****************************************
920 DATA 18,2,16,18,22,16,18,44,16,18,64,16
930 DATA 19,2,2,19,16,2,19,22,2,19,36,2
940 DATA 19,44,2,19,58,2,19,64,2,19,78,2
950 DATA 20,2,2,20,16,2,20,22,2,20,36,2
960 DATA 20,44,2,20,58,2,20,64,2,20,78,2
970 DATA 21,2,2,21,16,2,21,22,2,21,36,2
980 DATA 21,44,2,21,58,2,21,64,2,21,78,2
990 DATA 22,2,16,22,22,16,22,44,16,22,64,16
1000 '*****************************************
1010 '*             HORIZONTAL LINES           *
1020 '*****************************************
1030 DATA 8,11,60,16,11,60
1040 '*****************************************
1050 '*              VERTICAL LINES            *
1060 '*****************************************
1070 DATA 6,40,2,7,40,2,8,40,2,9,40,2,10,40,2
1080 DATA 11,40,2,12,40,2,13,40,2,14,40,2,15,40,2
1090 DATA 8,9,2,9,9,2,10,9,2
1100 DATA 16,9,2,17,9,2,18,9,2
1110 DATA 8,71,2,9,71,2,10,71,2
1120 DATA 16,71,2,17,71,2,18,71,2
1130 DATA 8,29,2,9,29,2,10,29,2
1140 DATA 16,29,2,17,29,2,18,29,2
1150 DATA 8,51,2,9,51,2,10,51,2
1160 DATA 16,51,2,17,51,2,18,51,2
1170 DATA 8,65,2,9,65,2,10,65,2
1180 DATA 16,65,2,17,65,2,18,65,2
```

There is only one really new instruction here. Statement 30 is called an OPTION BASE instruction. Recall from our discussion of DIMensioned arrays that there are such things as zero references, even though we didn't use them. OPTION BASE removes the memory allocation for those zero references, allowing reference from a specified base only. OPTION BASE applies to all DIMensioned arrays and must be specified *before* they are DIMensioned.

The concept here is that the screen matrix is itself the report. In much the same manner as we had previously located the boxes and words on the screen, we'll locate them in a matrix (REPORT.MATRIX$) that has been DIMensioned to the size of the screen. That size is 25 by 80, or 2000, and accounts for the CLEAR 2000 of statement 20. Since there are no other permanent string variables, the 2000 is sufficient. Thus, the 25 lines of 80 characters that will appear on the screen become the 25 lines of 80 characters that will appear as the printed output. Naturally, larger reports are possible but will require some very specific planning as to width and length characteristics. Reports wide than 80 characters require the use of one of the reduced print options previously discussed. For our present purposes, the 25 by 80 size is sufficient.

Examine the routine at statements 60-100. Its function is to load the matrix with spaces. When the DIMension is complete, the array is set to null rather than to spaces. A null equals "", with a length of zero. A space equals " ", with a length of 1. Therefore, the printer will not print a null. What isn't there can't be printed, and the result is that the print head will not move and the graphics output will be significantly distorted. Therefore, before anything is overlaid in the matrix, it must be loaded with spaces. You'll know to do that because of the message at statement 50.

As before, the coordinates of the boxes and lines are obtained from DATA statements. The fact that their positioning will be in a matrix rather than LOCATEd on a screen is of no consequence – almost, that is. It's different in a couple of ways. Now examine the coding in statements 260 through 320. The row, column, and length are read from DATA lines, just as before. But this time something different happens. Look at statement 290. Note that the Y in the FOR . . . NEXT look now has a range of 0 to one less than the length extracted from the DATA statement even though the total number of positions is the same (recall that zero is a number). The reason for the difference is what is known as *address compounding*. Statement 200 uses address compounding. The location of the row is the major location within the matrix. The location of the column, however, becomes a function of the column location in the DATA statement *plus* the offset from that location, which is a function of the length. Therefore (B + 0) is the same as B, or the first columnar position. All well and good, you say, but the same thing holds true for the screen. Yes, you're right, with one significant exception. When you LOCATEd the variable on the screen, you'll recall that the address of the variable was incremented by the computer itself. That is not true, however, when you are loading a matrix one character at a time.

The same occurs when words are placed in the matrix. Examine statement 470, which says that we wish to locate the words MAIN MENU beginning with 3,36. The concept is that "M" goes to 3,36; "A" goes to 3,37; "I" goes to 3,38, and so on. Unfortunately, it doesn't work that way. When you say you wish to locate the string variable MAIN MENU at 3,36, that's where it goes, but 3,37 is another matter. If you omit statements 620 and 640, you'll see what the difference really is. If you're into mazes, you'll be pleased with the result, but it won't look like what you had reason to expect.

Because the words MAIN MENU occupy nine positions on the printed output and only one position in the matrix, it becomes necessary to adjust the spacing by the length of the variable. Rather than simply compensating for the *known* length of the variable, we'd prefer to be able to make the adjustment based on the length of *any* variable. This is the reason for the instructions in statements 620 and 640, and you'll note that they are adjusted downward in a way that is commonly called *inclusive*. For example, there are eleven numbers from 0 to 10, inclusive.

The same concept can be applied to the sales report previously discussed. If you know the point, you can place the character into the array and then print it. The examples given here utilize the histogram approach, primarily because this is not intended to be a mathematical text. If, however, you wish to develop curves based on mathematical functions, the only really important thing to remember is that when a curve increases (rises on the paper), the row attribute of the matrix decreases. When the curve decreases (drops on the paper), the row attribute of the matrix increases. Otherwise, the left-to-right concept remains valid. Recall that you build a matrix one character at a time.

SUMMARY

We can now add the following to the list of commands, instructions, and functions we have already used:

Non-I/O Statements

OPTION BASE — Sets the minimum value for subscripted arrays.

I/O Statements

CLOSE — Is used to close a file, specifying buffer number.

INPUT # — Is used for reading a sequential file.

OPEN — Makes a file available for reading or writing. The mode of operation must be specified.

PRINT # — Is used for writing a sequential file.

Miscellaneous

EOF — Is used to determine that the end of file condition has been encountered.

FRE — Determines available memory.

5
Disks and the
Disk Operating System

In the last chapter the concept of a sequential file on disk was introduced. If by chance you have never been introduced to the Disk Operating System (DOS), you would no doubt have had a little difficulty there, but the routines were included because they are essentially the same as cassette routines. Before we begin using diskettes more extensively, it will be necessary to explain some additional concepts.

Technically, the media placed in the diskette drive is a *diskette*. A diskette is a 5 1/4-in. sheet of mylar, punched in the shape of a doughnut (or 45 rpm record), and mounted inside a sleeve. There are larger (8-in.) diskettes, and there have been experiments with smaller (3-in.) diskettes. Diskettes, like their larger computer counterparts, are a storage medium for data and programs. Highly accessible, they can be "read" or "written" at moderate speed. By and large, the general term applied to them is simply *disk*.

Take a program — any program — and seal it in a small envelope. Mark that envelope BASIC. Take that envelope and seal it in a larger envelope marked DOS. Do all this figuratively, at least. If you can conceptualize that this program solves a problem in a language called BASIC and functions through an operating system called the DOS, then you pretty much have the idea. In technical terms, the operating system *executes* the BASIC program. It does so as shown in the chart.

We've been discussing the DOS as if you already knew how to turn it on, and chances are that you've learned that much from the manual. In case you haven't, let's hit a few of the high points. First, the IBM system is one of the few systems in which it is possible to leave a diskette when the system is off. You can power up the system with a diskette already in place and you can remove power under the same conditions. Simply throw the red switch.

Recall that a previous discussion stated that if you did not have disk, then the system would power up with Cassette BASIC. Cassette BASIC is stored within

DOS

BASIC

FRAME (PC-5-1.BAS)

PC-5-2.BAS
BREAKEVEN ANALYSIS

PC-5-3.BAS
ENGLISH TO METRIC CONVERSION

PC-5-4.BAS
TWENTY-THREE MATCHES

PC-5-5.BAS
GRADE SCHOOL MATH

ROOT PROGRAM

ADD

SUB

MUL

DIV

the machine itself in what is known as Read Only Memory (ROM). Once you have your disk drives installed, you can still turn the system on in the same way. Note that when you do so, however, the computer knows of the presence of the disk drives and will attempt to read the diskette in the left drive (known as Drive A). Drive A is known as the *default drive*, and the hardware will always go to Drive A for direction if no other instructions have been received. After it tries to find the DOS diskette and doesn't (or finds something else), only then will it begin Cassette BASIC. If, at that time, you choose to do your work under the Disk Operating System instead, you must insert the diskette in Drive A (be sure to follow the directions exactly) and then hold down the ALT and CTL keys with the left hand and the DEL key with the right hand to boot the system. *Booting the system* is the term used to denote placing the system into disk mode. If you had left the diskette in the drive (or placed it there) before power came up, the system would have booted itself.

In any event, the first thing you must do is provide the system with the date. The "Guide to Operations" spells out the rules for entering the date. Interestingly, you can provide the system with the date under DOS and later have access to it with the DATE$ command in BASIC. We'll do that for one program in this chapter — not that we want the date for its own sake (TIME$ is also available) but because we will use it to reseed the random number generator. Give the system a valid Day, Month, Year date, as follows:

```
Enter today's date (m-d-y): 05/06/82
```

As soon as you provide the date, you'll see a prompt (probably "A") with a right carat, as follows:

```
Enter today's date (m-d-y): 05/06/82

The IBM Personal Computer DOS
Version 1.00 (C)Copyright IBM Corp 1981

A>
```

You can change that to utilize drive B as default, but you would only want to do so if drive A were inoperative and had to be taken out of the cabinet (the instructions show you how) for repairs. At this point, you have two disk-based BASIC options — regular Disk BASIC (BASIC) and Advanced BASIC (BASICA). Unless you are using the color monitor, you'll have no need for BASICA, and you can ERASE it *from your backup working copy only*. It occupies a lot of space on the diskette. Also, on your working diskette, you can get rid of *all* the demonstration programs very simply, as follows:

1. You must be *in* DOS mode. To get there, boot the system in the described manner, or, if you are already in BASIC, enter SYSTEM.
2. ERASE *.BAS

The ERASE command is DOS' way to remove files from the diskette. *But*, whenever you remove anything from a media, do so *gingerly*. Many, many hours can be lost by careless handling of media programs and data. When it's gone, moreover, it's gone forever. There's no resurrecting it unless you have a 96K system and full knowledge of the machine's assembly language. When you ERASE a file, you remove it from the directory. With DOS, you can ERASE many files with common attributes merely by using the wild card (*). In the above example, the ERASE command removed *all* BASIC programs.

ERASE has a counterpart in BASIC – the KILL command. It permits you to KILL only one file at a time and requires that the file name be specified in quotation marks.

We will discuss each of the DOS facilities at length within this chapter. By and large, however, we're going to concentrate on programs stored on disk, which do not read and write disk files, per se, but which either call another disk-based program or are combined from other programs that reside on disk. In the process, we'll also study one business program (Breakeven Analysis), one conversion tool (English to Metric Conversion), one game (Twenty-Three Matches), and one educational program (Grade School Math) with a root and four segments.

While you are still in DOS, enter DIR, and you will see on the screen a directory of all files located on the diskette. These are program files, as opposed to data files. As a matter of convention, IBM gives its system programs a name with a suffix of .COM. It expects that all BASIC programs will have a name with a suffix of .BAS, and if you don't specify .BAS, it is added for you. Now press the CAPS LOCK key and respond to the prompt with BASIC, producing this:

```
Enter today's date (m-d-y): 05/06/82

The IBM Personal Computer DOS
Version 1.00 (C)Copyright IBM Corp 1981

A>BASIC
```

Add the KEY OFF command (which can also be part of your program), and the line of lighted function keys at the bottom of the screen will be erased.

To load a program, press F3. It will generate the keyword LOAD". Note the trailing quote on the keyword. It is required because all files accessed *from inside BASIC* must be set off in quotes. They need not be terminated by a quote, however. If you try to load a file not on the disk, DOS will tell you so, as in the example that follows. Once you load a file properly, the BASIC prompt (Ok) will tell you that you have done so. Any time you decide to store a program on disk, simply press F4. It will generate SAVE" in the same manner. In this example, if the .BAS had been omitted, DOS would have added it to the diskette, and it would be required for a subsequent LOAD":

```
The IBM Personal Computer Basic
Version D1.00 Copyright IBM Corp. 1981
41156 Bytes free
Ok
KEY OFF
Ok
LOAD"PC-5-1.BAS
File not found
Ok
LOAD"PC-5-6.BAS
Ok
SAVE"PC-5-6.BAS
Ok
```

Once "out of DOS" and back "in BASIC," enter FILES. You'll note that even if the format is slightly different, the result is the same, that is, you can still determine what's on the diskette. A word of caution. As you are doing the initial preparations, prepare *two* diskettes, and always stay one diskette ahead of where you need to be. At some point you will find that you have just completed a very long and difficult program only to find that there is insufficient room when you try to save it to the diskette. If you must then stop and format a diskette, you will lose what is in memory while you do so. Be prepared. There is an alternative. If you are in BASIC, you may use KILL "BASICA.COM". If you are in BASICA, you may do the equivalent to BASIC. Later, as you become more versed in your job, you will no doubt keep application programs (those you have developed yourself) off the system disk and use Drive B for programs exclusively, thereby working with disks on which no systems programs have been placed.

DOS has, in addition to its executive routines, certain other functions of a utility nature. Two of these are of immediate importance: FORMAT and DISKCOPY.

In order to place *anything* on a disk, it's an absolute must to *format* that disk. Formatting is a routine that places address markers on the diskette. Find the illustration of the disk in the DOS section of the "Guide to Operations." Note that the diskette is made up of a series of concentric circles and that there is a smaller hole beside the larger hole near its center. On a corresponding concentric track on the diskette itself is a smaller hole. When the smaller holes align and photoelectric contact is made, the position corresponds to the start of each track on the diskette. From that point, the diskette is divided into *sectors*, or pie-shaped wedges, on which data is recorded. Thus, before you can understand anything in this chapter, you must look up the FORMAT routine in the IBM manual and format several diskettes.

The next thing to do is make at least two copies of the DOS diskette with the DOS DISKCOPY command, which is also explained in the "Guide to Operations." Put one copy in a safe place within your business or home and a second copy off premises. Both should be stored in a cool, dust-free area free of magnetic interference.

In this chapter we will not deal with the use of disk for data files. We will, however, talk about combining segments of programs into one program and about transferring control from one program to another. We will also discuss passing information from one program to another.

The programs we will deal with are as follows:

1. A frame program, which is a program that exists simply as a mechanism to call other programs. It is stored on the author's disk as PC-5-1.BAS.
2. The four other programs that the frame program can call, as follows:
   a. PC-5-2.BAS — Breakeven Point Calculator
   b. PC-5-3.BAS — English-to-Metric Conversion
   c. PC-5-4.BAS — Twenty-Three Matches
   d. PC-5-5.BAS — Grade School Math (consisting of a root segment with four routines that must be merged with it prior to running)

The frame program operates within BASIC, which operates within DOS — the envelope concept previously discussed.

Frame program PC-5-1 produces the following screen:

```
THIS IS A FRAME PROGRAM.    YOU MAY SELECT ONE OF THESE PROGRAMS:

             1.    BREAKEVEN ANALYSIS

             2.    ENGLISH TO METRIC CONVERSION

             3.    TWENTY-THREE MATCHES

             4.    GRADE-SCHOOL MATH




SELECT:
```

The entire program is as follows:

```
10 CLS
20 CLEAR 5000
30 KEY OFF
40 COMMON USER.NAME$
50 INPUT "ENTER YOUR NAME: ",USER.NAME$
60 LOCATE 10,10
70 PRINT "THIS IS A FRAME PROGRAM.  YOU MAY SELECT ";
80 PRINT "ONE OF THESE PROGRAMS:";
90 LOCATE 12,20
100 PRINT "1.  BREAKEVEN ANALYSIS";
110 LOCATE 14,20
120 PRINT "2.  ENGLISH TO METRIC CONVERSION";
130 LOCATE 16,20
140 PRINT "3.  TWENTY-THREE MATCHES";
150 LOCATE 18,20
160 PRINT "4.  GRADE-SCHOOL MATH";
170 LOCATE 24,10
180 PRINT "SELECT: ";
190 Z$ = INKEY$:IF Z$ = "" THEN 190
200 PROGRAM = VAL(Z$)
210 IF (PROGRAM < 1) OR (PROGRAM > 4) THEN 300
220 PRINT PROGRAM;
230 ON PROGRAM GOTO 250,260,270,280
240 GOTO 300
250 CHAIN "A:PC-5-2.BAS"
260 CHAIN "A:PC-5-3.BAS"
270 CHAIN "A:PC-5-4.BAS"
280 CHAIN "A:PC-5-5.BAS"
290 GOTO 10
300 BEEP
310 LOCATE 24,1
320 PRINT SPACE$(79);
330 GOTO 170
```

From this short program several things may be learned. First, observe statement 20: CLEAR 5000. The number, in itself, is not significant, but any *large* CLEAR number *is*. Examine statement 40: COMMON USER.NAME$. The COMMON instruction advises BASIC that a variable specified within its statement will be passed to another program. The hitch, however, is that if the receiving program has its own CLEAR, the variable will be destroyed upon entering the subprogram. Thus, the other programs − PC-5-2, PC-5-3, PC-5-4, PC-5-5 − do not have independent CLEAR statements. This particular variable, (USER. NAME$), is requested in statement 50 and is displayed in the other programs only so that you will know for certain that it has been passed.

Control passes to another program as a function of the CHAIN command (see statements 250-280). In this instance, because of statement 230, control is passed to one of the four programs residing on disk drive A. Unless otherwise directed, the CHAIN command will call in the requested program and commence execution at the first statement (as if you had typed RUN or pressed F2, as previously discussed). Try entering this program and running it. If the other programs are not present, you'll receive an error message. Later you will learn that it's possible to call for a program from Drive A only to find that it isn't there. The error can be circummented, however, with an ON ERROR command that permits you to specify the same command for the other drive. The ON

ERROR command requires you to test for the presence of a specific error line (IF ERL =) or error code (IF ERR =).

Now on to the second program, PC-5-2.BAS – the Breakeven Point Calculator:

```
1000 CLS
1010 PRINT "HELLO, ";USER.NAME$
1020 LOCATE 3,10
1030 PRINT "B R E A K E V E N   P O I N T   C A L C U L A T O R"
1040 LOCATE 6,31
1050 A$ = ""
1060 PRINT "ENTER FIXED COSTS: ";
1070 Z$ = INKEY$:IF Z$ = "" THEN 1070
1080 IF Z$ = CHR$(13) THEN 1120
1090 PRINT Z$;
1100 A$ = A$ + Z$
1110 GOTO 1070
1120 LOCATE 6,31
1130 FIXED.COSTS = VAL(A$)
1140 PRINT "ENTER FIXED COSTS: ";FIXED.COSTS
1150 IF FIXED.COSTS < 0 THEN BEEP:GOTO 1040
1160 A$ = ""
1170 LOCATE 9,20
1180 PRINT "ENTER VARIABLE COST PER UNIT: ";
1190 Z$ = INKEY$:IF Z$ = "" THEN 1190
1200 IF Z$ = CHR$(13) THEN 1240
1210 PRINT Z$;
1220 A$ = A$ + Z$
1230 GOTO 1190
1240 LOCATE 9,20
1250 VARIABLE.COST.PER.UNIT = VAL(A$)
1260 PRINT "ENTER VARIABLE COST PER UNIT: ";VARIABLE.COST.PER.UNIT
1270 IF VARIABLE.COST.PER.UNIT < 0 THEN BEEP:GOTO 1170
1280 A$ = ""
1290 LOCATE 12,29
1300 PRINT "ENTER THE UNIT PRICE: ";
1310 Z$ = INKEY$:IF Z$ = "" THEN 1310
1320 IF Z$ = CHR$(13) THEN 1360
1330 PRINT Z$;
1340 A$ = A$ + Z$
1350 GOTO 1310
1360 LOCATE 12,29
1370 UNIT.PRICE = VAL(A$)
1380 PRINT "ENTER THE UNIT PRICE: ";UNIT.PRICE
1390 IF UNIT.PRICE <0 THEN BEEP:GOTO 1290
1400 QUANTITY = (FIXED.COSTS/(UNIT.PRICE - VARIABLE.COST.PER.UNIT))
1410 IF QUANTITY < 0 THEN QUANTITY = 1:QUANTITY.FLAG$ = "*":FLAG$ = "*"
1420 TOTAL.VARIABLE.COSTS = VARIABLE.COST.PER.UNIT * QUANTITY
1430 SALES.AT.BREAKEVEN = UNIT.PRICE * QUANTITY
1440 TOTAL.COSTS = FIXED.COSTS + (VARIABLE.COST.PER.UNIT * QUANTITY)
1450 UNIT.COST = TOTAL.COSTS/QUANTITY
1460 IF UNIT.COST < 0 THEN UNIT.COST = 1:UNIT.COST.FLAG$ = "*":FLAG$ = "*"
1470 CLS
1480 LOCATE 8,1
1490 PRINT STRING$(79,223);
1500 LOCATE 10,20
1510 PRINT "B R E A K E V E N   A N A L Y S I S"
1520 LOCATE 12,20
1530 PRINT "BREAKEVEN QUANTITY: ";TAB(43);
1540 PRINT USING "##,###";QUANTITY;
1550 PRINT TAB(52);QUANTITY.FLAG$;
1560 LOCATE 13,20
1570 PRINT "BREAKEVEN SALES: ";TAB(40);
1580 PRINT USING "$$,###.##";SALES.AT.BREAKEVEN;
1590 LOCATE 16,20
1600 PRINT "FIXED COSTS: ";TAB(40);
1610 PRINT USING "$$,###.##";FIXED.COSTS;
```

```
1620 LOCATE 17,20
1630 PRINT "VARIABLE COSTS: ";TAB(40);
1640 PRINT USING "##,###.##";TOTAL.VARIABLE.COSTS;
1650 LOCATE 18,20
1660 PRINT "";TAB(40);STRING$(10,22);
1670 LOCATE 19,20
1680 PRINT "TOTAL COSTS: ";TAB(40);
1690 PRINT USING "$$,###.##";TOTAL.COSTS;
1700 LOCATE 21,20
1710 PRINT "UNIT COST: ";TAB(40);
1720 PRINT USING "$$,###.##";UNIT.COST;
1730 PRINT TAB(52);UNIT.COST.FLAG$;
1740 LOCATE 22,1
1750 PRINT STRING$(79,223);
1760 LOCATE 23,20
1770 IF FLAG$ = "*" THEN PRINT "* INDICATES THAT THE FIELD WAS < 0";
1780 LOCATE 25,1
1790 PRINT "DO YOU WISH TO DO ANOTHER CALCULATION (Y/N)? ";
1800 Z$ = INKEY$:IF Z$ = "" THEN 1800
1810 IF Z$ = "Y" THEN 1000
1820 CHAIN "A:PC-5-1.BAS"
```

This is a straightforward little program for determining breakeven points. (Note that the variable passed from the frame program — USER.NAME$) — is printed at 1010. No attempt has been made to do any sophisticated programming to intercept bogus values; thus, if you use bonafide numbers, you will get a bonafide answer. The single exception to this rule occurs when a figure is derived that is smaller than 1; such a figure is *forced* to be 1 and is flagged.

We've dealt with the subject of screen editing before. Please examine statements 1540, 1580, 1610, 1640, 1690, and 1710. These instructions contain editing to enforce figure alignment on the screen. The ones with the double dollar sign float that sign to a position to the left of the highest number in the dollar field, assuming that the dollar field is smaller or equal in length to the *edit mask*, the $'s and #'s.

When you are asked if you require another calculation and you do, the program is repeated. If you do not, the program CHAINs back to the frame program in statement 1820.

There is nothing significantly different about the English-to-Metric Conversion program, except that the exit from this program (and return to the frame program) is accomplished by means of a zero option. It makes little difference whether the internal branching is a function of an alphabetic menu or a numeric menu, except that an alphabetic menu is ordinarily used whenever the alphabetics have meaning. Such is the case, as we shall see, in the program called Grade School Math, PC-5-5.BAS.

The English-to-Metric Conversion program is as follows:

```
1000 CLS
1010 PRINT "HELLO, ";USER.NAME$
1020 DIM A(17)
1030 PRINT "ENGLISH TO METRIC CONVERSION":PRINT
1040 PRINT " 0 .";TAB(10);"END THE PROGRAM"
```

```
1050 FOR N = 1 TO 17:READ A(N),A$,B$
1060 PRINT N;".";TAB(10);A$;" TO ";B$
1070 NEXT N
1080 RESTORE
1090 PRINT
1100 INPUT "WHICH CONVERSION DO YOU NEED";N
1110 IF N = 0 THEN CHAIN "A:PC-5-1.BAS"
1120 IF N > 17 THEN 1100
1130 FOR Z = 1 TO N:READ A(N),A$,B$:NEXT Z
1140 RESTORE
1150 INPUT "VALUE TO BE CONVERTED: ",I
1160 R = I*A(N):IF N = 17 THEN R =(I-32) * 5/9
1170 PRINT
1180 PRINT I;" ";A$;" ="R;" ";B$
1190 INPUT "PRESS ENTER TO GO AGAIN",B$:GOTO 1000
1200 DATA 2.54,INCHES,CENTIMETERS
1210 DATA 30.48,FEET,CENTIMETERS
1220 DATA .3048,FEET,METERS
1230 DATA .9144,YARDS,METERS
1240 DATA 1.609,MILES,KILOMETERS
1250 DATA 4.929,TSP.,CUBIC CM.
1260 DATA 14.788,TBSP,CUBIC CM.
1270 DATA .2366,CUPS,LITERS
1280 DATA .4732,PINTS,LITERS
1290 DATA .9463,QUARTS,LITERS
1300 DATA 3.785,GALLONS,LITERS
1310 DATA 35.24,BUSHELS,LITERS
1320 DATA 8.809,PECKS,LITERS
1330 DATA 28.3495,OUNCES,GRAMS
1340 DATA .4536,POUNDS,KILOGRAMS
1350 DATA 907.2,TONS,KILOGRAMS
1360 DATA .6214,DEGREES F.,DEGREES C.
```

Note that all these subprograms begin at statement 1000. There is no particular reason for this; it is merely a matter of distinction. Later, if it were determined that the programs should be combined (rather than called as a function of CHAINing), this combination could be provided by the MERGE facilities of the BASIC language. We'll do that very thing with the Grade School Math program later on.

Of course, since we didn't want this book to be completely about business, we've included a game (Twenty-Three Matches) as well as an educational program (the Grade School Math), both of which should be fun for any children in your life. The program for the game is as follows:

```
1000 CLS
1010 KEY OFF
1020 PRINT "HELLO, ";USER.NAME$
1030 ROW = 1
1040 LOCATE ROW + 1,30
1050 PRINT "THIS IS THE GAME OF 23 MATCHES"
1060 LOCATE ROW + 3,10
1070 PRINT "I WILL PLACE 23 MATCHES ON THE SCREEN.  ";
1080 PRINT "WE WILL TAKE TURNS REMOVING";
1090 LOCATE ROW + 4,10
1100 PRINT "ONE, TWO, OR THREE MATCHES.  ";
```

```
1110 PRINT "IF YOU MUST REMOVE THE LAST MATCH, YOU";
1120 LOCATE ROW + 5,10
1130 PRINT "WILL BE THE ";
1140 X = 1
1150 LOCATE ROW + 5,22
1160 PRINT SPACE$(X);"LOSER...";
1170 FOR Z = 1 TO 50:NEXT Z
1180 X = X + 1
1190 IF X = 48 THEN 1200 ELSE 1150
1200 FOR Z = 1 TO 1000:NEXT Z
1210 MATCHES = 23
1220 MOVE = 1
1230 GOSUB 1330          'DRAW THE MATCHES
1240 PLAYER$ = "X":COMPUTER$ = ""
1250 GOSUB 1540          'DRAW THE SCOREBOARD
1260 GOSUB 1680          'MAKE THE PLAYER'S MOVE
1270 GOSUB 1330          'DRAW THE MATCHES
1280 PLAYER$ = "":COMPUTER$ = "X"
1290 GOSUB 1540          'DRAW THE SCOREBOARD
1300 GOSUB 1930          'MAKE THE COMPUTER'S MOVE
1310 GOSUB 1330          'DRAW THE MATCHES
1320 GOTO 1240
1330 '********************************
1340 '* DRAW THE MATCHES AND FLAMES *
1350 '********************************
1360 CLS
1370 BUMP = 0
1380 FOR COLUMN = 7 TO 74 STEP 3
1390     FOR ROW = 4 TO 14
1400         LOCATE ROW,COLUMN
1410         PRINT CHR$(219);
1420     NEXT ROW
1430     BUMP = BUMP + 1
1440     IF BUMP = MATCHES THEN BUMP = 0:GOTO 1460
1450 NEXT COLUMN
1460 FOR COLUMN = 7 TO 74 STEP 3
1470     ROW = 3
1480     LOCATE ROW,COLUMN
1490     PRINT CHR$(127);
1500     BUMP = BUMP + 1
1510     IF BUMP = MATCHES THEN BUMP = 0:GOTO 1530
1520 NEXT COLUMN
1530 RETURN
1540 '****************************
1550 '* POSITION THE SCOREBOARD *
1560 '****************************
1570 LOCATE 18,15
1580 PRINT "MOVE      MATCHES REMAINING      YOUR MOVE      MY MOVE"
1590 LOCATE 20,15
1600 PRINT MOVE
1610 LOCATE 20,30
1620 PRINT MATCHES
1630 LOCATE 20,50
1640 PRINT PLAYER$
1650 LOCATE 20,62
1660 PRINT COMPUTER$
1670 RETURN
1680 '*************************************
1690 '* ROUTINE TO GAIN THE PLAYER'S MOVE *
1700 '*************************************
1710 MOVE = MOVE + 1
1720 LOCATE 22,10
1730 PRINT "HOW MANY MATCHES DO YOU WISH TO REMOVE (1, 2, OR 3)? ";
1740 Z$ = INKEY$:IF Z$ = "" THEN 1740
1750 PRINT Z$
1760 FOR Z = 1 TO 1500:NEXT Z
1770 A = VAL(Z$)
1780 IF (A > 0) AND (A < 4) THEN 1880
1790 LOCATE 25,10
```

```
1800 PRINT "INVALID - RETRY";
1810 BEEP
1820 FOR Z = 1 TO 1500:NEXT Z
1830 LOCATE 22,1
1840 PRINT SPACE$(79);
1850 LOCATE 25,1
1860 PRINT SPACE$(79);
1870 GOTO 1720
1880 MATCHES = MATCHES - A
1890 IF MATCHES = 3 THEN MATCHES = 4
1900 GOSUB 2130
1910 RETURN
1920 IF A > MATCHES THEN 1790
1930 '****************************************
1940 '* ROUTINE TO GAIN THE COMPUTER'S MOVE *
1950 '****************************************
1960 RANDOMIZE(-MATCHES)
1970 MOVE = MOVE + 1
1980 LOCATE 22,7
1990 PRINT "I'M DECIDING HOW MANY MATCHES TO REMOVE.   ";
2000 FOR Z = 1 TO 1500:NEXT Z
2010 IF (MATCHES > 3) AND (MATCHES < 5) THEN 2100
2020 REMOVE = INT(RND(MATCHES)*10)
2030 IF (REMOVE > 3) OR (REMOVE < 1) THEN 2020
2040 MATCHES = MATCHES - REMOVE
2050 PRINT "I WILL REMOVE";REMOVE;
2060 IF REMOVE = 1 THEN PRINT "MATCH.";:GOTO 2090
2070 PRINT "MATCHES.";
2080 GOSUB 2130
2090 FOR Z = 1 TO 1500:NEXT Z:RETURN
2100 REMOVE = MATCHES - 1
2110 MATCHES = 1
2120 GOTO 2050
2130 '********************
2140 '* SCORING ROUTINE *
2150 '********************
2160 IF (PLAYER$ = "X") AND (MATCHES < 2) THEN 2190
2170 IF (COMPUTER$ = "X") AND (MATCHES < 2) THEN 2220
2180 RETURN
2190 GOSUB 1330:GOSUB 1540
2200 LOCATE 24,1
2210 PRINT "THE PLAYER WINS";:GOTO 2250
2220 GOSUB 1330:GOSUB 1540
2230 LOCATE 24,1
2240 PRINT "THE COMPUTER WINS";
2250 LOCATE 25,1
2260 PRINT "DO YOU WISH TO PLAY AGAIN (Y/N)? ";
2270 Z$ = INKEY$:IF Z$ = "" THEN 2270
2280 PRINT Z$
2290 IF Z$ = "Y" THEN 1000
2300 CHAIN "A:PC-5-1.BAS"
```

Enter and play this game, and you'll find that it's not particularly difficult, partly because complex strategic logic has been kept out of it. The game itself is a very old one. In England it is known as *nim*, and a junior high school teacher named Leo Christopherson is reputed to have changed its matches to robots, animated them, added sound, published *Android Nim*, and become quite wealthy in the process. You never know where the most simple game will lead. Of note in this program is the spanning of the screen by the single word "LOSER" in the opening routine.

Now add the following statement and watch the program work:

1200 STOP

After doing so, you can retype statement 1200 or simply touch F5 (CONT). The instruction at 1200 merely instigates a delay loop. As you work through the author's programs, you'll note that he likes to add counters called *bumps* ("bump a counter," that is, "increment a counter," is an old DP expression).

Before we can use the Grade School Math program within the Frame program, there is some work to be done. First we must enter and save the root segment with this command:

SAVE"ROOT.BAS",A

The ,A suffix provides the way for a *text file* — stored in *ASCII format* — to be created. Program parts that we wish to combine must always be in ASCII format.

The root segment of the Grade School Math program is as follows:

```
1000 CLS
1005 PRINT "HELLO, ";USER.NAME$
1010 BYPASS.RANDOMIZE.SWITCH$ = "OFF"
1020 KEY OFF
1030 LOCATE 4,5
1040 PRINT "THIS IS A MATH EXERCISE BASED ON ";
1050 PRINT "WHOLE NUMBERS IN THE RANGE OF 0 - 12";
1060 LOCATE 6,8
1070 PRINT "IT WILL ALSO DEMONSTRATE THE WAY ";
1080 PRINT "TO MERGE PROGRAMS AS REQUIRED";
1090 LOCATE 8,23
1100 PRINT "SELECT EXERCISE YOU WISH TO USE ";
1110 LOCATE 10,30
1120 PRINT "<A>DDITION";
1130 LOCATE 12,30
1140 PRINT "<S>UBTRACTION";
1150 LOCATE 14,30
1160 PRINT "<M>ULTIPLICATION";
1170 LOCATE 16,30
1180 PRINT "<D>IVISION";
1190 LOCATE 18,29
1200 PRINT "E<X>IT THE PROGRAM";
1210 LOCATE 20,23
1220 PRINT "SELECT: ";
1230 Z$ = INKEY$:IF Z$ = "" THEN 1230
1240 IF Z$ = "A" THEN PRINT Z$:GOTO 3000
1250 IF Z$ = "S" THEN PRINT Z$:GOTO 4000
1260 IF Z$ = "M" THEN PRINT Z$:GOTO 5000
1270 IF Z$ = "D" THEN PRINT Z$:GOTO 6000
1280 IF Z$ = "X" THEN PRINT Z$:CHAIN "A:PC-5-1.BAS"
1290 GOTO 1230
1300 '************************
1310 '* THE NUMBER GENERATOR *
1320 '************************
1330 X = 1:Y = 2
1340 IF BYPASS.RANDOMIZE.SWITCH$ = "ON" THEN 1360
1350 RANDOMIZE (ASC(DATE$))
1360 A = INT(RND(X) * 20)
1370 IF (A < 1) OR (A > 12) THEN 1360
1380 B = INT(RND(Y) * 20)
1390 IF (B < 1) OR (B > 12) THEN 1380
1400 X = X + 1:Y = Y + 2
1410 RETURN
```

Now we must store the addition routine with the command,

SAVE"ADD.BAS",A

This routine is as follows:

```
3000 '**************************
3010 '* THE ADDITION ROUTINE *
3020 '**************************
3030 BYPASS.RANDOMIZE.SWITCH$ = "ON"
3040 FOR Z = 1 TO 1000:NEXT Z
3050 GOSUB 1300
3060 CLS
3070 LOCATE 10,10
3080 PRINT "ADD: ";A;" + ";B;" = ";STRING$(2,219);
3090 LOCATE 15,10
3100 PRINT "WHAT IS YOUR ANSWER? ";:INPUT "",C
3110 IF ABS(C) < > A + B THEN 3180
3120 LOCATE 20,10
3130 PRINT "CORRECT";SPACE$(40);
3140 LOCATE 24,10
3150 PRINT "DO YOU WISH TO DO ANOTHER ADDITION PROBLEM (Y/N)? ";
3160 Z$ = INKEY$:IF Z$ = "" THEN 3160
3170 IF Z$ = "Y" THEN 3050 ELSE 1000
3180 LOCATE 20,10
3190 PRINT "NOT CORRECT - TRY AGAIN";
3200 LOCATE 15,1
3210 PRINT SPACE$(79);
3220 GOTO 3090
```

Next we store the subtraction routine with the commands,

SAVE"SUB.BAS",A

This routine is as follows:

```
4000 '*****************************
4010 '* THE SUBTRACTION ROUTINE *
4020 '*****************************
4030 BYPASS.RANDOMIZE.SWITCH$ = "ON"
4040 FOR Z = 1 TO 1000:NEXT Z
4050 GOSUB 1300
4060 CLS
4070 IF B > A THEN SWAP A,B
4080 LOCATE 10,10
4090 PRINT "SUBTRACT: ";A;" - ";B;" = ";STRING$(2,219);
4100 LOCATE 15,10
4110 PRINT "WHAT IS YOUR ANSWER? ";:INPUT "",C
4120 IF ABS(C) < > A - B THEN 4190
4130 LOCATE 20,10
4140 PRINT "CORRECT";SPACE$(40);
4150 LOCATE 24,10
4160 PRINT "DO YOU WISH TO DO ANOTHER SUBTRACTION PROBLEM (Y/N)? ";
4170 Z$ = INKEY$:IF Z$ = "" THEN 4170
4180 IF Z$ = "Y" THEN 4050 ELSE 1000
4190 LOCATE 20,10
4200 PRINT "NOT CORRECT - TRY AGAIN";
4210 LOCATE 15,1
4220 PRINT SPACE$(79);
4230 GOTO 4100
```

Then we store the multiplication routine with the command,

SAVE"MUL.BAS",A

This routine is as follows:

```
5000 '*******************************
5010 '* THE MULTIPLICATION ROUTINE *
5020 '*******************************
5030 BYPASS.RANDOMIZE.SWITCH$ = "ON"
5040 FOR Z = 1 TO 1000:NEXT Z
5050 GOSUB 1300
5060 CLS
5070 LOCATE 10,10
5080 PRINT "MULTIPLY: ";A;" * ";B;" = ";STRING$(2,219);
5090 LOCATE 15,10
5100 PRINT "WHAT IS YOUR ANSWER? ";:INPUT "",C
5110 IF ABS(C) < > A * B THEN 5180
5120 LOCATE 20,10
5130 PRINT "CORRECT";SPACE$(40);
5140 LOCATE 24,10
5150 PRINT "DO YOU WISH TO DO ANOTHER MULTIPLICATION PROBLEM (Y/N)? ";
5160 Z$ = INKEY$:IF Z$ = "" THEN 5160
5170 IF Z$ = "Y" THEN 5050 ELSE 1000
5180 LOCATE 20,10
5190 PRINT "NOT CORRECT - TRY AGAIN";
5200 LOCATE 15,1
5210 PRINT SPACE$(79);
5220 GOTO 5090
```

Finally, we store the division routine with the command,

SAVE"DIV.BAS",A

This routine (note the use of the SWAP command) is as follows:

```
6000 '**************************
6010 '* THE DIVISION ROUTINE *
6020 '**************************
6030 BYPASS.RANDOMIZE.SWITCH$ = "ON"
6040 FOR Z = 1 TO 1000:NEXT Z
6050 GOSUB 1300
6060 CLS
6070 IF B > A THEN SWAP A,B
6080 LOCATE 10,10
6090 PRINT "DIVIDE: ";A;" / ";B;" = ";STRING$(2,219);
6100 PRINT "  QUOTIENT,  ";STRING$(2,219);"  REMAINDER";
6110 LOCATE 15,10
6120 PRINT "WHAT IS THE QUOTIENT? ";:INPUT Q:Q = ABS(Q)
6130 LOCATE 16,10
6140 PRINT "WHAT IS THE REMAINDER? ";:INPUT R:R = ABS(R)
6150 IF A < > ((Q * B) + R) THEN 6220
6160 LOCATE 20,10
6170 PRINT "CORRECT";SPACE$(40);
6180 LOCATE 24,10
6190 PRINT "DO YOU WISH TO DO ANOTHER DIVISION PROBLEM (Y/N)? ";
6200 Z$ = INKEY$:IF Z$ = "" THEN 6200
6210 IF Z$ = "Y" THEN 6050 ELSE 1000
6220 LOCATE 20,10
6230 PRINT "NOT CORRECT - TRY AGAIN";
6240 LOCATE 15,1
6250 PRINT SPACE$(79);
```

```
6260 LOCATE 16,1
6270 PRINT SPACE$(79);
6280 GOTO 6110
```

The SWAP command simply exchanges variables.

Now, to put these routines all together, follow this sequence:

LOAD"ROOT.BAS

MERGE"ADD.BAS

MERGE"SUB.BAS

MERGE"MUL.BAS

MERGE"DIV.BAS

SAVE"PC-5-5.BAS

The properly combined program is then as follows:

```
1000 CLS
1005 PRINT "HELLO, ";USER.NAME$
1010 BYPASS.RANDOMIZE.SWITCH$ = "OFF"
1020 KEY OFF
1030 LOCATE 4,5
1040 PRINT "THIS IS A MATH EXERCISE BASED ON ";
1050 PRINT "WHOLE NUMBERS IN THE RANGE OF 0 - 12";
1060 LOCATE 6,8
1070 PRINT "IT WILL ALSO DEMONSTRATE THE WAY ";
1080 PRINT "TO MERGE PROGRAMS AS REQUIRED";
1090 LOCATE 8,23
1100 PRINT "SELECT EXERCISE YOU WISH TO USE ";
1110 LOCATE 10,30
1120 PRINT "<A>DDITION";
1130 LOCATE 12,30
1140 PRINT "<S>UBTRACTION";
1150 LOCATE 14,30
1160 PRINT "<M>ULTIPLICATION";
1170 LOCATE 16,30
1180 PRINT "<D>IVISION";
1190 LOCATE 18,29
1200 PRINT "E<X>IT THE PROGRAM";
1210 LOCATE 20,23
1220 PRINT "SELECT: ";
1230 Z$ = INKEY$:IF Z$ = "" THEN 1230
1240 IF Z$ = "A" THEN PRINT Z$:GOTO 3000
1250 IF Z$ = "S" THEN PRINT Z$:GOTO 4000
1260 IF Z$ = "M" THEN PRINT Z$:GOTO 5000
1270 IF Z$ = "D" THEN PRINT Z$:GOTO 6000
1280 IF Z$ = "X" THEN PRINT Z$:CHAIN "A:PC-5-1.BAS"
1290 GOTO 1230
1300 '************************
1310 '* THE NUMBER GENERATOR *
1320 '************************
1330 X = 1:Y = 2
1340 IF BYPASS.RANDOMIZE.SWITCH$ = "ON" THEN 1360
1350 RANDOMIZE (ASC(DATE$))
1360 A = INT(RND(X) * 20)
1370 IF (A < 1) OR (A > 12) THEN 1360
1380 B = INT(RND(Y) * 20)
1390 IF (B < 1) OR (B > 12) THEN 1380
1400 X = X + 1:Y = Y + 2
1410 RETURN
3000 '************************
```

```
3010 '* THE ADDITION ROUTINE *
3020 '************************
3030 BYPASS.RANDOMIZE.SWITCH$ = "ON"
3040 FOR Z = 1 TO 1000:NEXT Z
3050 GOSUB 1300
3060 CLS
3070 LOCATE 10,10
3080 PRINT "ADD: ";A;" + ";B;" = ";STRING$(2,219);
3090 LOCATE 15,10
3100 PRINT "WHAT IS YOUR ANSWER? ";:INPUT "",C
3110 IF ABS(C) < > A + B THEN 3180
3120 LOCATE 20,10
3130 PRINT "CORRECT";SPACE$(40);
3140 LOCATE 24,10
3150 PRINT "DO YOU WISH TO DO ANOTHER ADDITION PROBLEM (Y/N)? ";
3160 Z$ = INKEY$:IF Z$ = "" THEN 3160
3170 IF Z$ = "Y" THEN 3050 ELSE 1000
3180 LOCATE 20,10
3190 PRINT "NOT CORRECT - TRY AGAIN";
3200 LOCATE 15,1
3210 PRINT SPACE$(79);
3220 GOTO 3090
4000 '*****************************
4010 '* THE SUBTRACTION ROUTINE *
4020 '*****************************
4030 BYPASS.RANDOMIZE.SWITCH$ = "ON"
4040 FOR Z = 1 TO 1000:NEXT Z
4050 GOSUB 1300
4060 CLS
4070 IF B > A THEN SWAP A,B
4080 LOCATE 10,10
4090 PRINT "SUBTRACT: ";A;" - ";B;" = ";STRING$(2,219);
4100 LOCATE 15,10
4110 PRINT "WHAT IS YOUR ANSWER? ";:INPUT "",C
4120 IF ABS(C) < > A - B THEN 4190
4130 LOCATE 20,10
4140 PRINT "CORRECT";SPACE$(40);
4150 LOCATE 24,10
4160 PRINT "DO YOU WISH TO DO ANOTHER SUBTRACTION PROBLEM (Y/N)? ";
4170 Z$ = INKEY$:IF Z$ = "" THEN 4170
4180 IF Z$ = "Y" THEN 4050 ELSE 1000
4190 LOCATE 20,10
4200 PRINT "NOT CORRECT - TRY AGAIN";
4210 LOCATE 15,1
4220 PRINT SPACE$(79);
4230 GOTO 4100
5000 '*******************************
5010 '* THE MULTIPLICATION ROUTINE *
5020 '*******************************
5030 BYPASS.RANDOMIZE.SWITCH$ = "ON"
5040 FOR Z = 1 TO 1000:NEXT Z
5050 GOSUB 1300
5060 CLS
5070 LOCATE 10,10
5080 PRINT "MULTIPLY: ";A;" * ";B;" = ";STRING$(2,219);
5090 LOCATE 15,10
5100 PRINT "WHAT IS YOUR ANSWER? ";:INPUT "",C
5110 IF ABS(C) < > A * B THEN 5180
5120 LOCATE 20,10
5130 PRINT "CORRECT";SPACE$(40);
5140 LOCATE 24,10
5150 PRINT "DO YOU WISH TO DO ANOTHER MULTIPLICATION PROBLEM (Y/N)? ";
5160 Z$ = INKEY$:IF Z$ = "" THEN 5160
5170 IF Z$ = "Y" THEN 5050 ELSE 1000
5180 LOCATE 20,10
5190 PRINT "NOT CORRECT - TRY AGAIN";
5200 LOCATE 15,1
5210 PRINT SPACE$(79);
5220 GOTO 5090
```

```
6000 '************************
6010 '* THE DIVISION ROUTINE *
6020 '************************
6030 BYPASS.RANDOMIZE.SWITCH$ = "ON"
6040 FOR Z = 1 TO 1000:NEXT Z
6050 GOSUB 1300
6060 CLS
6070 IF B > A THEN SWAP A,B
6080 LOCATE 10,10
6090 PRINT "DIVIDE: ";A;" / ";B;" = ";STRING$(2,219);
6100 PRINT "  QUOTIENT,  ";STRING$(2,219);"  REMAINDER";
6110 LOCATE 15,10
6120 PRINT "WHAT IS THE QUOTIENT? ";:INPUT Q:Q = ABS(Q)
6130 LOCATE 16,10
6140 PRINT "WHAT IS THE REMAINDER? ";:INPUT R:R = ABS(R)
6150 IF A < > ((Q * B) + R) THEN 6220
6160 LOCATE 20,10
6170 PRINT "CORRECT";SPACE$(40);
6180 LOCATE 24,10
6190 PRINT "DO YOU WISH TO DO ANOTHER DIVISION PROBLEM (Y/N)? ";
6200 Z$ = INKEY$:IF Z$ = "" THEN 6200
6210 IF Z$ = "Y" THEN 6050 ELSE 1000
6220 LOCATE 20,10
6230 PRINT "NOT CORRECT - TRY AGAIN";
6240 LOCATE 15,1
6250 PRINT SPACE$(79);
6260 LOCATE 16,1
6270 PRINT SPACE$(79);
6280 GOTO 6110
```

You are now in a position to LOAD'PC-5-1.BAS (the frame), and everything will work as planned. Note from your examination of the various modules comprising Grade School Math that each has a different set of statement numbers. Had they had the same statement numbers, the most recent statement numbers would have overridden any corresponding numbers previously in memory, and *on a corresponding number basis*. For example:

Replace This	With This	You'll Get This
1100	1100	1100
1105	–	1105
1110	1110	1110

Obviously, you might just end up with a program whose contents are less than predictable.

MORE DOS COMMANDS

It is not our intention to familiarize you with all the capabilities of DOS or of the PC Assembly Language, for which much of the DOS facility exists. It is our purpose, however, to give you sufficient information for your success as a BASIC programmer. We will therefore introduce you to several more DOS commands.

FAT CITY

Occasionally it's useful to know just how many disk files you have, how much space is occupied on the disk, and what is available both on the disk and in memory. You can find out with the CHKDSK command. Check Disk (CHKDSK) will give you a status report, as follows:

```
Enter today's date (m-d-y): 05/10/82

The IBM Personal Computer DOS
Version 1.00 (C)Copyright IBM Corp 1981

A>CHKDSK
         38 disk files
     160256 bytes total disk space
          0 bytes remain available

      65536 bytes total memory
      53392 bytes free

A>
```

It does so by analysis of the diskette's director and file allocation table (frequently called the *FAT table*). If you enter CHKDSK only, you'll get statistics based on the default drive of A. If you wish to know about B, simply enter CHKDSK B:. Don't forget the colon. In fact, any time you must check anything not on the default drive, you must specify the drive, followed by a colon.

COMPARE, COMPARE

Frequently when it is necessary to copy a file or a diskette, it's useful to compare the copy against the original to see if a true copy has been made. This comparison is accomplished with the two DOS commands, COMP and DISKCOMP. Suppose we have copied ADD.BAS from drive A to drive B. To compare it, we use the command,

COMP ADD.BAS B:ADD.BAS

The copying of a disk is a function merely of specifying which drive is to be compared against which drive. The *from* disk is specified first; the *to* disk is specified second; and the command is as follows:

DISKCOMP A: B:

COPYCAT

Of course, one need compare only when something has been copied. The copying process may be done at the file level or at the diskette level. At the file level, the command would be

COPY ADD.BAS B:ADD.BAS

In this instance, drive B has been specified as the receiving drive for a program *of the same name.* Suppose, however, that we wanted a second copy of the same program on the default disk. If we entered COPY ADD.BAS ADD.BAS, we would merely overwrite the same program. However, if we entered COPY ADD.BAS PROG.BAS, a second copy of the program would appear on the default disk but with another name. Note that no quotes are used with these files names because we are in DOS-mode.

To copy at the diskette level (whether for a single- or a multiple-drive copy), you use the command DISKCOPY. For example, if you want a two-drive copy, use the command,

DISKCOPY A: B

If you want a one-drive copy, use the command,

DISKCOPY A: A:

HOW'S ABOUT A DATE?

As you know it is always necessary to specify a date when opening the system. Occasionally, however, it's important that yet another date be entered. The DOS command DATE will allow you to do so after you are already in DOS, either from a *batch file* (which will not be covered in this text) or from the DATE$ command in BASIC.

ANYTIME

In the same manner as you can specify a date (and *must* in order to get into the system), you can set the system clock with the TIME command of DOS or with the TIME$ command of BASIC. Time is kept in an hour:minute:second: hundredths-of-second format. Once set, the clock will run so long as the system is running.

DIRECTORIES

As has been previously stated, you can determine the contents of a diskette by simply entering DIR. If you wish to check drive B, then enter DIR B: (remember to insert the colon). Suppose that you want to know if a specific program is on the disk. No problem. Simply enter DIR ADD.BAS (using your program name). Recall that the BASIC counterpart for this command is FILES. Similarly, FILES"ADD.BAS does what you would expect it to do.

ERASE ALL MEMORY

We are speaking here of erasing all *auxiliary memory*, that is, which is the technical name for diskettes. Think back about our discussion of the wild card (∗). You can erase an entire disk with the command,

ERASE ∗.∗

Or you can specify a specific file, as follows:

ERASE ADD.BAS

You might as well take the subprograms of PC-5-5.BAS off the diskette now with the command: ERASE ROOT.∗, ADD.∗, SUB.∗, MUL.∗, and DIV.∗.

YOU CAN'T WRITE THE DATA WITHOUT A FORMAT

As has been previously mentioned, you must FORMAT a diskette to allow addresses to be stored on it. The format of the FORMAT is command,

FORMAT B: or   FORMAT A:

The system will tell you where to insert diskettes and when. If you suspect that there is a bad track, append /S to the command, as follows:

FORMAT B:/S

A NAME BY ANY OTHER ROSE

Occasionally you may change your mind about a file's name. If it's a program file, you could LOAD it, SAVE it to another name, and then ERASE or KILL the original file. The job is a little more tricky with a data file. The best way is simply to rename it. For example:

RENAME B:PETUNIA.BAS ROSE.BAS

FOR THE WANT OF A SYSTEM

As a market develops for the PC, you'll be able to obtain software. This software will be sold, however, without a DOS (else somebody will have to pay some royalties to IBM). So long as you have DOS in Drive A and the program in Drive B, that's OK. Suppose, however, that a program calls for two drives. It then becomes important to put enough of the DOS on the program diskette to get the work done, and you would use the command,

SYS B: (or A:)

In order for the SYS command to be effective, it is necessary the /S form of the FORMAT statement to have been used on the receiving diskette.

WHAT TYPE ARE YOU?

Occasionally it's important to get a quick look at a file. If that file is a data file or a file stored in ASCII, then the following command will work:

TYPE ADD.BAS

Apply that command to a program, however, and you'll get gobbledegook.

There are other DOS commands, of course, but they essentially apply to the color features or the batch features of DOS. For that reason, they will not be described here.

SUMMARY

In addition to the new DOS commands just discussed, we can add the following BASIC instructions found in this chapter:

Commands

FILES	Displays the directory and can be used either as a command function or from within the program.
KILL	Removes the specified file from the directory.

MERGE	Is used to merge a saved program (in ASCII format) with one located in memory.
NAME	Functions in the same manner as the DOS RENAME but from *inside* BASIC.
RESET	CLOSEs all diskette files.
SYSTEM	Leaves BASIC and returns to DOS.

Non-I/O Statements

CHAIN	Calls another program, with overlay or run line options.
COMMON	Specifies the list of variables to be used in a CHAINed program. Where a COMMON has been used, the variables are cleared by a CLEAR within the calling program. COMMON is used in the *sending* program only.
DATE$	Is used to access the date and can be the source or object of a command.
ON ERROR	Allows trapping of an error code for processing.
SWAP	Is used to exchange variables. (Look back at the subtraction and divide routines of Grade School Math for an example.)
TIME$	Is used to access the time and can be the source or object of a command.

Numeric Functions

ABS	Absolute value (no signs).
INT	The integer (whole number) portion of a number.
RND	Generates a random number.

Numeric Functions Not Used in This Book

ATN	Arctangent.
CDBL	Converts to double precision.
CINT	Converts to an integer by rounding.
COS	Cosine.
CSNG	Converts to single precision.
EXP	Exponentiates.
FIX	Truncates to an integer.

SGN	Sign.
SIN	Sine.
SQR	Square root.
TAN	Tangent.

Numeric functions are the intrinsic functions of the machine itself. See the BASIC reference manual if you must use any of them.

String-Related and String Functions

| ASC | Obtains the ASCII code for the first character of a string. |

Miscellaneous

| ERL | Error line number. |
| ERR | Error code number. |

6
Disk Applications

We can now begin to concentrate on using the disk for applications useful to business purposes. The program that follows is a scheduling program for a golf course. Faced with having to keep a book of reservations, the Lazy Daze Golf Course has decided to use the PC to computerize a day's schedule. As you review this program, please keep in mind that we are inventorying players in a slot called *tee-off time*. We could just as easily be inventorying widgets in a slot called *part number* or people in the seats of an airplane. You get the picture.

Before we start, a few thoughts about using disk in a *random* fashion: "Random" is technically a misnomer for this system for the simple reason that its capability is *finite*. Every record placed on a disk has some common identifying feature, usually a sequence number close enough to other similar numbers to allow efficient allocation of the storage. In an employee personnel file, for instance, a small business might have 10 people, numbered from 1 (the owner) to 10 (the latest trainee). That would be fine. But suppose that it is now more than 10 years since the company was formed and that the current crop of employees are numbered 1000 to 1100 but numbers 1, 2, and 3 still exist. The numbers in the sequence would obviously contain a large "hole." When holes are present in a sequence, a different method of accounting must be used. Here is the list of tee-off times for the Lazy Daze Golf Course (LDGC):

```
2190 '****************
2200 '* STARTING TIMES *
2210 '****************
2220 DATA 0800,0815,0830,0845
2230 DATA 0900,0915,0930,0945
2240 DATA 1000,1015,1030,1045
2250 DATA 1100,1115,1130,1145
2260 DATA 1200,1215,1230,1245
2270 DATA 1300,1315,1330,1345
2280 DATA 1400,1415,1430,1445
2290 DATA 1500,1515,1530,1545
2300 DATA 1600,1615,1630,1645
2310 DATA 1700,1715,1730,1745
2320 DATA 9999,9999,9999,9999
```

Note that there are 40 starting times, staggered in 15-minute intervals, commencing at 0800 (8 A.M.) and ending at 1745 (5:45 P.M.). For convenience, 24-hour clock time is used in this program. Note also that there is a sentinel row at the end. As we will see later, these numbers are read as integer types but must be converted to string variables, producing curious attributes of length. That subject will be discussed later.

Now, if the file were set up on a time basis, the key field range would require nearly 1800 records (sequence numbers 0001 to 1745), only 40 of which would have to be used. If we place these times in DATA statements, thereby creating a table of starting times, we can use only 40 records on the disk and thus save much space and search time. The key field 0800 is relative record 1, and 0815 is relative record 2. By "relative record" we mean that records are counted from zero. More on that as necessary.

In order to write to disk or read from it, its file must be OPENed. Recall that when we wrote a sequential file, it was necessary to identify whether it would be OPENed for INPUT or OUTPUT. It is possible, but not necessary, to specify RANDOM. If the mode of the file is not specified, it is assumed to be random, meaning that you may read from it or write to it at will. Unless otherwise instructed, BASIC reserves buffer space for three files. A *buffer* is a temporary storage space for data targeted either for the disk or for a recent arrival — a sort of Ellis Island for data. The OPEN command must therefore specify a buffer. Disks, as stated before, are organized into sectors. Each sector accepts 512 characters, or *bytes*. Since the standard buffer size is 128 bytes, the DOS can fit four 128-byte buffers into one sector. Since we need only 63 bytes in the LDGC problem, the buffer size can be shortened, giving DOS more room to pack data at eight records per sector. Thus only five sectors are needed to hold the data from the LDGC. In order to *use* the data in a buffer (or to *load* the data into it), it is necessary to identify the positions of the buffer with a FIELD statement. The opening coding with a FIELD statement is as follows:

```
10 CLS
20 KEY OFF
30 '****************************
40 '* OPEN AND DEFINE THE FILE *
50 '****************************
60 OPEN "TEEOFF.DAT" AS #1 LEN=63
70 FIELD #1,1 AS F$,15 AS N1$,15 AS N2$,15 AS N3$,15 AS N4$,2 AS NR$
```

As you examine the FIELD statement, here's what you'll find:

#1   The buffer number.

F$ This one-position variable functions as a flag. If the record has been used, the flag will be set to ASCII zero; if not, to ASCII 255, which is 11111111 in binary.

N1$-N4$ The names of the players scheduled for the foursome.

NR$ The numbers of the players scheduled for the foursome.

Note that every specification is a string variable and that the length of these variables is specified (one position *known as* F$; 15 positions *known as* N1$). *Do not* use these variables as targets of the LET instruction. *Do not* say INPUT N1$. These variables are assigned to the buffer and must be loaded with special commands (LSET and RSET). If used as the target of a LET, *even though LET is not specified*, they will become associated with variable space allocation and *not* with buffer space allocation.

You'll learn in time that the mode of data as it's moved to and from the disk is very important. NR$ is specified at two positions even though the number will never be greater than 4 since the conversion instruction creates a two-byte field, as we shall see. This FIELD will be used both for reading (GET) the file and for writing (PUT). If, perchance, you wanted to apply a *second FIELD* specification to the same buffer, you could do so, for example, when your records are of a mixed format or when you want to refer to the buffer by one name.

Here is the opening menu for the LDGC program and the selection routine:

```
80 '******************************
90 '* PRESENT THE SELECTION MENU *
100 '******************************
110 CLS
120 NAME.1$ = ""
130 NAME.2$ = ""
140 NAME.3$ = ""
150 NAME.4$ = ""
160 PRINT:PRINT TAB(30);"LAZY DAZE GOLF COURSE"
170 PRINT STRING$(79,220)
180 PRINT :PRINT TAB(36);"OPTIONS:"
190 PRINT:PRINT TAB(18);"<I>NITIALIZE THE FILE (CAUTION: REMOVES ALL DATA)"
200 PRINT:PRINT TAB(18);"<C>REATE A NEW STARTING TIME"
210 PRINT:PRINT TAB(18);"<D>ISPLAY A STARTING TIME"
220 PRINT:PRINT TAB(18);"<A>DD (OR DELETE) A PERSON'S STARTING TIME"
230 PRINT:PRINT TAB(18);"<R>EMOVE A FOURSOME FROM A STARTING TIME"
240 PRINT:PRINT TAB(18);"<L>IST RESERVATIONS WITH FEWER THAN FOUR PLAYERS"
250 PRINT:PRINT TAB(18);"<P>RINT AND DISPLAY THE DAY'S SCHEDULE"
260 PRINT:PRINT TAB(18);"<E>ND THE PROGRAM"
270 PRINT:PRINT "SELECT: ";
280 Z$ = INKEY$:IF Z$ = "" THEN 280
290 PRINT Z$;
300 IF Z$ = "I" THEN PRINT "NITIALIZE":SELECTION = 1:GOTO 470
310 IF Z$ = "i" THEN PRINT "nitialize":SELECTION = 1:GOTO 470
320 IF Z$ = "C" THEN PRINT "REATE":SELECTION = 2:GOTO 470
330 IF Z$ = "c" THEN PRINT "reate":SELECTION = 2:GOTO 470
340 IF Z$ = "D" THEN PRINT "ISPLAY":SELECTION = 3:GOTO 470
350 IF Z$ = "d" THEN PRINT "isplay":SELECTION = 3:GOTO 470
360 IF Z$ = "A" THEN PRINT "DD":SELECTION = 4:GOTO 470
370 IF Z$ = "a" THEN PRINT "dd":SELECTION = 4:GOTO 470
380 IF Z$ = "R" THEN PRINT "EPLACE":SELECTION = 5:GOTO 470
390 IF Z$ = "r" THEN PRINT "eplace":SELECTION = 5:GOTO 470
400 IF Z$ = "L" THEN PRINT "IST":SELECTION = 6:GOTO 470
410 IF Z$ = "l" THEN PRINT "ist":SELECTION = 6:GOTO 470
420 IF Z$ = "P" THEN PRINT "RINT":SELECTION = 7:GOTO 470
```

```
430 IF Z$ = "p" THEN PRINT "rint":SELECTION = 7:GOTO 470
440 IF Z$ = "E" THEN PRINT "ND":SELECTION = 8:GOTO 470
450 IF Z$ = "e" THEN PRINT "nd":SELECTION = 8:GOTO 470
460 GOTO 110
470 ON SELECTION GOSUB 1990,510,880,1060,1520,1650,2600,2150
480 PRINT "PRESS ANY KEY TO CONTINUE";
490 Z$ = INKEY$:IF Z$ = "" THEN 490
50C GOTO 110
```

This, like previous programs, has an alphabetically controlled menu. Statements 120 to 150 define what the four main input and display variables will be, and then the heading is placed onto the screen. Statements 300 through 450 allow the operator to specify his answer in either upper- or lower-case and then complete the word before establishing the value that will be used in statement 470. When you first power up the machine, it is automatically in lower-case and must be changed for use in upper-case by means of the CAPS LOCK key. When in capital mode, you can switch to lower-case simply by pressing the shift key.

Since the purpose of this program is to allocate a golf foursome to a specific playing time, we'll deal first with the routine that accepts and then uses the entered time:

```
1840 '****************************
1850 '* OBTAIN THE PLAYING TIME *
1860 '****************************
1870 NO.FIND.SWITCH = 0
1880 INPUT "PLAYING TIME";PLAYTIME%
1890     TIME.TIME$ = STR$(PLAYTIME%)
1900     TIME.TIME$ = RIGHT$(TIME.TIME$,4)
1910     TEE.TIME$=LEFT$(TIME.TIME$,2)+":"+RIGHT$(TIME.TIME$,2)
1920 GOSUB 2330
1930 IF NO.FIND.SWITCH = 1 THEN 1960
1940 IF (PLAYTIME% < 1) OR (PLAYTIME% > 40) THEN 1960
1950 GET #1,PLAYTIME%:RETURN
1960 PRINT "BAD STARTING TIME"
1970 NO.FIND.SWITCH = 0
1980 GOTO 1880
```

The first thing in the routine is the setting of the NO.FIND.SWITCH, which occurs when the DATA table is searched and the desired value (argument) is not located. The setting of this switch permits the program to learn, elsewhere, that a specific argument has not been located in the table (that is, that the specified starting time is invalid). You'll be able to recognize that once you have the program running.

Look at statement 1880. It seems straightforward enough, but just wait a minute! What's the % at the end of the variable PLAYTIME? Remember that when you're using diskette, funny things are bound to happen to numeric values.

The % indicates that the numeric variable you're dealing with is in *integer mode*. Since integer mode takes two bytes to express a numeric value, NR$ is specified as two bytes in the FIELD statement.

Study statements 1890 through 1910 before we discuss them. Remember that PLAYTIME% has come directly from the keyboard in response to an INPUT statement that requests a *numeric* value. Since we are using 24-hour clock time, the response will be in four digits, ranging from 0800 to 1745. The first thing we do, therefore, is to get the playtime into a string variable with the STR$ instruction. A curious transformation takes place when this occurs, however. You may very well have entered 1245 at the keyboard, but when statement 1890 is executed, variable TIME.TIME$ has a length of 5. You must realize that every number has an intrinsic *positive* sign even though it has not been specified. When a signed numeric is converted to a string variable, *it brings the sign position with it*. We get rid of that position with statement 1900. In other words, what *was* +1245 is now simply 1245. The function of statement 1910 is simply to insert a colon between the left two characters and the right two characters of the time. Statements 1890-1910 are indented for emphasis; some of their coding is repeated in other parts of the program.

We'll get to statement 2330 in a minute. It is a routine that selects a relative record number on the basis of the starting time in the DATA table. What isn't immediately obvious is that PLAYTIME% has received a new value in the range of 1 to 40, the latter of which, as you will recall, is the number of records in the file. If there were no find in the DATA statements, moreover, the switch would be tested, a message given, and the process repeated. In any event, when you come back from statement 2330, PLAYTIME% has the number of the record that contains the corresponding starting time, and that record will be obtained in statement 1950. Now let us proceed to statement 2330, which initiates the routine that determines the relative position of the starting time and allows that position to be used at statement 1950:

```
2330 '***********************************************************
2340 '* ROUTINE TO SELECT RECORD NUMBER BASED ON STARTING TIME *
2350 '***********************************************************
2360 RESTORE
2370 FOR CHECK.RECORD% = 1 TO 100
2380     READ WHICH.RECORD%
2390     IF WHICH.RECORD% = 9999 THEN 2440
2400     IF WHICH.RECORD% = PLAYTIME% THEN 2470
2410 NEXT CHECK.RECORD%
2420 PRINT "BAD TIME TABLE IN PROGRAM"
2430 END
2440 PRINT "TIME NOT AVAILABLE AS A STARTING TIME"
2450 NO.FIND.SWITCH = 1
2460 RETURN
2470 SWAP CHECK.RECORD%,PLAYTIME%
2480 GOTO 2460
```

The RESTORE in statement 2360 sets the pointer to the head of the DATA statements. The movement that will take place in the FOR . . . NEXT loop of statements 2370-2410 will be strictly linear, and although 100 is more than twice as large as the number required, we're really looking for the sentinel (9999) in statement 2390 to tell us when to stop. That way we can add new values to the table, assuming that we make the proper changes elsewhere. Values that arrive from the DATA lines do so as integer variables (WHICH.RECORD%). In a later routine the same values will be read as string variables. In any event, the selected DATA element is matched against the entered PLAYTIME%. If no find is made, we are notified. If a hit is encountered, however, we merely exchange the value of the count (which contains the DATA element number that matches) with the value of the time. We could have gotten away with making both of them equal to the value of CHECK.RECORD%, but that would have prevented us from using a nifty little instruction — SWAP.

The first option on the menu is to initialize the file. Technically, when a file is initialized, everything must be cleared. It would be simple enough merely to flag the F$ with 255 to indicate that a record is inoperative. We've gone one step further and cleared the entire record. As a result, if you need to review your files, they will be free of garbage. We do indeed flag F$ with 255 and then we clear N1$ through N4$. Irrespective of the number of characters you store in these variables, all of them consist of 15 bytes *as far as the disk is concerned*. Note that the buffer is set *once*, and then forty consecutive blank records are written (PUT). Because you should have a chance to confirm a desire to blank a disk, that question is asked in statement 2020. The initalizing routine is as follows:

```
1990 '***********************
2000 '* INITIALIZE THE FILE *
2010 '***********************
2020 PRINT "ARE YOU SURE(Y/N)? ";
2030 Z$ = INKEY$:IF Z$ = "" THEN 2030
2040 PRINT Z$
2050 IF Z$ < > "Y" THEN RETURN
2060 LSET F$=CHR$(255)
2070 LSET N1$ = SPACE$(15)
2080 LSET N2$ = SPACE$(15)
2090 LSET N3$ = SPACE$(15)
2100 LSET N4$ = SPACE$(15)
2110 FOR FILE.NUMBER = 1 TO 40
2120    PUT #1,FILE.NUMBER
2130 NEXT FILE.NUMBER
2140 RETURN
```

Next comes the creation option. Recall that the record on the disk file has already been initialized, and now we will select it by a record number based upon the starting time. Here is that routine:

```
510 '*******************
520 '* BUILD NEW ENTRY *
530 '*******************
540 GOSUB 1880
550 IF ASC(F$) = 255 THEN 600
560 PRINT "THE RECORD EXISTS - DO YOU WISH TO OVERWRITE (Y/N)?";
570 Z$ = INKEY$:IF Z$ = "" THEN 570
580 PRINT Z$
590 IF Z$ < > "Y" THEN RETURN
600 CLS
610 PRINT:PRINT TAB(30);"LAZY DAZE GOLF COURSE"
620 PRINT STRING$(79,220)
630 PRINT
640 TEE.TIME$=LEFT$(TIME.TIME$,2)+":"+RIGHT$(TIME.TIME$,2)
650 PRINT "RESERVATION TIME: ";TEE.TIME$
660 PRINT
670 NAME.1$ = ""
680 NAME.2$ = ""
690 NAME.3$ = ""
700 NAME.4$ = ""
710 LSET F$=CHR$(0)
720 LINE INPUT " FIRST PLAYER: ";NAME.1$
730 LSET N1$ = NAME.1$
740 LINE INPUT "SECOND PLAYER: ";NAME.2$
750 LSET N2$ = NAME.2$
760 LINE INPUT " THIRD PLAYER: ";NAME.3$
770 LSET N3$ = NAME.3$
780 LINE INPUT "FOURTH PLAYER: ";NAME.4$
790 LSET N4$ = NAME.4$
800 IF NAME.1$ < > "" THEN NUMBER.OF.PLAYERS% = NUMBER.OF.PLAYERS% + 1
810 IF NAME.2$ < > "" THEN NUMBER.OF.PLAYERS% = NUMBER.OF.PLAYERS% + 1
820 IF NAME.3$ < > "" THEN NUMBER.OF.PLAYERS% = NUMBER.OF.PLAYERS% + 1
830 IF NAME.4$ < > "" THEN NUMBER.OF.PLAYERS% = NUMBER.OF.PLAYERS% + 1
840 LSET NR$ = MKI$(NUMBER.OF.PLAYERS%)
850 NUMBER.OF.PLAYERS% = 0
860 PUT#1,PLAYTIME%
870 RETURN
```

Because it would be theoretically possible to enter an incorrect time and destroy a previously entered record, once you have determined that a record already exists, you are asked if you wish to overwrite it. If you respond with N, the main menu will be brought back. If your response is Y, the new record will overwrite the old one.

Because new names will be received, all name fields are set to null in statements 670-700. The presence or absence of these null codes will be the basis for counting how many players are registered by statements 800-830. One by one the names of the players are gained. Note the LINE INPUT statements. An INPUT statement terminates when it encounters a comma, expecting a second input. A LINE INPUT statement treats everything as an incoming string. Thus, if DOE, JOHN is entered, the comma will not interrupt the input.

The buffer is loaded by means of the instruction LSET. LSET means SET into the buffer field at the left side; RSET means to do the same as the right side. Using it sets the name (of whatever length) into the leftmost characters of the 15-character field. In a similar manner, the integer variable is set into the buffer with the MKI$ instruction of statement 840. The player count is reset in statement 850, and then the record is written (PUT) in statement 860.

The DISPLAY option functions are to get the desired starting time, select the record required, and present the data on the screen. Using the buffer for display is sufficient. In the modification routine, however, the buffer names are set back into the variable names. The CVI instruction allows the number to be obtained from the disk and presented. The routine is as follows:

```
880 '*********************
890 '* DISPLAY THE ENTRY *
900 '*********************
910 GOSUB 1880
920 IF ASC(F$) = 255 THEN PRINT "NOT RESERVED":RETURN
930 CLS
940 PRINT:PRINT TAB(30);"LAZY DAZE GOLF COURSE"
950 PRINT STRING$(79,220)
960 PRINT:PRINT TAB(30);"STARTING TIME: ";TEE.TIME$
970 PRINT:PRINT TAB(20);"PERSON #1:   ";N1$:NAME.1$ = N1$
980 PRINT:PRINT TAB(20);"PERSON #2:   ";N2$:NAME.2$ = N2$
990 PRINT:PRINT TAB(20);"PERSON #3:   ";N3$:NAME.3$ = N3$
1000 PRINT:PRINT TAB(20);"PERSON #4:   ";N4$:NAME.4$ = N4$
1010 PRINT:PRINT TAB(20);"SIZE OF GROUP:   ";CVI(NR$)
1020 PRINT
1030 PRINT STRING$(79,220)
1040 PRINT
1050 RETURN
```

The REPLACE (ADD or DELETE) option allows you to add or subtract a person from the foursome. All names are displayed, and you are asked which one you wish to modify (1, 2, 3, or 4). You can exit from this section by entering 9 to the question posed in statements 1300-1320. The determination of the size of the group for display purposes is a little more difficult since the name may be coming from either the disk or the keyboard and there will be a length difference. Therefore, a compound logical is used in statements 1210-1270 to ask for either a blank line of 15 characters (from the disk) or a length of zero (from the keyboard). The remainder of the routine is as before. The complete routine is as follows:

```
1060 '***************************************************
1070 '* ADD TO OR DELETE FROM AN EXISTING FOURSOME *
1080 '***************************************************
1090 GOSUB 1880
1100 IF ASC(F$) = 255 THEN PRINT "NOT RESERVED":RETURN
1110 NAME.1$ = N1$
1120 NAME.2$ = N2$
1130 NAME.3$ = N3$
1140 NAME.4$ = N4$
1150 CLS
1160 PRINT:PRINT TAB(30);"LAZY DAZE GOLF COURSE"
1170 PRINT STRING$(79,220)
1180 PRINT:PRINT TAB(30);"STARTING TIME: ";TEE.TIME$
```

```
1190 SIZE.OF.GROUP% = 0
1200 PRINT:PRINT TAB(20);"PERSON #1:   ";NAME.1$
1210 IF (NAME.1$ < > SPACE$(15)) AND (LEN(NAME.1$) < > 0)
          THEN SIZE.OF.GROUP% = SIZE.OF.GROUP% + 1
1220 PRINT:PRINT TAB(20);"PERSON #2:   ";NAME.2$
1230 IF (NAME.2$ < > SPACE$(15)) AND (LEN(NAME.2$) < > 0)
          THEN SIZE.OF.GROUP% = SIZE.OF.GROUP% + 1
1240 PRINT:PRINT TAB(20);"PERSON #3:   ";NAME.3$
1250 IF (NAME.3$ < > SPACE$(15)) AND (LEN(NAME.3$) < > 0)
          THEN SIZE.OF.GROUP% = SIZE.OF.GROUP% + 1
1260 PRINT:PRINT TAB(20);"PERSON #4:   ";NAME.4$
1270 IF (NAME.4$ < > SPACE$(15)) AND (LEN(NAME.4$) < > 0)
          THEN SIZE.OF.GROUP% = SIZE.OF.GROUP% + 1
1280 PRINT:PRINT TAB(20);"SIZE OF GROUP:   ";SIZE.OF.GROUP%
1290 PRINT
1300 PRINT:INPUT "WHICH NAME TO CHANGE (9 WHEN COMPLETE): ",WHICH.NAME
1310 PRINT
1320 IF WHICH.NAME = 9 THEN 1390
1330 IF WHICH.NAME = 1 THEN LINE INPUT "ENTER PERSON #1: ";NAME.1$:GOTO 1150
1340 IF WHICH.NAME = 2 THEN LINE INPUT "ENTER PERSON #2: ";NAME.2$:GOTO 1150
1350 IF WHICH.NAME = 3 THEN LINE INPUT "ENTER PERSON #3: ";NAME.3$:GOTO 1150
1360 IF WHICH.NAME = 4 THEN LINE INPUT "ENTER PERSON #4: ";NAME.4$:GOTO 1150
1370 CLS
1380 GOTO 1130
1390 PRINT
1400 NUMBER.OF.PLAYERS% = 0
1410 IF NAME.1$ < > "" THEN NUMBER.OF.PLAYERS% = NUMBER.OF.PLAYERS% + 1
1420 IF NAME.2$ < > "" THEN NUMBER.OF.PLAYERS% = NUMBER.OF.PLAYERS% + 1
1430 IF NAME.3$ < > "" THEN NUMBER.OF.PLAYERS% = NUMBER.OF.PLAYERS% + 1
1440 IF NAME.4$ < > "" THEN NUMBER.OF.PLAYERS% = NUMBER.OF.PLAYERS% + 1
1450 LSET NR$ = MKI$(NUMBER.OF.PLAYERS%)
1460 LSET N1$ = NAME.1$
1470 LSET N2$ = NAME.2$
1480 LSET N3$ = NAME.3$
1490 LSET N4$ = NAME.4$
1500 PUT#1,PLAYTIME%
1510 RETURN
```

Occasionally an entire foursome may cancel its scheduled time. The following routine will remove this foursome from the file. Although it would have been sufficient simply to perform statement 1570 followed by 1630; it's generally good practice to neutralize the entire record. Whenever the time comes to print the entire file, information in the record might prove confusing.

```
1520 '********************************
1530 '* REMOVE FOURSOME FROM THE FILE *
1540 '********************************
1550 GOSUB 1880
1560 IF ASC(F$) = 255 THEN PRINT "NOT RESERVED":RETURN
1570 LSET T$=CHR$(255)
1580 LSET NR$ = "  "
1590 LSET N1$ = SPACE$(15)
1600 LSET N2$ = SPACE$(15)
1610 LSET N3$ = SPACE$(15)
1620 LSET N4$ = SPACE$(15)
1630 PUT#1,PLAYTIME%
1640 RETURN
```

Suppose that you're busy at work and a customer comes in and asks, "Have you got an open time and a foursome I can join?" You tell him "Sure" and press the "L" option on your menu, invoking a routine whose only function is to survey the files for foursomes with fewer than four people. As presently programmed, statement 1770 does not permit the listing of the totally open times. You may wish to change that limitation. In any event, with the following option, your customer can join a developing foursome:

```
1650 '*******************************************
1660 '* LIST FOURSOMES WITHOUT FULL COMPLEMENTS *
1670 '*******************************************
1680 CLS
1690 PRINT:PRINT TAB(30);"LAZY DAZE GOLF COURSE"
1700 PRINT STRING$(79,220)
1710 PRINT:PRINT TAB(20);"FOURSOMES WITHOUT FULL COMPLEMENTS"
1720 PRINT STRING$(79,220)
1730 PRINT
1740 FOR FILE.NUMBER = 1 TO 40
1750     GOSUB 2490
1760     GET #1,FILE.NUMBER
1770     IF F$ = CHR$(255) THEN 1820
1780     TIME.TIME$ = STR$(WHICH.RECORD%)
1790     TIME.TIME$ = RIGHT$(TIME.TIME$,4)
1800     TEE.TIME$=LEFT$(TIME.TIME$,2)+":"+RIGHT$(TIME.TIME$,2)
1810     IF CVI(NR$) < 4 THEN PRINT
                "TEE TIME: ";TEE.TIME$,"NR OF PLAYERS: ";CVI(NR$)
1820 NEXT FILE.NUMBER
1830 RETURN
```

Finally, the program provides a printed schedule by selecting menu option "P." The schedule looks like the following:

```
LAZY DAZE GOLF COURSE TEE-OFF SCHEDULE FOR: 05-08-1982

    1           08:00           MERRILL
                                LYNCH
                                PIERCE
                                FENNER

    5           09:00           SMITH
                                KLINE
                                FRENCH

    9           10:00           WINKIN
                                BLINKIN
                                NOD

   13           11:00           DASHER
                                DANCER
                                PRANCER
                                VIXEN

   17           12:00           COMET
                                CUPID
                                DONDER
                                BLITZEN
```

The coding for the schedule is as follows:

```
2600 '*****************************************************************
2610 '* ROUTINE TO DISPLAY AND HARDCOPY PRINT A DAY'S SCHEDULE *
2620 '*****************************************************************
2630 LPRINT "LAZY DAZE GOLF COURSE TEE-OFF SCHEDULE FOR: ";DATE$
2640 LPRINT
2650 RESET
2660 OPEN "TEEOFF.DAT" AS #1 LEN=63
2670 FIELD #1,1 AS F$,15 AS N1$,15 AS N2$,15 AS N3$,15 AS N4$,2 AS NR$
2680 RESTORE
2690 FOR FILE.NUMBER = 1 TO 40
2700     GET #1,FILE.NUMBER
2710     READ DISPLAY.TIME$
2720     TEE.TIME$ = RIGHT$(DISPLAY.TIME$,4)
2730     TEE.TIME$ = LEFT$(TEE.TIME$,2) + ":" + RIGHT$(TEE.TIME$,2)
2740     IF F$ = CHR$(255) THEN 2850
2750     PRINT FILE.NUMBER,TEE.TIME$,N1$
2760     PRINT ,,N2$
2770     PRINT ,,N3$
2780     PRINT ,,N4$
2790     PRINT
2800     LPRINT FILE.NUMBER,TEE.TIME$,N1$
2810     LPRINT ,,N2$
2820     LPRINT ,,N3$
2830     LPRINT ,,N4$
2840     LPRINT
2850 NEXT FILE.NUMBER
2860 LPRINT CHR$(12)
2870 RETURN
```

This coding completes the discussion of the LAZY DAZE GOLF COURSE reservation system. Here is the entire program:

```
10 CLS
20 KEY OFF
30 '*****************************
40 '* OPEN AND DEFINE THE FILE *
50 '*****************************
60 OPEN "TEEOFF.DAT" AS #1 LEN=63
70 FIELD #1,1 AS F$,15 AS N1$,15 AS N2$,15 AS N3$,15 AS N4$,2 AS NR$
80 '*****************************
90 '* PRESENT THE SELECTION MENU *
100 '*****************************
110 CLS
120 NAME.1$ = ""
130 NAME.2$ = ""
140 NAME.3$ = ""
150 NAME.4$ = ""
160 PRINT:PRINT TAB(30);"LAZY DAZE GOLF COURSE"
170 PRINT STRING$(79,220)
180 PRINT :PRINT TAB(36);"OPTIONS:"
190 PRINT:PRINT TAB(18);"<I>NITIALIZE THE FILE (CAUTION: REMOVES ALL DATA)"
200 PRINT:PRINT TAB(18);"<C>REATE A NEW STARTING TIME"
210 PRINT:PRINT TAB(18);"<D>ISPLAY A STARTING TIME"
220 PRINT:PRINT TAB(18);"<A>DD (OR DELETE) A PERSON'S STARTING TIME"
230 PRINT:PRINT TAB(18);"<R>EMOVE A FOURSOME FROM A STARTING TIME"
240 PRINT:PRINT TAB(18);"<L>IST RESERVATIONS WITH FEWER THAN FOUR PLAYERS"
250 PRINT:PRINT TAB(18);"<P>RINT AND DISPLAY THE DAY'S SCHEDULE"
260 PRINT:PRINT TAB(18);"<E>ND THE PROGRAM"
270 PRINT:PRINT "SELECT: ";
```

```
280 Z$ = INKEY$:IF Z$ = "" THEN 280
290 PRINT Z$;
300 IF Z$ = "I" THEN PRINT "NITIALIZE":SELECTION = 1:GOTO 470
310 IF Z$ = "i" THEN PRINT "nitialize":SELECTION = 1:GOTO 470
320 IF Z$ = "C" THEN PRINT "REATE":SELECTION = 2:GOTO 470
330 IF Z$ = "c" THEN PRINT "reate":SELECTION = 2:GOTO 470
340 IF Z$ = "D" THEN PRINT "ISPLAY":SELECTION = 3:GOTO 470
350 IF Z$ = "d" THEN PRINT "isplay":SELECTION = 3:GOTO 470
360 IF Z$ = "A" THEN PRINT "DD":SELECTION = 4:GOTO 470
370 IF Z$ = "a" THEN PRINT "dd":SELECTION = 4:GOTO 470
380 IF Z$ = "R" THEN PRINT "EPLACE":SELECTION = 5:GOTO 470
390 IF Z$ = "r" THEN PRINT "eplace":SELECTION = 5:GOTO 470
400 IF Z$ = "L" THEN PRINT "IST":SELECTION = 6:GOTO 470
410 IF Z$ = "l" THEN PRINT "ist":SELECTION = 6:GOTO 470
420 IF Z$ = "P" THEN PRINT "RINT":SELECTION = 7:GOTO 470
430 IF Z$ = "p" THEN PRINT "rint":SELECTION = 7:GOTO 470
440 IF Z$ = "E" THEN PRINT "ND":SELECTION = 8:GOTO 470
450 IF Z$ = "e" THEN PRINT "nd":SELECTION = 8:GOTO 470
460 GOTO 110
470 ON SELECTION GOSUB 1990,510,880,1060,1520,1650,2600,2150
480 PRINT "PRESS ANY KEY TO CONTINUE";
490 Z$ = INKEY$:IF Z$ = "" THEN 490
500 GOTO 110
510 '*********************
520 '* BUILD NEW ENTRY *
530 '*********************
540 GOSUB 1880
550 IF ASC(F$) = 255 THEN 600
560 PRINT "THE RECORD EXISTS - DO YOU WISH TO OVERWRITE (Y/N)?";
570 Z$ = INKEY$:IF Z$ = "" THEN 570
580 PRINT Z$
590 IF Z$ < > "Y" THEN RETURN
600 CLS
610 PRINT:PRINT TAB(30);"LAZY DAZE GOLF COURSE"
620 PRINT STRING$(79,220)
630 PRINT
640 TEE.TIME$=LEFT$(TIME.TIME$,2)+":"+RIGHT$(TIME.TIME$,2)
650 PRINT "RESERVATION TIME: ";TEE.TIME$
660 PRINT
670 NAME.1$ = ""
680 NAME.2$ = ""
690 NAME.3$ = ""
700 NAME.4$ = ""
710 LSET F$=CHR$(0)
720 LINE INPUT " FIRST PLAYER: ";NAME.1$
730 LSET N1$ = NAME.1$
740 LINE INPUT "SECOND PLAYER: ";NAME.2$
750 LSET N2$ = NAME.2$
760 LINE INPUT " THIRD PLAYER: ";NAME.3$
770 LSET N3$ = NAME.3$
780 LINE INPUT "FOURTH PLAYER: ";NAME.4$
790 LSET N4$ = NAME.4$
800 IF NAME.1$ < > "" THEN NUMBER.OF.PLAYERS% = NUMBER.OF.PLAYERS% + 1
810 IF NAME.2$ < > "" THEN NUMBER.OF.PLAYERS% = NUMBER.OF.PLAYERS% + 1
820 IF NAME.3$ < > "" THEN NUMBER.OF.PLAYERS% = NUMBER.OF.PLAYERS% + 1
830 IF NAME.4$ < > "" THEN NUMBER.OF.PLAYERS% = NUMBER.OF.PLAYERS% + 1
840 LSET NR$ = MKI$(NUMBER.OF.PLAYERS%)
850 NUMBER.OF.PLAYERS% = 0
860 PUT#1,PLAYTIME%
870 RETURN
880 '*********************
890 '* DISPLAY THE ENTRY *
900 '*********************
910 GOSUB 1880
920 IF ASC(F$) = 255 THEN PRINT "NOT RESERVED":RETURN
930 CLS
940 PRINT:PRINT TAB(30);"LAZY DAZE GOLF COURSE"
950 PRINT STRING$(79,220)
960 PRINT:PRINT TAB(30);"STARTING TIME: ";TEE.TIME$
```

```
970 PRINT:PRINT TAB(20);"PERSON #1:   ";N1$:NAME.1$ = N1$
980 PRINT:PRINT TAB(20);"PERSON #2:   ";N2$:NAME.2$ = N2$
990 PRINT:PRINT TAB(20);"PERSON #3:   ";N3$:NAME.3$ = N3$
1000 PRINT:PRINT TAB(20);"PERSON #4:   ";N4$:NAME.4$ = N4$
1010 PRINT:PRINT TAB(20);"SIZE OF GROUP:   ";CVI(NR$)
1020 PRINT
1030 PRINT STRING$(79,220)
1040 PRINT
1050 RETURN
1060 '***********************************************
1070 '* ADD TO OR DELETE FROM AN EXISTING FOURSOME *
1080 '***********************************************
1090 GOSUB 1880
1100 IF ASC(F$) = 255 THEN PRINT "NOT RESERVED":RETURN
1110 NAME.1$ = N1$
1120 NAME.2$ = N2$
1130 NAME.3$ = N3$
1140 NAME.4$ = N4$
1150 CLS
1160 PRINT:PRINT TAB(30);"LAZY DAZE GOLF COURSE"
1170 PRINT STRING$(79,220)
1180 PRINT:PRINT TAB(30);"STARTING TIME: ";TEE.TIME$
1190 SIZE.OF.GROUP% = 0
1200 PRINT:PRINT TAB(20);"PERSON #1:   ";NAME.1$
1210 IF (NAME.1$ < > SPACE$(15)) AND (LEN(NAME.1$) < > 0)
         THEN SIZE.OF.GROUP% = SIZE.OF.GROUP% + 1
1220 PRINT:PRINT TAB(20);"PERSON #2:   ";NAME.2$
1230 IF (NAME.2$ < > SPACE$(15)) AND (LEN(NAME.2$) < > 0)
         THEN SIZE.OF.GROUP% = SIZE.OF.GROUP% + 1
1240 PRINT:PRINT TAB(20);"PERSON #3:   ";NAME.3$
1250 IF (NAME.3$ < > SPACE$(15)) AND (LEN(NAME.3$) < > 0)
         THEN SIZE.OF.GROUP% = SIZE.OF.GROUP% + 1
1260 PRINT:PRINT TAB(20);"PERSON #4:   ";NAME.4$
1270 IF (NAME.4$ < > SPACE$(15)) AND (LEN(NAME.4$) < > 0)
         THEN SIZE.OF.GROUP% = SIZE.OF.GROUP% + 1
1280 PRINT:PRINT TAB(20);"SIZE OF GROUP:   ";SIZE.OF.GROUP%
1290 PRINT
1300 PRINT:INPUT "WHICH NAME TO CHANGE (9 WHEN COMPLETE): ",WHICH.NAME
1310 PRINT
1320 IF WHICH.NAME = 9 THEN 1390
1330 IF WHICH.NAME = 1 THEN LINE INPUT "ENTER PERSON #1: ";NAME.1$:GOTO 1150
1340 IF WHICH.NAME = 2 THEN LINE INPUT "ENTER PERSON #2: ";NAME.2$:GOTO 1150
1350 IF WHICH.NAME = 3 THEN LINE INPUT "ENTER PERSON #3: ";NAME.3$:GOTO 1150
1360 IF WHICH.NAME = 4 THEN LINE INPUT "ENTER PERSON #4: ";NAME.4$:GOTO 1150
1370 CLS
1380 GOTO 1130
1390 PRINT
1400 NUMBER.OF.PLAYERS% = 0
1410 IF NAME.1$ < > "" THEN NUMBER.OF.PLAYERS% = NUMBER.OF.PLAYERS% + 1
1420 IF NAME.2$ < >"" THEN NUMBER.OF.PLAYERS% = NUMBER.OF.PLAYERS% + 1
1430 IF NAME.3$ < > "" THEN NUMBER.OF.PLAYERS% = NUMBER.OF.PLAYERS% + 1
1440 IF NAME.4$ < > "" THEN NUMBER.OF.PLAYERS% = NUMBER.OF.PLAYERS% + 1
1450 LSET NR$ = MKI$(NUMBER.OF.PLAYERS%)
1460 LSET N1$ = NAME.1$
1470 LSET N2$ = NAME.2$
1480 LSET N3$ = NAME.3$
1490 LSET N4$ = NAME.4$
1500 PUT#1,PLAYTIME%
1510 RETURN
1520 '*********************************
1530 '* REMOVE FOURSOME FROM THE FILE *
1540 '*********************************
1550 GOSUB 1880
1560 IF ASC(F$) = 255 THEN PRINT "NOT RESERVED":RETURN
1570 LSET T$=CHR$(255)
1580 LSET NR$ = "  "
1590 LSET N1$ = SPACE$(15)
1600 LSET N2$ = SPACE$(15)
1610 LSET N3$ = SPACE$(15)
```

```
1620 LSET N4$ = SPACE$(15)
1630 PUT#1,PLAYTIME%
1640 RETURN
1650 '*********************************************
1660 '* LIST FOURSOMES WITHOUT FULL COMPLEMENTS *
1670 '*********************************************
1680 CLS
1690 PRINT:PRINT TAB(30);"LAZY DAZE GOLF COURSE"
1700 PRINT STRING$(79,220)
1710 PRINT:PRINT TAB(20);"FOURSOMES WITHOUT FULL COMPLEMENTS"
1720 PRINT STRING$(79,220)
1730 PRINT
1740 FOR FILE.NUMBER = 1 TO 40
1750      GOSUB 2490
1760      GET #1,FILE.NUMBER
1770      IF F$ = CHR$(255) THEN 1820
1780      TIME.TIME$ = STR$(WHICH.RECORD%)
1790      TIME.TIME$ = RIGHT$(TIME.TIME$,4)
1800      TEE.TIME$=LEFT$(TIME.TIME$,2)+":"+RIGHT$(TIME.TIME$,2)
1810      IF CVI(NR$) < 4 THEN PRINT
                "TEE TIME: ";TEE.TIME$,"NR OF PLAYERS: ";CVI(NR$)
1820 NEXT FILE.NUMBER
1830 RETURN
1840 '*****************************
1850 '* OBTAIN THE PLAYING TIME *
1860 '*****************************
1870 NO.FIND.SWITCH = 0
1880 INPUT "PLAYING TIME";PLAYTIME%
1890      TIME.TIME$ = STR$(PLAYTIME%)
1900      TIME.TIME$ = RIGHT$(TIME.TIME$,4)
1910      TEE.TIME$=LEFT$(TIME.TIME$,2)+":"+RIGHT$(TIME.TIME$,2)
1920 GOSUB 2330
1930 IF NO.FIND.SWITCH = 1 THEN 1960
1940 IF (PLAYTIME% < 1) OR (PLAYTIME% > 40) THEN 1960
1950 GET #1,PLAYTIME%:RETURN
1960 PRINT "BAD STARTING TIME"
1970 NO.FIND.SWITCH = 0
1980 GOTO 1880
1990 '************************
2000 '* INITIALIZE THE FILE *
2010 '************************
2020 PRINT "ARE YOU SURE(Y/N)? ";
2030 Z$ = INKEY$:IF Z$ = "" THEN 2030
2040 PRINT Z$
2050 IF Z$ < > "Y" THEN RETURN
2060 LSET F$=CHR$(255)
2070 LSET N1$ = SPACE$(15)
2080 LSET N2$ = SPACE$(15)
2090 LSET N3$ = SPACE$(15)
2100 LSET N4$ = SPACE$(15)
2110 FOR FILE.NUMBER = 1 TO 40
2120      PUT #1,FILE.NUMBER
2130 NEXT FILE.NUMBER
2140 RETURN
2150 '************************
2160 '* END THE APPLICATION *
2170 '************************
2180 CLOSE:END
2190 '******************
2200 '* STARTING TIMES *
2210 '******************
2220 DATA 0800,0815,0830,0845
2230 DATA 0900,0915,0930,0945
2240 DATA 1000,1015,1030,1045
2250 DATA 1100,1115,1130,1145
2260 DATA 1200,1215,1230,1245
2270 DATA 1300,1315,1330,1345
2280 DATA 1400,1415,1430,1445
2290 DATA 1500,1515,1530,1545
```

```
2300 DATA 1600,1615,1630,1645
2310 DATA 1700,1715,1730,1745
2320 DATA 9999,9999,9999,9999
2330 '**********************************************************
2340 '* ROUTINE TO SELECT RECORD NUMBER BASED ON STARTING TIME *
2350 '**********************************************************
2360 RESTORE
2370 FOR CHECK.RECORD% = 1 TO 100
2380      READ WHICH.RECORD%
2390      IF WHICH.RECORD% = 9999 THEN 2440
2400      IF WHICH.RECORD% = PLAYTIME% THEN 2470
2410 NEXT CHECK.RECORD%
2420 PRINT "BAD TIME TABLE IN PROGRAM"
2430 END
2440 PRINT "TIME NOT AVAILABLE AS A STARTING TIME"
2450 NO.FIND.SWITCH = 1
2460 RETURN
2470 SWAP CHECK.RECORD%,PLAYTIME%
2480 GOTO 2460
2490 '**********************************************************
2500 '* ROUTINE TO SELECT STARTING TIME BASED ON RECORD NUMBER *
2510 '**********************************************************
2520 RESTORE
2530 FOR CHECK.RECORD% = 1 TO FILE.NUMBER
2540      READ WHICH.RECORD%
2550      IF WHICH.RECORD% = 9999 THEN 2580
2560 NEXT CHECK.RECORD%
2570 RETURN
2580 PRINT "BAD TIME TABLE IN PROGRAM"
2590 END
2600 '**********************************************************
2610 '* ROUTINE TO DISPLAY AND HARDCOPY PRINT A DAY'S SCHEDULE *
2620 '**********************************************************
2630 LPRINT "LAZY DAZE GOLF COURSE TEE-OFF SCHEDULE FOR: ";DATE$
2640 LPRINT
2650 RESET
2660 OPEN "TEEOFF.DAT" AS #1 LEN=63
2670 FIELD #1,1 AS F$,15 AS N1$,15 AS N2$,15 AS N3$,15 AS N4$,2 AS NR$
2680 RESTORE
2690 FOR FILE.NUMBER = 1 TO 40
2700      GET #1,FILE.NUMBER
2710      READ DISPLAY.TIME$
2720      TEE.TIME$ = RIGHT$(DISPLAY.TIME$,4)
2730      TEE.TIME$ = LEFT$(TEE.TIME$,2) + ":" + RIGHT$(TEE.TIME$,2)
2740      IF F$ = CHR$(255) THEN 2850
2750      PRINT FILE.NUMBER,TEE.TIME$,N1$
2760      PRINT ,,N2$
2770      PRINT ,,N3$
2780      PRINT ,,N4$
2790      PRINT
2800      LPRINT FILE.NUMBER,TEE.TIME$,N1$
2810      LPRINT ,,N2$
2820      LPRINT ,,N3$
2830      LPRINT ,,N4$
2840      LPRINT
2850 NEXT FILE.NUMBER
2860 LPRINT CHR$(12)
2870 RETURN
```

SLEAZE, PLEASE

The Lazy Daze Golf Course problem was an inventory problem in which the inventory numbers were not contiguous but the record numbers had to be. Unless we have a considerable amount of media available, the use of noncontiguous product codes, inventory numbers, on the like, can lead to a great deal of wasted space. Therefore, building a DATA table of starting times and using their relative positions within the table as the location of the record corresponding to that time on the disk was our wisest possible move. What if it were indeed part or inventory numbers that concerned us and if adding or deleting a part number would mean modifying our program with each change? That wouldn't seem to be the wisest thing to do, and it isn't. Changes in approach would have to to be made. A second file of part numbers would be necessary, with a record of part numbers and their relative location on the inventory file. These techniques will be dealt with in the next chapter, which is devoted to a small business system.

For the balance of this chapter we're going to concentrate on a bonafide inventory application that is randomly organized. Imagine that you have just become the quartermaster of Camp Sleazy and that when you turn on your PC, the following is what you see:

```
                     CAMP SLEAZY QUARTERMASTER
━━━━━━━━━━━━━━━━━━━━━━━━━━━━━━━━━━━━━━━━━━━━━━━━━━━━━━━━━━━━━━━━━━━━━━━━

                     OPTIONS:

        <I>NITIALIZE THE FILE - (CAUTION: REMOVES ALL DATA)

        <C>REATE A NEW ENTRY

        <D>ISPLAY INVENTORY FOR ONE ITEM

        <A>DD TO STOCK

        <S>UBTRACT FROM STOCK

        <L>IST ITEMS BELOW REORDER LEVEL

        <P>RINT THE ENTIRE INVENTORY LIST

        <E>ND THE PROGRAM

SELECT:
```

In this example we do not find the inventory record by a two-step process as we did in the Lazy Daze Golf Course problem. Instead, we're assuming the presence of one hundred items, numbered sequentially from 1 to 100. Our discussion of this program will not be on a module by module basis because its similarities to the Lazy Daze program are great. The differences will be pointed out by reference to the program listing at the end of the discussion.

In this program, we want to determine the quantity of items on hand, the reorder level, the unit price, and the location of each. *Important note*: No routines have been included to change anything other than the quantity on hand. The inclusion of such options would not be a difficult task since it would follow precisely the technique by which the player's names were substituted in the Lazy Daze program.

The output from menu option "P" is as follows:

```
                    CAMP SLEAZY QUARTERMASTER
```
_____

```
BLANKETS, O.D.                QUANTITY 100        REORDER LEVEL 500
PONCHO                        QUANTITY 10         REORDER LEVEL 20
PRESS ANY KEY TO CONTINUE
```

The output from menu option "L" is as follows:

```
                    CAMP SLEAZY QUARTERMASTER
```
_____

```
                       INVENTORY FILE LIST
```
_____

```
ITEM NUMBER    1

    ITEM: COMBAT BOOTS

    QUANTITY ON HAND    100
    REORDER LEVEL        75
    UNIT PRICE        $5.55
    BIN LOCATION:       A45

ITEM NUMBER    3

    ITEM: BLANKETS, O.D.

    QUANTITY ON HAND    100
    REORDER LEVEL       500
    UNIT PRICE        $6.66
    BIN LOCATION:       C78

ITEM NUMBER    5

    ITEM: PONCHO

    QUANTITY ON HAND     10
    REORDER LEVEL        20
    UNIT PRICE        $4.44
    BIN LOCATION:       B23
```

The complete program is shown below. There are a few more figures involved in the data stored on disk (and converted both ways) and in the calculations. You'll notice that in particular when you stop to study the addition and subtraction routines located between statements 970 and 1280. The difference in both routines is that after a change has been made *a portion* of the display routine is invoked, allowing the change to be presented before the program goes back to the main menu again.

```
10 CLS
20 KEY OFF
30 '*****************************
40 '* OPEN AND DEFINE THE FILE *
50 '*****************************
60 OPEN "ITEMS.DAT" AS #1 LEN = 43
```

```
70 FIELD #1,1 AS FLAG$,30 AS FILE.DESCRIPTION$,2 AS FILE.QUANTITY$,
      2 AS FILE.REORDER.POINT$,4 AS FILE.UNIT.PRICE$,4 AS FILE.BIN.LOCATION$
80 '*******************************
90 '* PRESENT THE SELECTION MENU *
100 '*******************************
110 CLS
120 PRINT:PRINT TAB(30);"CAMP SLEAZY QUARTERMASTER"
130 PRINT STRING$(79,220)
140 PRINT:PRINT TAB(36);"OPTIONS:"
150 PRINT:PRINT TAB(18);"<I>NITIALIZE THE FILE - (CAUTION: REMOVES ALL DATA)"
160 PRINT:PRINT TAB(18);"<C>REATE A NEW ENTRY"
170 PRINT:PRINT TAB(18);"<D>ISPLAY INVENTORY FOR ONE ITEM"
180 PRINT:PRINT TAB(18);"<A>DD TO STOCK"
190 PRINT:PRINT TAB(18);"<S>UBTRACT FROM STOCK"
200 PRINT:PRINT TAB(18);"<L>IST ITEMS BELOW REORDER LEVEL"
210 PRINT:PRINT TAB(18);"<P>RINT THE ENTIRE INVENTORY LIST"
220 PRINT:PRINT TAB(18);"<E>ND THE PROGRAM"
230 PRINT:PRINT "SELECT: ";
240 Z$ = INKEY$:IF Z$ = "" THEN 240
250 PRINT Z$;
260 IF Z$ = "I" THEN PRINT "NITIALIZE":SELECTION = 1:GOTO 430
270 IF Z$ = "i" THEN PRINT "nitialize":SELECTION = 1:GOTO 430
280 IF Z$ = "C" THEN PRINT "REATE":SELECTION = 2:GOTO 430
290 IF Z$ = "c" THEN PRINT "reate":SELECTION = 2:GOTO 430
300 IF Z$ = "D" THEN PRINT "ISPLAY":SELECTION = 3:GOTO 430
310 IF Z$ = "d" THEN PRINT "isplay":SELECTION = 3:GOTO 430
320 IF Z$ = "A" THEN PRINT "DD":SELECTION = 4:GOTO 430
330 IF Z$ = "a" THEN PRINT "dd":SELECTION = 4:GOTO 430
340 IF Z$ = "S" THEN PRINT "UBTRACT":SELECTION = 5:GOTO 430
350 IF Z$ = "s" THEN PRINT "ubtract":SELECTION = 5:GOTO 430
360 IF Z$ = "L" THEN PRINT "IST":SELECTION = 6:GOTO 430
370 IF Z$ = "l" THEN PRINT "ist":SELECTION = 6:GOTO 430
380 IF Z$ = "P" THEN PRINT "RINT":SELECTION = 7:GOTO 430
390 IF Z$ = "p" THEN PRINT "rint":SELECTION = 7:GOTO 430
400 IF Z$ = "E" THEN PRINT "ND":SELECTION = 8:GOTO 430
410 IF Z$ = "e" THEN PRINT "nd":SELECTION = 8:GOTO 430
420 GOTO 110
430 ON SELECTION GOSUB 1460,470,780,970,1110,1290,1580,2010
440 PRINT "PRESS ANY KEY TO CONTINUE";
450 Z$ = INKEY$:IF Z$ = "" THEN 450
460 GOTO 110
470 '*********************
480 '* BUILD NEW ENTRY *
490 '*********************
500 CLS
510 PRINT:PRINT TAB(30);"CAMP SLEAZY QUARTERMASTER"
520 PRINT STRING$(79,220)
530 GOSUB 1440
540 IF ASC(FLAG$) = 255 THEN 590
550 PRINT "THE RECORD EXISTS - DO YOU WISH TO OVERWRITE (Y/N)? ";
560 Z$ = INKEY$:IF Z$ = "" THEN 560
570 PRINT Z$
580 IF Z$ < > "Y" THEN RETURN
590 LSET FLAG$=CHR$(0)
600 PRINT
610 LINE INPUT "ITEM DESCRIPTION: ";ITEM.DESCRIPTION$
620 LSET FILE.DESCRIPTION$ = ITEM.DESCRIPTION$
630 PRINT
640 INPUT "QUANTITY IN STOCK: ",QUANTITY.IN.STOCK%
650 LSET FILE.QUANTITY$ = MKI$(QUANTITY.IN.STOCK%)
660 PRINT
670 INPUT "REORDER POINT: ",REORDER.POINT%
680 LSET FILE.REORDER.POINT$ = MKI$(REORDER.POINT%)
690 PRINT
700 INPUT "UNIT PRICE: $",UNIT.PRICE
710 LSET FILE.UNIT.PRICE$ =MKS$(UNIT.PRICE)
720 PRINT
730 LINE INPUT "BIN LOCATION: ";BIN.LOCATION$
740 LSET FILE.BIN.LOCATION$ = BIN.LOCATION$
```

```
750 PRINT
760 PUT#1,ITEM%
770 RETURN
780 '***********************
790 '* DISPLAY THE ENTRY *
800 '***********************
810 CLS
820 PRINT:PRINT TAB(30);"CAMP SLEAZY QUARTERMASTER"
830 PRINT STRING$(79,220)
840 GOSUB 1440
850 IF ASC(FLAG$)= 255 THEN PRINT "NULL ENTRY":RETURN
860 PRINT
870 PRINT USING "ITEM NUMBER ###";ITEM%
880 PRINT
890 PRINT TAB(5);"ITEM: ";FILE.DESCRIPTION$
900 PRINT
910 PRINT TAB(5);"";:PRINT USING "QUANTITY ON HAND #####";CVI(FILE.QUANTITY$)
920 PRINT TAB(5);"";:PRINT USING "REORDER LEVEL    #####";
        CVI(FILE.REORDER.POINT$)
930 PRINT TAB(5);"";:PRINT USING "UNIT PRICE      $$##.##";CVS(FILE.UNIT.PRICE$)
940 PRINT TAB(5);"";:PRINT "BIN LOCATION:      ";FILE.BIN.LOCATION$
950 PRINT
960 RETURN
970 '*****************
980 '* ADD TO STOCK *
990 '*****************
1000 CLS
1010 PRINT:PRINT TAB(30);"CAMP SLEAZY QUARTERMASTER"
1020 PRINT STRING$(79,220)
1030 GOSUB 1440
1040 IF ASC(FLAG$) = 255 THEN PRINT "NULL ENTRY":RETURN
1050 PRINT FILE.DESCRIPTION$:INPUT "QUANTITY TO ADD ";QUANTITY.TO.ADD%
1060 QUANTITY% = CVI(FILE.QUANTITY$) + QUANTITY.TO.ADD%
1070 LSET FILE.QUANTITY$=MKI$(QUANTITY%)
1080 PUT#1,ITEM%
1090 GOSUB 860                    'USE PART OF THE DISPLAY ROUTINE
1100 RETURN
1110 '***********************
1120 '* REMOVE FROM STOCK *
1130 '***********************
1140 CLS
1150 PRINT:PRINT TAB(30);"CAMP SLEAZY QUARTERMASTER"
1160 PRINT STRING$(79,220)
1170 GOSUB 1440
1180 IF ASC(FLAG$) = 255 THEN PRINT "NULL ENTRY":RETURN
1190 PRINT FILE.DESCRIPTION$
1200 INPUT "QUANTITY TO SUBTRACT";QUANTITY.TO.SUBTRACT%
1210 QUANTITY%=CVI(FILE.QUANTITY$)
1220 IF (QUANTITY% - QUANTITY.TO.SUBTRACT%) < 0
        THEN PRINT "INSUFFICIENT QUANTITY - ONLY";QUANTITY%;
            " IN STOCK":GOTO 1200
1230 QUANTITY% = QUANTITY% - QUANTITY.TO.SUBTRACT%
1240 IF QUANTITY% = < CVI(FILE.REORDER.POINT$) THEN PRINT
        "QUANTITY NOW";QUANTITY%;" REORDER LEVEL";CVI(FILE.REORDER.POINT$)
1250 LSET FILE.QUANTITY$=MKI$(QUANTITY%)
1260 PUT #1,ITEM%
1270 GOSUB 860                    'USE PART OF THE DISPLAY ROUTINE
1280 RETURN
1290 '************************************
1300 '* LIST ITEMS BELOW REORDER LEVEL *
1310 '************************************
1320 CLS
1330 PRINT:PRINT TAB(30);"CAMP SLEAZY QUARTERMASTER"
1340 PRINT STRING$(79,220)
1350 PRINT
1360 FOR I = 1 TO 100
1370     GET #1,I
1380     IF CVI(FILE.QUANTITY$) < CVI(FILE.REORDER.POINT$) THEN PRINT
                FILE.DESCRIPTION$;"QUANTITY";CVI(FILE.QUANTITY$);TAB(50);
                    "REORDER LEVEL";CVI(FILE.REORDER.POINT$)
```

```
1390 NEXT I
1400 RETURN
1410 '****************************
1420 '* OBTAIN THE ITEM NUMBER *
1430 '****************************
1440 PRINT:INPUT "ITEM NUMBER";ITEM%
1450 IF (ITEM% < 1) OR (ITEM% > 100) THEN PRINT "BAD PART NUMBER":GOTO 1440
               ELSE GET #1,ITEM%:RETURN
1460 '************************
1470 '* INITIALIZE THE FILE *
1480 '************************
1490 PRINT "ARE YOU SURE (Y/N)? ";
1500 Z$ = INKEY$:IF Z$ = "" THEN 1500
1510 PRINT Z$
1520 IF Z$ < > "Y" THEN RETURN
1530 LSET FLAG$ = CHR$(255)
1540 FOR I = 1 TO 100
1550    PUT #1,I
1560 NEXT I
1570 RETURN
1580 '*******************************
1590 '* PRINT THE INVENTORY FILE *
1600 '*******************************
1610 CLS
1620 PRINT:PRINT TAB(30);"CAMP SLEAZY QUARTERMASTER"
1630 LPRINT:LPRINT TAB(30);"CAMP SLEAZY QUARTERMASTER"
1640 PRINT STRING$(79,220)
1650 PRINT
1660 LPRINT STRING$(79,220)
1670 LPRINT
1680 PRINT:PRINT TAB(33);"INVENTORY FILE LIST"
1690 PRINT STRING$(79,220)
1700 PRINT
1710 LPRINT:LPRINT TAB(33);"INVENTORY FILE LIST"
1720 LPRINT STRING$(79,220)
1730 LPRINT
1740 FOR I = 1 TO 100
1750    GET #1,I
1760    IF FLAG$ = CHR$(255) THEN 1950
1770    PRINT USING "ITEM NUMBER ###";I
1780    LPRINT USING "ITEM NUMBER ###";I
1790    PRINT
1800    LPRINT
1810    PRINT TAB(5);"ITEM: ";FILE.DESCRIPTION$
1820    LPRINT TAB(5);"ITEM: ";FILE.DESCRIPTION$
1830    PRINT
1840    LPRINT
1850    PRINT TAB(5);"";:PRINT USING "QUANTITY ON HAND #####";
               CVI(FILE.QUANTITY$)
1860    LPRINT TAB(5);"";:LPRINT USING "QUANTITY ON HAND #####";
               CVI(FILE.QUANTITY$)
1870    PRINT TAB(5);"";:PRINT USING "REORDER LEVEL    #####";
               CVI(FILE.REORDER.POINT$)
1880    LPRINT TAB(5);"";:LPRINT USING "REORDER LEVEL    #####";
               CVI(FILE.REORDER.POINT$)
1890    PRINT TAB(5);"";:PRINT USING "UNIT PRICE     $$##.##";
               CVS(FILE.UNIT.PRICE$)
1900    LPRINT TAB(5);"";:LPRINT USING "UNIT PRICE     $$##.##";
               CVS(FILE.UNIT.PRICE$)
1910    PRINT TAB(5);"";:PRINT "BIN LOCATION:     ";FILE.BIN.LOCATION$
1920    LPRINT TAB(5);"";:LPRINT "BIN LOCATION:     ";FILE.BIN.LOCATION$
1930    PRINT
1940    LPRINT
1950 NEXT I
1960 LPRINT CHR$(12)
1970 RETURN
1980 '************************
1990 '* END THE APPLICATION *
2000 '************************
2010 CLOSE:END
```

The handling of responses to the opening menu are well worth examining. Look at statements 260 through 410. You'll note that we have structured the evaluation of the response to accept either upper- or lower-case response. As stated before, when you first turn the PC on, you are automatically in lower-case. You must consciously press the capital shift key to get into upper-case. If you fail to do that, a perfectly valid lower-case response might be rejected. This program demonstrates this possibility, and when you list some of the demonstration programs supplied by IBM, you'll find the same to be true of them. Unfortunately, there is no way to perform an alphabetic shift inside the program in the same manner as KEY OFF affords. This is not to say that we couldn't develop a routine to convert the ASCII of lower-case response to the ASCII of upper-case response. We certainly could do that, but it would not change the display *as entered*. That's just one of the many things you'll learn as you work with the PC.

Permit the sharing of one other annoying thing. Unlike in COBOL, which is an English language programming language, references to BASIC statements are by line number, not by symbolic label. This means that if you choose to remove a line in BASIC, it disappears. If another instruction references that line, however, you'll be able to find the line only when you use that instruction. One way for this to happen is to execute the statement. To do so is usually OK since no harm is done. It will merely hang the program with an error message. The other way, and the most frustrating of all, is to use the RENUM operation. The RENUM operation will advise you that there is an unreferenced address in a statement number. When you call up that statement number with an EDIT or LIST, the unreferenced address is nowhere to be seen. What has happened is that the statement number displayed is from the program as it was *before* the renumbering was done. Because it's a hardware and not a software feature, there is no place else to store the program while it is being renumbered. The renumbering therefore proceeds, and the unreferenced line number becomes quite difficult to find. That's when you learn to make frequent lists of your program so that you will have something to which you may refer.

A couple of other discoveries may prove useful. If you haven't yet tried a trace (TRON and TROFF), try one now. It will destroy whatever you have on the screen, but it is extremely useful when you cannot find why a misfiring program is doing what it is doing. The simplest way is to include the command in your program. You can certainly use the function keys, but you must be in command mode when you do so. Thus, you can't arbitrarily turn the trace on when you think of it, particularly if the program is resting at an INPUT statement waiting for an answer. Next you'll learn that the trace appears only on the screen. It's sometimes nice to get it on paper so that you can study what has happened without ruining your eyes. There are two ways to do so. You can interrupt the trace (Ctrl/Scr Lock) and the print the screen (Capital Shift/PrtSc), or you can see to it that whatever appears on the screen gets to the printer merely by pressing (Ctrl/PrtSc). Just be certain to repeat the process to turn the trace off. This feature is also very useful when you are in DOS mode and want to TYPE the contents of a file.

SUMMARY

There aren't very many instructions left (non-COLOR-oriented instructions, that is), but we can add these to our list:

I/O Statements

LSET	Left justifies a string in a field (used for disk).
RSET	Right justifies a string in a field (used for disk).
FIELD	Defines fields in the random buffer.
GET	Reads a record from a random file (usually disk).
PUT	Writes a record to a random file (usually disk).
LINE INPUT	Used to accept data from keyboard, or from media without regard for punctuation. In this manner, commas can be given to the program within a data field, whereas with the INPUT statement, a comma would terminate the input (even though there is more input given), returning an "extra ignored" statement for the balance of the input.

The following instructions are not used in this book but may prove useful to you in non-COLOR applications. Some of them will be useful to anyone who knows his way around the machine's assembler language:

Commands

BLOAD	Loads binary data (a machine language program) into memory. As more entrepreneurs develop more proprietary software for this machine, some of it will be developed in assembler, and this will be the command necessary to load it.
BSAVE	If you do get into assembler, this command will store your binary data onto disk. It will give you unpredictable results from BASIC.

CONT   This command is also executed by a function key. It is used when you have inserted a STOP command in the program and want to get things going again.

COM   Someday you will be able to initiate a message (ON), terminate a message (OFF), or cease communications activity (STOP) with this instruction. Not yet.

CRSLIN This command will return the line on which the cursor is located. It is very useful for sophisticated light pen and editing functions.

DEF SEG With some knowledge of the assembler language, you can determine what is where and place a DEFinition upon it.

DEF USR Again, with assembler knowledge, a programmer can incorporate machine language subroutines in a BASIC program. Such routines frequently speed up execution but are really valid only for speeding up graphics, protecting software, etc.

ERROR   Most of the error trapping we do in this book is of the software type. Machine errors become important only when there is a possibility that they might occur. One such example is when you are deeply involved in a complex program, go to read the file, and find that it isn't there. To reset the program and to find and load the file means that all the processing up to that point must be redone. More sophisticated users will include traps for hardware errors. One of the problems with hardware errors is that they are difficult to simulate. ERROR allows you to simulate the number (discussed previously) of the error you are tracking down.

HEX$ Converts a decimal number to a hexadecimal (base 16) *alphabetic* string. It is great for debugging assembler-language subroutines.

INP   This command, the opposite of OUT, is used to INPut data from a port and is customarily employed in communications-oriented devices.

INSTR   This is the "in-string" function and is useful for a technique called *parsing*. Parsing is simply the process of isolating (identifying) a group of characters from a larger string, but you need to know what you're looking for.

LOC

If you do much sophisticated disk work, this command will become invaluable. It will return the next record number of a random file, the number of sectors read or written for a sequential file, or the number of characters in the communication buffer. This book's approach has been to do all work in arrays — an approach that you will find to be consistently successful.

LOF

Tells you how many bytes are in a file (in multiples of 128) or the number of free bytes in the communication buffer. People who use it are usually very knowledgeable about the machine.

LPOS

Returns the carriage position of the printer and will allow you to shift character sizes on the basis of the received string.

MOTOR

This command turns the cassette on and off. It can be used when data is read, when programs are merged, and so on, but it is usually not necessary for these purposes, particularly if the programmer keeps strict tabs on what he's doing. One interesting way it could be used would be to turn the cassette on and off during an audio-visual educational exercise. In this case, however, gaps between the audio recording must permit enough leeway to allow internal timing, since there would be no data flow to the machine and no way to sense whether spoken messages were complete.

OCT$

Converts a decimal number to an octal (base 8) *alphabetic* string. It is important if you find you must communicate with an octally based machine.

ON COM

This command is called an *enable trap* for communications. Along with several other communications-based instructions, it may prove useful.

ON KEY

Although the function keys are pre-set, their functions can be changed. If your program were run from the function keys instead of from responses the menu, this instruction would be useful.

ON PEN

The PC has routines to employ light pens that can reference screen data by touching the screen, rather than the operator's responding by key. Since it is possible to determine the location of any point on the screen, the light pen can easily be used for drawing lines.

ON STRIG	Why STRIG means *joystick* is not known, but a joystick is a game paddle that IBM doesn't supply with the PC. One can be obtained from Atari or Radio Shack or some other source to move your space ship to attack Klingons. There won't be too many Klingons in offices where the PC is employed.
OPEN "COM ...	Opens a communications file.
OUT	Is used to send data to an output port, such as a serial printer.
PEN ON/OFF STOP	Self-explanatory.
PEEK	Reads what is located at a known memory location. You must know some machine language and machine architecture to use this command. A great deal of what other micros must use PEEK for (and the associated POKE, below) is included in the standard functions of the PC.
PEN	Read the light pen.
POKE	Allows writing to a known memory location.
POS	Returns the column position of the cursor.
SCREEN	We have discussed screen option available to the monochrome display before. This command will do some of the same things and will also allow use of the PAGE keys you see on the numeric keypad. If you become involved with color or word processing, it may have some value.
SPC	Works just like SPACE$(n), but it is used, however, only in PRINT or LPRINT statements.
STICK	Returns the coordinates of the joystick.
STRIG	Gives the state of the joystick.
STRIG ON/OFf	Enables/disables the joystick.
USR	Is used to call machine language subroutines, a function also possible with the CALL command.
VARPTR	If you wish to write a sophisticated machine-language routine to provide a cross reference list of all variables, please do so. One doesn't exist as of this writing. But

if you do, you must use the **VARPTR** instruction since it tells you where the variables are located. Finding out *what* variables exist so that you can find out where they are is something else indeed. This instruction also returns the address of the file control block for the specified file.

WAIT

A communications command that enables an interruption by a communication line or item of hardware connected to an output port.

WEND

WEND closes the following loop.

WHILE

A WHILE . . . WEND loop is the frame equivalent of a FOR . . . NEXT loop except that it is used to control the entire process so long as a given expression is true. Such an expression could mean that a condition is true until the end-of-file is reached on some input data file.

WRITE

You can speed up the display process if you know everything you intend to display and display the entire screen at one time. This command is also useful when sending blocks of data to a file.

7
A Small Business System

We have now reached the point at which this book was designed to arrive. The PC is basically a business machine, any way you look at it. Already advertisements are appearing to attract people to use the PC in business establishments. You may rest assured that businesses are not seeking to hire PC programmers for their abilities to kill Klingons in the office environment.

Here's something else that's quite interesting – the early statistics, at least, indicate that more monochrome displays than color displays are being sold. For this reason, IBM has not come into the marketplace with its own color monitor. The monochrome display is a Japanese monitor designed to integrate to the system. In like manner, the PC begins its life in Boca Raton, FL, as a 48K one-disk system. You cannot (as yet) purchase light pens, game paddles, or cassettes with the system. The facility is there to use all three, but even the cassette cable must be fabricated at a retail output. The Computerland outlets are a known supplier, but it is not known whether Sears, IBM, and other outlets are yet in stock.

Insofar as PC technique is concerned, most of it has been already surveyed. There are a few new things in this chapter, but its major purpose is to walk you through the development of a small business system.

The system that we will consider is not a simple one. It has aspects that will make you think differently about your business and about how you may wish to employ a computer to support it. Furthermore, no two businesses are exactly alike because they have differing needs for information. The system presented here, then, is only the skeletal structure of what yours should be. Therefore, as we dissect each piece, we will take note of where the program(s) can serve your purposes and where they should be modified for a closer fit.

Our system consists of eleven major building blocks, some of which have several component building blocks. The major blocks are as follows:

BUSINESS.BAS   This is the frame program – the one that operates the menu which provides access to the other blocks of

the system. It is *the one* place where the name of the organization is placed. That name is then carried throughout the entire system.

CHART.BAS   This program is used to build the chart of accounts. The chart of accounts is required essentially for income statement and balance sheet purposes but also serves as the repository of account types and titles as required by the accounts receivable operation. The feeds exist to do the same in the accounts payable operation. This file is used jointly with the account file discussed next.

VALUE.BAS   As the system is set up, there is an account file for every period to be considered. This account file is the one file whose name must be specified to the program. In order for it to work with the income statement and the balance sheet programs, values must be loaded into it. The important thing to remember is that this is a *small business* system and there-fore requires certain manual operations and interfaces. One of the things not built into it is an ability to combine account files over a long period. You may wish to develop such a program. More probably, other programs will be modified for multiple file input.

CUSTOMER.BAS If you are to have an accounts receivable system, then it is necessary to have a customer file. This pro-gram is used to develop a sequential customer file. For purposes of this book, only rudimentary infor-mation is designed into the system. You may wish to modify the system to gather more information about your customers.

VENDOR.BAS The accounts payable portion of the system is not a full-fledged A/P system, and for a very basic reason: The small business simply does not have enough accounts payable to have to worry about discount dates and automated generation of checks. However, in anticipation of such an activity, a vendor file has been established. Later, when you get into the accounts payable subsystem, you may wish to change the given approach to tie it to the vendor file in much the same manner as the accounts receivable applica-tion is tied to the customer file.

MAILLIST.BAS As the name implies, this program allows selection of either the customer file or the vendor file for the purposes of preparing mailing labels. The spacing worked into the program will fit popular-size labels.

PRODUCT.BAS The system includes a rudimentary inventory control mechanism. This file is used with accounts receivable invoices and statements. It might further be used should you wish to develop purchase order, inventory movement, and replenishment reports.

RECIVBLE.BAS The accounts receivable system is perhaps the most important of all to the small business. Therefore, the A/R subsystem of the small business system is quite extensive. This program provides three of the seven services incorporated in the system: Initial entry, addition of invoices and production of invoices. A

64K system was used to develop this subsystem. The reader with a smaller system will need to break this program down into its component parts and duplicate in several programs some of the commonly used routines. Details on that process will be included later on. The remaining four services called by this program include the production of A/R reports, the posting of account records, the production of monthly statements, and the aging of accounts.

PAYABLE.BAS

The accounts payable implemented here is *not* a complete accounts payable subsystem. Having been in a small business for many years, the author has found that the accounts payable features required by a larger company are not really relevant to the small business. What *is* relevant is the ability to control the cash *outflow*. For that reason, the accounts payable application as contained here is devoted entirely to checkbook entry (what a larger company would call the "purchases journal"), maintenance, reporting, and balancing.

INCOME.BAS

This program simply produces an income statement using the prestored totals from the account file selected and using the titles from the chart of accounts. As previously stated, the system is designed to accept one data file at a time. Changing it to accept others is not difficult.

BALANCE.BAS

This program produces the accompanying balance sheet. All considerations that are applicable to the income statement also apply here.

The interrelationship of these building blocks is shown in Fig. 7-1.

BUSINESS.BAS

The entire process begins with this program — BUSINESS.BAS — which is simply a 46 statement frame. If you will examine it now — the program immediately follows this discussion — what is to be said here will be far more meaningful.

First, the CLEAR statement is set up for 5,000 positions (bytes) of memory. This is sufficient, but if your memory size is constrained, you might give serious

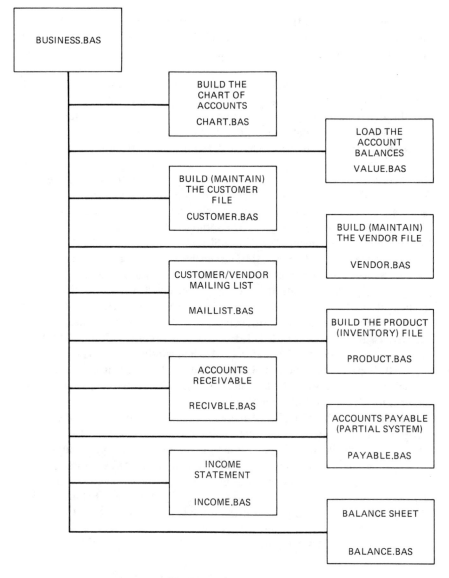

Fig. 7-1 Business System

consideration to reducing it. Much will depend upon the size of your customer and vendor files. If they are small, the value may be reduced.

Statement 30 turns off the function key display at the bottom of the screen, and then the variable COMPANY.NAME$ is established as COMMON. We've selected a very pertinent company name – SMALL BUSINESS ENTERPRISE, INC.

Look at statement 60. Since the screen is 80 characters wide, and since the length of COMPANY.NAME$ would be known, it's easy enough to determine the difference in the lengths, divide that by 2, and determine the starting point of the heading, as in statements 80 and 90. Thus, if you change COMPANY. NAME$ to ABC, it will be as centered as an odd-length heading on an even-length screen.

There are ten options plus a termination option. As the system is entirely integrated, the latter will be the only exit from the system, unless, of course, a program ceases to function or you purposely interrupt it. At statements 220 through 270, the response "X" will terminate the program.

Now look at statement 280. The ASCII value of the letter "A" is 65. The ON . . . GOTO of statement 300 must make the varying branch on the basis of a *numeric* value. It is therefore necessary to take the alphabetic response of A through J and transmute it to a number that will work with that variable (called PROGRAM). Therefore, if the letter "A" is the response, 65(A) less 64 will leave the result of 1, producing a branch to 320. The same is true for the letter "B" – a result of 2 – is letter "C" – a result of 3, etc. There is an error trap in statement 290 that will not allow anything less than 1 nor more than 10 to pass. Protection is also provided by the fact that there are but 10 branching addresses in 300. Statement 310 is an unnecessary instruction; it is entered for clarity and further protection – just in case.

In statements 320 through 410, there are CHAINs to carry you to the selected program. Again, statement 420 will undoubtedly never occur. It is not a bad idea to occasionally include an instruction whose necessity you doubt. In 20 years in the business, the author has learned that Murphy's Law is omnipresent. The idea of the CHAIN is that the selected program is drawn into memory, *replacing the program that CHAINed to it* – in this case, BUSINESS.BAS. All that will remain of BUSINESS.BAS until it is recalled will be the COMPANY. NAME$ – Small Business Enterprise, Inc.

Here is program BUSINESS.BAS:

```
10 CLS
20 CLEAR 5000
30 KEY OFF
40 COMMON COMPANY.NAME$
50 COMPANY.NAME$ = "SMALL BUSINESS ENTERPRISE, INC."
60 X = ((80 - LEN(COMPANY.NAME$)) / 2)
70 CLS
80 LOCATE 2,X
90 PRINT COMPANY.NAME$;
100 PRINT STRING$(79,220)
```

```
110 PRINT:PRINT TAB(20);"A.  CHART OF ACCOUNTS";
120 PRINT TAB(20);"B.  LOAD ACCOUNT BALANCES";
130 PRINT TAB(20);"C.  CREATE (MAINTAIN) CUSTOMER FILE";
140 PRINT TAB(20);"D.  CREATE (MAINTAIN) VENDOR FILE";
150 PRINT TAB(20);"E.  CUSTOMER/VENDOR MAILING LIST";
160 PRINT TAB(20);"F.  CREATE (MAINTAIN) PRODUCT (INVENTORY) FILE";
170 PRINT TAB(20);"G.  ACCOUNTS RECEIVABLE";
180 PRINT TAB(20);"H.  ACCOUNTS PAYABLE";
190 PRINT TAB(20);"I.  INCOME STATEMENT";
200 PRINT TAB(20);"J.  BALANCE SHEET";
210 LOCATE 25,1
220 PRINT "PRESS 'X' TO TERMINATE PROGRAM";
230 LOCATE 22,10
240 PRINT "SELECT: ";
250 Z$ = INKEY$:IF Z$ = "" THEN 250
260 PRINT Z$;
270 IF Z$ = "X" THEN END
280 PROGRAM = ASC(Z$) - 64
290 IF (PROGRAM < 1) OR (PROGRAM > 10) THEN 430
300 ON PROGRAM GOTO 320,330,340,350,360,370,380,390,400,410
310 GOTO 430
320 CHAIN "A:CHART.BAS"
330 CHAIN "A:VALUE.BAS"
340 CHAIN "A:CUSTOMER.BAS"
350 CHAIN "A:VENDOR.BAS"
360 CHAIN "A:MAILLIST.BAS"
370 CHAIN "A:PRODUCT.BAS"
380 CHAIN "A:RECIVBLE.BAS"
390 CHAIN "A:PAYABLE.BAS"
400 CHAIN "A:INCOME.BAS"
410 CHAIN "A:BALANCE.BAS"
420 GOTO 10
430 BEEP
440 LOCATE 22,1
450 PRINT SPACE$(79);
460 GOTO 230
```

CHART.BAS

Since the entire system is built around the Chart of Accounts, that's where the process must begin. The user has the opportunity to enter one or more account types and titles using this program. They must fall within five distinct categories: Asset, Liability, Capital, Income, and Expense; it can be seen that these are the headings that will appear on the Income Statement and Balance Sheet. Like every system, there is a first time option and a second and subsequent time option. If you respond to the program that this is an entirely new file, you will build the file from scratch. It is built in memory and not written to disk until you state that you've entered all the data. Therefore, if you have inadvertently begun a new file when one already exists, you can either interrupt the process or replace the disk. Throughout this chapter the programs will contain both programs and data for the default drive, A. The reason for this is that some purchasers will obtain one-disk systems. However, if you have two drives, it might be wise to maintain your programs on drive A and the data files on drive B, thereby requiring some changes to the programs. In any event, *always copy critical data files* before *beginning any work on them.* It's very difficult to reconstruct old data since once it's been changed. The cost of a few extra diskettes is far less than the cost of the time necessary to correct a 10-second mistake.

The program will accept keyboard input from the keyboard only (when no file previously exists) or input from an existing file plus the keyboard. It then writes the initial file or updates the previous file and, of course, displays the results of its work.

A block diagram of the Chart of Accounts program is shown in Fig. 7-2. The program narrative is as follows: The program accepts input from the keyboard,

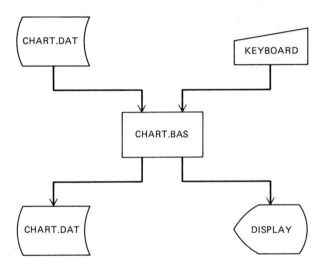

Fig. 7-2 Building the Chart of Accounts

or from the file and keyboard combined, and uses it to develop a new Chart of Accounts. Each account is coded with A (Asset), L (Liability), C (Capital), I (Income), or E (Expense) and is given an account title. These account titles will be used throughout the system and when income statements and balance sheets are prepared.

Before we show you the program, we should present its two major displays, as shown on the opposite page.

As usual, a little explanation is required. When you get to the complete program you will note that a paired INPUT statement is used but not a LINE INPUT. This means that titles must be devoid of punctuation. It also means that the program anticipates *two* responses before it can interpret the first one. Thus, the request for END,END is really a request for two operands. However, as for every good rule, there is an exception. Study the program and you'll find that it searches out only the first END and that the second could just as easily be satisfied by pressing the return key, only, however, *after* entering a

CHART OF ACCOUNT MAINTENANCE

```
ENTER THE ACCOUNTS IN THE FOLLOWING FORM (INCLUDE THE COMMA):
   ACCOUNT TYPE (ONE LETTER), ACCOUNT NAME (WITHOUT PUNCTUATION)

TYPES  A=ASSETS, L=LIABILITIES, C=CAPITAL, I=INCOME, E=EXPENSE
EXAMPLE INPUTS: A,CASH   OR   L,ACCOUNTS PAYABLE

ENTER INFORMATION NOW - TYPE 'END,END' TO TERMINATE INPUT
? A,CASH
? A,ACCOUNTS RECEIVABLE
? A,EQUIPMENT
? A,PREPAID INSURANCE
? A,ROLLING STOCK
? L,ACCOUNTS PAYABLE
? L,NOTES PAYABLE
? C,SBE DRAW
? I,SALES INCOME
? I,RENTAL INCOME
? I,ROYALTY INCOME
? E,RENT EXPENSE
? E,TELEPHONE EXPENSE
? E,TRAVEL EXPENSE
```

SMALL BUSINESS ENTERPRISE, INC.

CHART OF ACCOUNT MAINTENANCE

ACCOUNT #	TYPE	NAME
1	A	CASH
2	A	ACCOUNTS RECEIVABLE
3	A	EQUIPMENT
4	A	PREPAID INSURANCE
5	A	ROLLING STOCK
6	L	ACCOUNTS PAYABLE
7	L	NOTES PAYABLE
8	C	SBE DRAW
9	I	SALES INCOME
10	I	RENTAL INCOME
11	I	ROYALTY INCOME
12	E	RENT EXPENSE
13	E	TELEPHONE EXPENSE
14	E	TRAVEL EXPENSE

ARE THERE OTHER ACCOUNTS TO BE ADDED (Y/N)

comma. If you'll look back to the first of the previous pair of print-outs, you'll note that the data entered is preceded by a question mark. It is a feature of PC BASIC that the question mark may be suppressed. In this instance, we decided not to do so so that it would be perfectly obvious that an input was requested. The first response is one of the five codes A, L, C, I, or E. Those codes could be entered in any order.

In this example, fourteen accounts have been created. In a later program you will note that the number of accounts has grown to 15, as the program itself adds a new account, INTEREST INCOME. The Account Number given represents the record number of the account in the sequential file CHART.DAT.

That file exists as a part of internal program design and is written with the record that you see plus one additional record that precedes the whole thing — the first record, which contains the count of the records to follow. Thus, throughout this entire small business system, the disk files are sequential (they're not large enough to require random access), and they each have an initial record that specifies the number of records to follow. This arrangement is possible because all the work is done in arrays and the record count is known before the file is written. In some cases throughout this discussion you will note that the DIMensioning of the array used to handle the data will not take place at the beginning of the program but is delayed until the size of the file is known.

Here is the program CHART.BAS:

```
10 CLS
20 GOSUB 1360
30 '*********************************************************************
40 '* T$ HOLDS THE ACCOUNT TYPE; N$ HOLDS THE ACCOUNT NAME.  BS$ IS USED   *
50 '* TO DETERMINE THE SEQUENCE IN WHICH THE ACCOUNTS ARE WRITTEN TO DISK. *
60 '* THIS WILL BE IMPORTANT FOR THE CONSTRUCTION OF A BALANCE SHEET       *
70 '*********************************************************************
80 DIM T$(25),N$(25),BS$(5)
90 BS$(1) = "A"
100 BS$(2) = "L"
110 BS$(3) = "C"
120 BS$(4) = "I"
130 BS$(5) = "E"
140 '*********************************************************************
150 PRINT
160 PRINT
170 PRINT "WILL THE CHART OF ACCOUNTS BE ENTERED FROM THE FILE (Y/N) ";
180 Z$ = INKEY$:IF Z$ = "" THEN 180
190 PRINT Z$
200 IF Z$ < > "Y" THEN 230
210 GOSUB 1140
220 GOTO 500
230 '************************************
240 '* ENTER ACCOUNTS FROM THE KEYBOARD *
250 '************************************
260 PRINT
270 CLS
280 GOSUB 1360
290 PRINT "ENTER THE ACCOUNTS IN THE FOLLOWING FORM (INCLUDE THE COMMA): "
300 PRINT TAB(5);"ACCOUNT TYPE (ONE LETTER), ACCOUNT NAME (WITHOUT PUNCTUATION)
310 PRINT
320 PRINT "TYPES  A=ASSETS, L=LIABILITIES, C=CAPITAL, I=INCOME, E=EXPENSE"
330 PRINT "EXAMPLE INPUTS: A,CASH   OR   L,ACCOUNTS PAYABLE"
340 PRINT
350 PRINT "ENTER INFORMATION NOW - TYPE 'END,END' TO TERMINATE INPUT"
360 I = 1
370     T$(I)=""
380     INPUT T$(I),N$(I)
390     IF T$(I) = "END" THEN 480
400     IF T$(I) = "A" THEN 460
410     IF T$(I) = "L" THEN 460
420     IF T$(I) = "C" THEN 460
430     IF T$(I) = "I" THEN 460
440     IF T$(I) = "E" THEN 460
450     PRINT "ENTRY NOT ACCEPTABLE - REPEAT":GOTO 690
460     I = I + 1
470 GOTO 370
480 N = I - 1    'THIS COUNT WILL BE WRITTEN AS THE FIRST RECORD ON THE DISK
490 '****************************
500 '* PRINT THE ACCOUNT NAMES *
510 '****************************
```

```
520 CLS
530 GOSUB 1360
540 PRINT
550 PRINT " ACCOUNT #      TYPE          NAME"
560 FOR I = 1 TO N
570     PRINT I;TAB(17);T$(I);TAB(23);N$(I)
580 NEXT I
590 '************************
600 '* ADDING NEW ACCOUNTS *
610 '************************
620 PRINT
630 PRINT "ARE THERE OTHER ACCOUNTS TO BE ADDED (Y/N) ";
640 Z$ = INKEY$:IF Z$ = "" THEN 640
650 PRINT Z$
660 IF Z$ < > "Y" THEN 820
670 PRINT "ENTER NEW ACCOUNTS - TYPE 'END,END' WHEN FINISHED"
680 N = N + 1
690 T$(N) = " "
700 INPUT T$(N),N$(N)
710 IF T$(N) = "END" THEN 790
720     IF T$(N) = "A" THEN 780
730     IF T$(N) = "L" THEN 780
740     IF T$(N) = "C" THEN 780
750     IF T$(N) = "I" THEN 780
760     IF T$(N) = "E" THEN 780
770     PRINT "ENTRY NOT ACCEPTABLE - REPEAT":GOTO 690
780 GOTO 680
790 N = N - 1     'THIS COUNT WILL BE WRITTEN AS THE FIRST RECORD ON THE DISK
800 GOTO 500
810 '******************************
820 '* CHANGING EXISTING ACCOUNTS *
830 '******************************
840 PRINT "ARE THERE ANY ITEMS TO CHANGE (Y/N)? ";
850 Z$ = INKEY$:IF Z$ = "" THEN 850
860 PRINT Z$
870 IF Z$ < > "Y" THEN 1000
880 PRINT "ENTER THE ACCOUNT # TO BE CHANGED FOLLOWED BY (COMMA),"
890 PRINT " THE NEW TYPE (COMMA), THE ACCOUNT NAME"
900 INPUT Z,T$(Z),N$(Z)
910 CLS
920 GOSUB 1360
930 PRINT
940 PRINT " #      TYPE          NAME"
950 FOR I = 1 TO N
960     PRINT I;TAB(9);T$(I);TAB(15);N$(I)
970 NEXT I
980 GOTO 840
990 '************************
1000 '* SAVING ARRAY IN FILE *
1010 '************************
1020 FILE.NAME$ = "CHART.DAT"
1030 GOSUB 1250
1040 '************************
1050 '* PROGRAM TERMINATION *
1060 '************************
1070 PRINT
1080 PRINT
1090 PRINT "CHART OF ACCOUNTS IS COMPLETE"
1100 CHAIN "A:BUSINESS.BAS"
1110 '************************
1120 '* SUBROUTINES FOLLOW *
1130 '**************************
1140 '* OPEN AND INPUT NAME FILE *
1150 '**************************
1160 FILE.NAME$ = "CHART.DAT"
1170 OPEN "I",1,FILE.NAME$
1180 INPUT #1,N  'OBTAIN THE RECORD COUNT PREVIOUSLY STORED
1190 FOR I = 1 TO N
1200     INPUT #1,T$(I),N$(I)
1210 NEXT I
1220 CLOSE 1
```

```
1230 RETURN
1240 '****************************
1250 '* OPEN AND WRITE TO FILE *
1260 '****************************
1270 OPEN "O",2,FILE.NAME$
1280 PRINT #2,N            'WRITE THE RECORD COUNT
1290 FOR J = 1 TO 5
1300     FOR I = 1 TO N
1310         IF BS$(J) = T$(I) THEN PRINT #2,T$(I);",";N$(I)
1320     NEXT I
1330 NEXT J
1340 CLOSE 2
1350 RETURN
1360 '*********************************
1370 '* HEADING USED FOR THE DISPLAY *
1380 '*********************************
1390 X = ((80 - LEN(COMPANY.NAME$)) / 2)
1400 LOCATE 2,X
1410 PRINT COMPANY.NAME$
1420 PRINT STRING$(79,220):PRINT
1430 PRINT TAB(27);"CHART OF ACCOUNT MAINTENANCE"
1440 PRINT STRING$(79,220)
1450 RETURN
```

In this program, there are three tables: T$, which will permit up to 25 account codes; N$, which will permit up to 25 account names; and B$, which will hold the five acceptable code types loaded in statements 90 through 130.

Examine the routine from 360 through 470. You'll note that it *looks* like a traditional FOR . . . NEXT loop, and it is — almost. Because we knew that T$ was DIMensioned at 25, we could have used a 1 to 25 FOR . . . NEXT loop. Suppose, however, that you wish to have 37 accounts? Two methods are possible. The FOR . . . NEXT loop can be established as a number larger than would ever be possible, as we do in a later program, or it can be established merely linearly, with I being set initially at 1 (statement 360) and then being incremented with each iteration of the loop (460). (*Iteration* is a computerese term that simply means a movement through the loop.) When the last entry has been made and the END is received, the count (less 1, as it will have been incremented too far) is stored in the variable N to permit it to be used later.

Some mention must be made of the one-letter variables that find their way into common use. Such variables as Z$, Z, N, I, J, K, L, etc., are frequently used by programmers as *work variables*. By themselves, the variables have no specific meaning, such as a variable like COMPANY.NAME$ would. There are times, however, when a utility variable is required as a means to count. Generally in this programming, the variable I is used for *I*ndexing through an array. Where there are more than one array in concurrent or simultaneous use, the variables J, K, etc., will be used. In a later program discussion we will show you how to compress the contents of an array while indexing through the *source* array with one variable and through the *destination* array with a second. Interestingly enough, we'll find that we're using the same array.

At this point, the variable N contains the size of the loaded arrays. This value then becomes the maximum to which any further work on the arrays will range. In this application, when a file is read into the program and records are added to the end, it becomes necessary to go beyond. Now, a word of caution: Look through the program and you will see that the file reading routine at statements 1130-1230 reads the size of the record at 1180 and then reads *that many* records in the loop 1190-1210. The variable N here has the same use as the variable N in statement 480. In later programs we will substitute a name for N — xxxx.FILE.SIZE, with a name replacing xxxx.

There is an interesting concept in statement 1310. Statement 1310 says that if the entry to the array contains one of the codes in array B$, then it may be written to the file. Although protection is provided the entry process in statements 720 through 760, if for some reason that protection is changed, only the values loaded into B$ may be used. The routine from statements 1290 to 1350 demonstrates the two-variable concept for array positioning. (In this instance, variable J is used to move through the five-position array B$ while variable I moves through the range of 1 to N, previously discussed).

VALUE.BAS

The Chart of Accounts is nothing more than a pattern to be used for corresponding data on one or more account files. It's important to note that both the Chart of Accounts file and the account files (which could more properly be called *account value files*) are in the same configuration *as far as the account value file goes.* As mentioned before, the Chart of Accounts file has 14 records. Thus, it's possible that you will develop data on 14 accounts for several months before you suddenly discover that a new one is needed. From that point on, 15 accounts will be required, *but the first 14 will always be the same.* Thus, you can see that it's not very good business to change the sequence of accounts in the Chart of Accounts once the process has begun. It's not important what sequence the Chart of Accounts is in originally. When the Income Statement and the Balance Sheet are developed, they'll be in the proper sequence.

The block diagram in Fig. 7-3 summarizes the capabilities of the file load we call VALUE.BAS. This program passes the Chart of Accounts file for the purpose of developing an account file with balances that correspond to the accounts listed in the chart. This function will be particularly useful when the INCOME statement and BALANCE sheet are prepared. The name of the output file must first be specified from the keyboard (*), will be combined with ".DAT" within the program, and will then produce a file that will be used in the referenced runs and also with the Accounts Receivable subsystem.

The chart file is read and loaded into arrays T$ and N$. Then, one by one, they are passed upon the screen, and the operator is asked to give a value to them. In practice, the opening balances should be where your accountant says they should be. Since there is no transition from period to period (e.g., month or quarter), then the final balances of one period become the opening balances of

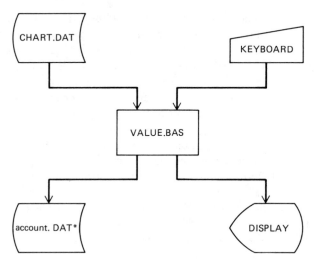

Fig. 7-3 Loading an Account File

the new period. You can accomplish this with either a value load or with a DISKCOPY operation in DOS, changing the name. Thus, if the present file is MAY82.DAT, you need only copy it to JUN82.DAT to have a new file with which to begin the new period — in this case, a month.

Using this application, changes may be made to existing codes and account titles, and, of course, the amounts are added to the array. Then, when the process is complete, you are asked for the *stub* of the file name. It is the convention of this system that program names are suffixed with .BAS and data files are suffixed with .DAT. In any event, you are asked for the stub in statement 440, and then the *program* combines it with .DAT.

Here is the program VALUE.BAS:

```
10 CLS
20 GOSUB 800
30 '**************************************************************************
40 '* T$ HOLDS THE ACCOUNT TYPE; N$ HOLDS THE ACCOUNT NAME.  A IS USED     *
50 '* TO STORE THE BALANCE OF THE ACCOUNTS WHICH HAVE BEEN ENTERED BY THE  *
60 '* PROGRAM CHART.BAS.                                                   *
70 '**************************************************************************
80 DIM T$(25),N$(25),A(25)
90 PRINT
100 GOSUB 580
110 PRINT "ENTER AMOUNTS FOR THE ACCOUNTS SHOWN"
120 PRINT
130 FOR I = 1 TO N
140     PRINT T$(I),N$(I),"$";
150     INPUT "",A(I)
160 NEXT I
```

```
170 '**********************
180 '* PRINT THE RESULTS *
190 '**********************
200 GOSUB 800
210 PRINT
220 PRINT "ACCOUNT #";TAB(15);"ACCOUNT TYPE";TAB(30);
230 PRINT "ACCOUNT TITLE";TAB(55);"AMOUNT"
240 PRINT
250 FOR I = 1 TO N
260     PRINT I;TAB(20);T$(I);TAB(30);N$(I);TAB(55);A(I)
270 NEXT I
280 PRINT
290 '******************************
300 '* CHANGING EXISTING ACCOUNTS *
310 '******************************
320 PRINT
330 PRINT "ARE THERE ANY ITEMS TO CHANGE (Y/N)? ";
340 Z$ = INKEY$:IF Z$ = "" THEN 340
350 PRINT Z$
360 IF Z$ < > "Y" THEN 410
370 PRINT "ENTER THE ACCOUNT # TO BE CHANGED FOLLOWED BY (COMMA AND)";
380 PRINT " THE NEW AMOUNT"
390 INPUT Z,A(Z)
400 GOTO 170
410 '**************************
420 '* SAVING ARRAY IN FILE *
430 '**************************
440 PRINT "ENTER THE FILE NAME FOR THIS DATA (I WILL COMBINE WITH .DAT)";
450 INPUT FILE.NAME$
460 FILE.NAME$ = FILE.NAME$ + ".DAT"
470 GOSUB 690
480 '**************************
490 '* PROGRAM TERMINATION *
500 '**************************
510 PRINT
520 PRINT
530 PRINT "LOADING OF ACCOUNT VALUES IS COMPLETE"
540 CHAIN "A:BUSINESS.BAS"
550 '**********************
560 '* SUBROUTINES FOLLOW *
570 '**************************
580 '* OPEN AND INPUT NAME FILE *
590 '**************************
600 FILE.NAME$ = "CHART.DAT"
610 OPEN "I",1,FILE.NAME$
620 INPUT #1,N  'OBTAIN THE RECORD COUNT PREVIOUSLY STORED
630 FOR I = 1 TO N
640     INPUT #1,T$(I),N$(I)
650 NEXT I
660 CLOSE 1
670 RETURN
680 '**************************
690 '* OPEN AND WRITE TO FILE *
700 '**************************
710 OPEN "O",2,FILE.NAME$
720 PRINT #2,N          'WRITE THE RECORD COUNT
740 FOR I = 1 TO N
750     PRINT #2,A(I)
760 NEXT I
780 CLOSE 2
790 RETURN
800 '******************************
810 '* HEADING USED FOR THE DISPLAY *
820 '******************************
830 CLS
840 X = ((80 - LEN(COMPANY.NAME$)) / 2)
850 LOCATE 2,X
860 PRINT COMPANY.NAME$
870 PRINT STRING$(79,220):PRINT
880 PRINT TAB(28);"ACCOUNT BALANCE DATA ENTRY"
890 PRINT STRING$(79,220)
900 RETURN
```

CUSTOMER.BAS

A small business has a customer list — particularly if it is in the business of selling something, which makes it, by definition, a business. Such a list ordinarily proves to be extremely useful. In the small business sytstem presented here, it's essential, because without it the accounts receivable subsystem cannot function. If you have a small number of customers, the list may be very informal, and the PC, and this book, will probably not mean very much to you.

There are many ways to develop a customer list. The most expeditious is to use a devoted application to develop and maintain a customer list, which may then be used in other applications. Our particular application allows for initial development of the file, additions to the file, and changes to the file. It does not allow for the removal of a customer from the file as it's currently constituted. There are a couple of reasons for this omission, the chief one being that since a small business needs all the customers it can get, it seldom gives up on any client. This application also stores the names onto a file that will be used later for mail list purposes.

A block diagram for building and maintaining the customer file is shown in Figure 7-4. The program accepts input from the keyboard, or from the file and keyboard combined, and uses it to develop a Customer Master File. This Customer Master File is used in several other places in the system, specifically in the Accounts Receivable subsystem. A list of customers and pertinent data may be obtained. You may wish to augment the customer file with other pertinent data.

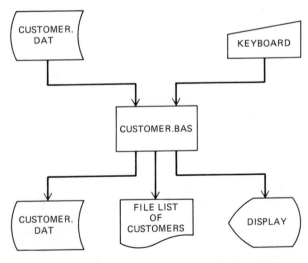

Fig. 7-4 Building and Maintaining the Customer File

The opening message of the program is extremely important. If you respond that the file has never been built before, the program will create a new file with the same name. So long as you are entering information from the keyboard, you need not be concerned about interruption or changing the disk. When input is terminated, however, the new file is written. As in the other examples, the data is handled through arrays.

When the file already exists, the proper response will cause the current CUSTOMER.DAT to be read to memory; additions are made by increasing the length of the array. For safety's sake, the file size and array sizes are reserved at 1,000 bytes each, even though that much space may not be needed. In this particular program, 1,000 bytes are set aside. In a later application, the DIMensioning is done as a function of the file size *plus* 1,000 bytes. Both approaches work well and are illustrated to show you the variety possible.

Observe the FOR . . . NEXT loop at statements 220-290. In this instance, we have asked for a name, four lines of address, and customer terms. Each of the items requested exists in its own array (as DIMensioned in the routine in statements 410-470). Only rudimentary information is asked for; there is no request for a telephone number or any other information. Moreover, the item customer terms is given as an alphabetic string, allowing text but not a numeric value. Furthermore, note that everything is done with INPUT rather than with LINE INPUT. If you should wish to imbed commas anywhere, it will be necessary to change INPUT to LINE INPUT. If you wish to use customer terms as a calculation variable (this system uses a fixed 1 1/2% factor), then you must change the customer terms variable and build it into your programs. Note that once a file is built, the LINE INPUT feature is used. The explanation for the seeming inconsistency is that it protects you should you choose to add programs to the system that will produce changes to, or input for, the customer file.

This application, as programmed, allows for the listing of the file. The system is currently programmed to print four customer records per page of printed out-put, the printed out-put looking as follows:

```
RECORD NUMBER:    1

CUSTOMER NAME:       SEARS
CUSTOMER ADDRESS:    SEARSLAND
                     100 LUNENBERG PARKWAY
                     LEOMINSTER,
                     MASSACHUSETTS 01377
CUSTOMER TERMS:      CASH


-----------------------------------------------------------------------


RECORD NUMBER:    2

CUSTOMER NAME:       MASSACHUSETTS ELECTRIC
CUSTOMER ADDRESS:    95 MECHANIC STREET
                     GARDNER,
                     MASSACHUSETTS 01440
```

```
CUSTOMER TERMS:     NET 30 DAYS


-----------------------------------------------------------------------------


RECORD NUMBER:   3

CUSTOMER•NAME:      GIRARD CONSTRUCTION COMPANY
CUSTOMER·ADDRESS:   35 GOODRICH STREET
                    WINCHENDON,
                    MASSACHUSETTS 01475

CUSTOMER TERMS:     1.5% ON UNPAID BALANCE


-----------------------------------------------------------------------------
```

Here is the program CUSTOMER.BAS:

```
10 GOSUB 2120
20 ARRAY.SIZE = 1000
30 FILE.SIZE = 1000
40 GOSUB 410
50 BASE = 1
60 PRINT
70 PRINT "TWO FORMS OF INPUT ARE POSSIBLE IN THIS PROGRAM: INPUT FROM EITHER"
80 PRINT "DISK OR THE KEYBOARD.  IF YOU CHOOSE NOT TO OBTAIN THE INPUT FROM"
90 PRINT "THE DISK, THE PROGRAM WILL ASSUME THAT YOU WISH TO ENTER FROM THE"
100 PRINT "KEYBOARD, DESTROYING ANY DISK FILE.  IF YOU WISH TO ADD TO THE FILE"
110 PRINT "WHICH ALREADY EXISTS, YOU MUST ANSWER 'Y' TO THIS QUESTION:"
120 PRINT:PRINT "WILL INPUT BE FROM THE DISK FILE (Y/N)? ";
130 Z$ = INKEY$:IF Z$ = "" THEN 130
140 PRINT Z$
150 IF Z$ < > "Y" THEN 530
160 '*****************************
170 '* OPEN AND INPUT NAME FILE *
180 '*****************************
190 FILE.NAME$ = "CUSTOMER.DAT"
200 OPEN "I",1,FILE.NAME$
210 INPUT #1,FILE.SIZE        'OBTAIN THE RECORD COUNT PREVIOUSLY STORED
220 FOR I = 1 TO FILE.SIZE
230      INPUT #1,CUSTOMER.NAME$(I)
240      INPUT #1,CUSTOMER.ADDR.1$(I)
250      INPUT #1,CUSTOMER.ADDR.2$(I)
260      INPUT #1,CUSTOMER.ADDR.3$(I)
270      INPUT #1,CUSTOMER.ADDR.4$(I)
280      INPUT #1,CUSTOMER.TERMS$(I)
290 NEXT I
300 RECORD.COUNT = I - 1
310 CLOSE 1
320 PRINT:PRINT "WILL THERE BE ADDITIONS TO THE FILE (Y/N)? ";
330 Z$ = INKEY$:IF Z$ = "" THEN 330
340 PRINT Z$
350 IF Z$ < > "Y" THEN 830
360 BASE = I
370 GOTO 530
380 '*********************************************************************
390 '* THE DIMENSIONING IS ESTABLISHED AS A THOUSAND RECORDS. *
400 '*********************************************************************
410 DIM CUSTOMER.NAME$(ARRAY.SIZE)
420 DIM CUSTOMER.ADDR.1$(ARRAY.SIZE)
430 DIM CUSTOMER.ADDR.2$(ARRAY.SIZE)
440 DIM CUSTOMER.ADDR.3$(ARRAY.SIZE)
450 DIM CUSTOMER.ADDR.4$(ARRAY.SIZE)
460 DIM CUSTOMER.TERMS$(ARRAY.SIZE)
470 RETURN
```

```
480 '*************************************************************
490 '* THIS IS THE ROUTINE TO ACCEPT TOTAL INPUT OF THE FILE FROM  *
500 '* THE KEYBOARD.  IT IS NOT THE ROUTINE TO ADD TO AN EXISTING  *
510 '* FILE.  FILE SIZE IS DEFAULTED TO 1000 RECORDS MAXIMUM.      *
520 '*************************************************************
530 FOR I = BASE TO ARRAY.SIZE
540     GOSUB 2120
550     PRINT
560     PRINT "ENTER 'END' UNDER CUSTOMER NAME TO TERMINATE ENTRY."
570     PRINT
580     LINE INPUT "CUSTOMER NAME:            ";CUSTOMER.NAME$(I)
590     IF (CUSTOMER.NAME$(I) = "END") AND RECORD.COUNT < 1 THEN 690
600     IF CUSTOMER.NAME$(I) = "END" THEN 760
610     LINE INPUT "CUSTOMER ADDRESS LINE 1:   ";CUSTOMER.ADDR.1$(I)
620     LINE INPUT "CUSTOMER ADDRESS LINE 2:   ";CUSTOMER.ADDR.2$(I)
630     LINE INPUT "CUSTOMER ADDRESS LINE 3:   ";CUSTOMER.ADDR.3$(I)
640     LINE INPUT "CUSTOMER ADDRESS LINE 4:   ";CUSTOMER.ADDR.4$(I)
650     INPUT "CUSTOMER TERMS:            ",CUSTOMER.TERMS$(I)
660     PRINT:PRINT "ACCEPTABLE (Y/N)? "
670     Z$ = INKEY$:IF Z$ = "" THEN 670
680     IF Z$ = "Y" THEN 740
690     LOCATE 25,1
700     PRINT "ENTRY REJECTED";
710     BEEP
720     FOR Z = 1 TO 1000:NEXT Z
730     GOTO 540
740 RECORD.COUNT = RECORD.COUNT + 1
750 NEXT I
760 FILE.SIZE = I - 1
770 GOSUB 1980            'ROUTINE TO WRITE THE FILE
780 '*************************************************************
790 '* THE FILE IS WRITTEN AND CLOSED.  IT MUST BE OPENED AGAIN IF *
800 '* THE USER DETERMINES TO GET A LISTING OF THE FILE EITHER IN  *
810 '* DISPLAY FORM ON IN HARDCOPY FORM.                          *
820 '*************************************************************
830 GOSUB 2120
840 FOUR.TO.A.PAGE = 0
850 PRINT:PRINT "DO YOU WISH TO SEE THE CONTENTS OF THE FILE (Y/N)? ";
860 Z$ = INKEY$:IF Z$ = "" THEN 860
870 PRINT Z$
880 IF Z$ < > "Y" THEN 1720
890 PRINT "DO YOU WISH A HARDCOPY OUTPUT (Y/N)? ";
900 Z$ = INKEY$:IF Z$ = "" THEN 900
910 PRINT Z$
920 IF Z$ < > "Y" THEN HARDCOPY$ = "NO":GOTO 940
930 HARDCOPY$ = "YES"
940 PRINT "UNINTERRUPTED PRINTING - 'N' CAUSES PAUSE WITH EACH - (Y/N)? ";
950 Z$ = INKEY$:IF Z$ = "" THEN 950
960 PRINT Z$
970 IF Z$ < > "Y" THEN CONTINUE$ = "NO":GOTO 990
980 CONTINUE$ = "YES"
990 FILE.NAME$ = "CUSTOMER.DAT"
1000 OPEN "I",1,FILE.NAME$
1010 INPUT #1,FILE.SIZE        'OBTAIN THE RECORD COUNT PREVIOUSLY STORED
1020 FOR I = 1 TO FILE.SIZE
1030     LINE INPUT #1,CUSTOMER.NAME$(I)
1040     LINE INPUT #1,CUSTOMER.ADDR.1$(I)
1050     LINE INPUT #1,CUSTOMER.ADDR.2$(I)
1060     LINE INPUT #1,CUSTOMER.ADDR.3$(I)
1070     LINE INPUT #1,CUSTOMER.ADDR.4$(I)
1080     LINE INPUT #1,CUSTOMER.TERMS$(I)
1090 NEXT I
1100 CLOSE 1
1110 FOR I = 1 TO FILE.SIZE
1120     IF CONTINUE$ = "YES" THEN 1140
1130     Z$ = INKEY$:IF Z$ = "" THEN 1130
1140     PRINT
1150     PRINT STRING$(79,"-")
1160     PRINT
```

```
1170      PRINT "RECORD NUMBER: ";I
1180      PRINT "CUSTOMER NAME:";TAB(20);CUSTOMER.NAME$(I)
1190      PRINT "CUSTOMER ADDRESS:";TAB(20);CUSTOMER.ADDR.1$(I)
1200      PRINT TAB(20);CUSTOMER.ADDR.2$(I)
1210      PRINT TAB(20);CUSTOMER.ADDR.3$(I)
1220      PRINT TAB(20);CUSTOMER.ADDR.4$(I)
1230      PRINT "CUSTOMER TERMS:";TAB(20);CUSTOMER.TERMS$(I)
1240      PRINT
1250      PRINT
1260      IF HARDCOPY$ = "NO" THEN 1420
1270      LPRINT "RECORD NUMBER: ";I
1280      LPRINT
1290      LPRINT "CUSTOMER NAME:";TAB(20);CUSTOMER.NAME$(I)
1300      LPRINT "CUSTOMER ADDRESS:";TAB(20);CUSTOMER.ADDR.1$(I)
1310      LPRINT TAB(20);CUSTOMER.ADDR.2$(I)
1320      LPRINT TAB(20);CUSTOMER.ADDR.3$(I)
1330      LPRINT TAB(20);CUSTOMER.ADDR.4$(I)
1340      LPRINT "CUSTOMER TERMS:";TAB(20);CUSTOMER.TERMS$(I)
1350      LPRINT
1360      LPRINT
1370      LPRINT STRING$(79,"-")
1380      LPRINT
1390      LPRINT
1400      FOUR.TO.A.PAGE = FOUR.TO.A.PAGE +1
1410      IF FOUR.TO.A.PAGE = 4 THEN LPRINT CHR$(12):FOUR.TO.A.PAGE = 0
1420 NEXT I
1430 IF HARDCOPY$ = "YES" THEN LPRINT CHR$(12)
1440 GOSUB 2120
1450 PRINT:PRINT "DO YOU WISH TO MAKE CORRECTIONS (Y/N)? ";
1460 Z$ = INKEY$:IF Z$ = "" THEN 1460
1470 PRINT Z$
1480 IF Z$ < > "Y" THEN GOSUB 1970:GOTO 1720
1490 PRINT:INPUT "WHICH RECORD DO YOU WISH TO CHANGE? ";I
1500 PRINT
1510 LINE INPUT "CUSTOMER NAME:              ",TEMPORARY.CUSTOMER.NAME$
1520 LINE INPUT "CUSTOMER ADDRESS LINE 1:    ",TEMPORARY.CUSTOMER.ADDR.1$
1530 LINE INPUT "CUSTOMER ADDRESS LINE 2:    ",TEMPORARY.CUSTOMER.ADDR.2$
1540 LINE INPUT "CUSTOMER ADDRESS LINE 3:    ",TEMPORARY.CUSTOMER.ADDR.3$
1550 LINE INPUT "CUSTOMER ADDRESS LINE 4:    ",TEMPORARY.CUSTOMER.ADDR.4$
1560 LINE INPUT "CUSTOMER TERMS:             ",TEMPORARY.CUSTOMER.TERMS$
1570 PRINT:PRINT "ACCEPTABLE (Y/N)? ";
1580 Z$ = INKEY$:IF Z$ = "" THEN 1580
1590 PRINT Z$
1600 IF Z$ < > "Y" THEN 1440
1610 CUSTOMER.NAME$(I) = TEMPORARY.CUSTOMER.NAME$
1620 CUSTOMER.ADDR.1$(I) = TEMPORARY.CUSTOMER.ADDR.1$
1630 CUSTOMER.ADDR.2$(I) = TEMPORARY.CUSTOMER.ADDR.2$
1640 CUSTOMER.ADDR.3$(I) = TEMPORARY.CUSTOMER.ADDR.3$
1650 CUSTOMER.ADDR.4$(I) = TEMPORARY.CUSTOMER.ADDR.4$
1660 CUSTOMER.TERMS$(I) = TEMPORARY.CUSTOMER.TERMS$
1670 GOTO 1440
1680 '***********************************************
1690 '* ALL CORRECTIONS ARE MADE - REWRITE THE FILE *
1700 '***********************************************
1710 GOSUB 1980
1720 '************************
1730 '* PROGRAM TERMINATION *
1740 '************************
1750 PRINT
1760 PRINT "LOADING OF CUSTOMER FILE IS COMPLETE"
1770 PRINT
1780 PRINT "DO YOU WISH TO REVIEW THE FILE (Y/N)? ";
1790 Z$ = INKEY$:IF Z$ = "" THEN 1790
1800 PRINT Z$
1810 IF Z$ = "Y" THEN 830
1820 PRINT
1830 PRINT "DO YOU WISH TO REPEAT THE PROGRAM (Y/N)? ";
1840 Z$ = INKEY$:IF Z$ = "" THEN 1840
1850 PRINT Z$
```

```
1860 IF Z$ < > "Y" THEN 1940
1870 ERASE CUSTOMER.NAME$
1880 ERASE CUSTOMER.ADDR.1$
1890 ERASE CUSTOMER.ADDR.2$
1900 ERASE CUSTOMER.ADDR.3$
1910 ERASE CUSTOMER.ADDR.4$
1920 ERASE CUSTOMER.TERMS$
1930 GOTO 10
1940 CHAIN "A:BUSINESS.BAS"
1950 '***********************
1960 '* SUBROUTINES FOLLOW *
1970 '***************************
1980 '* OPEN AND WRITE TO FILE *
1990 '***************************
2000 OPEN "O",2,"CUSTOMER.DAT"
2010 PRINT #2,FILE.SIZE           'WRITE THE RECORD COUNT
2020 FOR I = 1 TO FILE.SIZE
2030    PRINT #2,CUSTOMER.NAME$(I)
2040    PRINT #2,CUSTOMER.ADDR.1$(I)
2050    PRINT #2,CUSTOMER.ADDR.2$(I)
2060    PRINT #2,CUSTOMER.ADDR.3$(I)
2070    PRINT #2,CUSTOMER.ADDR.4$(I)
2080    PRINT #2,CUSTOMER.TERMS$(I)
2090 NEXT I
2100 CLOSE 2
2110 RETURN
2120 '*********************************
2130 '* HEADING USED FOR THE DISPLAY *
2140 '*********************************
2150 CLS
2160 X = ((80 - LEN(COMPANY.NAME$)) / 2)
2170 LOCATE 2,X
2180 PRINT COMPANY.NAME$
2190 PRINT STRING$(79,220):PRINT
2200 PRINT TAB(29);"CUSTOMER FILE DATA ENTRY"
2210 PRINT STRING$(79,220)
2220 RETURN
```

VENDOR.BAS

If you look at VENDOR.BAS carefully, you'll notice some similarities between it and CUSTOMER.BAS. You'll also notice similarities between it and PRODUCT. BAS, a program that will come along later in the discussion. A close inspection will show a valid reason for this: They're the same program. Well, not entirely the same, of course, but close enough to be near copies, which, of course, they are. Recall that in our discussion of MERGE in a prior chapter we said that we could store commonly used routines and combine them with a program being developed in order to save a lot of time. But wait a minute! If we used that approach this time, why are the routines at different statement numbers? The definition of a file, for instance, would have had to be combined with each program *at the same statement number.* That's entirely true. Generally what you will do is (1) save your commonly used definitions and routines with a high statement number, (2) MERGE them with your program in the place where you want them (before later statements are developed) or make the additions necessary for their use as subroutines, and then (3) RENUMber them.

A block diagram for the building and maintenance of the vendor is shown in Fig. 7-5. The program accepts input from the keyboard, or from the file

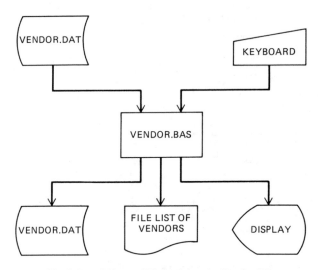

Fig. 7-5 Building and Maintaining the Vendor File

and keyboard combined, and uses it to develop a Vendor File. This Vendor File is used in other places in the system and is structured for use should the Accounts Payable subsystem be expanded. You may wish to augment the Vendor File with other pertinent data.

The similarity in the output with that of the customer file can be seen in the following (for simplicity, we have used the same people as both customers and vendors):

```
RECORD NUMBER:   1

VENDOR NAME:       SEARS
VENDOR ADDRESS:    SEARSLAND
                   100 LUNENBERG PARKWAY
                   LEOMINSTER,
                   MASSACHUSETTS 01377
VENDOR TERMS:      CASH


-----------------------------------------------------------------------


RECORD NUMBER:   2

VENDOR NAME:       MASSACHUSETTS ELECTRIC
VENDOR ADDRESS:    95 MECHANIC STREET
                   GARDNER,
                   MASSACHUSETTS

VENDOR TERMS:      NET 30 DAYS


-----------------------------------------------------------------------
```

```
RECORD NUMBER:   3

VENDOR NAME:        GIRARD CONSTRUCTION COMPANY
VENDOR ADDRESS:     35 GOODRICH STREET
                    WINCHENDON,
                    MASSACHUSETTS 01475

VENDOR TERMS:       1.5% ON UNPAID BALANCE
```

Because the program is a near copy of the previous one, we'll not chew our cabbage a second time, but we would like to draw your attention to statements 1870-1920. While the memory is reserved in the frame program (BUSINESS. BAS), the DIMensioning is done whereever needed. When you attempt to execute a program a second time, however, some adjustments will be required. ERASE is the BASIC statement to remove DIMensioning from the arrays and neutralize or reset the arrays. Another approach to take, of course, would be to set the arrays to null or zero with a routine designed precisely for that purpose. ERASE is the simplest way to do it, however, and absolutely necessary to do before you reDIMension the arrays; otherwise, your program will cease functioning and send you a message that you tried to double DIMension.

By the way, should you choose to interrupt the process, you may restart (RUN − F2) the program that is in memory. But if you do so, you will lose the COMPANY.NAME$ that had been supplied by BUSINESS.BAS.

Here is the program VENDOR.BAS:

```
10 GOSUB 2120
20 ARRAY.SIZE = 1000
30 FILE.SIZE = 1000
40 GOSUB 410
50 BASE = 1
60 PRINT
70 PRINT "TWO FORMS OF INPUT ARE POSSIBLE IN THIS PROGRAM: INPUT FROM EITHER"
80 PRINT "DISK OR THE KEYBOARD.  IF YOU CHOOSE NOT TO OBTAIN THE INPUT FROM"
90 PRINT "THE DISK, THE PROGRAM WILL ASSUME THAT YOU WISH TO ENTER FROM THE"
100 PRINT "KEYBOARD, DESTROYING ANY DISK FILE.  IF YOU WISH TO ADD TO THE FILE"
110 PRINT "WHICH ALREADY EXISTS, YOU MUST ANSWER 'Y' TO THIS QUESTION:"
120 PRINT:PRINT "WILL INPUT BE FROM THE DISK FILE (Y/N)? ";
130 Z$ = INKEY$:IF Z$ = "" THEN 130
140 PRINT Z$
150 IF Z$ < > "Y" THEN 530
160 '***************************
170 '* OPEN AND INPUT NAME FILE *
180 '***************************
190 FILE.NAME$ = "VENDOR.DAT"
200 OPEN "I",1,FILE.NAME$
210 INPUT #1,FILE.SIZE        'OBTAIN THE RECORD COUNT PREVIOUSLY STORED
220 FOR I = 1 TO FILE.SIZE
230     INPUT #1,VENDOR.NAME$(I)
240     INPUT #1,VENDOR.ADDR.1$(I)
250     INPUT #1,VENDOR.ADDR.2$(I)
260     INPUT #1,VENDOR.ADDR.3$(I)
```

```
270      INPUT #1,VENDOR.ADDR.4$(I)
280      INPUT #1,VENDOR.TERMS$(I)
290 NEXT I
300 RECORD.COUNT = I - 1
310 CLOSE 1
320 PRINT:PRINT "WILL THERE BE ADDITIONS TO THE FILE (Y/N)? ";
330 Z$ = INKEY$:IF Z$ = "" THEN 330
340 PRINT Z$
350 IF Z$ < > "Y" THEN 830
360 BASE = I
370 GOTO 530
380 '***********************************************************
390 '* THE DIMENSIONING IS ESTABLISHED AS A THOUSAND RECORDS. *
400 '***********************************************************
410 DIM VENDOR.NAME$(ARRAY.SIZE)
420 DIM VENDOR.ADDR.1$(ARRAY.SIZE)
430 DIM VENDOR.ADDR.2$(ARRAY.SIZE)
440 DIM VENDOR.ADDR.3$(ARRAY.SIZE)
450 DIM VENDOR.ADDR.4$(ARRAY.SIZE)
460 DIM VENDOR.TERMS$(ARRAY.SIZE)
470 RETURN
480 '***********************************************************
490 '* THIS IS THE ROUTINE TO ACCEPT TOTAL INPUT OF THE FILE FROM *
500 '* THE KEYBOARD.  IT IS NOT THE ROUTINE TO ADD TO AN EXISTING *
510 '* FILE.  FILE SIZE IS DEFAULTED TO 1000 RECORDS MAXIMUM.    *
520 '***********************************************************
530 FOR I = BASE TO ARRAY.SIZE
540      GOSUB 2120
550      PRINT
560      PRINT "ENTER 'END' UNDER VENDOR NAME TO TERMINATE ENTRY."
570      PRINT
580      LINE INPUT "VENDOR NAME:            ";VENDOR.NAME$(I)
590      IF (VENDOR.NAME$(I) = "END") AND RECORD.COUNT < 1 THEN 690
600      IF VENDOR.NAME$(I) = "END" THEN 760
610      LINE INPUT "VENDOR ADDRESS LINE 1:    ";VENDOR.ADDR.1$(I)
620      LINE INPUT "VENDOR ADDRESS LINE 2:    ";VENDOR.ADDR.2$(I)
630      LINE INPUT "VENDOR ADDRESS LINE 3:    ";VENDOR.ADDR.3$(I)
640      LINE INPUT "VENDOR ADDRESS LINE 4:    ";VENDOR.ADDR.4$(I)
650      INPUT "VENDOR TERMS:            ",VENDOR.TERMS$(I)
660      PRINT:PRINT "ACCEPTABLE (Y/N)? "
670      Z$ = INKEY$:IF Z$ = "" THEN 670
680      IF Z$ = "Y" THEN 740
690      LOCATE 25,1
700      PRINT "ENTRY REJECTED";
710      BEEP
720      FOR Z = 1 TO 1000:NEXT Z
730      GOTO 540
740 RECORD.COUNT = RECORD.COUNT + 1
750 NEXT I
760 FILE.SIZE = I - 1
770 GOSUB 1980            'ROUTINE TO WRITE THE FILE
780 '***********************************************************
790 '* THE FILE IS WRITTEN AND CLOSED.  IT MUST BE OPENED AGAIN IF *
800 '* THE USER DETERMINES TO GET A LISTING OF THE FILE EITHER IN  *
810 '* DISPLAY FORM ON IN HARDCOPY FORM.                          *
820 '***********************************************************
830 GOSUB 2120
840 FOUR.TO.A.PAGE = 0
850 PRINT:PRINT "DO YOU WISH TO SEE THE CONTENTS OF THE FILE (Y/N)? ";
860 Z$ = INKEY$:IF Z$ = "" THEN 860
870 PRINT Z$
880 IF Z$ < > "Y" THEN 1720
890 PRINT "DO YOU WISH A HARDCOPY OUTPUT (Y/N)? ";
900 Z$ = INKEY$:IF Z$ = "" THEN 900
910 PRINT Z$
920 IF Z$ < > "Y" THEN HARDCOPY$ = "NO":GOTO 940
930 HARDCOPY$ = "YES"
940 PRINT "UNINTERRUPTED PRINTING - 'N' CAUSES PAUSE WITH EACH - (Y/N)? ";
950 Z$ = INKEY$:IF Z$ = "" THEN 950
```

```
960 PRINT Z$
970 IF Z$ < > "Y" THEN CONTINUE$ = "NO":GOTO 990
980 CONTINUE$ = "YES"
990 FILE.NAME$ = "VENDOR.DAT"
1000 OPEN "I",1,FILE.NAME$
1010 INPUT #1,FILE.SIZE          'OBTAIN THE RECORD COUNT PREVIOUSLY STORED
1020 FOR I = 1 TO FILE.SIZE
1030      LINE INPUT #1,VENDOR.NAME$(I)
1040      LINE INPUT #1,VENDOR.ADDR.1$(I)
1050      LINE INPUT #1,VENDOR.ADDR.2$(I)
1060      LINE INPUT #1,VENDOR.ADDR.3$(I)
1070      LINE INPUT #1,VENDOR.ADDR.4$(I)
1080      LINE INPUT #1,VENDOR.TERMS$(I)
1090 NEXT I
1100 CLOSE 1
1110 FOR I = 1 TO FILE.SIZE
1120      IF CONTINUE$ = "YES" THEN 1140
1130      Z$ = INKEY$:IF Z$ = "" THEN 1130
1140      PRINT
1150      PRINT STRING$(79,"-")
1160      PRINT
1170      PRINT "RECORD NUMBER: ";I
1180      PRINT "VENDOR NAME:";TAB(20);VENDOR.NAME$(I)
1190      PRINT "VENDOR ADDRESS:";TAB(20);VENDOR.ADDR.1$(I)
1200      PRINT TAB(20);VENDOR.ADDR.2$(I)
1210      PRINT TAB(20);VENDOR.ADDR.3$(I)
1220      PRINT TAB(20);VENDOR.ADDR.4$(I)
1230      PRINT "VENDOR TERMS:";TAB(20);VENDOR.TERMS$(I)
1240      PRINT
1250      PRINT
1260      IF HARDCOPY$ = "NO" THEN 1420
1270      LPRINT "RECORD NUMBER: ";I
1280      LPRINT
1290      LPRINT "VENDOR NAME:";TAB(20);VENDOR.NAME$(I)
1300      LPRINT "VENDOR ADDRESS:";TAB(20);VENDOR.ADDR.1$(I)
1310      LPRINT TAB(20);VENDOR.ADDR.2$(I)
1320      LPRINT TAB(20);VENDOR.ADDR.3$(I)
1330      LPRINT TAB(20);VENDOR.ADDR.4$(I)
1340      LPRINT "VENDOR TERMS:";TAB(20);VENDOR.TERMS$(I)
1350      LPRINT
1360      LPRINT
1370      LPRINT STRING$(79,"-")
1380      LPRINT
1390      LPRINT
1400      FOUR.TO.A.PAGE = FOUR.TO.A.PAGE +1
1410      IF FOUR.TO.A.PAGE = 4 THEN LPRINT CHR$(12):FOUR.TO.A.PAGE = 0
1420 NEXT I
1430 IF HARDCOPY$ = "YES" THEN LPRINT CHR$(12)
1440 GOSUB 2120
1450 PRINT:PRINT "DO YOU WISH TO MAKE CORRECTIONS (Y/N)? ";
1460 Z$ = INKEY$:IF Z$ = "" THEN 1460
1470 PRINT Z$
1480 IF Z$ < > "Y" THEN GOSUB 1970:GOTO 1720
1490 PRINT:INPUT "WHICH RECORD DO YOU WISH TO CHANGE? ";I
1500 PRINT
1510 LINE INPUT "VENDOR NAME:                  ",TEMPORARY.VENDOR.NAME$
1520 LINE INPUT "VENDOR ADDRESS LINE 1:        ",TEMPORARY.VENDOR.ADDR.1$
1530 LINE INPUT "VENDOR ADDRESS LINE 2:        ",TEMPORARY.VENDOR.ADDR.2$
1540 LINE INPUT "VENDOR ADDRESS LINE 3:        ",TEMPORARY.VENDOR.ADDR.3$
1550 LINE INPUT "VENDOR ADDRESS LINE 4:        ",TEMPORARY.VENDOR.ADDR.4$
1560 LINE INPUT "VENDOR TERMS:                 ",TEMPORARY.VENDOR.TERMS$
1570 PRINT:PRINT "ACCEPTABLE (Y/N)? ";
1580 Z$ = INKEY$:IF Z$ = "" THEN 1580
1590 PRINT Z$
1600 IF Z$ < > "Y" THEN 1440
1610 VENDOR.NAME$(I) = TEMPORARY.VENDOR.NAME$
1620 VENDOR.ADDR.1$(I) = TEMPORARY.VENDOR.ADDR.1$
1630 VENDOR.ADDR.2$(I) = TEMPORARY.VENDOR.ADDR.2$
1640 VENDOR.ADDR.3$(I) = TEMPORARY.VENDOR.ADDR.3$
```

```
1650 VENDOR.ADDR.4$(I) = TEMPORARY.VENDOR.ADDR.4$
1660 VENDOR.TERMS$(I) = TEMPORARY.VENDOR.TERMS$
1670 GOTO 1440
1680 '***********************************************
1690 '* ALL CORRECTIONS ARE MADE - REWRITE THE FILE *
1700 '***********************************************
1710 GOSUB 1980
1720 '************************
1730 '* PROGRAM TERMINATION *
1740 '************************
1750 PRINT
1760 PRINT "LOADING OF VENDOR FILE IS COMPLETE"
1770 PRINT
1780 PRINT "DO YOU WISH TO REVIEW THE FILE (Y/N)? ";
1790 Z$ = INKEY$:IF Z$ = "" THEN 1790
1800 PRINT Z$
1810 IF Z$ = "Y" THEN 830
1820 PRINT
1830 PRINT "DO YOU WISH TO REPEAT THE PROGRAM (Y/N)? ";
1840 Z$ = INKEY$:IF Z$ = "" THEN 1840
1850 PRINT Z$
1860 IF Z$ < > "Y" THEN 1940
1870 ERASE VENDOR.NAME$
1880 ERASE VENDOR.ADDR.1$
1890 ERASE VENDOR.ADDR.2$
1900 ERASE VENDOR.ADDR.3$
1910 ERASE VENDOR.ADDR.4$
1920 ERASE VENDOR.TERMS$
1930 GOTO 10
1940 CHAIN "A:BUSINESS.BAS"
1950 '************************
1960 '* SUBROUTINES FOLLOW *
1970 '*************************
1980 '* OPEN AND WRITE TO FILE *
1990 '*************************
2000 OPEN "O",2,"VENDOR.DAT"
2010 PRINT #2,FILE.SIZE          'WRITE THE RECORD COUNT
2020 FOR I = 1 TO FILE.SIZE
2030     PRINT #2,VENDOR.NAME$(I)
2040     PRINT #2,VENDOR.ADDR.1$(I)
2050     PRINT #2,VENDOR.ADDR.2$(I)
2060     PRINT #2,VENDOR.ADDR.3$(I)
2070     PRINT #2,VENDOR.ADDR.4$(I)
2080     PRINT #2,VENDOR.TERMS$(I)
2090 NEXT I
2100 CLOSE 2
2110 RETURN
2120 '***********************************
2130 '* HEADING USED FOR THE DISPLAY *
2140 '***********************************
2150 CLS
2160 X = ((80 - LEN(COMPANY.NAME$)) / 2)
2170 LOCATE 2,X
2180 PRINT COMPANY.NAME$
2190 PRINT STRING$(79,220):PRINT
2200 PRINT TAB(30);"VENDOR FILE DATA ENTRY"
2210 PRINT STRING$(79,220)
2220 RETURN
```

MAILLIST.BAS

This program contains the one joke in the entire system; it asks if you want a hardcopy. Of course, there would be no point in running a mail list program were it not for the purpose of acquiring a hardcopy list or labels. Throughout the design of this system, the author placed the output listings on the screen as well as the printer. Occasionally, it may be necessary to run a program when the printer has slipped a cog and gone into the shop for a cog-replacement. It's generally good programming practice to allow the user to specify if a printer is to be used. There are, of course, sophisticated error-trapping routines that allow a programmer to determine if, in fact, a system has no printer attached (either physically or electronically) at the time it is needed. The PC, however, is a one-user system. It's assumed that the user will know if a printer is required. If a printer is not available and it has been *selected* (computer term for *demanded*), you'll know it soon enough. You'll be told that it's out of paper, when in fact it may not even be in the room. But if the printer is attached and not made *ready*, the program will hang waiting for it unless you have included the routines for bypassing it.

This is not a complex program to understand. It merely reads the file into an array and then works its way through the array producing output to the display and/or printer. A block diagram for the program is shown in Fig. 7-6.

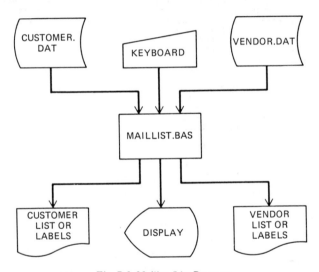

Fig. 7-6 Mailing List Program

The program takes the Customer Files and Vendor Files, and, with a menu selection, produces a display and, if one is selected, either of the lists. Proper spacing is established in the program to permit use of commonly available pressure-sensitive labels. The program will work for your Christmas card list so long as your friends are loaded as customers or vendors.

Here is the program MAILLIST.BAS:

```
10 GOSUB 1000
20 PRINT
30 PRINT "TWO DIFFERENT MAILING LISTS MAY BE OBTAINED WITH THIS PROGRAM. "
40 PRINT "YOU MAY PRODUCE A MAILING LIST FOR EITHER YOUR CUSTOMERS OR YOUR"
```

```
 50 PRINT "VENDORS.   YOU HAVE THE OPPORTUNITY TO VIEW THEM ON THE SCREEN AND"
 60 PRINT "TO OBTAIN A HARDCOPY REPORT ON PAPER (OR LABELS) FOR YOUR USE."
 70 PRINT
 80 PRINT "YOU MAY SELECT EITHER THE <C>USTOMER FILE OR THE <V>ENDOR FILE"
 90 PRINT "MERELY BY PRESSING THE LETTER."
100 PRINT
110 Z$ = INKEY$:IF Z$ = "" THEN 110
120 PRINT Z$;
130 IF Z$ = "C" THEN PRINT "USTOMER FILE WAS SELECTED":PRINT
140 IF Z$ = "V" THEN PRINT "ENDOR FILE WAS SELECTED":PRINT
150 IF Z$ = "C" THEN FILE.NAME$ = "CUSTOMER.DAT":GOTO 230
160 IF Z$ = "V" THEN FILE.NAME$ = "VENDOR.DAT":GOTO 230
170 LOCATE 25,1
180 PRINT "INVALID CODE";
190 BEEP
200 FOR Z = 1 TO 1000:NEXT Z
210 GOSUB 1000
220 GOTO 20
230 '*****************************
240 '* OPEN AND INPUT NAME FILE *
250 '*****************************
260 OPEN "I",1,FILE.NAME$
270 INPUT #1,FILE.SIZE        'OBTAIN THE RECORD COUNT PREVIOUSLY STORED
280 '************************************************************************
290 '* THE DIMENSIONING IS ESTABLISHED ON THE BASIS OF THE FIRST RECORD *
300 '************************************************************************
310 DIM LABEL.NAME$(FILE.SIZE)
320 DIM LABEL.ADDR.1$(FILE.SIZE)
330 DIM LABEL.ADDR.2$(FILE.SIZE)
340 DIM LABEL.ADDR.3$(FILE.SIZE)
350 DIM LABEL.ADDR.4$(FILE.SIZE)
360 DIM LABEL.TERMS$(FILE.SIZE)
370 FOR I = 1 TO FILE.SIZE
380     LINE INPUT #1,LABEL.NAME$(I)
390     LINE INPUT #1,LABEL.ADDR.1$(I)
400     LINE INPUT #1,LABEL.ADDR.2$(I)
410     LINE INPUT #1,LABEL.ADDR.3$(I)
420     LINE INPUT #1,LABEL.ADDR.4$(I)
430     LINE INPUT #1,LABEL.TERMS$(I)
440 NEXT I
450 CLOSE 1
460 '****************************
470 '* LABEL PRINTING ROUTINE *
480 '****************************
490 GOSUB 1000
500 PRINT
510 PRINT "DO YOU WISH A HARDCOPY OUTPUT (Y/N)? ";
520 Z$ = INKEY$:IF Z$ = "" THEN 520
530 PRINT Z$
540 IF Z$ < > "Y" THEN HARDCOPY$ = "NO":GOTO 560
550 HARDCOPY$ = "YES"
560 PRINT "UNINTERRUPTED PRINTING - 'N' CAUSES PAUSE WITH EACH - (Y/N)? ";
570 Z$ = INKEY$:IF Z$ = "" THEN 570
580 PRINT Z$
590 IF Z$ < > "Y" THEN CONTINUE$ = "NO":GOTO 610
600 CONTINUE$ = "YES"
610 FOR I = 1 TO FILE.SIZE
620     PRINT
630     PRINT
640     PRINT LABEL.NAME$(I)
650     PRINT LABEL.ADDR.1$(I)
660     PRINT LABEL.ADDR.2$(I)
670     PRINT LABEL.ADDR.3$(I)
680     PRINT LABEL.ADDR.4$(I)
690     IF CONTINUE$ = "YES" THEN 710
700     Z$ = INKEY$:IF Z$ = "" THEN 700
710     IF HARDCOPY$ = "NO" THEN 790
720     LPRINT
730     LPRINT
```

```
740      LPRINT LABEL.NAME$(I)
750      LPRINT LABEL.ADDR.1$(I)
760      LPRINT LABEL.ADDR.2$(I)
770      LPRINT LABEL.ADDR.3$(I)
780      LPRINT LABEL.ADDR.4$(I)
790 NEXT I
800 IF HARDCOPY$ = "YES" THEN LPRINT CHR$(12)
810 '*************************
820 '* PROGRAM TERMINATION *
830 '*************************
840 PRINT
850 IF FILE.NAME$ = "CUSTOMER.DAT" THEN
        PRINT "PRINTING OF THE CUSTOMER FILE IS COMPLETE"
860 IF FILE.NAME$ = "VENDOR.DAT" THEN
        PRINT "PRINTING OF THE VENDOR FILE IS COMPLETE"
870 PRINT
880 PRINT "DO YOU WISH TO REPEAT THE PROGRAM (Y/N)? ";
890 Z$ = INKEY$:IF Z$ = "" THEN 890
900 PRINT Z$
910 IF Z$ < > "Y" THEN 990
920 ERASE LABEL.NAME$
930 ERASE LABEL.ADDR.1$
940 ERASE LABEL.ADDR.2$
950 ERASE LABEL.ADDR.3$
960 ERASE LABEL.ADDR.4$
970 ERASE LABEL.TERMS$
980 GOTO 10
990 CHAIN "A:BUSINESS.BAS"
1000 '*********************************
1010 '* HEADING USED FOR THE DISPLAY *
1020 '*********************************
1030 CLS
1040 X = ((80 - LEN(COMPANY.NAME$)) / 2)
1050 LOCATE 2,X
1060 PRINT COMPANY.NAME$
1070 PRINT STRING$(79,220):PRINT
1080 PRINT TAB(25);"MAILING LIST PRINT PROGRAM"
1090 PRINT STRING$(79,220)
1100 RETURN
```

PRODUCT.BAS

As if we haven't had enough inventory programs in this book, here is yet another. This one is integrated with the system and uses sequential files, a technique not previously employed. A block diagram is shown in Fig. 7-7. The program accepts input from the keyboard, or from the file and keyboard combined, and uses it to develop a Product (Inventory) File. This file is used with the Accounts Receivable subsystem. At the moment, since it contains the bare minimum of information needed, you may wish to augment it for further use.

An inventory file is, of course, a suitable place for storing information about double-sided framistan-oriented widgets and octagonal, centrifugal gizmos, as we shall demonstrate. More importantly, it is a place where you can store descriptive information *once* and call upon it forever after, as required. If you are able to reduce the number of keystrokes, your operation cannot help but be improved. If your business involves products and inventory, this file is the way to save the labor of typing each invoice individually. You need only ensure the initial accuracy of the descriptive information, and it will be accurate until all the purple cows come home.

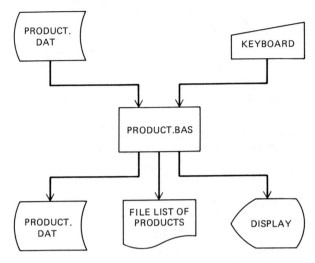

Fig. 7-7 Building and Maintaining the Product File

Some additional information appears in this application. We've included a unit of measure, a location within your storage facility, the quantity on hand, the reorder point, and room for any special shipping instructions. Although it wasn't brought up during the discussion of the customer file, you might want to include a mechanism to separate *types* of product *by shipping method.* Thus, you might wish to invoice on one piece of paper all products to be shipped by mail in order to distinguish them from those to be shipped by motor transport, for instance. That facility is not present in this system as designed. In order to add it, you would have to replace the narrative included in the shipping instructions with some standardized code: "A" could mean special handling; "B" could mean ship by motor freight; "C" could mean dangerous cargo, etc. You would need only to string together enough codes to describe the shipping method required and then use the INSTRing facility to determine the codes stored there.

Here are a couple examples of an inventory listing:

```
ITEM NUMBER:    1

PRODUCT:                WIDGET

PRODUCT DESCRIPTION:    DOUBLE-SIDED, FRAMISTAN-ORIENTED
UNIT OF MEASURE:        100 BUSHEL
LOCATION:               B45
QUANTITY ON HAND:       500
REORDER POINT:          200
SHIPPING INSTR:         SHIP ONLY IN GLASS CONTAINER

------------------------------------------------------------------
```

```
ITEM NUMBER:   2

PRODUCT:                 GIZMO

PRODUCT DESCRIPTION:     OCTAGONAL, CENTRIFUGAL
UNIT OF MEASURE:         1 EACH
LOCATION:                REAR WAREHOUSE, BIN 10
QUANTITY ON HAND:        5
REORDER POINT:           10
SHIPPING INSTR:          AIR MAIL SPECIAL DELIVERY
```

And now, the program. The assumption has been made that your inventory file will not exceed 1,000 items. As in previous programs, you are given a first-time option. If you respond incorrectly, you will develop a new file that will destroy the previous file. The work is done in the array, as before, and the new file will not be written until you indicate that no more input will be received. As a matter of practice, daily back-up copies of critical files is an absolute must. You'll find that a minimum of three cycles will be required. In the industry, that is known as the grandfather-father-son approach to protection.

As with previous programs also, there is the opportunity to obtain a listing of the inventory — either to the display or to hardcopy. Perhaps it should be mentioned — lest anybody get the wrong impression — that the author can't actually vouch for a high degree of mortality among cogs in a printer, but these cogs (which are the teeth of a gear) in most printers available nowadays are made of nylon. Cogs being wear parts, you can therefore expect that some wear will occur, depending upon how heavily you use the equipment.

There is one concept in this program that deserves special consideration. Look at statements 1600-1780. Whenever you are making changes to previously entered information in an array (information that you are not now entering), it's always wise to withhold the update of that information until such time as you are absolutely certain that the replacement record is accurate and that the change is indeed desirable. Everything else within the program conforms to what we have previously discussed:

Here is the program PRODUCT.BAS:

```
10 GOSUB 2250
20 ARRAY.SIZE = 1000
30 FILE.SIZE = 1000
40 GOSUB 420
50 BASE = 1
60 PRINT
70 PRINT "TWO FORMS OF INPUT ARE POSSIBLE IN THIS PROGRAM: INPUT FROM EITHER"
80 PRINT "DISK OR THE KEYBOARD.  IF YOU CHOOSE NOT TO OBTAIN THE INPUT FROM"
90 PRINT "THE DISK, THE PROGRAM WILL ASSUME THAT YOU WISH TO ENTER FROM THE"
100 PRINT "KEYBOARD, DESTROYING ANY DISK FILE.  IF YOU WISH TO ADD TO THE FILE"
110 PRINT "WHICH ALREADY EXISTS, YOU MUST ANSWER 'Y' TO THIS QUESTION:"
120 PRINT:PRINT "WILL INPUT BE FROM THE DISK FILE (Y/N)? ";
130 Z$ = INKEY$:IF Z$ = "" THEN 130
140 PRINT Z$
```

```
150 IF Z$ < > "Y" THEN 550
160 '****************************
170 '* OPEN AND INPUT NAME FILE *
180 '****************************
190 FILE.NAME$ = "PRODUCT.DAT"
200 OPEN "I",1,FILE.NAME$
210 INPUT #1,FILE.SIZE        'OBTAIN THE RECORD COUNT PREVIOUSLY STORED
220 FOR I = 1 TO FILE.SIZE
230     LINE INPUT #1,PRODUCT.NAME$(I)
240     LINE INPUT #1,PRODUCT.DESCR$(I)
250     LINE INPUT #1,PRODUCT.UNIT$(I)
260     LINE INPUT #1,PRODUCT.LOCATION$(I)
270     INPUT #1,PRODUCT.Q.O.H(I)
280     INPUT #1,PRODUCT.R.O.P(I)
290     LINE INPUT #1,PRODUCT.SHIP.INSTR$(I)
300 NEXT I
310 RECORD.COUNT = I - 1
320 CLOSE 1
330 PRINT:PRINT "WILL THERE BE ADDITIONS TO THE FILE (Y/N)? ";
340 Z$ = INKEY$:IF Z$ = "" THEN 340
350 PRINT Z$
360 IF Z$ < > "Y" THEN 860
370 BASE = I
380 GOTO 550
390 '***********************************************************
400 '* THE DIMENSIONING IS ESTABLISHED AS A THOUSAND RECORDS. *
410 '***********************************************************
420 DIM PRODUCT.NAME$(ARRAY.SIZE)
430 DIM PRODUCT.DESCR$(ARRAY.SIZE)
440 DIM PRODUCT.UNIT$(ARRAY.SIZE)
450 DIM PRODUCT.LOCATION$(ARRAY.SIZE)
460 DIM PRODUCT.Q.O.H(ARRAY.SIZE)
470 DIM PRODUCT.R.O.P(ARRAY.SIZE)
480 DIM PRODUCT.SHIP.INSTR$(ARRAY.SIZE)
490 RETURN
500 '***********************************************************
510 '* THIS IS THE ROUTINE TO ACCEPT TOTAL INPUT OF THE FILE FROM *
520 '* THE KEYBOARD.  IT IS NOT THE ROUTINE TO ADD TO AN EXISTING *
530 '* FILE.  FILE SIZE IS DEFAULTED TO 1000 RECORDS MAXIMUM.     *
540 '***********************************************************
550 FOR I = BASE TO ARRAY.SIZE
560     GOSUB 2250
570     PRINT
580     PRINT "ENTER 'END' UNDER PRODUCT NAME TO TERMINATE ENTRY."
590     PRINT
600     LINE INPUT "PRODUCT NAME:                ";PRODUCT.NAME$(I)
610     IF (PRODUCT.NAME$(I) = "END") AND RECORD.COUNT < 1 THEN 720
620     IF PRODUCT.NAME$(I) = "END" THEN 790
630     LINE INPUT "PRODUCT DESCRIPTION:         ";PRODUCT.DESCR$(I)
640     LINE INPUT "PRODUCT UNIT OF MEASURE:     ";PRODUCT.UNIT$(I)
650     LINE INPUT "PRODUCT LOCATION:            ";PRODUCT.LOCATION$(I)
660     INPUT "PRODUCT QTY ON HAND:         ",PRODUCT.Q.O.H(I)
670     INPUT "PRODUCT REORDER POINT:       ",PRODUCT.R.O.P(I)
680     INPUT "SPECIAL SHIPPING INSTR:      ",PRODUCT.SHIP.INSTR$(I)
690     PRINT:PRINT "ACCEPTABLE (Y/N)? "
700     Z$ = INKEY$:IF Z$ = "" THEN 700
710     IF Z$ = "Y" THEN 770
720     LOCATE 25,1
730     PRINT "ENTRY REJECTED";
740     BEEP
750     FOR Z = 1 TO 1000:NEXT Z
760     GOTO 560
770 RECORD.COUNT = RECORD.COUNT + 1
780 NEXT I
790 FILE.SIZE = I - 1
800 GOSUB 2100          'ROUTINE TO WRITE THE FILE
810 '***********************************************************
820 '* THE FILE IS WRITTEN AND CLOSED.  IT MUST BE OPENED AGAIN IF *
830 '* THE USER DETERMINES TO GET A LISTING OF THE FILE EITHER IN  *
```

```
840 '* DISPLAY FORM ON IN HARDCOPY FORM.                                    *
850 '*****************************************************************
860 GOSUB 2250
870 FOUR.TO.A.PAGE = 0
880 PRINT:PRINT "DO YOU WISH TO SEE THE CONTENTS OF THE FILE (Y/N)? ";
890 Z$ = INKEY$:IF Z$ = "" THEN 890
900 PRINT Z$
910 IF Z$ < > "Y" THEN 1830
920 PRINT "DO YOU WISH A HARDCOPY OUTPUT (Y/N)? ";
930 Z$ = INKEY$:IF Z$ = "" THEN 930
940 PRINT Z$
950 IF Z$ < > "Y" THEN HARDCOPY$ = "NO":GOTO 970
960 HARDCOPY$ = "YES"
970 PRINT "UNINTERRUPTED PRINTING - 'N' CAUSES PAUSE WITH EACH - (Y/N)? ";
980 Z$ = INKEY$:IF Z$ = "" THEN 980
990 PRINT Z$
1000 IF Z$ < > "Y" THEN CONTINUE$ = "NO":GOTO 1020
1010 CONTINUE$ = "YES"
1020 FILE.NAME$ = "PRODUCT.DAT"
1030 OPEN "I",1,FILE.NAME$
1040 INPUT #1,FILE.SIZE          'OBTAIN THE RECORD COUNT PREVIOUSLY STORED
1050 FOR I = 1 TO FILE.SIZE
1060     LINE INPUT #1,PRODUCT.NAME$(I)
1070     LINE INPUT #1,PRODUCT.DESCR$(I)
1080     LINE INPUT #1,PRODUCT.UNIT$(I)
1090     LINE INPUT #1,PRODUCT.LOCATION$(I)
1100     INPUT #1,PRODUCT.Q.O.H(I)
1110     INPUT #1,PRODUCT.R.O.P(I)
1120     LINE INPUT #1,PRODUCT.SHIP.INSTR$(I)
1130 NEXT I
1140 CLOSE 1
1150 FOR I = 1 TO FILE.SIZE
1160     IF CONTINUE$ = "YES" THEN 1180
1170     Z$ = INKEY$:IF Z$ = "" THEN 1170
1180     PRINT
1190     PRINT STRING$(79,"-")
1200     PRINT
1210     PRINT "ITEM NUMBER: ";I
1220     PRINT
1230     PRINT "PRODUCT:";TAB(25);PRODUCT.NAME$(I)
1240     PRINT
1250     PRINT "PRODUCT DESCRIPTION:";TAB(25);PRODUCT.DESCR$(I)
1260     PRINT "UNIT OF MEASURE:";TAB(25);PRODUCT.UNIT$(I)
1270     PRINT "LOCATION:";TAB(25);PRODUCT.LOCATION$(I)
1280     PRINT "QUANTITY ON HAND:";TAB(25);PRODUCT.Q.O.H(I)
1290     PRINT "REORDER POINT:";TAB(25);PRODUCT.R.O.P(I)
1300     PRINT "SHIPPING INSTR:";TAB(25);PRODUCT.SHIP.INSTR$(I)
1310     PRINT
1320     PRINT
1330     IF HARDCOPY$ = "NO" THEN 1510
1340     LPRINT "ITEM NUMBER: ";I
1350     LPRINT
1360     LPRINT "PRODUCT:";TAB(25);PRODUCT.NAME$(I)
1370     LPRINT
1380     LPRINT "PRODUCT DESCRIPTION:";TAB(25);PRODUCT.DESCR$(I)
1390     LPRINT "UNIT OF MEASURE:";TAB(25);PRODUCT.UNIT$(I)
1400     LPRINT "LOCATION:";TAB(25);PRODUCT.LOCATION$(I)
1410     LPRINT "QUANTITY ON HAND:";TAB(25);PRODUCT.Q.O.H(I)
1420     LPRINT "REORDER POINT:";TAB(25);PRODUCT.R.O.P(I)
1430     LPRINT "SHIPPING INSTR:";TAB(25);PRODUCT.SHIP.INSTR$(I)
1440     LPRINT
1450     LPRINT
1460     LPRINT STRING$(79,"-")
1470     LPRINT
1480     LPRINT
1490     FOUR.TO.A.PAGE = FOUR.TO.A.PAGE +1
1500     IF FOUR.TO.A.PAGE = 4 THEN LPRINT CHR$(12):FOUR.TO.A.PAGE = 0
1510 NEXT I
1520 IF HARDCOPY$ = "YES" THEN LPRINT CHR$(12)
```

```
1530 GOSUB 2250
1540 PRINT:PRINT "DO YOU WISH TO MAKE CORRECTIONS (Y/N)? ";
1550 Z$ = INKEY$:IF Z$ = "" THEN 1550
1560 PRINT Z$
1570 IF Z$ < > "Y" THEN GOSUB 2090:GOTO 1830
1580 PRINT:INPUT "WHICH RECORD DO YOU WISH TO CHANGE? ";I
1590 PRINT
1600 LINE INPUT "PRODUCT NAME:               ",TEMPORARY.PRODUCT.NAME$
1610 LINE INPUT "PRODUCT DESCRIPTION:        ",TEMPORARY.PRODUCT.DESCR$
1620 LINE INPUT "PRODUCT UNIT OF MEASURE:    ",TEMPORARY.PRODUCT.UNIT$
1630 INPUT "PRODUCT LOCATION:          ",TEMPORARY.PRODUCT.LOCATION$
1640 INPUT "PRODUCT QUANTITY ON HAND:      ",TEMPORARY.PRODUCT.Q.O.H
1650 LINE INPUT "PRODUCT REORDER POINT:      ",TEMPORARY.PRODUCT.R.O.P
1660 LINE INPUT "PRODUCT SHIPPINT INSTR:     ",TEMPORARY.PRODUCT.SHIP.INSTR$
1670 PRINT:PRINT "ACCEPTABLE (Y/N)? ";
1680 Z$ = INKEY$:IF Z$ = "" THEN 1680
1690 PRINT Z$
1700 IF Z$ < > "Y" THEN 1530
1710 PRODUCT.NAME$(I) = TEMPORARY.PRODUCT.NAME$
1720 PRODUCT.DESCR$(I) = TEMPORARY.PRODUCT.DESCR$
1730 PRODUCT.UNIT$(I) = TEMPORARY.PRODUCT.UNIT$
1740 PRODUCT.LOCATION$(I) = TEMPORARY.PRODUCT.LOCATION$
1750 PRODUCT.Q.O.H(I) = TEMPORARY.PRODUCT.Q.O.H
1760 PRODUCT.R.O.P(I) = TEMPORARY.PRODUCT.R.O.P
1770 PRODUCT.SHIP.INSTR$(I) = TEMPORARY.PRODUCT.SHIP.INSTR$
1780 GOTO 1530
1790 '***********************************************
1800 '* ALL CORRECTIONS ARE MADE - REWRITE THE FILE *
1810 '***********************************************
1820 GOSUB 2100
1830 '************************
1840 '* PROGRAM TERMINATION *
1850 '************************
1860 PRINT
1870 PRINT "LOADING OF PRODUCT FILE IS COMPLETE"
1880 PRINT
1890 PRINT "DO YOU WISH TO REVIEW THE FILE (Y/N)? ";
1900 Z$ = INKEY$:IF Z$ = "" THEN 1900
1910 PRINT Z$
1920 IF Z$ = "Y" THEN 860
1930 PRINT
1940 PRINT "DO YOU WISH TO REPEAT THE PROGRAM (Y/N)? ";
1950 Z$ = INKEY$:IF Z$ = "" THEN 1950
1960 PRINT Z$
1970 IF Z$ < > "Y" THEN 2060
1980 ERASE PRODUCT.NAME$
1990 ERASE PRODUCT.DESCR$
2000 ERASE PRODUCT.UNIT$
2010 ERASE PRODUCT.LOCATION$
2020 ERASE PRODUCT.Q.O.H
2030 ERASE PRODUCT.R.O.P
2040 ERASE PRODUCT.SHIP.INSTR$
2050 GOTO 10
2060 CHAIN "A:BUSINESS.BAS"
2070 '***********************
2080 '* SUBROUTINES FOLLOW *
2090 '***********************
2100 '* OPEN AND WRITE TO FILE *
2110 '***************************
2120 OPEN "O",2,"PRODUCT.DAT"
2130 PRINT #2,FILE.SIZE            'WRITE THE RECORD COUNT
2140 FOR I = 1 TO FILE.SIZE
2150     PRINT #2,PRODUCT.NAME$(I)
2160     PRINT #2,PRODUCT.DESCR$(I)
2170     PRINT #2,PRODUCT.UNIT$(I)
2180     PRINT #2,PRODUCT.LOCATION$(I)
2190     PRINT #2,PRODUCT.Q.O.H(I)
2200     PRINT #2,PRODUCT.R.O.P(I)
2210     PRINT #2,PRODUCT.SHIP.INSTR$(I)
```

```
2220 NEXT I
2230 CLOSE 2
2240 RETURN
2250 '*********************************
2260 '* HEADING USED FOR THE DISPLAY *
2270 '*********************************
2280 CLS
2290 X = ((80 - LEN(COMPANY.NAME$)) / 2)
2300 LOCATE 2,X
2310 PRINT COMPANY.NAME$
2320 PRINT STRING$(79,220):PRINT
2330 PRINT TAB(26);"PRODUCT (INVENTORY) PROCESSING"
2340 PRINT STRING$(79,220)
2350 RETURN
```

RECIVBLE.BAS

The Accounts Receivable subsystem of the small business system is the largest, and by definition, the most complex of them all. It was developed on a 64K system and even with this capability, four of the seven services had to be separated into CHAINable programs. Throughout the book the programs have taken advantage of the documentation capabilities of the BASIC language as implemented on the PC. The statements have been made as simple as possible. Multiple statements have not been placed on a line, a practice, of course, that makes a program longer than it has to be. Moreover, there is considerable commenting and use of asterisk lines to separate routines. Any of these can be done away with if it is necessary to reduce the memory consumption of any program.

The Accounts Receivable application provides the following services:

1. Initial entry of data for an A/R file
2. Adding entries to the A/R file
3. Posting of payments to the A/R file
4. Production of invoices
5. Production of statements
6. Production of A/R reports
7. Aging the accounts

The seven services are distributed in this manner:

RECIVBLE.BAS – Initial entry of data
                Additional entry of data
                Production of A/R reports

INVOICE.BAS – Production of invoices

POSTREC.BAS – Posting the payment of accounts

STATMENT.BAS – Production of the monthly statement

AGEING.BAS – Aging the accounts

The opening menu to the application, which we arrive at as a result of a selection made in BUSINESS.BAS, is as follows:

```
               SMALL BUSINESS ENTERPRISE, INC.

▬▬▬▬▬▬▬▬▬▬▬▬▬▬▬▬▬▬▬▬▬▬▬▬▬▬▬▬▬▬▬▬▬▬▬▬▬▬▬▬▬▬▬▬

            ACCOUNTS RECEIVABLE PROCESSING PROGRAM

▬▬▬▬▬▬▬▬▬▬▬▬▬▬▬▬▬▬▬▬▬▬▬▬▬▬▬▬▬▬▬▬▬▬▬▬▬▬▬▬▬▬▬▬

MAY 24, 1982

THIS APPLICATION WILL ALLOW :

   1.   INITIAL ENTRY OF DATA FOR AN ACCOUNTS RECEIVABLE FILE.
   2.   ADDING INVOICE ENTRIES TO THE ACCOUNTS RECEIVABLE FILE.
   3.   REMOVAL OF INVOICE ENTRIES FROM THE FILES WHEN PAID.
   4.   PRODUCING THE INVOICE WHICH WILL BE SENT TO THE CUSTOMER.
   5.   PRODUCING THE CUSTOMERS' MONTHLY STATEMENTS
   6.   PRODUCING REPORTS OF ACCOUNTS RECEIVABLE.
   7.   AGEING THE ACCOUNTS RECEIVABLE FILE AND APPLYING INTEREST.
   8.   TERMINATE THE PROGRAM

SELECT:
```

The big difficulty, of course, of having to subdivide a large problem is that commonly used subroutines, such as those used in the loading or writing of files or of displaying data on the screen, must be copied into the new program. That is true of this program, and you will find routines in INVOICE.BAS, POSTREC.BAS, STATMENT.BAS, and AGEING.BAS appearing in each other as well as in RECIVBLE.BAS, probably at entirely different sequence numbers. Unless you mix BASIC with Assembler Language, there's not much way around that difficulty.

The first two options differ only in the manner in which they are entered. In the program following this discussion, follow them through the ON . . . GOTO at statements 1050-1150 and then 1210. You will see that the only difference between the two is that in the case of the first, no file is read into the program, whereas in the second, the file is read into the array and the new data is then added to the end.

On the opposite page is a *linear screen* — that is, after the first portion appears, the screen builds one statement at a time until it is completed.

The screen's development, of course, traces the development of the program. The opening entry advises the operator that there will be a question at the end of each entry as to whether or not the process will be terminated, which it is after the entered record has been accepted.

Next, the operator is asked if it is necessary to review the customer file. If it is, the routines necessary to pass the customer file onto the screen (with a hardcopy option) are invoked, before returning to the opening entry. The whole purpose is to allow the mechanism to determine the customer number before proceeding to the next required entry, which is, coincidentally, where

```
                    SMALL BUSINESS ENTERPRISE, INC.
████████████████████████████████████████████████████████████████████

                 ACCOUNTS RECEIVABLE PROCESSING PROGRAM
████████████████████████████████████████████████████████████████████

INPUT IS TERMINATED BY QUESTION AT THE END OF EACH ENTRY

DO YOU NEED TO REVIEW THE CUSTOMER FILE (Y/N)? N

ENTER CUSTOMER NUMBER:    1
CUSTOMER.NAME:            SEARS
CUSTOMER ADDRESS:         SEARSLAND
                          100 LUNENBERG PARKWAY
                          LEOMINSTER,
                          MASSACHUSETTS 01377

CORRECT (Y/N)? Y

DO YOU NEED TO REVIEW THE PRODUCT FILE (Y/N)? N

HOW MANY ITEMS ON THIS INVOICE (MAXIMUM 4)? 2

ENTER PRODUCT NUMBER:     1
PRODUCT.NAME:             WIDGET
DESCRIPTION:              DOUBLE-SIDED, FRAMISTAN-ORIENTED
SHIPPING INSTRUCTIONS:    SHIP ONLY IN GLASS CONTAINER

CORRECT (Y/N)? Y
HOW MANY WILL BE INVOICED? 1
UNIT PRICE? $111.11

ENTER PRODUCT NUMBER:     2
PRODUCT.NAME:             GIZMO
DESCRIPTION:              OCTAGONAL, CENTRIFUGAL
SHIPPING INSTRUCTIONS:    AIR MAIL SPECIAL DELIVERY

CORRECT (Y/N)? Y
HOW MANY WILL BE INVOICED? 2
UNIT PRICE? $222.22
```

you will enter the customer number. When you have entered the customer number, the customer information is displayed and you are given the opportunity to confirm that it pertains to the customer to whom this invoice is to be assigned.

The program now asks if you wish to review the product file. If you do, then a side trip is taken to allow you to determine which products to request without having to specify them. You are then asked how many products are to be listed on the invoice (the maximum is set at four). Having responded to that question, you may enter the product number for each in turn. As each is selected, the product name, description, and shipping instructions are displayed. You are then asked to confirm that each item is the one you wish to invoice. Once you do, you are asked how many will be invoiced and at what unit price.

In the designing of any system, some fundamental questions must be asked. One of these is whether or not a small business offers the same price to every client for a product. If the product is tangible, it often happens that it's against the law to sell it at a different price to different clients. In this case, the unit price could be made a part of the product master file. Some small businesses get around this restriction by charging the same basic unit price but adding a mark-up based on customer terms. In this case, the invoicing would have to be tied to the customer terms of the customer file. If charges are made on the basis of estimate or proposal and therefore differ among clients, an override must be built into the application. The author chose to avoid any question of this possibility simply by building the request for the unit price into the invoicing application itself.

In this process, you are asked to assign an invoice number. Although not prevented from using a previous invoice number, you are advised of the highest number currently on file. This arrangement could lead to a problem. Suppose that invoice 555 is presented as the highest number in the file, that you had generated invoice 556, and that it had already been paid for. In this case, you might inadvertently use 556 again. Again, there was a design choice. It would be easy enough to store the latest number in the area of the file where the number of records in the file is stored, but there would also be maintenance requirements for changing it. Thus, it was decided that most small businesses no doubt keep a register of invoices or at least duplicate invoices and would therefore know what the next invoice number in the sequence would be.

Once completed, the invoice is prepared, and the operator is asked if it is acceptable. If it *is* acceptable, then the invoice, shown below, may be printed.

```
DATE:  05-24-1982                       INVOICE NUMBER:  555
CUSTOMER.NAME:        SEARS
CUSTOMER ADDRESS:     SEARSLAND
                      100 LUNENBERG PARKWAY
                      LEOMINSTER,
                      MASSACHUSETTS 01377


ITEM      QUANTITY          DESCRIPTION           PRICE      EXTENSION
-----------------------------------------------------------------------
 1           1               WIDGET              111.11        111.11
 2           2               GIZMO               222.22        444.44
AMOUNT DUE:                                                   $555.55
                                                            ==============

ACCEPTABLE (Y/N)?
```

As stated, since the second option is the first option entered without first loading the file, there is nothing new to say about it. The same is almost true of the A/R reports. If you'll look at the routine that begins at statement 2340, you'll note that a list of invoice data and customer data is produced. In this instance, it is a work list; no care has been taken to make it a fancy report. The invoice number is presented, its date, and its amount, followed by the customer's name and address. Itemized purchases are not a part of this report. As before, you are given the option of reviewing this report either on the display screen or with a hardcopy added. At the end, the total number of invoices produced is given.

Here is the program RECIVBLE.BAS:

```
10 GOSUB 3440
20 INVOICE.MONTH$ = LEFT$(DATE$,2)
30 INVOICE.DAY$ = MID$(DATE$,4,2)
40 INVOICE.YEAR$ = RIGHT$(DATE$,4)
50 IF VAL(INVOICE.MONTH$) = 1 THEN INVOICE.MONTH$ = "JANUARY"
60 IF VAL(INVOICE.MONTH$) = 2 THEN INVOICE.MONTH$ = "FEBRUARY"
70 IF VAL(INVOICE.MONTH$) = 3 THEN INVOICE.MONTH$ = "MARCH"
80 IF VAL(INVOICE.MONTH$) = 4 THEN INVOICE.MONTH$ = "APRIL"
90 IF VAL(INVOICE.MONTH$) = 5 THEN INVOICE.MONTH$ = "MAY"
100 IF VAL(INVOICE.MONTH$) = 6 THEN INVOICE.MONTH$ = "JUNE"
110 IF VAL(INVOICE.MONTH$) = 7 THEN INVOICE.MONTH$ = "JULY"
120 IF VAL(INVOICE.MONTH$) = 8 THEN INVOICE.MONTH$ = "AUGUST"
130 IF VAL(INVOICE.MONTH$) = 9 THEN INVOICE.MONTH$ = "SEPTEMBER"
140 IF VAL(INVOICE.MONTH$) = 10 THEN INVOICE.MONTH$ = "OCTOBER"
150 IF VAL(INVOICE.MONTH$) = 11 THEN INVOICE.MONTH$ = "NOVEMBER"
160 IF VAL(INVOICE.MONTH$) = 12 THEN INVOICE.MONTH$ = "DECEMBER"
170 INVOICE.MONTH$ = INVOICE.MONTH$ + " "
180 INVOICE.DATE$ = INVOICE.MONTH$ + INVOICE.DAY$ + ", " + INVOICE.YEAR$
190 PRINT
200 PRINT INVOICE.DATE$
210 '*********************************
220 '* DIMENSION THE RECEIVABLES FILE. *
230 '*********************************
240 DIM CUSTOMER.NUMBER(100)
250 DIM DATE.OF.INVOICE$(100)
260 DIM DOCUMENT.NUMBER(100)
270 DIM ITEM.1.NUMBER(100)
280 DIM ITEM.1.QTY(100)
290 DIM ITEM.1.UNIT.PRICE(100)
300 DIM ITEM.2.NUMBER(100)
310 DIM ITEM.2.QTY(100)
320 DIM ITEM.2.UNIT.PRICE(100)
330 DIM ITEM.3.NUMBER(100)
340 DIM ITEM.3.QTY(100)
350 DIM ITEM.3.UNIT.PRICE(100)
360 DIM ITEM.4.NUMBER(100)
370 DIM ITEM.4.QTY(100)
380 DIM ITEM.4.UNIT.PRICE(100)
390 DIM AMOUNT.OF.INVOICE(100)
400 DIM AMOUNT.LESS.THAN.30.DAYS(100)
410 DIM AMOUNT.AT.30.DAYS(100)
420 DIM AMOUNT.AT.60.DAYS(100)
430 DIM AMOUNT.AT.90.DAYS(100)
440 '*******************************
450 '* DIMENSION THE PRODUCT FILE. *
460 '*******************************
470 DIM PRODUCT.NAME$(100)
480 DIM PRODUCT.DESCR$(100)
490 DIM PRODUCT.UNIT$(100)
500 DIM PRODUCT.LOCATION$(100)
510 DIM PRODUCT.Q.O.H(100)
520 DIM PRODUCT.R.O.P(100)
530 DIM PRODUCT.SHIP.INSTR$(100)
540 '*******************************
550 '* DIMENSION THE CUSTOMER FILE. *
560 '*******************************
570 DIM CUSTOMER.NAME$(100)
580 DIM CUSTOMER.ADDR.1$(100)
590 DIM CUSTOMER.ADDR.2$(100)
600 DIM CUSTOMER.ADDR.3$(100)
610 DIM CUSTOMER.ADDR.4$(100)
620 DIM CUSTOMER.TERMS$(100)
630 '*******************************
640 '* DIMENSION THE ACCOUNT FILE. *
650 '*******************************
660 DIM T$(100)
670 DIM N$(100)
```

```
680 DIM A(100)
690 '****************
700 '* OPENING MENU *
710 '*******************************************************************************
720 PRINT
730 PRINT "THIS APPLICATION WILL ALLOW :"
740 PRINT
750 PRINT "    1.   INITIAL ENTRY OF DATA FOR AN ACCOUNTS RECEIVABLE FILE."
760 PRINT "    2.   ADDING INVOICE ENTRIES TO THE ACCOUNTS RECEIVABLE FILE."
770 PRINT "    3.   REMOVAL OF INVOICE ENTRIES FROM THE FILES WHEN PAID."
780 PRINT "    4.   PRODUCING THE INVOICE WHICH WILL BE SENT TO THE CUSTOMER."
790 PRINT "    5.   PRODUCING THE CUSTOMERS' MONTHLY STATEMENTS"
800 PRINT "    6.   PRODUCING REPORTS OF ACCOUNTS RECEIVABLE."
810 PRINT "    7.   AGEING THE ACCOUNTS RECEIVABLE FILE AND APPLYING INTEREST."
820 PRINT "    8.   TERMINATE THE PROGRAM"
830 PRINT
840 '*******************************************************************************
850 PRINT:PRINT "SELECT: ";
860 Z$ = INKEY$:IF Z$ = "" THEN 860
870 PRINT Z$:PRINT
880 IF Z$ = "1" THEN PRINT "INITIAL ENTRY OF A/R DATA":PRINT
890 IF Z$ = "2" THEN PRINT "ADD INVOICE ENTRIES TO THE A/R FILE":PRINT
900 IF Z$ = "3" THEN PRINT "POST PAYMENTS TO A/R FILE":PRINT
910 IF Z$ = "4" THEN PRINT "PRODUCE CUSTOMER INVOICE":PRINT
920 IF Z$ = "5" THEN PRINT "PRODUCE CUSTOMER STATEMENTS":PRINT
930 IF Z$ = "6" THEN PRINT "PRODUCE A/R REPORTS":PRINT
940 IF Z$ = "7" THEN PRINT "AGE THE ACCOUNTS":PRINT
950 IF Z$ = "8" THEN 2970
960 FOR Z = 1 TO 1000:NEXT Z
970 MENU.SELECTION = VAL(Z$)
980 IF (MENU.SELECTION > 0) AND (MENU.SELECTION < 8) THEN 1050
990 LOCATE 25,1
1000 PRINT "INVALID CODE";
1010 BEEP
1020 FOR Z = 1 TO 1000:NEXT Z
1030 GOSUB 3440
1040 GOTO 720
1050 ON MENU.SELECTION GOTO 1150,1210,2810,2930,2850,2380,2890
1060 GOTO 990
1070 '*******************************************************************************
1080 '* THIS IS THE ROUTINE FOR ENTRY OF ACCOUNTS RECEIVABLE.   THE POINT OF *
1090 '* ENTRY TO THE ROUTINE DETERMINES IF A NEW FILES IS BEING CREATED OR  *
1100 '* IF AN EXISTING FILE IS TO BE USED.                                   *
1110 '*******************************************************************************
1120 '* ENTRY HERE (NEW FILE) REQUIRES ARRAY COUNT TO BE SET TO 0 TO         *
1130 '* ALLOW RELATIVE INCREMENTATION (RFS).                                 *
1140 '*******************************************************************************
1150 RECEIVE.FILE.SIZE = 0
1160 GOTO 1250
1170 '*******************************************************************************
1180 '* ENTRY HERE (ADD TO FILE) REQUIRES ARRAY COUNT TO BE SET TO FILE      *
1190 '* TO ALLOW RELATIVE INCREMENTATION (RFS).                              *
1200 '*******************************************************************************
1210 GOSUB 3550          'GET THE RECEIVABLES FILE
1220 FOR I = 1 TO RECEIVE.FILE.SIZE
1230      IF DOCUMENT.NUMBER(I) > HIGHEST.NUMBER THEN
                HIGHEST.NUMBER = DOCUMENT.NUMBER(I)
1240 NEXT I
1250 GOSUB 3440          'GET THE DISPLAY HEADING
1260 PRINT:PRINT "HIGHEST INVOICE IN THE FILE IS: ";HIGHEST.NUMBER
1270 PRINT:INPUT "ENTER THE BEGINNING INVOICE NUMBER: ",INVOICE.NUMBER
1280 IF INVOICE.NUMBER = 0 THEN BEEP:GOTO 1250
1290 IF INVOICE.NUMBER < = HIGHEST.NUMBER THEN BEEP:GOTO 1250
1300 INVOICE.NUMBER = INT(INVOICE.NUMBER)
1310 PRINT:PRINT "CORRECT (Y/N)? ";
1320 Z$ = INKEY$:IF Z$ = "" THEN 1320
1330 PRINT Z$
1340 IF Z$ < > "Y" THEN BEEP:GOTO 1250
1350 GOSUB 4320              'GET THE CUSTOMER FILE
```

```
1360 GOSUB 4150              'GET THE PRODUCT FILE
1370 GOSUB 3440              'GET THE DISPLAY HEADING
1380 PRINT:PRINT "INPUT IS TERMINATED BY QUESTION AT THE END OF EACH ENTRY"
1390 PRINT:PRINT "DO YOU NEED TO REVIEW THE CUSTOMER FILE (Y/N)? ";
1400 Z$ = INKEY$:IF Z$ = "" THEN 1400
1410 PRINT Z$
1420 IF Z$ = "Y" THEN GOSUB 4630:GOTO 1370
1430 PRINT
1440 PRINT "ENTER CUSTOMER NUMBER:";TAB(25);:INPUT "",WHICH.CUSTOMER
1450 IF (WHICH.CUSTOMER < 1) OR (WHICH.CUSTOMER > CUSTOMER.FILE.SIZE) THEN
          PRINT "CUSTOMER NUMBER INVALID":GOTO 1430
1460 GOSUB 5530
1470 IF ALREADY.ACCEPTED$ = "YES" THEN ALREADY.ACCEPTED$ = "NO":GOTO 1530
1480 PRINT:PRINT "CORRECT (Y/N)? ";
1490 Z$ = INKEY$:IF Z$ = "" THEN 1490
1500 PRINT Z$
1510 IF Z$ < > "Y" THEN BEEP:GOTO 1370
1520 ALREADY.ACCEPTED$ = "YES"
1530 PRINT:PRINT "DO YOU NEED TO REVIEW THE PRODUCT FILE (Y/N)? ";
1540 Z$ = INKEY$:IF Z$ = "" THEN 1540
1550 PRINT Z$
1560 IF Z$ = "Y" THEN GOSUB 5070:GOSUB 3440:GOSUB 5530:GOTO 1470
1570 PRINT
1580 INPUT "HOW MANY ITEMS ON THIS INVOICE (MAXIMUM 4)? ",INVOICE.ITEMS
1590 IF (INVOICE.ITEMS < 1) OR (INVOICE.ITEMS > 4) THEN PRINT
          "INVALID ENTRY - REPEAT":GOTO 1580
1600 BILLED.ITEMS = 1
1610 RFS = RECEIVE.FILE.SIZE + 1
1620 PRINT
1630 PRINT "ENTER PRODUCT NUMBER:";TAB(25);:INPUT "",WHICH.PRODUCT
1640 IF (WHICH.PRODUCT < 1) OR (WHICH.PRODUCT > PRODUCT.FILE.SIZE) THEN PRINT
          "INVALID PRODUCT NUMBER - REPEAT":GOTO 1620
1650 PRINT "PRODUCT.NAME:";TAB(25);PRODUCT.NAME$(WHICH.PRODUCT)
1660 PRINT "DESCRIPTION:";TAB(25);PRODUCT.DESCR$(WHICH.PRODUCT)
1670 PRINT "SHIPPING INSTRUCTIONS:";TAB(25);PRODUCT.SHIP.INSTR$(WHICH.PRODUCT)
1680 PRINT:PRINT "CORRECT (Y/N)? ";
1690 Z$ = INKEY$:IF Z$ = "" THEN 1690
1700 PRINT Z$
1710 IF Z$ < > "Y" THEN BEEP:GOTO 1620
1720 IF BILLED.ITEMS = 2 THEN 1850
1730 IF BILLED.ITEMS = 3 THEN 1950
1740 IF BILLED.ITEMS = 4 THEN 2050
1750 ITEM.1.NUMBER(RFS) = WHICH.PRODUCT
1760 ITEM.NAME.1$ = PRODUCT.NAME$(WHICH.PRODUCT)
1770 INPUT "HOW MANY WILL BE INVOICED? ",ITEM.1.QTY(RFS)
1780 IF ITEM.1.QTY(RFS) = 0 THEN 1770
1790 ITEM.1.QTY = INT(ITEM.1.QTY(RFS))
1800 INPUT "UNIT PRICE? $",ITEM.1.UNIT.PRICE(RFS)
1810 IF ITEM.1.UNIT.PRICE(RFS) = 0 THEN 1800
1820 IF BILLED.ITEMS = INVOICE.ITEMS THEN 2120
1830 BILLED.ITEMS = BILLED.ITEMS + 1
1840 GOTO 1620
1850 ITEM.2.NUMBER(RFS) = WHICH.PRODUCT
1860 ITEM.NAME.2$ = PRODUCT.NAME$(WHICH.PRODUCT)
1870 INPUT "HOW MANY WILL BE INVOICED? ",ITEM.2.QTY(RFS)
1880 IF ITEM.2.QTY(RFS) = 0 THEN 1870
1890 ITEM.2.QTY = INT(ITEM.2.QTY(RFS))
1900 INPUT "UNIT PRICE? $",ITEM.2.UNIT.PRICE(RFS)
1910 IF ITEM.2.UNIT.PRICE(RFS) = 0 THEN 1900
1920 IF BILLED.ITEMS = INVOICE.ITEMS THEN 2120
1930 BILLED.ITEMS = BILLED.ITEMS + 1
1940 GOTO 1620
1950 ITEM.3.NUMBER(RFS) = WHICH.PRODUCT
1960 ITEM.NAME.3$ = PRODUCT.NAME$(WHICH.PRODUCT)
1970 INPUT "HOW MANY WILL BE INVOICED? ",ITEM.3.QTY(RFS)
1980 IF ITEM.3.QTY(RFS) = 0 THEN 1970
1990 ITEM.3.QTY = INT(ITEM.3.QTY(RFS))
2000 INPUT "UNIT PRICE? $",ITEM.3.UNIT.PRICE(RFS)
2010 IF ITEM.3.UNIT.PRICE(RFS) = 0 THEN 2000
```

```
2020 IF BILLED.ITEMS = INVOICE.ITEMS THEN 2120
2030 BILLED.ITEMS = BILLED.ITEMS + 1
2040 GOTO 1620
2050 ITEM.4.NUMBER(RFS) = WHICH.PRODUCT
2060 ITEM.NAME.4$ = PRODUCT.NAME$(WHICH.PRODUCT)
2070 INPUT "HOW MANY WILL BE INVOICED? ",ITEM.4.QTY(RFS)
2080 IF ITEM.4.QTY(RFS) = 0 THEN 2070
2090 ITEM.4.QTY = INT(ITEM.4.QTY(RFS))
2100 INPUT "UNIT PRICE? $",ITEM.4.UNIT.PRICE(RFS)
2110 IF ITEM.4.UNIT.PRICE(RFS) = 0 THEN 2100
2120 '***********************************************************
2130 '* NOW THE INVOICE IS ASSEMBLED.  IT IS SHOWN FOR ACCEPTANCE *
2140 '***********************************************************
2150 PRINT CHR$(12)
2160 DATE.OF.INVOICE$(RFS) = INVOICE.DATE$
2170 DOCUMENT.NUMBER(RFS) = INVOICE.NUMBER
2180 CUSTOMER.NUMBER(RFS) = WHICH.CUSTOMER
2190 PRINT "DATE: ";DATE$;TAB(50);"INVOICE NUMBER: ";INVOICE.NUMBER
2200 GOSUB 5530
2210 PRINT
2220 GOSUB 5710
2230 PRINT "ACCEPTABLE (Y/N)? ";
2240 Z$ = INKEY$:IF Z$ = "" THEN 2240
2250 PRINT Z$
2260 IF Z$ < > "Y" THEN 1370
2270 RECEIVE.FILE.SIZE = RFS
2280 PRINT "DO YOU NOW WISH TO TERMINATE INPUT (Y/N)? ";
2290 Z$ = INKEY$:IF Z$ = "" THEN 2290
2300 PRINT Z$
2310 IF Z$ = "Y" THEN 2350
2320 INVOICE.NUMBER = INVOICE.NUMBER + 1
2330 GOTO 1370
2340 '***********************************************************
2350 GOSUB 3850                    'WRITE THE A/R FILE
2360 GOSUB 3440                    'GET THE HEADING
2370 GOTO 690                      'RETURN TO MAIN MENU
2380 '***********************************************************
2390 '* ROUTINE TO PRODUCE ACCOUNTS RECEIVABLE REPORTS *
2400 '***********************************************************
2410 GOSUB 4320          'GET THE CUSTOMER FILE
2420 GOSUB 3550          'GET THE RECEIVABLE FILE
2430 GOSUB 3440          'GET THE HEADING
2440 PRINT:PRINT "ACCOUNTS RECEIVABLE REPORT - DO YOU WANT A HARDCOPY (Y/N)? ";
2450 Z$ = INKEY$:IF Z$ = "" THEN 2450
2460 PRINT Z$
2470 IF Z$ < > "Y" THEN HARDCOPY$ = "NO":GOTO 2490
2480 HARDCOPY$ = "YES"
2490 PRINT
2500 FOR I = 1 TO RECEIVE.FILE.SIZE
2510     TOTAL.AMT.OF.INVOICES = TOTAL.AMT.OF.INVOICES + AMOUNT.OF.INVOICE(I)
2520     PRINT DOCUMENT.NUMBER(I),DATE.OF.INVOICE$(I),;
2530     PRINT USING "$$###,###.##";AMOUNT.OF.INVOICE(I)
2540     PRINT
2550     PRINT CUSTOMER.NAME$(CUSTOMER.NUMBER(I))
2560     PRINT CUSTOMER.ADDR.1$(CUSTOMER.NUMBER(I))
2570     PRINT CUSTOMER.ADDR.2$(CUSTOMER.NUMBER(I))
2580     PRINT CUSTOMER.ADDR.3$(CUSTOMER.NUMBER(I))
2590     PRINT CUSTOMER.ADDR.4$(CUSTOMER.NUMBER(I))
2600     PRINT
2610     PRINT STRING$(79,"-")
2620     PRINT
2630     IF HARDCOPY$ = "YES" THEN 2650
2640     FOR Z = 1 TO 1500:NEXT Z:GOTO 2760
2650     LPRINT DOCUMENT.NUMBER(I),DATE.OF.INVOICE$(I),;
2660     LPRINT USING "$$###,###.##";AMOUNT.OF.INVOICE(I)
2670     LPRINT
2680     LPRINT CUSTOMER.NAME$(CUSTOMER.NUMBER(I))
2690     LPRINT CUSTOMER.ADDR.1$(CUSTOMER.NUMBER(I))
2700     LPRINT CUSTOMER.ADDR.2$(CUSTOMER.NUMBER(I))
```

```
2710     LPRINT CUSTOMER.ADDR.3$(CUSTOMER.NUMBER(I))
2720     LPRINT CUSTOMER.ADDR.4$(CUSTOMER.NUMBER(I))
2730     LPRINT
2740     LPRINT STRING$(79,"-")
2750     LPRINT
2760 NEXT I
2770     PRINT USING "TOTAL VALUE OF INVOICES: $$##,###.##";
             TOTAL.AMT.OF.INVOICES
2780     IF HARDCOPY$ = "YES" THEN
             LPRINT USING "TOTAL VALUE OF INVOICES: $$##,###.##";
             TOTAL.AMT.OF.INVOICES:LPRINT CHR$(12)
2790 GOSUB 3440                         'GET THE HEADING
2800 GOTO 690                           'RETURN TO MAIN MENU
2810 '*****************************
2820 '* ROUTINE TO POST PAYMENTS *
2830 '*****************************
2840 CHAIN "A:POSTREC.BAS"
2850 '**********************************
2860 '* ROUTINE TO PRODUCE A STATEMENT *
2870 '**********************************
2880 CHAIN "A:STATMENT.BAS"
2890 '********************************
2900 '* ROUTINE TO AGE THE ACCOUNTS *
2910 '********************************
2920 CHAIN "A:AGEING.BAS"
2930 '*********************************************
2940 '* INVOICE DISPLAY AND PRINTING ROUTINE *
2950 '*********************************************
2960 CHAIN "A:INVOICE.BAS"
2970 '***************************
2980 '* PROGRAM TERMINATION *
2990 '***************************
3000 PRINT
3010 PRINT "INVOICE PREPARATION IS COMPLETE"
3020 PRINT
3030 PRINT "DO YOU WISH TO REPEAT THE PROGRAM (Y/N)? ";
3040 Z$ = INKEY$:IF Z$ = "" THEN 3040
3050 PRINT Z$
3060 IF Z$ < > "Y" THEN 3430
3070 ERASE CUSTOMER.NUMBER
3080 ERASE DATE.OF.INVOICE$
3090 ERASE DOCUMENT.NUMBER
3100 ERASE ITEM.1.NUMBER
3110 ERASE ITEM.1.QTY
3120 ERASE ITEM.1.UNIT.PRICE
3130 ERASE ITEM.2.NUMBER
3140 ERASE ITEM.2.UNIT.PRICE
3150 ERASE ITEM.3.NUMBER
3160 ERASE ITEM.3.QTY
3170 ERASE ITEM.3.UNIT.PRICE
3180 ERASE ITEM.4.NUMBER
3190 ERASE ITEM.4.QTY
3200 ERASE ITEM.4.UNIT.PRICE
3210 ERASE AMOUNT.OF.INVOICE
3220 ERASE AMOUNT.LESS.THAN.30.DAYS
3230 ERASE AMOUNT.AT.30.DAYS
3240 ERASE AMOUNT.AT.60.DAYS
3250 ERASE AMOUNT.AT.90.DAYS
3260 ERASE PRODUCT.NAME$
3270 ERASE PRODUCT.DESCR$
3280 ERASE PRODUCT.UNIT$
3290 ERASE PRODUCT.LOCATION$
3300 ERASE PRODUCT.Q.O.H
3310 ERASE PRODUCT.R.O.P
3320 ERASE PRODUCT.SHIP.INSTR$
3330 ERASE CUSTOMER.NAME$
3340 ERASE CUSTOMER.ADDR.1$
3350 ERASE CUSTOMER.ADDR.2$
3360 ERASE CUSTOMER.ADDR.3$
```

```
3370 ERASE CUSTOMER.ADDR.4$
3380 ERASE CUSTOMER.TERMS$
3390 ERASE T$
3400 ERASE N$
3410 ERASE A
3420 GOTO 10
3430 CHAIN "A:BUSINESS.BAS"
3440 '*********************************
3450 '* HEADING USED FOR THE DISPLAY *
3460 '*********************************
3470 CLS
3480 X = ((80 - LEN(COMPANY.NAME$)) / 2)
3490 LOCATE 2,X
3500 PRINT COMPANY.NAME$
3510 PRINT STRING$(79,220):PRINT
3520 PRINT TAB(19);"ACCOUNTS RECEIVABLE PROCESSING PROGRAM"
3530 PRINT STRING$(79,220)
3540 RETURN
3550 '*********************************
3560 '* OPEN AND INPUT RECEIVABLE FILE *
3570 '*********************************
3580 PRINT:PRINT "LOADING THE RECEIVABLES FILE"
3590 OPEN "I",1,"RECEIVE.DAT"
3600 INPUT #1,RECEIVE.FILE.SIZE          'OBTAIN THE RECORD COUNT
3610 FOR I = 1 TO RECEIVE.FILE.SIZE
3620       INPUT #1,CUSTOMER.NUMBER(I)
3630       LINE INPUT #1,DATE.OF.INVOICE$(I)
3640       INPUT #1,DOCUMENT.NUMBER(I)
3650       INPUT #1,ITEM.1.NUMBER(I)
3660       INPUT #1,ITEM.1.QTY(I)
3670       INPUT #1,ITEM.1.UNIT.PRICE(I)
3680       INPUT #1,ITEM.2.NUMBER(I)
3690       INPUT #1,ITEM.2.QTY(I)
3700       INPUT #1,ITEM.2.UNIT.PRICE(I)
3710       INPUT #1,ITEM.3.NUMBER(I)
3720       INPUT #1,ITEM.3.QTY(I)
3730       INPUT #1,ITEM.3.UNIT.PRICE(I)
3740       INPUT #1,ITEM.4.NUMBER(I)
3750       INPUT #1,ITEM.4.QTY(I)
3760       INPUT #1,ITEM.4.UNIT.PRICE(I)
3770       INPUT #1,AMOUNT.OF.INVOICE(I)
3780       INPUT #1,AMOUNT.LESS.THAN.30.DAYS(I)
3790       INPUT #1,AMOUNT.AT.30.DAYS(I)
3800       INPUT #1,AMOUNT.AT.60.DAYS(I)
3810       INPUT #1,AMOUNT.AT.90.DAYS(I)
3820 NEXT I
3830 CLOSE 1
3840 RETURN
3850 '*************************************
3860 '* OPEN AND OUTPUT RECEIVABLE FILE *
3870 '*************************************
3880 PRINT:PRINT "WRITING THE RECEIVABLES FILE"
3890 OPEN "O",1,"RECEIVE.DAT"
3900 PRINT #1,RECEIVE.FILE.SIZE          'STORE THE RECORD COUNT
3910 FOR I = 1 TO RECEIVE.FILE.SIZE
3920       PRINT #1,CUSTOMER.NUMBER(I)
3930       PRINT #1,DATE.OF.INVOICE$(I)
3940       PRINT #1,DOCUMENT.NUMBER(I)
3950       PRINT #1,ITEM.1.NUMBER(I)
3960       PRINT #1,ITEM.1.QTY(I)
3970       PRINT #1,ITEM.1.UNIT.PRICE(I)
3980       PRINT #1,ITEM.2.NUMBER(I)
3990       PRINT #1,ITEM.2.QTY(I)
4000       PRINT #1,ITEM.2.UNIT.PRICE(I)
4010       PRINT #1,ITEM.3.NUMBER(I)
4020       PRINT #1,ITEM.3.QTY(I)
4030       PRINT #1,ITEM.3.UNIT.PRICE(I)
4040       PRINT #1,ITEM.4.NUMBER(I)
4050       PRINT #1,ITEM.4.QTY(I)
```

```
4060      PRINT #1,ITEM.4.UNIT.PRICE(I)
4070      PRINT #1,AMOUNT.OF.INVOICE(I)
4080      PRINT #1,AMOUNT.LESS.THAN.30.DAYS(I)
4090      PRINT #1,AMOUNT.AT.30.DAYS(I)
4100      PRINT #1,AMOUNT.AT.60.DAYS(I)
4110      PRINT #1,AMOUNT.AT.90.DAYS(I)
4120 NEXT I
4130 CLOSE 1
4140 RETURN
4150 '********************************
4160 '* OPEN AND INPUT PRODUCT FILE *
4170 '********************************
4180 PRINT:PRINT "LOADING THE PRODUCT FILE"
4190 OPEN "I",1,"PRODUCT.DAT"
4200 INPUT #1,PRODUCT.FILE.SIZE        'OBTAIN THE RECORD COUNT
4210 FOR J = 1 TO PRODUCT.FILE.SIZE
4220      LINE INPUT #1,PRODUCT.NAME$(J)
4230      LINE INPUT #1,PRODUCT.DESCR$(J)
4240      LINE INPUT #1,PRODUCT.UNIT$(J)
4250      LINE INPUT #1,PRODUCT.LOCATION$(J)
4260      INPUT #1,PRODUCT.Q.O.H(J)
4270      INPUT #1,PRODUCT.R.O.P(J)
4280      LINE INPUT #1,PRODUCT.SHIP.INSTR$(J)
4290 NEXT J
4300 CLOSE 1
4310 RETURN
4320 '********************************
4330 '* OPEN AND INPUT CUSTOMER FILE *
4340 '********************************
4350 PRINT:PRINT "LOADING THE CUSTOMER FILE"
4360 OPEN "I",1,"CUSTOMER.DAT"
4370 INPUT #1,CUSTOMER.FILE.SIZE       'OBTAIN THE RECORD COUNT
4380 FOR K = 1 TO CUSTOMER.FILE.SIZE
4390      LINE INPUT #1,CUSTOMER.NAME$(K)
4400      LINE INPUT #1,CUSTOMER.ADDR.1$(K)
4410      LINE INPUT #1,CUSTOMER.ADDR.2$(K)
4420      LINE INPUT #1,CUSTOMER.ADDR.3$(K)
4430      LINE INPUT #1,CUSTOMER.ADDR.4$(K)
4440      LINE INPUT #1,CUSTOMER.TERMS$(K)
4450 NEXT K
4460 CLOSE 1
4470 RETURN
4480 '********************************
4490 '* OPEN AND INPUT ACCOUNT FILE *
4500 '********************************
4510 PRINT:PRINT "LOADING THE ACCOUNT FILE"
4520 PRINT:INPUT "SPECIFY THE ACCOUNT FILE TO BE USED: ",SPECIFIED.FILE$
4530 SPECIFIED.FILE$ = SPECIFIED.FILE$ + ".DAT"
4540 OPEN "I",1,SPECIFIED.FILE$
4550 INPUT #1,SPECIFIED.FILE.SIZE      'OBTAIN THE RECORD COUNT
4560 FOR L = 1 TO SPECIFIED.FILE.SIZE
4570      LINE INPUT #1,T$(L)
4580      LINE INPUT #1,N$(L)
4590      INPUT #1,A(L)
4600 NEXT L
4610 CLOSE 1
4620 RETURN
4630 '**********************************************************************
4640 '* REVIEW THE MATRIX IN WHICH THE CUSTOMER FILE HAS BEEN STORED *
4650 '**********************************************************************
4660 PRINT:PRINT "DO YOU WISH CONTINUOUS DISPLAY (Y/N)? ";
4670 Z$ = INKEY$:IF Z$ = "" THEN 4670
4680 PRINT Z$
4690 IF Z$ = "Y" THEN CONTINUE$ = "YES":GOTO 4710
4700 CONTINUE$ = "NO"
4710 PRINT:PRINT "DO YOU WISH TO OBTAIN A HARD COPY (Y/N)? ";
4720 Z$ = INKEY$:IF Z$ = "" THEN 4720
4730 PRINT Z$
4740 IF Z$ = "Y" THEN HARDCOPY$ = "YES":GOTO 4760
```

```
4750 HARDCOPY$ = "NO"
4760 FOR I = 1 TO CUSTOMER.FILE.SIZE
4770     PRINT
4780     PRINT "CUSTOMER NUMBER: ";I
4790     PRINT
4800     PRINT "CUSTOMER NAME:";TAB(25);CUSTOMER.NAME$(I)
4810     PRINT
4820     PRINT "CUSTOMER ADDRESS:";TAB(25);CUSTOMER.ADDR.1$(I)
4830     PRINT TAB(25);CUSTOMER.ADDR.2$(I)
4840     PRINT TAB(25);CUSTOMER.ADDR.3$(I)
4850     PRINT TAB(25);CUSTOMER.ADDR.4$(I)
4860     PRINT
4870     IF CONTINUE$ = "YES" THEN 4910
4880     PRINT "PRESS 'X' TO EXIT -- ANY OTHER KEY TO CONTINUE"
4890     Z$ = INKEY$:IF Z$ = "" THEN 4890
4900     IF Z$ = "X" THEN 5060
4910     IF (HARDCOPY$ = "NO") AND (CONTINUE$ = "NO") THEN 4930
4920     FOR Z = 1 TO 1500:NEXT Z
4930     IF HARDCOPY$ = "NO" THEN 5050
4940     LPRINT
4950     LPRINT
4960     LPRINT "CUSTOMER NUMBER: ";I
4970     LPRINT
4980     LPRINT "CUSTOMER NAME:";TAB(25);CUSTOMER.NAME$(I)
4990     LPRINT
5000     LPRINT "CUSTOMER ADDRESS:";TAB(25);CUSTOMER.ADDR.1$(I)
5010     LPRINT TAB(25);CUSTOMER.ADDR.2$(I)
5020     LPRINT TAB(25);CUSTOMER.ADDR.3$(I)
5030     LPRINT TAB(25);CUSTOMER.ADDR.4$(I)
5040     LPRINT
5050 NEXT I
5060 RETURN
5070 '**********************************************************************
5080 '* REVIEW THE MATRIX IN WHICH THE PRODUCT FILE HAS BEEN STORED *
5090 '**********************************************************************
5100 PRINT:PRINT "DO YOU WISH CONTINUOUS DISPLAY (Y/N)? ";
5110 Z$ = INKEY$:IF Z$ = "" THEN 5110
5120 PRINT Z$
5130 IF Z$ = "Y" THEN CONTINUE$ = "YES":GOTO 5150
5140 CONTINUE$ = "NO"
5150 PRINT:PRINT "DO YOU WISH TO OBTAIN A HARD COPY (Y/N)? ";
5160 Z$ = INKEY$:IF Z$ = "" THEN 5160
5170 PRINT Z$
5180 IF Z$ = "Y" THEN HARDCOPY$ = "YES":GOTO 5200
5190 HARDCOPY$ = "NO"
5200 FOR J = 1 TO PRODUCT.FILE.SIZE
5210     PRINT
5220     PRINT "PRODUCT NUMBER: ";J
5230     PRINT
5240     PRINT "PRODUCT NAME:";TAB(25);PRODUCT.NAME$(J)
5250     PRINT
5260     PRINT "DESCRIPTION:";TAB(25);PRODUCT.DESCR$(J)
5270     PRINT "UNIT OF MEASURE:";TAB(25);PRODUCT.UNIT$(J)
5280     PRINT "LOCATION:";TAB(25);PRODUCT.UNIT$(J)
5290     PRINT "QUANTITY ON HAND:";TAB(25);PRODUCT.Q.O.H(J)
5300     PRINT "REORDER POINT:";TAB(25);PRODUCT.R.O.P(J)
5310     PRINT "SHIPPING INSTRUCTIONS:";TAB(25);PRODUCT.SHIP.INSTR$(J)
5320     PRINT
5330     IF CONTINUE$ = "YES" THEN 5370
5340     PRINT "PRESS 'X' TO EXIT -- ANY OTHER KEY TO CONTINUE"
5350     Z$ = INKEY$:IF Z$ = "" THEN 5350
5360     IF Z$ = "X" THEN 5520
5370     IF (HARDCOPY$ = "NO") AND (CONTINUE$ = "NO") THEN 5390
5380     FOR Z = 1 TO 1500:NEXT Z
5390     IF HARDCOPY$ = "NO" THEN 5510
5400     LPRINT
5410     LPRINT
5420     LPRINT "PRODUCT NAME:";TAB(25);PRODUCT.NAME$(J)
5430     LPRINT
```

```
5440      LPRINT "DESCRIPTION:";TAB(25);PRODUCT.DESCR$(J)
5450      LPRINT "UNIT OF MEASURE:";TAB(25);PRODUCT.UNIT$(J)
5460      LPRINT "LOCATION:";TAB(25);PRODUCT.UNIT$(J)
5470      LPRINT "QUANTITY ON HAND:";TAB(25);PRODUCT.Q.O.H(J)
5480      LPRINT "REORDER POINT:";TAB(25);PRODUCT.R.O.P(J)
5490      LPRINT "SHIPPING INSTRUCTIONS:";TAB(25);PRODUCT.SHIP.INSTR$(J)
5500      LPRINT
5510 NEXT J
5520 RETURN
5530 '**********************************************************************
5540 '* THIS IS A ROUTINE USED MORE THAN ONCE TO DISPLAY THE CUSTOMER INFO *
5550 '**********************************************************************
5560 PRINT "CUSTOMER.NAME:";TAB(25);CUSTOMER.NAME$(WHICH.CUSTOMER)
5570 PRINT "CUSTOMER ADDRESS:";TAB(25);CUSTOMER.ADDR.1$(WHICH.CUSTOMER)
5580 PRINT TAB(25);CUSTOMER.ADDR.2$(WHICH.CUSTOMER)
5590 PRINT TAB(25);CUSTOMER.ADDR.3$(WHICH.CUSTOMER)
5600 PRINT TAB(25);CUSTOMER.ADDR.4$(WHICH.CUSTOMER)
5610 RETURN
5620 '**********************************************************************
5630 '* THIS IS A ROUTINE USED MORE THAN ONCE TO PRINT THE CUSTOMER INFO *
5640 '**********************************************************************
5650 LPRINT "CUSTOMER.NAME:";TAB(25);CUSTOMER.NAME$(WHICH.CUSTOMER)
5660 LPRINT "CUSTOMER ADDRESS:";TAB(25);CUSTOMER.ADDR.1$(WHICH.CUSTOMER)
5670 LPRINT TAB(25);CUSTOMER.ADDR.2$(WHICH.CUSTOMER)
5680 LPRINT TAB(25);CUSTOMER.ADDR.3$(WHICH.CUSTOMER)
5690 LPRINT TAB(25);CUSTOMER.ADDR.4$(WHICH.CUSTOMER)
5700 RETURN
5710 '********************************************
5720 '* ROUTINE TO DISPLAY THE INVOICE DETAIL *
5730 '********************************************
5740 PRINT "ITEM";TAB(10);"QUANTITY";TAB(30);"DESCRIPTION";
5750 PRINT TAB(60);"PRICE";TAB(70);"EXTENSION"
5760 ITEM.1.EXTENSION = (ITEM.1.QTY(RFS) * ITEM.1.UNIT.PRICE(RFS))
5770 ITEM.2.EXTENSION = (ITEM.2.QTY(RFS) * ITEM.2.UNIT.PRICE(RFS))
5780 ITEM.3.EXTENSION = (ITEM.3.QTY(RFS) * ITEM.3.UNIT.PRICE(RFS))
5790 ITEM.4.EXTENSION = (ITEM.4.QTY(RFS) * ITEM.4.UNIT.PRICE(RFS))
5800 PRINT STRING$(79,"-")
5810 PRINT ITEM.1.NUMBER(RFS);TAB(13);ITEM.1.QTY(RFS);TAB(30);
5820 PRINT ITEM.NAME.1$;TAB(55);
5830 PRINT USING "##,###.##";ITEM.1.UNIT.PRICE(RFS);
5840 PRINT TAB(70);"";:PRINT USING "##,###.##";ITEM.1.EXTENSION
5850 IF ITEM.NAME.2$ = "" THEN 6010
5860 PRINT ITEM.2.NUMBER(RFS);TAB(13);ITEM.2.QTY(RFS);TAB(30);
5870 PRINT ITEM.NAME.2$;TAB(55);
5880 PRINT USING "##,###.##";ITEM.2.UNIT.PRICE(RFS);
5890 PRINT TAB(70);"";:PRINT USING "##,###.##";ITEM.2.EXTENSION
5900 IF ITEM.NAME.3$ = "" THEN 6010
5910 PRINT ITEM.3.NUMBER(RFS);TAB(13);ITEM.3.QTY(RFS);TAB(30);
5920 PRINT ITEM.NAME.3$;TAB(55);
5930 PRINT USING "##,###.##";ITEM.3.UNIT.PRICE(RFS);
5940 PRINT TAB(70);"";:PRINT USING "##,###.##";ITEM.3.EXTENSION
5950 IF ITEM.NAME.4$ = "" THEN 6010
5960 PRINT ITEM.4.NUMBER(RFS);TAB(13);ITEM.4.QTY(RFS);TAB(30);
5970 PRINT ITEM.NAME.4$;TAB(55);
5980 PRINT USING "##,###.##";ITEM.4.UNIT.PRICE(RFS);
5990 PRINT TAB(70);"";:PRINT USING "##,###.##";ITEM.4.EXTENSION
6000 PRINT TAB(68);"--------------"
6010 AMOUNT.OF.INVOICE(RFS) = 0
6020 AMOUNT.OF.INVOICE(RFS) = AMOUNT.OF.INVOICE(RFS) + ITEM.1.EXTENSION
6030 AMOUNT.OF.INVOICE(RFS) = AMOUNT.OF.INVOICE(RFS) + ITEM.2.EXTENSION
6040 AMOUNT.OF.INVOICE(RFS) = AMOUNT.OF.INVOICE(RFS) + ITEM.3.EXTENSION
6050 AMOUNT.OF.INVOICE(RFS) = AMOUNT.OF.INVOICE(RFS) + ITEM.4.EXTENSION
6060 PRINT "AMOUNT DUE:";
6070 PRINT TAB(68);"";:PRINT USING "$$###,###.##";AMOUNT.OF.INVOICE(RFS)
6080 AMOUNT.LESS.THAN.30.DAYS(RFS) = AMOUNT.OF.INVOICE(RFS)
6090 PRINT TAB(68);"============="
6100 RETURN
6110 '******************************************
6120 '* ROUTINE TO PRINT THE INVOICE DETAIL *
```

```
6130 '*****************************************
6140 LPRINT "ITEM";TAB(10);"QUANTITY";TAB(30);"DESCRIPTION";
6150 LPRINT TAB(60);"PRICE";TAB(70);"EXTENSION"
6160 ITEM.1.EXTENSION = (ITEM.1.QTY(RFS) * ITEM.1.UNIT.PRICE(RFS))
6170 ITEM.2.EXTENSION = (ITEM.2.QTY(RFS) * ITEM.2.UNIT.PRICE(RFS))
6180 ITEM.3.EXTENSION = (ITEM.3.QTY(RFS) * ITEM.3.UNIT.PRICE(RFS))
6190 ITEM.4.EXTENSION = (ITEM.4.QTY(RFS) * ITEM.4.UNIT.PRICE(RFS))
6200 PRINT STRING$(79,"-")
6210 LPRINT ITEM.1.NUMBER(RFS);TAB(13);ITEM.1.QTY(RFS);TAB(30);
6220 LPRINT ITEM.NAME.1$;TAB(55);
6230 LPRINT USING "##,###.##";ITEM.1.UNIT.PRICE(RFS);
6240 LPRINT TAB(70);"";:PRINT USING "##,###.##";ITEM.1.EXTENSION
6250 IF ITEM.NAME.2$ = "" THEN 6430
6260 LPRINT
6270 LPRINT ITEM.2.NUMBER(RFS);TAB(13);ITEM.2.QTY(RFS);TAB(30);
6280 LPRINT ITEM.NAME.2$;TAB(55);
6290 LPRINT USING "##,###.##";ITEM.2.UNIT.PRICE(RFS);
6300 LPRINT TAB(70);"";:PRINT USING "##,###.##";ITEM.2.EXTENSION
6310 IF ITEM.NAME.3$ = "" THEN 6430
6320 LPRINT
6330 LPRINT ITEM.3.NUMBER(RFS);TAB(13);ITEM.3.QTY(RFS);TAB(30);
6340 LPRINT ITEM.NAME.3$;TAB(55);
6350 LPRINT USING "##,###.##";ITEM.3.UNIT.PRICE(RFS);
6360 LPRINT TAB(70);"";:PRINT USING "##,###.##";ITEM.3.EXTENSION
6370 IF ITEM.NAME.4$ = "" THEN 6430
6380 LPRINT
6390 LPRINT ITEM.4.NUMBER(RFS);TAB(13);ITEM.4.QTY(RFS);TAB(30);
6400 LPRINT ITEM.NAME.4$;TAB(55);
6410 LPRINT USING "##,###.##";ITEM.4.UNIT.PRICE(RFS);
6420 LPRINT TAB(70);"";:PRINT USING "##,###.##";ITEM.4.EXTENSION
6430 LPRINT TAB(68);"--------------"
6440 LPRINT
6450 AMOUNT.OF.INVOICE(RFS) = 0
6460 AMOUNT.OF.INVOICE(RFS) = AMOUNT.OF.INVOICE(RFS) + ITEM.1.EXTENSION
6470 AMOUNT.OF.INVOICE(RFS) = AMOUNT.OF.INVOICE(RFS) + ITEM.2.EXTENSION
6480 AMOUNT.OF.INVOICE(RFS) = AMOUNT.OF.INVOICE(RFS) + ITEM.3.EXTENSION
6490 AMOUNT.OF.INVOICE(RFS) = AMOUNT.OF.INVOICE(RFS) + ITEM.4.EXTENSION
6500 PRINT "AMOUNT DUE:";
6510 PRINT TAB(68);"";:PRINT USING "$$##,###.##";AMOUNT.OF.INVOICE(RFS)
6520 AMOUNT.LESS.THAN.30.DAYS(RFS) = AMOUNT.OF.INVOICE(RFS)
6530 PRINT TAB(68);"============="
6540 RETURN
6550 '*****************************************
6560 '* ROUTINE TO DISPLAY THE AGEING DETAIL *
6570 '*****************************************
6580 PRINT STRING$(79,"-")
6590 PRINT "30 DAYS OR LESS";TAB(20);"30 - 60 DAYS";TAB(40);
6600 PRINT "60 - 90 DAYS";TAB(60);"90 DAYS AND OVER"
6610 PRINT USING "$$##,###.##";AMOUNT.LESS.THAN.30.DAYS(I);
6620 PRINT TAB(20);"";
6630 PRINT USING "$$##,###.##";AMOUNT.AT.30.DAYS(I);
6640 PRINT TAB(37);"";
6650 PRINT USING "$$##,###.##";AMOUNT.AT.60.DAYS(I);
6660 PRINT TAB(57);"";
6670 PRINT USING "$$##,###.##";AMOUNT.AT.90.DAYS(I)
6680 PRINT STRING$(79,"-")
6690 RETURN
6700 '*****************************************
6710 '* ROUTINE TO PRINT THE AGEING DETAIL *
6720 '*****************************************
6730 LPRINT STRING$(79,"-")
6740 LPRINT "30 DAYS OR LESS";TAB(20);"30 - 60 DAYS";TAB(40);
6750 LPRINT "60 - 90 DAYS";TAB(60);"90 DAYS AND OVER"
6760 LPRINT USING "$$##,###.##";AMOUNT.LESS.THAN.30.DAYS(I);
6770 LPRINT TAB(20);"";
6780 LPRINT USING "$$##,###.##";AMOUNT.AT.30.DAYS(I);
6790 LPRINT TAB(37);"";
6800 LPRINT USING "$$##,###.##";AMOUNT.AT.60.DAYS(I);
6810 LPRINT TAB(57);"";
```

```
6820 LPRINT USING "$$###,###.##";AMOUNT.AT.90.DAYS(I)
6830 LPRINT
6840 LPRINT STRING$(79,"-")
6850 RETURN
```

The opening of this program differs somewhat from what we've become accustomed to. The DATE$ facility of DOS and BASIC gives you back a date that looks like MM-DD-YYYY. May 25, 1982, for instance, looks like 05-25-1982 on the PC. For much of what is done with the machine, that presentation is sufficient. However, since some people like their dates to look a little different, the instructions from statement 50 through 200 are designed to provide the difference. Think of the date in the following manner:

05-25-1982

1234567890

Thus, it can be seen that the date takes up ten positions. Now look at statement 20, and you'll see that the first two positions are isolated in a place called INVOICE.MONTH$. Note in all cases that we are dealing with a string variable. Thus, LEFT$(DATE$,2) separates the *string* 05. Next, we use the MID$ of statement 30 to select the two characters that begin in the fourth position, which are 25. Finally we use the RIGHT$ of statement 40 to select the four characters that specify the year. Because the month is in string form, it was decided to change it to a numeric comparand. To do so wasn't really important, as a string comparand would have worked just as well. In any event, a word is produced for the month, the day and the punctuation are then combined with it, and finally the year is added before the date is displayed.

In statements 880-950, the words corresponding to the line number selected are displayed, and the display is frozen by statement 960. The response is then changed from a string variable to a numeric variable and used both in the range check of statement 980 and in the ON . . . GOTO of statement 1050.

The CHAIN statements to call programs that are not incorporated are located in statements 2810-2960. It is possible to repeat the program, but the DIMensioning must be removed to do so, and that is done between statements 3070 and 3420. If the program is terminated, the frame program is called in statement 3430.

The commonly used routines begin in 3440. Note the contents of the receivables file, as defined in statements 3550-3840. There is a customer number (which can be different from the record number, as we have previously discussed), the date of the invoice, the number of the invoice, and the provision of four items. Again, the maximum was set at four items — a design choice made because of the size of the system and the available media. You may wish to change the posting program so that it will merely separate records to a dead file rather than cancel them. If you do so, you will have the basis for developing sales statistics over an extended and cyclical period.

The aging information is part of the record. Note that the aging is performed at the invoice level. You will see later that it is done within category and that the accumulated interest is reflected as an additional line item to the statement. We'll have more to say about that when the POSTREC.BAS, STATMENT.BAS, and AGEING.BAS programs are discussed.

The rest of this program is fairly straightforward and easily understood. Two block diagrams that describe it are shown in Figs. 7-8(A) and 7-8(B). The program either builds RECEIVE.DAT from scratch or adds to it. The invoice data combines information from the customer and product files in the preparation of invoice data. The actual production of the invoice takes place in INVOICE.BAS. In like manner, statements are produced in the program STATMENT.BAS. Records are posted and aged in the subordinate programs POSTREC.BAS and AGEING.BAS, respectively.

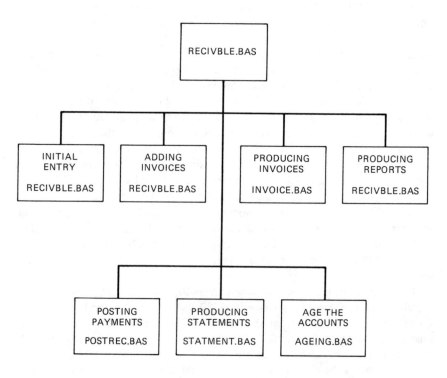

Fig. 7-8(A) Accounts Receivable Subsystem

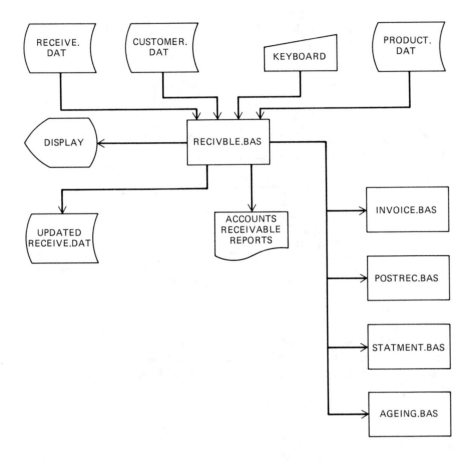

Fig. 7-8(B) Accounts Receivable Subsystem

INVOICE.BAS

The invoicing program takes the file developed in RECIVBLE.BAS and transfers it to paper. If you look at statements 20 through 200, you'll see that the same routine is used to develop the date that does onto the invoice.

It is possible to specify a beginning place: either those invoices that have been produced on the date of the run or a beginning invoice number if you are unable to run the invoices on the day they are prepared.

In the same manner as the invoices are displayed on the screen, they are transferred to paper, with the exception that the paper is ejected between in-

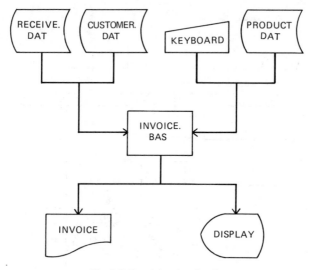

Fig. 7-9 Invoicing Application

voices. This is the purpose of the LPRINT CHR$(12) at statement 1230. A
block diagram for the invoicing application appears in Fig. 7-9. This program,
which is subordinate to RECIVBLE.BAS, takes the information written to
file by that program and produces displayed and paper output. If a given
starting place is desired, it may be specified; else, the invoices for the entire
file are produced.

The invoice produced looks as follows:

```
INVOICE.NUMBER 555                              DATE: MAY 24, 1982
CUSTOMER.NAME:          SEARS
CUSTOMER ADDRESS:       SEARSLAND
                        100 LUNENBERG PARKWAY
                        LEOMINSTER,
                        MASSACHUSETTS 01377

------------------------------------------------------------------------------

ITEM       QUANTITY              DESCRIPTION              PRICE     EXTENSION
1          1                     WIDGET                  111.11        111.11

2          2                     GIZMO                   222.22        444.44
                                                                   --------------

AMOUNT DUE:                                                          $555.55
                                                                   ==============


------------------------------------------------------------------------------
30 DAYS OR LESS     30 - 60 DAYS       60 - 90 DAYS     90 DAYS AND OVER
    $555.55             $0.00              $0.00             $0.00

------------------------------------------------------------------------------
```

One of the things you'll learn as you do more and more programming is that you'll have to plan for many contingencies. Since there is a possibility that the invoice application will become tied to the statement application, a routine has been included to obtain input from the specified account file. That particular routine (statements 2780-2920) is not invoked in the program; it is merely there in case it is needed.

Note that when the program is complete, it CHAINs back to RECIVBLE. BAS, *not* to BUSINESS.BAS. In other words, the chain is followed in both directions.

Here is the program INVOICE.BAS:

```
10 GOSUB 1740
20 INVOICE.MONTH$ = LEFT$(DATE$,2)
30 INVOICE.DAY$ = MID$(DATE$,4,2)
40 INVOICE.YEAR$ = RIGHT$(DATE$,4)
50 IF VAL(INVOICE.MONTH$) = 1 THEN INVOICE.MONTH$ = "JANUARY"
60 IF VAL(INVOICE.MONTH$) = 2 THEN INVOICE.MONTH$ = "FEBRUARY"
70 IF VAL(INVOICE.MONTH$) = 3 THEN INVOICE.MONTH$ = "MARCH"
80 IF VAL(INVOICE.MONTH$) = 4 THEN INVOICE.MONTH$ = "APRIL"
90 IF VAL(INVOICE.MONTH$) = 5 THEN INVOICE.MONTH$ = "MAY"
100 IF VAL(INVOICE.MONTH$) = 6 THEN INVOICE.MONTH$ = "JUNE"
110 IF VAL(INVOICE.MONTH$) = 7 THEN INVOICE.MONTH$ = "JULY"
120 IF VAL(INVOICE.MONTH$) = 8 THEN INVOICE.MONTH$ = "AUGUST"
130 IF VAL(INVOICE.MONTH$) = 9 THEN INVOICE.MONTH$ = "SEPTEMBER"
140 IF VAL(INVOICE.MONTH$) = 10 THEN INVOICE.MONTH$ = "OCTOBER"
150 IF VAL(INVOICE.MONTH$) = 11 THEN INVOICE.MONTH$ = "NOVEMBER"
160 IF VAL(INVOICE.MONTH$) = 12 THEN INVOICE.MONTH$ = "DECEMBER"
170 INVOICE.MONTH$ = INVOICE.MONTH$ + " "
180 INVOICE.DATE$ = INVOICE.MONTH$ + INVOICE.DAY$ + ", " + INVOICE.YEAR$
190 PRINT
200 PRINT INVOICE.DATE$
210 '*********************************
220 '* DIMENSION THE RECEIVABLES FILE. *
230 '*********************************
240 DIM CUSTOMER.NUMBER(100)
250 DIM DATE.OF.INVOICE$(100)
260 DIM DOCUMENT.NUMBER(100)
270 DIM ITEM.1.NUMBER(100)
280 DIM ITEM.1.QTY(100)
290 DIM ITEM.1.UNIT.PRICE(100)
300 DIM ITEM.2.NUMBER(100)
310 DIM ITEM.2.QTY(100)
320 DIM ITEM.2.UNIT.PRICE(100)
330 DIM ITEM.3.NUMBER(100)
340 DIM ITEM.3.QTY(100)
350 DIM ITEM.3.UNIT.PRICE(100)
360 DIM ITEM.4.NUMBER(100)
370 DIM ITEM.4.QTY(100)
380 DIM ITEM.4.UNIT.PRICE(100)
390 DIM AMOUNT.OF.INVOICE(100)
400 DIM AMOUNT.LESS.THAN.30.DAYS(100)
410 DIM AMOUNT.AT.30.DAYS(100)
420 DIM AMOUNT.AT.60.DAYS(100)
430 DIM AMOUNT.AT.90.DAYS(100)
440 '*******************************
450 '* DIMENSION THE PRODUCT FILE. *
460 '*******************************
470 DIM PRODUCT.NAME$(100)
480 DIM PRODUCT.DESCR$(100)
490 DIM PRODUCT.UNIT$(100)
500 DIM PRODUCT.LOCATION$(100)
```

```
510 DIM PRODUCT.Q.O.H(100)
520 DIM PRODUCT.R.O.P(100)
530 DIM PRODUCT.SHIP.INSTR$(100)
540 '*********************************
550 '* DIMENSION THE CUSTOMER FILE. *
560 '*********************************
570 DIM CUSTOMER.NAME$(100)
580 DIM CUSTOMER.ADDR.1$(100)
590 DIM CUSTOMER.ADDR.2$(100)
600 DIM CUSTOMER.ADDR.3$(100)
610 DIM CUSTOMER.ADDR.4$(100)
620 DIM CUSTOMER.TERMS$(100)
630 '********************************
640 '* DIMENSION THE ACCOUNT FILE. *
650 '********************************
660 DIM T$(100)
670 DIM N$(100)
680 DIM A(100)
690 '********************************************
700 '* INVOICE DISPLAY AND PRINTING ROUTINE *
710 '********************************************
720 GOSUB 2450          'GET THE PRODUCT FILE
730 GOSUB 2620          'GET THE CUSTOMER FILE
740 GOSUB 1850          'GET THE RECEIVABLES FILE
750 PRINT:PRINT "DO YOU WISH TO BEGIN WITH TODAY'S INVOICE (Y/N)? ";
760 Z$ = INKEY$:IF Z$ = "" THEN 760
770 PRINT Z$
780 IF Z$ < > "Y" THEN SPECIFIED.INVOICE$ = "NO":GOTO 800
790 SPECIFIED.INVOICE$ = "YES"
800 GOSUB 1740          'GET THE HEADING
810 PRINT
820 PRINT "DO YOU WISH A HARDCOPY OUTPUT (Y/N)? ";
830 Z$ = INKEY$:IF Z$ = "" THEN 830
840 PRINT Z$
850 IF Z$ < > "Y" THEN HARDCOPY$ = "NO":GOTO 870
860 HARDCOPY$ = "YES"
870 PRINT "UNINTERRUPTED PRINTING - 'N' CAUSES PAUSE WITH EACH - (Y/N)? ";
880 Z$ = INKEY$:IF Z$ = "" THEN 880
890 PRINT Z$
900 IF Z$ < > "Y" THEN CONTINUE$ = "NO":GOTO 920
910 CONTINUE$ = "YES"
920 FOR I = 1 TO RECEIVE.FILE.SIZE
930     ITEM.NAME.1$ = PRODUCT.NAME$(ITEM.1.NUMBER(I))
940     ITEM.NAME.2$ = PRODUCT.NAME$(ITEM.2.NUMBER(I))
950     ITEM.NAME.3$ = PRODUCT.NAME$(ITEM.3.NUMBER(I))
960     ITEM.NAME.4$ = PRODUCT.NAME$(ITEM.4.NUMBER(I))
970     WHICH.CUSTOMER = I
980     RFS = I
990     IF SPECIFIED.INVOICE$ = "NO" THEN 1010
1000     IF DOCUMENT.NUMBER(I) < INVOICE.NUMBER THEN 1240
1010     PRINT
1020     PRINT "ACCOUNT NUMBER: ";I
1030     PRINT "INVOICE.NUMBER";DOCUMENT.NUMBER(I);
1040     PRINT TAB(50);"DATE: ";DATE.OF.INVOICE$(I)
1050     GOSUB 2930
1060     PRINT STRING$(79,"-")
1070     GOSUB 3110
1080     GOSUB 3960
1090     IF CONTINUE$ = "YES" THEN 1110
1100     Z$ = INKEY$:IF Z$ = "" THEN 1100
1110     IF HARDCOPY$ = "NO" THEN 1240
1120     LPRINT
1130     LPRINT
1140     LPRINT "INVOICE.NUMBER";DOCUMENT.NUMBER(I);
1150     LPRINT TAB(50);"DATE: ";DATE.OF.INVOICE$(I)
1160     GOSUB 3020
1170     LPRINT
1180     LPRINT STRING$(79,"-")
1190     LPRINT
```

```
1200      GOSUB 3510
1210      LPRINT
1220      GOSUB 4110
1230      LPRINT CHR$(12)
1240 NEXT I
1250 GOSUB 1740                    'GET THE HEADING
1260 '***********************
1270 '* PROGRAM TERMINATION *
1280 '***********************
1290 PRINT
1300 PRINT "INVOICE PREPARATION IS COMPLETE"
1310 PRINT
1320 PRINT "DO YOU WISH TO REPEAT THE PROGRAM (Y/N)? ";
1330 Z$ = INKEY$:IF Z$ = "" THEN 1330
1340 PRINT Z$
1350 IF Z$ < > "Y" THEN 1730
1360 ERASE CUSTOMER.NUMBER
1370 ERASE DATE.OF.INVOICE$
1380 ERASE DOCUMENT.NUMBER
1390 ERASE ITEM.1.NUMBER
1400 ERASE ITEM.1.QTY
1410 ERASE ITEM.1.UNIT.PRICE
1420 ERASE ITEM.2.NUMBER
1430 ERASE ITEM.2.QTY
1440 ERASE ITEM.2.UNIT.PRICE
1450 ERASE ITEM.3.NUMBER
1460 ERASE ITEM.3.QTY
1470 ERASE ITEM.3.UNIT.PRICE
1480 ERASE ITEM.4.NUMBER
1490 ERASE ITEM.4.QTY
1500 ERASE ITEM.4.UNIT.PRICE
1510 ERASE AMOUNT.OF.INVOICE
1520 ERASE AMOUNT.LESS.THAN.30.DAYS
1530 ERASE AMOUNT.AT.30.DAYS
1540 ERASE AMOUNT.AT.60.DAYS
1550 ERASE AMOUNT.AT.90.DAYS
1560 ERASE PRODUCT.NAME$
1570 ERASE PRODUCT.DESCR$
1580 ERASE PRODUCT.UNIT$
1590 ERASE PRODUCT.LOCATION$
1600 ERASE PRODUCT.Q.O.H
1610 ERASE PRODUCT.R.O.P
1620 ERASE PRODUCT.SHIP.INSTR$
1630 ERASE CUSTOMER.NAME$
1640 ERASE CUSTOMER.ADDR.1$
1650 ERASE CUSTOMER.ADDR.2$
1660 ERASE CUSTOMER.ADDR.3$
1670 ERASE CUSTOMER.ADDR.4$
1680 ERASE CUSTOMER.TERMS$
1690 ERASE T$
1700 ERASE N$
1710 ERASE A
1720 GOTO 10
1730 CHAIN "A:RECIVBLE.BAS"
1740 '********************************
1750 '* HEADING USED FOR THE DISPLAY *
1760 '********************************
1770 CLS
1780 X = ((80 - LEN(COMPANY.NAME$)) / 2)
1790 LOCATE 2,X
1800 PRINT COMPANY.NAME$
1810 PRINT STRING$(79,220):PRINT
1820 PRINT TAB(19);"ACCOUNTS RECEIVABLE PROCESSING PROGRAM"
1830 PRINT STRING$(79,220)
1840 RETURN
1850 '********************************
1860 '* OPEN AND INPUT RECEIVABLE FILE *
1870 '********************************
1880 PRINT:PRINT "LOADING THE RECEIVABLES FILE"
```

```
1890 OPEN "I",1,"RECEIVE.DAT"
1900 INPUT #1,RECEIVE.FILE.SIZE        'OBTAIN THE RECORD COUNT
1910 FOR I = 1 TO RECEIVE.FILE.SIZE
1920     INPUT #1,CUSTOMER.NUMBER(I)
1930     LINE INPUT #1,DATE.OF.INVOICE$(I)
1940     INPUT #1,DOCUMENT.NUMBER(I)
1950     INPUT #1,ITEM.1.NUMBER(I)
1960     INPUT #1,ITEM.1.QTY(I)
1970     INPUT #1,ITEM.1.UNIT.PRICE(I)
1980     INPUT #1,ITEM.2.NUMBER(I)
1990     INPUT #1,ITEM.2.QTY(I)
2000     INPUT #1,ITEM.2.UNIT.PRICE(I)
2010     INPUT #1,ITEM.3.NUMBER(I)
2020     INPUT #1,ITEM.3.QTY(I)
2030     INPUT #1,ITEM.3.UNIT.PRICE(I)
2040     INPUT #1,ITEM.4.NUMBER(I)
2050     INPUT #1,ITEM.4.QTY(I)
2060     INPUT #1,ITEM.4.UNIT.PRICE(I)
2070     INPUT #1,AMOUNT.OF.INVOICE(I)
2080     INPUT #1,AMOUNT.LESS.THAN.30.DAYS(I)
2090     INPUT #1,AMOUNT.AT.30.DAYS(I)
2100     INPUT #1,AMOUNT.AT.60.DAYS(I)
2110     INPUT #1,AMOUNT.AT.90.DAYS(I)
2120 NEXT I
2130 CLOSE 1
2140 RETURN
2150 '************************************
2160 '* OPEN AND OUTPUT RECEIVABLE FILE *
2170 '************************************
2180 PRINT:PRINT "WRITING THE RECEIVABLES FILE"
2190 OPEN "O",1,"RECEIVE.DAT"
2200 PRINT #1,RECEIVE.FILE.SIZE        'STORE THE RECORD COUNT
2210 FOR I = 1 TO RECEIVE.FILE.SIZE
2220     PRINT #1,CUSTOMER.NUMBER(I)
2230     PRINT #1,DATE.OF.INVOICE$(I)
2240     PRINT #1,DOCUMENT.NUMBER(I)
2250     PRINT #1,ITEM.1.NUMBER(I)
2260     PRINT #1,ITEM.1.QTY(I)
2270     PRINT #1,ITEM.1.UNIT.PRICE(I)
2280     PRINT #1,ITEM.2.NUMBER(I)
2290     PRINT #1,ITEM.2.QTY(I)
2300     PRINT #1,ITEM.2.UNIT.PRICE(I)
2310     PRINT #1,ITEM.3.NUMBER(I)
2320     PRINT #1,ITEM.3.QTY(I)
2330     PRINT #1,ITEM.3.UNIT.PRICE(I)
2340     PRINT #1,ITEM.4.NUMBER(I)
2350     PRINT #1,ITEM.4.QTY(I)
2360     PRINT #1,ITEM.4.UNIT.PRICE(I)
2370     PRINT #1,AMOUNT.OF.INVOICE(I)
2380     PRINT #1,AMOUNT.LESS.THAN.30.DAYS(I)
2390     PRINT #1,AMOUNT.AT.30.DAYS(I)
2400     PRINT #1,AMOUNT.AT.60.DAYS(I)
2410     PRINT #1,AMOUNT.AT.90.DAYS(I)
2420 NEXT I
2430 CLOSE 1
2440 RETURN
2450 '********************************
2460 '* OPEN AND INPUT PRODUCT FILE *
2470 '********************************
2480 PRINT:PRINT "LOADING THE PRODUCT FILE"
2490 OPEN "I",1,"PRODUCT.DAT"
2500 INPUT #1,PRODUCT.FILE.SIZE        'OBTAIN THE RECORD COUNT
2510 FOR J = 1 TO PRODUCT.FILE.SIZE
2520     LINE INPUT #1,PRODUCT.NAME$(J)
2530     LINE INPUT #1,PRODUCT.DESCR$(J)
2540     LINE INPUT #1,PRODUCT.UNIT$(J)
2550     LINE INPUT #1,PRODUCT.LOCATION$(J)
2560     INPUT #1,PRODUCT.Q.O.H(J)
2570     INPUT #1,PRODUCT.R.O.P(J)
```

```
2580     LINE INPUT #1,PRODUCT.SHIP.INSTR$(J)
2590 NEXT J
2600 CLOSE 1
2610 RETURN
2620 '*********************************
2630 '* OPEN AND INPUT CUSTOMER FILE *
2640 '*********************************
2650 PRINT:PRINT "LOADING THE CUSTOMER FILE"
2660 OPEN "I",1,"CUSTOMER.DAT"
2670 INPUT #1,CUSTOMER.FILE.SIZE       'OBTAIN THE RECORD COUNT
2680 FOR K = 1 TO CUSTOMER.FILE.SIZE
2690     LINE INPUT #1,CUSTOMER.NAME$(K)
2700     LINE INPUT #1,CUSTOMER.ADDR.1$(K)
2710     LINE INPUT #1,CUSTOMER.ADDR.2$(K)
2720     LINE INPUT #1,CUSTOMER.ADDR.3$(K)
2730     LINE INPUT #1,CUSTOMER.ADDR.4$(K)
2740     LINE INPUT #1,CUSTOMER.TERMS$(K)
2750 NEXT K
2760 CLOSE 1
2770 RETURN
2780 '********************************
2790 '* OPEN AND INPUT ACCOUNT FILE *
2800 '********************************
2810 PRINT:PRINT "LOADING THE ACCOUNT FILE"
2820 PRINT:INPUT "SPECIFY THE ACCOUNT FILE TO BE USED: ",SPECIFIED.FILE$
2830 SPECIFIED.FILE$ = SPECIFIED.FILE$ + ".DAT"
2840 OPEN "I",1,SPECIFIED.FILE$
2850 INPUT #1,SPECIFIED.FILE.SIZE       'OBTAIN THE RECORD COUNT
2860 FOR L = 1 TO SPECIFIED.FILE.SIZE
2870     LINE INPUT #1,T$(L)
2880     LINE INPUT #1,N$(L)
2890     INPUT #1,A(L)
2900 NEXT L
2910 CLOSE 1
2920 RETURN
2930 '***********************************************************************
2940 '* THIS IS A ROUTINE USED MORE THAN ONCE TO DISPLAY THE CUSTOMER INFO *
2950 '***********************************************************************
2960 PRINT "CUSTOMER.NAME:";TAB(25);CUSTOMER.NAME$(WHICH.CUSTOMER)
2970 PRINT "CUSTOMER ADDRESS:";TAB(25);CUSTOMER.ADDR.1$(WHICH.CUSTOMER)
2980 PRINT TAB(25);CUSTOMER.ADDR.2$(WHICH.CUSTOMER)
2990 PRINT TAB(25);CUSTOMER.ADDR.3$(WHICH.CUSTOMER)
3000 PRINT TAB(25);CUSTOMER.ADDR.4$(WHICH.CUSTOMER)
3010 RETURN
3020 '**********************************************************************
3030 '* THIS IS A ROUTINE USED MORE THAN ONCE TO PRINT THE CUSTOMER INFO *
3040 '**********************************************************************
3050 LPRINT "CUSTOMER.NAME:";TAB(25);CUSTOMER.NAME$(WHICH.CUSTOMER)
3060 LPRINT "CUSTOMER ADDRESS:";TAB(25);CUSTOMER.ADDR.1$(WHICH.CUSTOMER)
3070 LPRINT TAB(25);CUSTOMER.ADDR.2$(WHICH.CUSTOMER)
3080 LPRINT TAB(25);CUSTOMER.ADDR.3$(WHICH.CUSTOMER)
3090 LPRINT TAB(25);CUSTOMER.ADDR.4$(WHICH.CUSTOMER)
3100 RETURN
3110 '*********************************************
3120 '* ROUTINE TO DISPLAY THE INVOICE DETAIL *
3130 '*********************************************
3140 PRINT "ITEM";TAB(10);"QUANTITY";TAB(30);"DESCRIPTION";
3150 PRINT TAB(60);"PRICE";TAB(70);"EXTENSION"
3160 ITEM.1.EXTENSION = (ITEM.1.QTY(RFS) * ITEM.1.UNIT.PRICE(RFS))
3170 ITEM.2.EXTENSION = (ITEM.2.QTY(RFS) * ITEM.2.UNIT.PRICE(RFS))
3180 ITEM.3.EXTENSION = (ITEM.3.QTY(RFS) * ITEM.3.UNIT.PRICE(RFS))
3190 ITEM.4.EXTENSION = (ITEM.4.QTY(RFS) * ITEM.4.UNIT.PRICE(RFS))
3200 PRINT STRING$(79,"-")
3210 PRINT ITEM.1.NUMBER(RFS);TAB(13);ITEM.1.QTY(RFS);TAB(30);
3220 PRINT ITEM.NAME.1$;TAB(55);
3230 PRINT USING "##,###.##";ITEM.1.UNIT.PRICE(RFS);
3240 PRINT TAB(70);"";:PRINT USING "##,###.##";ITEM.1.EXTENSION
3250 IF ITEM.NAME.2$ = "" THEN 3410
3260 PRINT ITEM.2.NUMBER(RFS);TAB(13);ITEM.2.QTY(RFS);TAB(30);
```

```
3270 PRINT ITEM.NAME.2$;TAB(55);
3280 PRINT USING "##,###.##";ITEM.2.UNIT.PRICE(RFS);
3290 PRINT TAB(70);"";:PRINT USING "##,###.##";ITEM.2.EXTENSION
3300 IF ITEM.NAME.3$ = "" THEN 3410
3310 PRINT ITEM.3.NUMBER(RFS);TAB(13);ITEM.3.QTY(RFS);TAB(30);
3320 PRINT ITEM.NAME.3$;TAB(55);
3330 PRINT USING "##,###.##";ITEM.3.UNIT.PRICE(RFS);
3340 PRINT TAB(70);"";:PRINT USING "##,###.##";ITEM.3.EXTENSION
3350 IF ITEM.NAME.4$ = "" THEN 3410
3360 PRINT ITEM.4.NUMBER(RFS);TAB(13);ITEM.4.QTY(RFS);TAB(30);
3370 PRINT ITEM.NAME.4$;TAB(55);
3380 PRINT USING "##,###.##";ITEM.4.UNIT.PRICE(RFS);
3390 PRINT TAB(70);"";:PRINT USING "##,###.##";ITEM.4.EXTENSION
3400 PRINT TAB(68);"---------------"
3410 AMOUNT.OF.INVOICE(RFS) = O
3420 AMOUNT.OF.INVOICE(RFS) = AMOUNT.OF.INVOICE(RFS) + ITEM.1.EXTENSION
3430 AMOUNT.OF.INVOICE(RFS) = AMOUNT.OF.INVOICE(RFS) + ITEM.2.EXTENSION
3440 AMOUNT.OF.INVOICE(RFS) = AMOUNT.OF.INVOICE(RFS) + ITEM.3.EXTENSION
3450 AMOUNT.OF.INVOICE(RFS) = AMOUNT.OF.INVOICE(RFS) + ITEM.4.EXTENSION
3460 PRINT "AMOUNT DUE:";
3470 PRINT TAB(68);"";:PRINT USING "$$###,###.##";AMOUNT.OF.INVOICE(RFS)
3480 AMOUNT.LESS.THAN.30.DAYS(RFS) = AMOUNT.OF.INVOICE(RFS)
3490 PRINT TAB(68);"============="
3500 RETURN
3510 '*****************************************
3520 '* ROUTINE TO PRINT THE INVOICE DETAIL *
3530 '*****************************************
3540 LPRINT "ITEM";TAB(10);"QUANTITY";TAB(30);"DESCRIPTION";
3550 LPRINT TAB(60);"PRICE";TAB(70);"EXTENSION"
3560 PRINT STRING$(79,"-")
3570 ITEM.1.EXTENSION = (ITEM.1.QTY(RFS) * ITEM.1.UNIT.PRICE(RFS))
3580 ITEM.2.EXTENSION = (ITEM.2.QTY(RFS) * ITEM.2.UNIT.PRICE(RFS))
3590 ITEM.3.EXTENSION = (ITEM.3.QTY(RFS) * ITEM.3.UNIT.PRICE(RFS))
3600 ITEM.4.EXTENSION = (ITEM.4.QTY(RFS) * ITEM.4.UNIT.PRICE(RFS))
3610 PRINT STRING$(79,"-")
3620 LPRINT ITEM.1.NUMBER(RFS);TAB(13);ITEM.1.QTY(RFS);TAB(30);
3630 LPRINT ITEM.NAME.1$;TAB(55);
3640 LPRINT USING "##,###.##";ITEM.1.UNIT.PRICE(RFS);
3650 LPRINT TAB(70);"";:LPRINT USING "##,###.##";ITEM.1.EXTENSION
3660 IF ITEM.NAME.2$ = "" THEN 3840
3670 LPRINT
3680 LPRINT ITEM.2.NUMBER(RFS);TAB(13);ITEM.2.QTY(RFS);TAB(30);
3690 LPRINT ITEM.NAME.2$;TAB(55);
3700 LPRINT USING "##,###.##";ITEM.2.UNIT.PRICE(RFS);
3710 LPRINT TAB(70);"";:LPRINT USING "##,###.##";ITEM.2.EXTENSION
3720 IF ITEM.NAME.3$ = "" THEN 3840
3730 LPRINT
3740 LPRINT ITEM.3.NUMBER(RFS);TAB(13);ITEM.3.QTY(RFS);TAB(30);
3750 LPRINT ITEM.NAME.3$;TAB(55);
3760 LPRINT USING "##,###.##";ITEM.3.UNIT.PRICE(RFS);
3770 LPRINT TAB(70);"";:LPRINT USING "##,###.##";ITEM.3.EXTENSION
3780 IF ITEM.NAME.4$ = "" THEN 3840
3790 LPRINT
3800 LPRINT ITEM.4.NUMBER(RFS);TAB(13);ITEM.4.QTY(RFS);TAB(30);
3810 LPRINT ITEM.NAME.4$;TAB(55);
3820 LPRINT USING "##,###.##";ITEM.4.UNIT.PRICE(RFS);
3830 LPRINT TAB(70);"";:LPRINT USING "##,###.##";ITEM.4.EXTENSION
3840 LPRINT TAB(68);"---------------"
3850 LPRINT
3860 AMOUNT.OF.INVOICE(RFS) = O
3870 AMOUNT.OF.INVOICE(RFS) = AMOUNT.OF.INVOICE(RFS) + ITEM.1.EXTENSION
3880 AMOUNT.OF.INVOICE(RFS) = AMOUNT.OF.INVOICE(RFS) + ITEM.2.EXTENSION
3890 AMOUNT.OF.INVOICE(RFS) = AMOUNT.OF.INVOICE(RFS) + ITEM.3.EXTENSION
3900 AMOUNT.OF.INVOICE(RFS) = AMOUNT.OF.INVOICE(RFS) + ITEM.4.EXTENSION
3910 LPRINT "AMOUNT DUE:";
3920 LPRINT TAB(68);"";:LPRINT USING "$$###,###.##";AMOUNT.OF.INVOICE(RFS)
3930 AMOUNT.LESS.THAN.30.DAYS(RFS) = AMOUNT.OF.INVOICE(RFS)
3940 LPRINT TAB(68);"============="
3950 RETURN
```

```
3960 '*****************************************
3970 '* ROUTINE TO DISPLAY THE AGEING DETAIL *
3980 '*****************************************
3990 PRINT STRING$(79,"-")
4000 PRINT "30 DAYS OR LESS";TAB(20);"30 - 60 DAYS";TAB(40);
4010 PRINT "60 - 90 DAYS";TAB(60);"90 DAYS AND OVER"
4020 PRINT USING "$$##,###.##";AMOUNT.LESS.THAN.30.DAYS(I);
4030 PRINT TAB(20);"";
4040 PRINT USING "$$##,###.##";AMOUNT.AT.30.DAYS(I);
4050 PRINT TAB(37);"";
4060 PRINT USING "$$##,###.##";AMOUNT.AT.60.DAYS(I);
4070 PRINT TAB(57);"";
4080 PRINT USING "$$##,###.##";AMOUNT.AT.90.DAYS(I)
4090 PRINT STRING$(79,"-")
4100 RETURN
4110 '*****************************************
4120 '* ROUTINE TO PRINT THE AGEING DETAIL *
4130 '*****************************************
4140 LPRINT STRING$(79,"-")
4150 LPRINT "30 DAYS OR LESS";TAB(20);"30 - 60 DAYS";TAB(40);
4160 LPRINT "60 - 90 DAYS";TAB(60);"90 DAYS AND OVER"
4170 LPRINT USING "$$##,###.##";AMOUNT.LESS.THAN.30.DAYS(I);
4180 LPRINT TAB(20);"";
4190 LPRINT USING "$$##,###.##";AMOUNT.AT.30.DAYS(I);
4200 LPRINT TAB(37);"";
4210 LPRINT USING "$$##,###.##";AMOUNT.AT.60.DAYS(I);
4220 LPRINT TAB(57);"";
4230 LPRINT USING "$$##,###.##";AMOUNT.AT.90.DAYS(I)
4240 LPRINT
4250 LPRINT STRING$(79,"-")
4260 RETURN
```

POSTREC.BAS

The posting of the payments involves the same files as the other programs, and its opening menu provides the key to the way it works, as follows:

```
              ACCOUNTS RECEIVABLE PROCESSING PROGRAM

POSTING METHODS:

    1.   POST PAYMENT BY CUSTOMER

    2.   POST PAYMENT BY INVOICE

    3.   VIEW ACCOUNTS BY CUSTOMER NUMBER

    4.   VIEW ACCOUNTS BY INVOICE NUMBER

    5.   REWRITE FILES, POST ACCOUNTS, AND TERMINATE

SELECT:
```

Looking at options 3 and 4 first, let's simply state that all payments are against invoice. However, on the possibility that you don't know what the invoice number and amount are, option 3 will summarize the outstanding invoices by customer number. Each invoice can then be viewed separately. The same is true of the posting. If the posting is done by invoice, then the in-

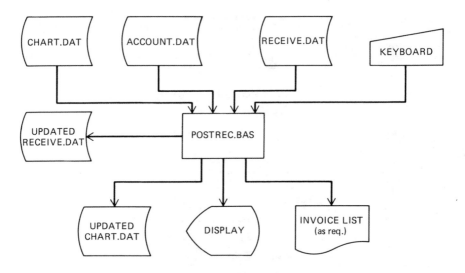

Fig. 7-10 Posting Application

voice number is specified. If it's done by customer, then you apply the customer number toward the invoice. However you slice it, the payment will be made by invoice. When you tell the computer how much money it has to spend, it will continue to process payment requests until it runs out of money. If the payment is the right amount, the program simply adjusts its balance towards zero. If interest is paid, the accumulated interest is posted to the INTEREST INCOME account. If there is no such account, the program creates one for you. If the payment is too small, posting of the account attacks the oldest money first, leaving the unpaid balance in the youngest money. As you will find when we discuss the aging process, the money is aged and incremented where it is.

A block diagram for the posting application is shown in Fig. 7-10. This program takes the Chart of Accounts, the Receivables File, and the Account File for the period and allows the operator to post against the files. Payments are then posted individually or in groups. When all payments have been posted, the updated files are written back to media. Posting of accounts is detailed in the display and before and after application balances are shown to the operator.

When the program opens, an important message is presented: a display of those accounts on the Chart of Accounts and the balances from the Account File. The program will create new accounts for Cash Income for the Interest Income. For the present, no other accounts are needed if you take the specific approach offered by this system. If, however, you wish for something more complex and want other accounts to be posted, it will be necessary to ensure that the proper account type and title have been loaded into the Chart of Accounts. Remember that the balances on the account file must be in the same sequence. A typical display of accounts and balances is as follows:

```
                ACCOUNTS RECEIVABLE PROCESSING PROGRAM
```
▬▬▬

```
I M P O R T A N T ! ! !
IF THE PAYMENT CANNOT BE POSTED TO THESE ACCOUNTS, YOU MUST TERMINATE
HERE AND RETURN TO CHART.BAS, FOLLOWED BY VALUE.BAS, TO ESTABLISH THE ACCOUNT:
-------------------------------------------------------------------------
A,CASH                         101.23
A,ACCOUNTS RECEIVABLE        1,000.47
A,EQUIPMENT                    200.00
A,PREPAID INSURANCE            400.00
A,ROLLING STOCK              4,000.00
L,ACCOUNTS PAYABLE             637.34
L,NOTES PAYABLE              1,245.78
C,SBE DRAW                     209.88
I,SALES INCOME              30,000.00
I,RENTAL INCOME                473.00
I,ROYALTY INCOME            20,000.00
E,RENT EXPENSE                 600.00
E,TELEPHONE EXPENSE            225.00
E,TRAVEL EXPENSE               110.47

DO YOU WISH TO TERMINATE (Y/N)?
```

The invoice is presented in the following manner:

▬▬▬

```
                ACCOUNTS RECEIVABLE PROCESSING PROGRAM
```
▬▬▬

```
ENTER THE INVOICE NUMBER: 555

CUSTOMER:  1
CUSTOMER NAME:          SEARS
CUSTOMER ADDRESS:       SEARSLAND
                        100 LUNENBERG PARKWAY
                        LEOMINSTER,
                        MASSACHUSETTS 01377

DATE OF INVOICE: MAY 24, 1982           INVOICE NUMBER:   555

AMOUNT OF INVOICE:                      5.55
ACCUMULATED INTEREST:                   0.00

TOTAL DUE:                              $5.55
-------------------------------------------------------------------------
PRESS ANY KEY TO CONTINUE
```

Here is the program POSTREC.BAS:

```
10 '**********************************
20 '* DIMENSION THE RECEIVABLES FILE. *
30 '**********************************
40 DIM CUSTOMER.NUMBER(100)
50 DIM DATE.OF.INVOICE$(100)
60 DIM DOCUMENT.NUMBER(100)
70 DIM ITEM.1.NUMBER(100)
80 DIM ITEM.1.QTY(100)
90 DIM ITEM.1.UNIT.PRICE(100)
100 DIM ITEM.2.NUMBER(100)
110 DIM ITEM.2.QTY(100)
120 DIM ITEM.2.UNIT.PRICE(100)
130 DIM ITEM.3.NUMBER(100)
140 DIM ITEM.3.QTY(100)
150 DIM ITEM.3.UNIT.PRICE(100)
```

```
160 DIM ITEM.4.NUMBER(100)
170 DIM ITEM.4.QTY(100)
180 DIM ITEM.4.UNIT.PRICE(100)
190 DIM AMOUNT.OF.INVOICE(100)
200 DIM AMOUNT.LESS.THAN.30.DAYS(100)
210 DIM AMOUNT.AT.30.DAYS(100)
220 DIM AMOUNT.AT.60.DAYS(100)
230 DIM AMOUNT.AT.90.DAYS(100)
240 '*********************************
250 '* DIMENSION THE CUSTOMER FILE. *
260 '*********************************
270 DIM CUSTOMER.NAME$(100)
280 DIM CUSTOMER.ADDR.1$(100)
290 DIM CUSTOMER.ADDR.2$(100)
300 DIM CUSTOMER.ADDR.3$(100)
310 DIM CUSTOMER.ADDR.4$(100)
320 DIM CUSTOMER.TERMS$(100)
330 '***********************************************
340 '* DIMENSION THE CHART OF ACCOUNTS FILE *
350 '***********************************************
360 DIM T$(25),N$(25)
370 '*********************************
380 '* DIMENSION THE ACCOUNT FILE *
390 '*********************************
400 DIM A(25)
410 '*****************************
420 '* ROUTINE TO POST PAYMENTS *
430 '*****************************
440 COMMON COMPANY.NAME$
450 GOSUB 4930
460 PRINT TAB(17);"P O S T    P A Y M E N T S    R E C E I V E D"
470 GOSUB 4150              'GET THE CUSTOMER FILE
480 GOSUB 3550              'GET THE RECEIVABLES FILE
490 GOSUB 4310              'GET THE CHART OF ACCOUNTS FILE
500 PRINT:INPUT "ENTER THE ACCOUNT FILE NAME (I'LL ADD .DAT): ",ACCOUNT.FILE$
510 ACCOUNT.FILE$ = ACCOUNT.FILE$ + ".DAT"
520 GOSUB 4530             'GET THE ACCOUNT FILE
530 GOSUB 4930
540 PRINT:PRINT"I M P O R T A N T ! ! !"
550 PRINT "IF THE PAYMENT CANNOT BE POSTED TO THESE ACCOUNTS, YOU MUST ";
560 PRINT "TERMINATE HERE"
570 PRINT "AND RETURN TO CHART.BAS, FOLLOWED BY VALUE.BAS, TO ESTABLISH ";
580 PRINT "THE ACCOUNT:"
590 PRINT STRING$(79,"-")
600 FOR I = 1 TO CHART.FILE.SIZE
610      PRINT T$(I);TAB(30);
620      PRINT USING "##,###.##";A(I)
630 NEXT I
640 PRINT
650 PRINT "DO YOU WISH TO TERMINATE (Y/N)? ";
660 Z$ = INKEY$:IF Z$ = "" THEN 660
670 IF Z$ = "Y" THEN 3540
680 GOSUB 4930
690 PRINT:PRINT "POSTING METHODS:"
700 PRINT
710 PRINT TAB(5);"1.  POST PAYMENT BY CUSTOMER"
720 PRINT
730 PRINT TAB(5);"2.  POST PAYMENT BY INVOICE"
740 PRINT
750 PRINT TAB(5);"3.  VIEW ACCOUNTS BY CUSTOMER NUMBER"
760 PRINT
770 PRINT TAB(5);"4.  VIEW ACCOUNTS BY INVOICE NUMBER"
780 PRINT
790 PRINT TAB(5);"5.  REWRITE FILES, POST ACCOUNTS, AND TERMINATE"
800 PRINT
810 PRINT "SELECT: ";
820 Z$ = INKEY$:IF Z$ = "" THEN 820
830 IF Z$ = "1" THEN PRINT "POST PAYMENT BY CUSTOMER"
840 IF Z$ = "2" THEN PRINT "POST PAYMENT BY INVOICE"
```

```
850 IF Z$ = "3" THEN PRINT "VIEW ACCOUNTS BY CUSTOMER NUMBER"
860 IF Z$ = "4" THEN PRINT "VIEW ACCOUNTS BY INVOICE NUMBER"
870 IF Z$ = "5" THEN PRINT "POSTING ACCOUNTS"
880 FOR Z = 1 TO 1500:NEXT Z
890 A = VAL(Z$)
900 ON A GOSUB 920,1280,2060,2900,3250
910 GOTO 680
920 '*****************************
930 '* POST PAYMENT BY CUSTOMER *
940 '*****************************
950 GOSUB 4930
960 PRINT:INPUT "ENTER THE CUSTOMER NUMBER: ",WHICH.CUSTOMER
970 PRINT
980 GOSUB 4750
990 PRINT:PRINT "CORRECT (Y/N)? ";
1000 Z$ = INKEY$:IF Z$ = "" THEN 1000
1010 PRINT Z$
1020 IF Z$ < > "Y" THEN 440
1030 PRINT:INPUT "ENTER THE AMOUNT OF THE PAYMENT: ",AMOUNT.OF.PAYMENT
1040 CASH.ADJUSTMENT = CASH.ADJUSTMENT + AMOUNT.OF.PAYMENT
1050 GOSUB 4930
1060 PRINT "THESE ARE THE INVOICES FOR THIS CUSTOMER:":PRINT
1070 PRINT "PERHAPS YOU SHOULD TAKE NOTES":PRINT
1080 FOR J = 1 TO RECEIVE.FILE.SIZE
1090     IF CUSTOMER.NUMBER(J) < > WHICH.CUSTOMER THEN 1190
1100     PRINT "CUSTOMER: ";J;TAB(18);"DATE: ";DATE.OF.INVOICE$(J);
1110     PRINT TAB(42);"INVOICE: ";DOCUMENT.NUMBER(J);
1120     PRINT TAB(60);"AMOUNT: ";
1130     TOTAL.AGEING = 0
1140     TOTAL.AGEING = TOTAL.AGEING + AMOUNT.LESS.THAN.30.DAYS(J)
1150     TOTAL.AGEING = TOTAL.AGEING + AMOUNT.AT.30.DAYS(J)
1160     TOTAL.AGEING = TOTAL.AGEING + AMOUNT.AT.60.DAYS(J)
1170     TOTAL.AGEING = TOTAL.AGEING + AMOUNT.AT.90.DAYS(J)
1180     PRINT USING "##,###.##";TOTAL.AGEING
1190 NEXT J
1200 IF AMOUNT.OF.PAYMENT < 1 THEN AMOUNT.OF.PAYMENT = 0
1210 PRINT:PRINT "YOU HAVE ";
1220 PRINT USING "$$###,###.##";AMOUNT.OF.PAYMENT;
1230 PRINT " TO APPLY"
1240 FOR Z = 1 TO 1000:NEXT Z
1250 IF AMOUNT.OF.PAYMENT < = 0 THEN RETURN
1260 GOSUB 1340          'JUMP INTO MIDDLE OF POST PAYMENT BY INVOICE
1270 GOTO 1200
1280 '*****************************
1290 '* POST PAYMENT BY INVOICE *
1300 '*****************************
1310 GOSUB 4930
1320 PRINT:INPUT "ENTER THE AMOUNT OF THE PAYMENT: ",AMOUNT.OF.PAYMENT
1330 CASH.ADJUSTMENT = CASH.ADJUSTMENT + AMOUNT.OF.PAYMENT
1340 PRINT
1350 GOSUB 2940          'ENTER REVIEW ROUTINE AFTER THE BEGINNING
1360 INTEREST.DUE = (TOTAL.AGEING - AMOUNT.OF.INVOICE(J))
1370 PRINT
1380 PRINT "ACCOUNT BEFORE APPLYING PAYMENT"
1390 PRINT
1400 PRINT USING "  90 DAYS: ##,###.##";AMOUNT.AT.90.DAYS(J)
1410 PRINT USING "  60 DAYS: ##,###.##";AMOUNT.AT.60.DAYS(J)
1420 PRINT USING "  30 DAYS: ##,###.##";AMOUNT.AT.30.DAYS(J)
1430 PRINT USING "< 30 DAYS: ##,###.##";AMOUNT.LESS.THAN.30.DAYS(J)
1440 IF AMOUNT.OF.PAYMENT > = TOTAL.AGEING THEN 1970
1450 IF AMOUNT.OF.PAYMENT < AMOUNT.AT.90.DAYS(J) THEN 1520
1460 AMOUNT.OF.PAYMENT = (AMOUNT.OF.PAYMENT - AMOUNT.AT.90.DAYS(J))
1470 A.R.ADJUSTMENT = 0
1480 A.R.ADJUSTMENT = A.R.ADJUSTMENT + AMOUNT.AT.90.DAYS(J)
1490 AMOUNT.OF.INVOICE(J) = AMOUNT.OF.INVOICE(J) - AMOUNT.AT.90.DAYS(J)
1500 AMOUNT.AT.90.DAYS = 0
1510 GOTO 1550
1520 AMOUNT.AT.90.DAYS(J) = (AMOUNT.AT.90.DAYS(J) - AMOUNT.OF.PAYMENT)
1530 AMOUNT.OF.PAYMENT = 0
```

```
1540 GOTO 1780
1550 IF AMOUNT.OF.PAYMENT < AMOUNT.AT.60.DAYS(J) THEN 1610
1560 AMOUNT.OF.PAYMENT = (AMOUNT.OF.PAYMENT - AMOUNT.AT.60.DAYS(J))
1570 A.R.ADJUSTMENT = A.R.ADJUSTMENT + AMOUNT.AT.60.DAYS(J)
1580 AMOUNT.OF.INVOICE(J) = AMOUNT.OF.INVOICE(J) - AMOUNT.AT.60.DAYS(J)
1590 AMOUNT.AT.60.DAYS = 0
1600 GOTO 1640
1610 AMOUNT.AT.60.DAYS(J) = (AMOUNT.AT.60.DAYS(J) - AMOUNT.OF.PAYMENT)
1620 AMOUNT.OF.PAYMENT = 0
1630 GOTO 1780
1640 IF AMOUNT.OF.PAYMENT < AMOUNT.AT.30.DAYS(J) THEN 1700
1650 AMOUNT.OF.PAYMENT = (AMOUNT.OF.PAYMENT - AMOUNT.AT.30.DAYS(J))
1660 A.R.ADJUSTMENT = A.R.ADJUSTMENT + AMOUNT.AT.30.DAYS(J)
1670 AMOUNT.OF.INVOICE(J) = AMOUNT.OF.INVOICE(J) - AMOUNT.AT.30.DAYS(J)
1680 AMOUNT.AT.30.DAYS = 0
1690 GOTO 1730
1700 AMOUNT.AT.30.DAYS(J) = (AMOUNT.AT.30.DAYS(J) - AMOUNT.OF.PAYMENT)
1710 AMOUNT.OF.PAYMENT = 0
1720 GOTO 1780
1730 IF AMOUNT.OF.PAYMENT < AMOUNT.LESS.THAN.30.DAYS(J) THEN BEEP:PRINT
        "AMOUNT OF PAYMENT INSUFFICIENT - REJECTED":GOTO 1880
1740 AMOUNT.OF.PAYMENT = (AMOUNT.OF.PAYMENT - AMOUNT.LESS.THAN.30.DAYS(J))
1750 A.R.ADJUSTMENT = A.R.ADJUSTMENT + AMOUNT.LESS.THAN.30.DAYS(J)
1760 AMOUNT.OF.INVOICE(J) = AMOUNT.OF.INVOICE(J) - AMOUNT.LESS.THAN.30.DAYS(J)
1770 AMOUNT.LESS.THAN.30.DAYS = 0
1780 RECAST.INVOICE.AMOUNT = 0
1790 RECAST.INVOICE.AMOUNT = (RECAST.INVOICE.AMOUNT + AMOUNT.AT.90.DAYS(J))
1800 RECAST.INVOICE.AMOUNT = (RECAST.INVOICE.AMOUNT + AMOUNT.AT.60.DAYS(J))
1810 RECAST.INVOICE.AMOUNT = (RECAST.INVOICE.AMOUNT + AMOUNT.AT.30.DAYS(J))
1820 RECAST.INVOICE.AMOUNT =
        (RECAST.INVOICE.AMOUNT + AMOUNT.LESS.THAN.30.DAYS(J))
1830 INVOICE.AMOUNT(J) = RECAST.INVOICE.AMOUNT
1840 INTEREST.ADJUSTMENT = TOTAL.AGEING - A.R.ADJUSTMENT
1850 PRINT "INTEREST.ADJUSTMENT: ";INTEREST.ADJUSTMENT
1860 PRINT "TOTAL AGEING: ";TOTAL.AGEING
1870 PRINT "A.R. ADJUSTMENT: ";A.R.ADJUSTMENT
1880 PRINT
1890 PRINT "ACCOUNT AFTER APPLYING PAYMENT"
1900 PRINT
1910 PRINT USING "  90 DAYS: ##,###.##";AMOUNT.AT.90.DAYS(J)
1920 PRINT USING "  60 DAYS: ##,###.##";AMOUNT.AT.60.DAYS(J)
1930 PRINT USING "  30 DAYS: ##,###.##";AMOUNT.AT.30.DAYS(J)
1940 PRINT USING "< 30 DAYS: ##,###.##";AMOUNT.LESS.THAN.30.DAYS(J)
1950 FOR Z = 1 TO 1500:NEXT Z
1960 RETURN
1970 AMOUNT.OF.PAYMENT = (AMOUNT.OF.PAYMENT - TOTAL.AGEING)
1980 A.R.ADJUSTMENT = A.R.ADJUSTMENT + TOTAL.AGEING
1990 INTEREST.RECEIVED = (TOTAL.AGEING - AMOUNT.OF.INVOICE(J))
2000 AMOUNT.AT.90.DAYS(J) = 0
2010 AMOUNT.AT.60.DAYS(J) = 0
2020 AMOUNT.AT.30.DAYS(J) = 0
2030 AMOUNT.LESS.THAN.30.DAYS(J) = 0
2040 AMOUNT.OF.INVOICE(J) = 0
2050 GOTO 1880
2060 '****************************************
2070 '* REVIEW ACCOUNTS BY CUSTOMER NUMBER *
2080 '****************************************
2090 GOSUB 4930
2100 PRINT "TO SEE ENTIRE FILE, ENTER FIRST CUSTOMER NUMBER AND MOVE FORWARD"
2110 PRINT:INPUT "ENTER THE CUSTOMER NUMBER: ",WHICH.CUSTOMER
2120 PRINT
2130 GOSUB 4750
2140 PRINT:PRINT "CORRECT (Y/N)? ";
2150 Z$ = INKEY$:IF Z$ = "" THEN 2150
2160 PRINT Z$
2170 IF Z$ = "Y" THEN 2240
2180 PRINT
2190 PRINT "DO YOU WISH TO REVIEW THE FILE (Y/N)? ";
2200 Z$ = INKEY$:IF Z$ = "" THEN 2200
```

```
2210 PRINT Z$
2220 IF Z$ = "Y" THEN 2240
2230 GOTO 2090
2240 PRINT
2250 PRINT "DO YOU WANT A HARD COPY (Y/N)? ";
2260 Z$ = INKEY$:IF Z$ = "" THEN 2260
2270 PRINT Z$
2280 PRINT
2290 IF Z$ = "Y" THEN HARDCOPY$ = "YES":GOTO 2310
2300 HARDCOPY$ = "NO"
2310 FOR I = 1 TO CUSTOMER.FILE.SIZE
2320     PRINT "CUSTOMER NUMBER:";TAB(20);I
2330     GOSUB 4750
2340     PRINT
2350     IF HARDCOPY$ = "NO" THEN 2390
2360     LPRINT "CUSTOMER NUMBER:";TAB(20);I
2370     GOSUB 4840
2380     LPRINT
2390     PRINT:PRINT "PRESS 'A' TO ACCEPT"
2400     PRINT "PRESS 'X' TO ESCAPE"
2410     PRINT "PRESS ANY OTHER KEY TO CONTINUE"
2420     PRINT
2430     Z$ = INKEY$:IF Z$ = "" THEN 2430
2440     IF Z$ = "A" THEN 2480
2450     IF Z$ = "X" THEN 2090
2460 NEXT I
2470 GOTO 2090
2480 PRINT
2490 PRINT:PRINT "NOTE THE ACCOUNT NUMBERS":PRINT
2500 FOR J = 1 TO RECEIVE.FILE.SIZE
2510     IF CUSTOMER.NUMBER(J) < > WHICH.CUSTOMER THEN 2880
2520     PRINT CUSTOMER.NUMBER(J),;
2530     PRINT CUSTOMER.NAME$(I)
2540     PRINT
2550     PRINT "DATE OF INVOICE: ";DATE.OF.INVOICE$(J),;
2560     PRINT "INVOICE NUMBER: ";DOCUMENT.NUMBER(J)
2570     PRINT
2580     PRINT "AMOUNT OF INVOICE:";TAB(40);
2590     PRINT USING "##,###.##";AMOUNT.OF.INVOICE(J)
2600     PRINT "ACCUMULATED INTEREST:";TAB(40);
2610     TOTAL.AGEING = 0
2620     TOTAL.AGEING = TOTAL.AGEING + AMOUNT.LESS.THAN.30.DAYS(J)
2630     TOTAL.AGEING = TOTAL.AGEING + AMOUNT.AT.30.DAYS(J)
2640     TOTAL.AGEING = TOTAL.AGEING + AMOUNT.AT.60.DAYS(J)
2650     TOTAL.AGEING = TOTAL.AGEING + AMOUNT.AT.90.DAYS(J)
2660     ACCUMULATED.INTEREST = TOTAL.AGEING - AMOUNT.OF.INVOICE(J)
2670     PRINT USING "##,###.##";ACCUMULATED.INTEREST
2680     PRINT
2690     PRINT "TOTAL DUE:";TAB(38);
2700     PRINT USING "$$##,###.##";TOTAL.AGEING
2710     PRINT STRING$(79,"-")
2720     PRINT "PRESS ANY KEY TO CONTINUE"
2730     Z$ = INKEY$:IF Z$ = "" THEN 2730
2740     IF HARDCOPY$ = "NO" THEN 2880
2750     LPRINT CUSTOMER.NUMBER(J),;
2760     LPRINT CUSTOMER.NAME$(I)
2770     LPRINT
2780     LPRINT "DATE OF INVOICE: ";DATE.OF.INVOICE$(J),;
2790     LPRINT "INVOICE NUMBER: ";DOCUMENT.NUMBER(J)
2800     LPRINT "AMOUNT OF INVOICE:";TAB(30);
2810     LPRINT USING "##,###.##";AMOUNT.OF.INVOICE(J)
2820     LPRINT "ACCUMULATED INTEREST:";TAB(30);
2830     LPRINT USING "##,###.##";ACCUMULATED.INTEREST
2840     LPRINT
2850     LPRINT "TOTAL DUE:";TAB(28);
2860     LPRINT USING "$$##,###.##";ACCUMULATED.INTEREST
2870     LPRINT STRING$(79,"-")
2880 NEXT J
2890 RETURN
```

```
2900 '****************************************
2910 '* REVIEW ACCOUNTS BY INVOICE NUMBER *
2920 '****************************************
2930 GOSUB 4930
2940 PRINT:INPUT "ENTER THE INVOICE NUMBER: ",WHICH.INVOICE
2950 PRINT
2960 FOR J = 1 TO RECEIVE.FILE.SIZE
2970     IF DOCUMENT.NUMBER(J) = WHICH.INVOICE THEN 3020
2980 NEXT J
2990 PRINT "THE INVOICE NUMBER DOES NOT EXIST"
3000 FOR Z = 1 TO 1000:NEXT Z
3010 GOTO 680
3020 WHICH.CUSTOMER = CUSTOMER.NUMBER(J)
3030 PRINT "CUSTOMER: ";CUSTOMER.NUMBER(J)
3040 GOSUB 4750
3050'PRINT
3060 PRINT "DATE OF INVOICE: ";DATE.OF.INVOICE$(J),;
3070 PRINT "INVOICE NUMBER: ";DOCUMENT.NUMBER(J)
3080 PRINT:PRINT "AMOUNT OF INVOICE:";TAB(40);
3090 PRINT USING "##,###.##";AMOUNT.OF.INVOICE(J)
3100 PRINT "ACCUMULATED INTEREST:";TAB(40);
3110 TOTAL.AGEING = 0
3120 TOTAL.AGEING = TOTAL.AGEING + AMOUNT.LESS.THAN.30.DAYS(J)
3130 TOTAL.AGEING = TOTAL.AGEING + AMOUNT.AT.30.DAYS(J)
3140 TOTAL.AGEING = TOTAL.AGEING + AMOUNT.AT.60.DAYS(J)
3150 TOTAL.AGEING = TOTAL.AGEING + AMOUNT.AT.90.DAYS(J)
3160 ACCUMULATED.INTEREST = TOTAL.AGEING - AMOUNT.OF.INVOICE(J)
3170 PRINT USING "##,###.##";ACCUMULATED.INTEREST
3180 PRINT
3190 PRINT "TOTAL DUE:";TAB(38);
3200 PRINT USING "$$###,###.##";TOTAL.AGEING
3210 PRINT STRING$(79,"-")
3220 PRINT "PRESS ANY KEY TO CONTINUE"
3230 Z$ = INKEY$:IF Z$ = "" THEN 3230
3240 RETURN
3250 '********************************************************************
3260 '* ROUTINE TO POST THE ACCOUNT FILE, REWRITE THE RECEIVABLES FILE *
3270 '********************************************************************
3280 FOR J = 1 TO CHART.FILE.SIZE
3290     IF T$(J) = "A,ACCOUNTS RECEIVABLE" THEN 3350
3300 NEXT J
3310 PRINT "NO ACCOUNTS RECEIVABLE ENTRY TO CHART FILE - BEING ADDED"
3320 CHART.FILE.SIZE = J
3330 ACCOUNT.FILE.SIZE = J
3340 T$(J) = "A,ACCOUNTS RECEIVABLE"
3350 A(J) = A.R.ADJUSTMENT
3360 FOR J = 1 TO CHART.FILE.SIZE
3370     IF T$(J) = "A,CASH" THEN 3430
3380 NEXT J
3390 PRINT "NO ACCOUNTS RECEIVABLE ENTRY TO CHART FILE - BEING ADDED"
3400 CHART.FILE.SIZE = J
3410 ACCOUNT.FILE.SIZE = J
3420 T$(J) = "A,CASH"
3430 A(J) = CASH.ADJUSTMENT
3440 FOR J = 1 TO CHART.FILE.SIZE
3450     IF T$(J) = "I,INTEREST INCOME" THEN 3480
3460 NEXT J
3470 CHART.FILE.SIZE = J
3480 ACCOUNT.FILE.SIZE = J
3490 T$(J) = "I,INTEREST INCOME"
3500 A(J) = INTEREST.ADJUSTMENT
3510 GOSUB 4420                        'REWRITE CHART FILE
3520 GOSUB 4640                        'REWRITE ACCOUNT FILE
3530 GOSUB 3850                        'REWRITE RECEIVABLE FILE
3540 CHAIN "A:RECIVBLE.BAS"
3550 '*********************************************************
3560 '* ROUTINE TO OPEN AND INPUT THE RECEIVABLES FILE *
3570 '*********************************************************
3580 PRINT:PRINT "LOADING THE RECEIVABLES FILE"
```

```
3590 OPEN "I",1,"RECEIVE.DAT"
3600 INPUT #1,RECEIVE.FILE.SIZE          'OBTAIN THE RECORD COUNT
3610 FOR I = 1 TO RECEIVE.FILE.SIZE
3620     INPUT #1,CUSTOMER.NUMBER(I)
3630     LINE INPUT #1,DATE.OF.INVOICE$(I)
3640     INPUT #1,DOCUMENT.NUMBER(I)
3650     INPUT #1,ITEM.1.NUMBER(I)
3660     INPUT #1,ITEM.1.QTY(I)
3670     INPUT #1,ITEM.1.UNIT.PRICE(I)
3680     INPUT #1,ITEM.2.NUMBER(I)
3690     INPUT #1,ITEM.2.QTY(I)
3700     INPUT #1,ITEM.2.UNIT.PRICE(I)
3710     INPUT #1,ITEM.3.NUMBER(I)
3720     INPUT #1,ITEM.3.QTY(I)
3730     INPUT #1,ITEM.3.UNIT.PRICE(I)
3740     INPUT #1,ITEM.4.NUMBER(I)
3750     INPUT #1,ITEM.4.QTY(I)
3760     INPUT #1,ITEM.4.UNIT.PRICE(I)
3770     INPUT #1,AMOUNT.OF.INVOICE(I)
3780     INPUT #1,AMOUNT.LESS.THAN.30.DAYS(I)
3790     INPUT #1,AMOUNT.AT.30.DAYS(I)
3800     INPUT #1,AMOUNT.AT.60.DAYS(I)
3810     INPUT #1,AMOUNT.AT.90.DAYS(I)
3820 NEXT I
3830 CLOSE 1
3840 RETURN
3850 '************************************************************
3860 '* ROUTINE TO OPEN AND OUTPUT THE RECEIVABLES FILE *
3870 '************************************************************
3880 PRINT:PRINT "WRITING THE RECEIVABLES FILE"
3890 OPEN "O",1,"RECEIVE.DAT"
3900 PRINT #1,CUSTOMER.FILE.SIZE          'WRITE THE RECORD COUNT
3910 FOR I = 1 TO RECEIVE.FILE.SIZE
3920     PRINT #1,CUSTOMER.NUMBER(I)
3930     PRINT #1,DATE.OF.INVOICE$(I)
3940     PRINT #1,DOCUMENT.NUMBER(I)
3950     PRINT #1,ITEM.1.NUMBER(I)
3960     PRINT #1,ITEM.1.QTY(I)
3970     PRINT #1,ITEM.1.UNIT.PRICE(I)
3980     PRINT #1,ITEM.2.NUMBER(I)
3990     PRINT #1,ITEM.2.QTY(I)
4000     PRINT #1,ITEM.2.UNIT.PRICE(I)
4010     PRINT #1,ITEM.3.NUMBER(I)
4020     PRINT #1,ITEM.3.QTY(I)
4030     PRINT #1,ITEM.3.UNIT.PRICE(I)
4040     PRINT #1,ITEM.4.NUMBER(I)
4050     PRINT #1,ITEM.4.QTY(I)
4060     PRINT #1,ITEM.4.UNIT.PRICE(I)
4070     PRINT #1,AMOUNT.OF.INVOICE(I)
4080     PRINT #1,AMOUNT.LESS.THAN.30.DAYS(I)
4090     PRINT #1,AMOUNT.AT.30.DAYS(I)
4100     PRINT #1,AMOUNT.AT.60.DAYS(I)
4110     PRINT #1,AMOUNT.AT.90.DAYS(I)
4120 NEXT I
4130 CLOSE 1
4140 RETURN
4150 '**********************************
4160 '* OPEN AND INPUT CUSTOMER FILE *
4170 '**********************************
4180 PRINT:PRINT "LOADING THE CUSTOMER FILE"
4190 OPEN "I",1,"CUSTOMER.DAT"
4200 INPUT #1,CUSTOMER.FILE.SIZE          'OBTAIN THE RECORD COUNT
4210 FOR K = 1 TO CUSTOMER.FILE.SIZE
4220     LINE INPUT #1,CUSTOMER.NAME$(K)
4230     LINE INPUT #1,CUSTOMER.ADDR.1$(K)
4240     LINE INPUT #1,CUSTOMER.ADDR.2$(K)
4250     LINE INPUT #1,CUSTOMER.ADDR.3$(K)
4260     LINE INPUT #1,CUSTOMER.ADDR.4$(K)
4270     LINE INPUT #1,CUSTOMER.TERMS$(K)
```

```
4280 NEXT K
4290 CLOSE 1
4300 RETURN
4310 '****************************************
4320 '* OPEN AND INPUT CHART OF ACCOUNTS FILE *
4330 '****************************************
4340 PRINT:PRINT "LOADING THE CHART OF ACCOUNTS"
4350 OPEN "I",1,"CHART.DAT"
4360 INPUT #1,CHART.FILE.SIZE          'OBTAIN THE RECORD COUNT
4370 FOR J = 1 TO CHART.FILE.SIZE
4380     LINE INPUT #1,T$(J)
4390 NEXT J
4400 CLOSE 1
4410 RETURN
4420 '****************************************
4430 '* OPEN AND OUTPUT CHART OF ACCOUNTS FILE *
4440 '****************************************
4450 PRINT:PRINT "WRITING THE CHART OF ACCOUNTS"
4460 OPEN "O",1,"CHART.DAT"
4470 PRINT #1,CHART.FILE.SIZE          'WRITE THE RECORD COUNT
4480 FOR J = 1 TO CHART.FILE.SIZE
4490     PRINT #1,T$(J)
4500 NEXT J
4510 CLOSE 1
4520 RETURN
4530 '****************************************
4540 '* OPEN AND INPUT THE ACCOUNT FILE *
4550 '****************************************
4560 PRINT:PRINT "LOADING THE ACCOUNT FILE"
4570 OPEN "I",1,ACCOUNT.FILE$
4580 INPUT #1,ACCOUNT.FILE.SIZE
4590 FOR J = 1 TO ACCOUNT.FILE.SIZE
4600     INPUT #1,A(J)
4610 NEXT J
4620 CLOSE 1
4630 RETURN
4640 '****************************************
4650 '* OPEN AND OUTPUT THE ACCOUNT FILE *
4660 '****************************************
4670 PRINT:PRINT "WRITING THE ACCOUNT FILE"
4680 OPEN "O",1,ACCOUNT.FILE$
4690 PRINT #1,ACCOUNT.FILE.SIZE
4700 FOR J = 1 TO ACCOUNT.FILE.SIZE
4710     PRINT #1,A(J)
4720 NEXT J
4730 CLOSE 1
4740 RETURN
4750 '****************************************************************************
4760 '* THIS IS A ROUTINE USED MORE THAN ONCE TO DISPLAY THE CUSTOMER INFO *
4770 '****************************************************************************
4780 PRINT "CUSTOMER NAME:";TAB(25);CUSTOMER.NAME$(WHICH.CUSTOMER)
4790 PRINT "CUSTOMER ADDRESS:";TAB(25);CUSTOMER.ADDR.1$(WHICH.CUSTOMER)
4800 PRINT TAB(25);CUSTOMER.ADDR.2$(WHICH.CUSTOMER)
4810 PRINT TAB(25);CUSTOMER.ADDR.3$(WHICH.CUSTOMER)
4820 PRINT TAB(25);CUSTOMER.ADDR.4$(WHICH.CUSTOMER)
4830 RETURN
4840 '****************************************************************************
4850 '* THIS IS A ROUTINE USED MORE THAN ONCE TO PRINT THE CUSTOMER INFO *
4860 '****************************************************************************
4870 LPRINT "CUSTOMER NAME:";TAB(25);CUSTOMER.NAME$(WHICH.CUSTOMER)
4880 LPRINT "CUSTOMER ADDRESS:";TAB(25);CUSTOMER.ADDR.1$(WHICH.CUSTOMER)
4890 LPRINT TAB(25);CUSTOMER.ADDR.2$(WHICH.CUSTOMER)
4900 LPRINT TAB(25);CUSTOMER.ADDR.3$(WHICH.CUSTOMER)
4910 LPRINT TAB(25);CUSTOMER.ADDR.4$(WHICH.CUSTOMER)
4920 RETURN
4930 '********************************
4940 '* HEADING USED FOR THE DISPLAY *
4950 '********************************
4960 CLS
```

```
4970 X = ((80 - LEN(COMPANY.NAME$)) / 2)
4980 LOCATE 2,X
4990 PRINT COMPANY.NAME$
5000 PRINT STRING$(79,220):PRINT
5010 PRINT TAB(19);"ACCOUNTS RECEIVABLE PROCESSING PROGRAM"
5020 PRINT STRING$(79,220)
5030 RETURN
```

STATMENT.BAS

The production of a statement is not unlike the production of an invoice, but there are some significant differences:

1. It is usually done monthly or for some other fiscal period.
2. It will list *all* invoices that are current to that date.
3. It will list any accumulated interest (which is the difference between the total developed in the aging figures and the original amount of the invoice).
4. It will usually be run *after* account aging has been accomplished.

The statement that follows involves only one invoice, since only one was left on file at the time the statement was made. Note, however, that the aging has been accomplished (incremented by 1 1/2 percent) and that the invoice has developed $8.33 in interest.

```
                        S T A T E M E N T


CUSTOMER NAME:          SEARS
CUSTOMER ADDRESS:       SEARSLAND
                        100 LUNENBERG PARKWAY
                        LEOMINSTER,
                        MASSACHUSETTS 01377


 555         MAY 17, 1982         555.00

ACCUMULATED INTEREST:             $8.33


TOTAL DUE:                      $555.00

-----------------------------------------------------------------------
30 DAYS OR LESS      30 - 60 DAYS      60 - 90 DAYS      90 DAYS AND OVER
     $0.00              $563.33            $0.00              $0.00
-----------------------------------------------------------------------
```

A block diagram of the statement production is shown in Fig. 7-11. Using the input from the receivables file and from the customer file, this program will produce statements reflecting the balance status of the account. The invoices on which charges remain are presented, along with their respective balances. The differences in the aging charges and the amount of the invoice(s) reflect the accumulated interest charges.

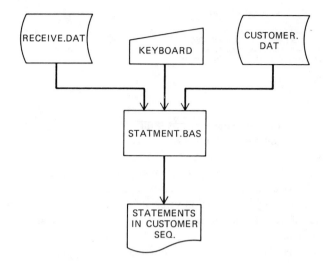

Fig. 7-11 Statement Production

```
10 '***********************************
20 '* DIMENSION THE RECEIVABLES FILE. *
30 '***********************************
40 DIM CUSTOMER.NUMBER(100)
50 DIM DATE.OF.INVOICE$(100)
60 DIM DOCUMENT.NUMBER(100)
70 DIM ITEM.1.NUMBER(100)
80 DIM ITEM.1.QTY(100)
90 DIM ITEM.1.UNIT.PRICE(100)
100 DIM ITEM.2.NUMBER(100)
110 DIM ITEM.2.QTY(100)
120 DIM ITEM.2.UNIT.PRICE(100)
130 DIM ITEM.3.NUMBER(100)
140 DIM ITEM.3.QTY(100)
150 DIM ITEM.3.UNIT.PRICE(100)
160 DIM ITEM.4.NUMBER(100)
170 DIM ITEM.4.QTY(100)
180 DIM ITEM.4.UNIT.PRICE(100)
190 DIM AMOUNT.OF.INVOICE(100)
200 DIM AMOUNT.LESS.THAN.30.DAYS(100)
210 DIM AMOUNT.AT.30.DAYS(100)
220 DIM AMOUNT.AT.60.DAYS(100)
230 DIM AMOUNT.AT.90.DAYS(100)
240 '********************************
250 '* DIMENSION THE CUSTOMER FILE. *
260 '********************************
270 DIM CUSTOMER.NAME$(100)
280 DIM CUSTOMER.ADDR.1$(100)
290 DIM CUSTOMER.ADDR.2$(100)
300 DIM CUSTOMER.ADDR.3$(100)
310 DIM CUSTOMER.ADDR.4$(100)
320 DIM CUSTOMER.TERMS$(100)
330 '**********************************
340 '* ROUTINE TO PRODUCE A STATEMENT *
350 '**********************************
360 COMMON COMPANY.NAME$
370 PRINT TAB(20);"S T A T E M E N T   P R E P A R A T I O N"
```

```
380 GOSUB 1500           'GET THE CUSTOMER FILE
390 GOSUB 1200           'GET THE RECEIVABLES FILE
400 FOR I = 1 TO CUSTOMER.FILE.SIZE
410     BYPASS$ = "OFF"
420     GOSUB 1840
430     STATEMENT.AMOUNT = 0
440     WHICH.CUSTOMER = I
450     PRINT:PRINT:LPRINT
460     FOR J = 1 TO RECEIVE.FILE.SIZE
470         IF CUSTOMER.NUMBER(J) < > I THEN 670
480         IF AMOUNT.OF.INVOICE(J) = 0 THEN 670
490         IF BYPASS$ = "ON" THEN 570
500         LPRINT TAB(30);"S T A T E M E N T"
510         LPRINT:LPRINT
520         GOSUB 1660        'DISPLAY NAME INFORMATION
530         GOSUB 1750        'PRINT NAME INFORMATION
540         LPRINT:LPRINT
550         PRINT:PRINT
560         BYPASS$ = "ON"
570         STATEMENT.AMOUNT = STATEMENT.AMOUNT + AMOUNT.OF.INVOICE(J)
580         PRINT DOCUMENT.NUMBER(J),DATE.OF.INVOICE$(J),;
590         PRINT USING "  ##,###.##";AMOUNT.OF.INVOICE(J)
600         LPRINT DOCUMENT.NUMBER(J),DATE.OF.INVOICE$(J),;
610         LPRINT USING "  ##,###.##";AMOUNT.OF.INVOICE(J)
620         AGEING.FIGURE = 0
630         AGEING.FIGURE = AGEING.FIGURE + AMOUNT.LESS.THAN.30.DAYS(J)
640         AGEING.FIGURE = AGEING.FIGURE + AMOUNT.AT.30.DAYS(J)
650         AGEING.FIGURE = AGEING.FIGURE + AMOUNT.AT.60.DAYS(J)
660         AGEING.FIGURE = AGEING.FIGURE + AMOUNT.AT.90.DAYS(J)
670     NEXT J
680     IF BYPASS$ = "OFF" THEN 1120
690     PRINT
700     ACCUMULATED.INTEREST = (AGEING.FIGURE - STATEMENT.AMOUNT)
710     PRINT "ACCUMULATED INTEREST: ",;
720     PRINT USING "$$##,###.##";ACCUMULATED.INTEREST
730     PRINT
740     LPRINT
750     LPRINT "ACCUMULATED INTEREST: ",;
760     LPRINT USING "$$##,###.##";ACCUMULATED.INTEREST
770     LPRINT
780     PRINT "TOTAL DUE:",,;
790     PRINT USING "$$##,###.##";STATEMENT.AMOUNT + ACCUMULATED.INTEREST
800     LPRINT
810     LPRINT "TOTAL DUE:",,;
820     LPRINT USING "$$##,###.##";STATEMENT.AMOUNT
830     PRINT
840     PRINT STRING$(79,"-")
850     PRINT "30 DAYS OR LESS";TAB(20);"30 - 60 DAYS";TAB(40);
860     PRINT "60 - 90 DAYS";TAB(60);"90 DAYS AND OVER"
870     PRINT USING "$$##,###.##";AMOUNT.LESS.THAN.30.DAYS(I);
880     PRINT TAB(18);"";
890     PRINT USING "$$##,###.##";AMOUNT.AT.30.DAYS(I);
900     PRINT TAB(38);"";
910     PRINT USING "$$##,###.##";AMOUNT.AT.60.DAYS(I);
920     PRINT TAB(60);"";
930     PRINT USING "$$##,###.##";AMOUNT.AT.90.DAYS(I)
940     PRINT STRING$(79,"-")
950     LPRINT
960     LPRINT STRING$(79,"-")
970     LPRINT "30 DAYS OR LESS";TAB(20);"30 - 60 DAYS";TAB(40);
980     LPRINT "60 - 90 DAYS";TAB(60);"90 DAYS AND OVER"
990     LPRINT USING "$$##,###.##";AMOUNT.LESS.THAN.30.DAYS(I);
1000    LPRINT TAB(18);"";
1010    LPRINT USING "$$##,###.##";AMOUNT.AT.30.DAYS(I);
1020    LPRINT TAB(38);"";
1030    LPRINT USING "$$##,###.##";AMOUNT.AT.60.DAYS(I);
1040    LPRINT TAB(60);"";
1050    LPRINT USING "$$##,###.##";AMOUNT.AT.90.DAYS(I)
1060    LPRINT STRING$(79,"-")
1070    IF J > 10 THEN 1090
1080    FOR N = 1 TO (10 - J):LPRINT:NEXT N       'TO PREVENT TIMEOUT
```

```
1090     LPRINT CHR$(12)
1100     PRINT STRING$(79,"-")
1110     GRAND.TOTAL = GRAND.TOTAL + STATEMENT.AMOUNT
1120 NEXT I
1130 FOR N = 1 TO 30:LPRINT:NEXT N          'THWART THE PRINTER TIMEOUT
1140 LPRINT CHR$(12)
1150 LPRINT "TOTAL VALUE OF STATEMENTS:",,;
1160 PRINT "TOTAL VALUE OF STATEMENTS:",,;
1170 PRINT USING "$$##,###.##";GRAND.TOTAL
1180 LPRINT USING "$$##,###.##";GRAND.TOTAL
1190 CHAIN "A:RECIVBLE.BAS"
1200 '*********************************
1210 '* OPEN AND INPUT RECEIVABLE FILE *
1220 '*********************************
1230 PRINT:PRINT "LOADING THE RECEIVABLES FILE"
1240 OPEN "I",1,"RECEIVE.DAT"
1250 INPUT #1,RECEIVE.FILE.SIZE        'OBTAIN THE RECORD COUNT
1260 FOR I = 1 TO RECEIVE.FILE.SIZE
1270     INPUT #1,CUSTOMER.NUMBER(I)
1280     LINE INPUT #1,DATE.OF.INVOICE$(I)
1290     INPUT #1,DOCUMENT.NUMBER(I)
1300     INPUT #1,ITEM.1.NUMBER(I)
1310     INPUT #1,ITEM.1.QTY(I)
1320     INPUT #1,ITEM.1.UNIT.PRICE(I)
1330     INPUT #1,ITEM.2.NUMBER(I)
1340     INPUT #1,ITEM.2.QTY(I)
1350     INPUT #1,ITEM.2.UNIT.PRICE(I)
1360     INPUT #1,ITEM.3.NUMBER(I)
1370     INPUT #1,ITEM.3.QTY(I)
1380     INPUT #1,ITEM.3.UNIT.PRICE(I)
1390     INPUT #1,ITEM.4.NUMBER(I)
1400     INPUT #1,ITEM.4.QTY(I)
1410     INPUT #1,ITEM.4.UNIT.PRICE(I)
1420     INPUT #1,AMOUNT.OF.INVOICE(I)
1430     INPUT #1,AMOUNT.LESS.THAN.30.DAYS(I)
1440     INPUT #1,AMOUNT.AT.30.DAYS(I)
1450     INPUT #1,AMOUNT.AT.60.DAYS(I)
1460     INPUT #1,AMOUNT.AT.90.DAYS(I)
1470 NEXT I
1480 CLOSE 1
1490 RETURN
1500 '*********************************
1510 '* OPEN AND INPUT CUSTOMER FILE *
1520 '*********************************
1530 PRINT:PRINT "LOADING THE CUSTOMER FILE"
1540 OPEN "I",1,"CUSTOMER.DAT"
1550 INPUT #1,CUSTOMER.FILE.SIZE        'OBTAIN THE RECORD COUNT
1560 FOR K = 1 TO CUSTOMER.FILE.SIZE
1570     LINE INPUT #1,CUSTOMER.NAME$(K)
1580     LINE INPUT #1,CUSTOMER.ADDR.1$(K)
1590     LINE INPUT #1,CUSTOMER.ADDR.2$(K)
1600     LINE INPUT #1,CUSTOMER.ADDR.3$(K)
1610     LINE INPUT #1,CUSTOMER.ADDR.4$(K)
1620     LINE INPUT #1,CUSTOMER.TERMS$(K)
1630 NEXT K
1640 CLOSE 1
1650 RETURN
1660 '*****************************************************************************
1670 '* THIS IS A ROUTINE USED MORE THAN ONCE TO DISPLAY THE CUSTOMER INFO *
1680 '*****************************************************************************
1690 PRINT "CUSTOMER NAME:";TAB(25);CUSTOMER.NAME$(WHICH.CUSTOMER)
1700 PRINT "CUSTOMER ADDRESS:";TAB(25);CUSTOMER.ADDR.1$(WHICH.CUSTOMER)
1710 PRINT TAB(25);CUSTOMER.ADDR.2$(WHICH.CUSTOMER)
1720 PRINT TAB(25);CUSTOMER.ADDR.3$(WHICH.CUSTOMER)
1730 PRINT TAB(25);CUSTOMER.ADDR.4$(WHICH.CUSTOMER)
1740 RETURN
1750 '*****************************************************************************
1760 '* THIS IS A ROUTINE USED MORE THAN ONCE TO PRINT THE CUSTOMER INFO *
1770 '*****************************************************************************
```

```
1780 LPRINT "CUSTOMER NAME:";TAB(25);CUSTOMER.NAME$(WHICH.CUSTOMER)
1790 LPRINT "CUSTOMER ADDRESS:";TAB(25);CUSTOMER.ADDR.1$(WHICH.CUSTOMER)
1800 LPRINT TAB(25);CUSTOMER.ADDR.2$(WHICH.CUSTOMER)
1810 LPRINT TAB(25);CUSTOMER.ADDR.3$(WHICH.CUSTOMER)
1820 LPRINT TAB(25);CUSTOMER.ADDR.4$(WHICH.CUSTOMER)
1830 RETURN
1840 '*********************************
1850 '* HEADING USED FOR THE DISPLAY *
1860 '*********************************
1870 CLS
1880 X = ((80 - LEN(COMPANY.NAME$)) / 2)
1890 LOCATE 2,X
1900 PRINT COMPANY.NAME$
1910 PRINT STRING$(79,220):PRINT
1920 PRINT TAB(19);"ACCOUNTS RECEIVABLE PROCESSING PROGRAM"
1930 PRINT STRING$(79,220)
1940 RETURN
```

AGEING.BAS

The employment of an accounts aging process is a recognition that time is money and that money tied up in receivables actually costs money. This program assigns the rate at 18 percent, or 0.015 percent per month.

There's an interesting thing about computers: Their precision will drive you wacky. You'll find that out sometime when you try subtracting one number from another only to find peculiarly unexpected results. What you usually end up with is a number followed by several decimal places. If you pass that number through an editing mask (##,###.##), you'll find that the thousandth's place has been rounded since the final result permits display of only two positions to the right of the decimal. Generally speaking, the number is rounded by 0.005. If a carry develops, it is reflected in the hundredth's position, and so on. What do you do, however, if you want the number to be rounded *in memory* rather than at display time. You merely add 0.005. Now, look at statement 410 in the program of this section, and you find that the rounding is done with + 5.000001E-03. Take my word: *That's 0.005!* If you enter just 0.005, you will end up with the number in scientific notation.

A block diagram of the accounts aging process is shown in Fig. 7-12. This program applies a consistent 1 1/2 percent interest to accounts that have been outstanding for more than 30 days. The basic theory is to apply the interest to the money in its age category rather than to reflect the new interest charge in current charges.

The approach the program takes is to add the interest in place. If, for example, money has been owing for more than 90 days, then the interested is added to the more-than-90-day category. Afficionados of larger systems will dispute this approach, but its rationale is as follows: To begin with, since the interest figure on the statement is derived from adding *all* aging categories and then subtracting the amount of the original invoice, it doesn't really matter where the interest is reflected insofar as the statement is concerned. Next, since the payment posting is done from the oldest first, it seems better that the

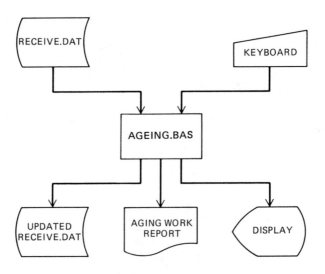

Fig. 7-12 Accounts Aging

oldest money should reflect its entire worth. This approach is not difficult to change.

A work list of accounts being aged is presented here. Because it is a work list, no editing has been done on the money fields other than rounding to position. It should be sufficient for your needs but can be easily modified if you'd like it to look prettier.

```
              A G E   T H E   A C C O U N T S

ACCOUNT #:  1
BEFORE:   555  AFTER:   563.33              INTEREST: 8.33
-------------------------------------------------------------------------

ACCOUNT #:  2
BEFORE:   814.79            AFTER:   827.01            INTEREST: 12.22
-------------------------------------------------------------------------

ACCOUNT #:  3
BEFORE:   494.19            AFTER:   501.6             INTEREST: 7.41
-------------------------------------------------------------------------

TOTAL INTEREST:   27.96
```

Here is the program AGEING.BAS, which completes the discussion of the accounts receivable subsystems:

```
10 '*********************************
20 '* DIMENSION THE RECEIVABLES FILE. *
30 '*********************************
40 DIM CUSTOMER.NUMBER(100)
50 DIM DATE.OF.INVOICE$(100)
60 DIM DOCUMENT.NUMBER(100)
```

```
70 DIM ITEM.1.NUMBER(100)
80 DIM ITEM.1.QTY(100)
90 DIM ITEM.1.UNIT.PRICE(100)
100 DIM ITEM.2.NUMBER(100)
110 DIM ITEM.2.QTY(100)
120 DIM ITEM.2.UNIT.PRICE(100)
130 DIM ITEM.3.NUMBER(100)
140 DIM ITEM.3.QTY(100)
150 DIM ITEM.3.UNIT.PRICE(100)
160 DIM ITEM.4.NUMBER(100)
170 DIM ITEM.4.QTY(100)
180 DIM ITEM.4.UNIT.PRICE(100)
190 DIM AMOUNT.OF.INVOICE(100)
200 DIM AMOUNT.LESS.THAN.30.DAYS(100)
210 DIM AMOUNT.AT.30.DAYS(100)
220 DIM AMOUNT.AT.60.DAYS(100)
230 DIM AMOUNT.AT.90.DAYS(100)
240 '*********************************
250 '* ROUTINE TO AGE THE RECEIVABLES *
260 '*********************************
270 COMMON COMPANY.NAME$
280 GOSUB 970            'GET THE HEADING
290 PRINT TAB(22);"A G E   T H E   A C C O U N T S"
300 LPRINT TAB(22);"A G E   T H E   A C C O U N T S"
310 LPRINT:LPRINT
320 GOSUB 670            'GET THE RECEIVABLES FILE
330 FOR J = 1 TO RECEIVE.FILE.SIZE
340    PRINT "ACCOUNT #: ";J
350    LPRINT "ACCOUNT #: ";J
360    BEFORE.AMOUNT = 0
370    BEFORE.AMOUNT = BEFORE.AMOUNT + AMOUNT.LESS.THAN.30.DAYS(J)
380    BEFORE.AMOUNT = BEFORE.AMOUNT + AMOUNT.AT.30.DAYS(J)
390    BEFORE.AMOUNT = BEFORE.AMOUNT + AMOUNT.AT.60.DAYS(J)
400    BEFORE.AMOUNT = BEFORE.AMOUNT + AMOUNT.AT.90.DAYS(J)
410    BEFORE.AMOUNT = (INT((BEFORE.AMOUNT + 5.000001E-03) * 100) / 100)
420    AMOUNT.AT.90.DAYS(J) = AMOUNT.AT.90.DAYS(J) + AMOUNT.AT.60.DAYS(J)
430    AMOUNT.AT.90.DAYS(J) = ((AMOUNT.AT.90.DAYS(J)) * 1.015)
440    AMOUNT.AT.60.DAYS(J) = ((AMOUNT.AT.30.DAYS(J)) * 1.015)
450    AMOUNT.AT.30.DAYS(J) = ((AMOUNT.LESS.THAN.30.DAYS(J)) * 1.015)
460    AMOUNT.LESS.THAN.30.DAYS(J) = 0
470    AFTER.AMOUNT = 0
480    AFTER.AMOUNT = AFTER.AMOUNT + AMOUNT.LESS.THAN.30.DAYS(J)
490    AFTER.AMOUNT = AFTER.AMOUNT + AMOUNT.AT.30.DAYS(J)
500    AFTER.AMOUNT = AFTER.AMOUNT + AMOUNT.AT.60.DAYS(J)
510    AFTER.AMOUNT = AFTER.AMOUNT + AMOUNT.AT.90.DAYS(J)
520    AFTER.AMOUNT = (INT((AFTER.AMOUNT + 5.000001E-03) * 100) / 100)
530    PRINT "BEFORE: ";BEFORE.AMOUNT,"AFTER: ";AFTER.AMOUNT,"INTEREST:";
              (INT(((AFTER.AMOUNT - BEFORE.AMOUNT) + 5.000001E-03) * 100) / 100)
540    LPRINT "BEFORE: ";BEFORE.AMOUNT,"AFTER: ";AFTER.AMOUNT,"INTEREST:";
              (INT(((AFTER.AMOUNT - BEFORE.AMOUNT) + 5.000001E-03) * 100) / 100)
550    TOTAL.INTEREST = TOTAL.INTEREST + (AFTER.AMOUNT - BEFORE.AMOUNT)
560    PRINT STRING$(79,"-")
570    LPRINT STRING$(79,"-")
580 NEXT J
590 PRINT
600 LPRINT
610 TOTAL.INTEREST = (INT((TOTAL.INTEREST + 5.000001E-03) * 100) / 100)
620 PRINT "TOTAL INTEREST: ";TOTAL.INTEREST
630 LPRINT "TOTAL INTEREST: ";TOTAL.INTEREST
640 LPRINT CHR$(12)
650 GOSUB 1080           'WRITE THE RECEIVABLES FILE
660 CHAIN "A:RECIVBLE.BAS"
670 '*********************************
680 '* OPEN AND INPUT RECEIVABLE FILE *
690 '*********************************
700 PRINT:PRINT "LOADING THE RECEIVABLES FILE"
710 OPEN "I",1,"RECEIVE.DAT"
720 INPUT #1,RECEIVE.FILE.SIZE      'OBTAIN THE RECORD COUNT
```

```
730 FOR I = 1 TO RECEIVE.FILE.SIZE
740      INPUT #1,CUSTOMER.NUMBER(I)
750      LINE INPUT #1,DATE.OF.INVOICE$(I)
760      INPUT #1,DOCUMENT.NUMBER(I)
770      INPUT #1,ITEM.1.NUMBER(I)
780      INPUT #1,ITEM.1.QTY(I)
790      INPUT #1,ITEM.1.UNIT.PRICE(I)
800      INPUT #1,ITEM.2.NUMBER(I)
810      INPUT #1,ITEM.2.QTY(I)
820      INPUT #1,ITEM.2.UNIT.PRICE(I)
830      INPUT #1,ITEM.3.NUMBER(I)
840      INPUT #1,ITEM.3.QTY(I)
850      INPUT #1,ITEM.3.UNIT.PRICE(I)
860      INPUT #1,ITEM.4.NUMBER(I)
870      INPUT #1,ITEM.4.QTY(I)
880      INPUT #1,ITEM.4.UNIT.PRICE(I)
890      INPUT #1,AMOUNT.OF.INVOICE(I)
900      INPUT #1,AMOUNT.LESS.THAN.30.DAYS(I)
910      INPUT #1,AMOUNT.AT.30.DAYS(I)
920      INPUT #1,AMOUNT.AT.60.DAYS(I)
930      INPUT #1,AMOUNT.AT.90.DAYS(I)
940 NEXT I
950 CLOSE 1
960 RETURN
970 '*********************************
980 '* HEADING USED FOR THE DISPLAY *
990 '*********************************
1000 CLS
1010 X = ((80 - LEN(COMPANY.NAME$)) / 2)
1020 LOCATE 2,X
1030 PRINT COMPANY.NAME$
1040 PRINT STRING$(79,220):PRINT
1050 PRINT TAB(19);"ACCOUNTS RECEIVABLE PROCESSING PROGRAM"
1060 PRINT STRING$(79,220)
1070 RETURN
1080 '*************************************
1090 '* OPEN AND OUTPUT RECEIVABLE FILE *
1100 '*************************************
1110 PRINT:PRINT "WRITING THE RECEIVABLES FILE"
1120 OPEN "O",1,"RECEIVE.DAT"
1130 PRINT #1,RECEIVE.FILE.SIZE          'PRODUCE THE RECORD COUNT
1140 FOR I = 1 TO RECEIVE.FILE.SIZE
1150      PRINT #1,CUSTOMER.NUMBER(I)
1160      PRINT #1,DATE.OF.INVOICE$(I)
1170      PRINT #1,DOCUMENT.NUMBER(I)
1180      PRINT #1,ITEM.1.NUMBER(I)
1190      PRINT #1,ITEM.1.QTY(I)
1200      PRINT #1,ITEM.1.UNIT.PRICE(I)
1210      PRINT #1,ITEM.2.NUMBER(I)
1220      PRINT #1,ITEM.2.QTY(I)
1230      PRINT #1,ITEM.2.UNIT.PRICE(I)
1240      PRINT #1,ITEM.3.NUMBER(I)
1250      PRINT #1,ITEM.3.QTY(I)
1260      PRINT #1,ITEM.3.UNIT.PRICE(I)
1270      PRINT #1,ITEM.4.NUMBER(I)
1280      PRINT #1,ITEM.4.QTY(I)
1290      PRINT #1,ITEM.4.UNIT.PRICE(I)
1300      PRINT #1,AMOUNT.OF.INVOICE(I)
1310      PRINT #1,AMOUNT.LESS.THAN.30.DAYS(I)
1320      PRINT #1,AMOUNT.AT.30.DAYS(I)
1330      PRINT #1,AMOUNT.AT.60.DAYS(I)
1340      PRINT #1,AMOUNT.AT.90.DAYS(I)
1350 NEXT I
1360 CLOSE 1
1370 RETURN
```

PAYABLE.BAS

The next major element of the small business system is the Accounts Payable activity. As previously mentioned, this is not a true A/P activity, in that the purchases journal, what we call a checkbook, is not developed and maintained in the strictest sense of the concept. Also, the portion of the system that would produce checks is not installed although it could be very easily within this system. Instead, recognizing that the owner of a small business controls his cash very carefully, the program offers the following options:

```
              SMALL BUSINESS ENTERPRISE, INC.

              ACCOUNTS PAYABLE APPLICATIONS

THESE APPLICATIONS ARE CURRENTLY AVAILABLE:

              1.  POST CHECKS AND DEPOSITS TO FILE

              2.  DRAW A CURRENT BALANCE FROM THE FILE

              3.  MAINTAIN CHECK FILE

              4.  DISPLAY / PRINT CHECK FILE

              5.  BALANCE CHECKBOOK

              6.  EXIT THE PROGRAM
SELECT:
```

The first option is the posting of check or deposits. As the system is designed, only checks and deposits find their way onto the file, CHECK.DAT. Thus, the selection of the first menu option will produce the following:

```
              SMALL BUSINESS ENTERPRISE, INC.

              ACCOUNTS PAYABLE APPLICATIONS

WHICH DO YOU WISH TO POST?

              <C>HECKS

              <D>EPOSITS
SELECT:
```

For purposes of illustration, we'll walk through a deposit. The following screen indicates that the deposit selection has been made and that a deposit of $100 has been confirmed. The application is programmed to allow for the entry of a specific date and the entry of the current date if the ENTER key has been pressed. Internally, the file is marked DEPOSIT, the date, and the amount.

```
                    SMALL BUSINESS ENTERPRISE, INC.

▬▬▬▬▬▬▬▬▬▬▬▬▬▬▬▬▬▬▬▬▬▬▬▬▬▬▬▬▬▬▬▬▬▬▬▬▬▬▬▬▬▬▬▬▬▬▬▬▬▬▬▬▬

                    ACCOUNTS PAYABLE APPLICATIONS

▬▬▬▬▬▬▬▬▬▬▬▬▬▬▬▬▬▬▬▬▬▬▬▬▬▬▬▬▬▬▬▬▬▬▬▬▬▬▬▬▬▬▬▬▬▬▬▬▬▬▬▬▬

WHICH DO YOU WISH TO POST?

          <C>HECKS

          <D>EPOSITS

SELECT: DEPOSITS

ENTER AMOUNT OF DEPOSIT: $100

CORRECT (Y/N)? Y

IF TODAY'S DATE, JUST PRESS ENTER KEY

ENTER DATE OF THE DEPOSIT:
DATE USED: 05-21-1982

TERMINATE THE INPUT (Y/N)?
```

The posting of checks works the same way. This application is *not* tied to the vendor file, predominantly because it was felt that the small business should not be faced with having to put a vendor on the vendor file in order to be able to issue a check to that vendor. In larger systems, such an approach is mandatory. Since the small business is small, we have provided the proprietor with the capability of entering the name of the PAYEE individually.

The second option allows you to draw a balance on the basis of the deposits and checks in the file. On the assumption that you have entered all your deposits and posted the file with the checks you have written, this option should produce a figure that matches your checkbook. The display is as follows:

```
                    SMALL BUSINESS ENTERPRISE, INC.

▬▬▬▬▬▬▬▬▬▬▬▬▬▬▬▬▬▬▬▬▬▬▬▬▬▬▬▬▬▬▬▬▬▬▬▬▬▬▬▬▬▬▬▬▬▬▬▬▬▬▬▬▬

                    ACCOUNTS PAYABLE APPLICATIONS

▬▬▬▬▬▬▬▬▬▬▬▬▬▬▬▬▬▬▬▬▬▬▬▬▬▬▬▬▬▬▬▬▬▬▬▬▬▬▬▬▬▬▬▬▬▬▬▬▬▬▬▬▬

CHECKBOOK CURRENT BALANCE ACCORDING TO THE FILE

READING THE CHECK FILE

CHECKBOOK BALANCE IS:      $190.00

PRESS ANY KEY TO RETURN TO MENU
```

In a larger system the auditors would go wild over the lack of an audit trail on the checkbook, but since the small business person will be keeping a check register anyway, the third option allows for the maintenance and modification of the check file. When you select option 3, you'll see the following:

```
                    SMALL BUSINESS ENTERPRISE, INC.
███████████████████████████████████████████████████████████████████████

                    ACCOUNTS PAYABLE APPLICATIONS
███████████████████████████████████████████████████████████████████████

CHECK FILE MAINTENANCE

DEPOSITS ARE ONLY AVAILABLE BY RECORD NUMBER
CHECKS ARE AVAILABLE BY EITHER CHECK NUMBER OF RECORD NUMBER

WHICH WAY: RESPOND <R>ECORD, <C>HECK NUMBER, OR E<X>IT: R

WHICH RECORD NUMBER DO YOU WISH TO SEE? 1
```

During maintenance, you have the option to make changes either by record number or by check number. You must know the record number that contains the deposit if you wish to make any changes since deposits are not numbered. The relevant record number, if you do not know it, may be obtained with option 4, to be discussed subsequently.

If you do select by record number, this is what you'll see:

```
                    SMALL BUSINESS ENTERPRISE, INC.
███████████████████████████████████████████████████████████████████████

                    ACCOUNTS PAYABLE APPLICATIONS
███████████████████████████████████████████████████████████████████████

THIS IS THE REQUESTED RECORD:

RECORD NUMBER:                1
DEPOSIT/CHECK NUMBER:         DEPOSIT
DATE:                         05-20-1982
AMOUNT:                          $100.00

YOU MAY:          <D>ELETE THE ENTIRE RECORD
                  <C>HANGE THE CONTENTS OF THE RECORD VIA RE-ENTRY
                  <R>ETURN TO THIS SECTION'S MENU
SELECT:
```

You can select a specific check for examination as follows:

```
                    SMALL BUSINESS ENTERPRISE, INC.
███████████████████████████████████████████████████████████████████████

                    ACCOUNTS PAYABLE APPLICATIONS
███████████████████████████████████████████████████████████████████████

CHECK FILE MAINTENANCE

DEPOSITS ARE ONLY AVAILABLE BY RECORD NUMBER
CHECKS ARE AVAILABLE BY EITHER CHECK NUMBER OF RECORD NUMBER

WHICH WAY: RESPOND <R>ECORD, <C>HECK NUMBER, OR E<X>IT: C

WHICH CHECK NUMBER DO YOU WISH TO SEE? 101
```

The displayed check will look as follows:

```
                    SMALL BUSINESS ENTERPRISE, INC.
███████████████████████████████████████████████████████████████████████

                    ACCOUNTS PAYABLE APPLICATIONS
███████████████████████████████████████████████████████████████████████

THIS IS THE REQUESTED RECORD:

RECORD NUMBER:              2
DEPOSIT/CHECK NUMBER:       101
DATE:                      05-20-1982
AMOUNT:                       $10.00

YOU MAY:         <D>ELETE THE ENTIRE RECORD
                 <C>HANGE THE CONTENTS OF THE RECORD VIA RE-ENTRY
                 <R>ETURN TO THIS SECTION'S MENU
SELECT:
```

The fourth option will produce a display/printout of the file in record number sequence. The program has purposely left off the name of the PAYEE because it was felt that manual records would be more than sufficient to provide the detail needed. It would not be difficult to modify the program to provide this data, as well, since it is already a part of the file.

```
                    SMALL BUSINESS ENTERPRISE, INC.
███████████████████████████████████████████████████████████████████████

                    ACCOUNTS PAYABLE APPLICATIONS
███████████████████████████████████████████████████████████████████████

DISPLAY / PRINT THE CHECK FILE

READING THE CHECK FILE

DO YOU WISH HARD COPY (Y/N)? N

RECORD NUMBER:              1
DEPOSIT/CHECK NUMBER       DEPOSIT
DATE:                      05-20-1982
DEPOSIT/CHECK AMOUNT:         $100.00
```

The fifth and final option is the checkbook reconciliation. In this reconciliation, you must first post the checks that have been returned. You do so by check number until you have posted the last check, after which you press "X" and thus enter the reconciliation phase. You are now asked for any credit memoranda, any debit memoranda, and the service charges. If there is a record without a proper code, you will be notified that there is a type problem. This particular message is shown in the following illustration, as the fourth record in the file is a null record, one used for end-of-file after RETURNED checks have been compressed:

```
ENTER 'X' WHEN YOU HAVE COMPLETED

ENTER CHECK NUMBER: X

ENTER THE TOTAL AMOUNT OF ANY CREDIT MEMO'S: 1.23

ENTER THE TOTAL AMOUNT OF ANY DEBIT MEMO'S: 2.34

ENTER SERVICE CHARGES: 2.00

WRITING THE CHECK FILE

RECORD 4  HAS A TYPE PROBLEM

CHECKBOOK BALANCE IS:              $190.00
PLUS CREDIT MEMO'S:                   1.23
LESS DEBIT MEMO'S:                   -2.34
LESS SERVICE CHARGES:               -2.00
RECONCILIATION:                    $186.89

YOUR CHECKBOOK TOTAL SHOULD MATCH THIS FIGURE

PRESS ANY KEY TO RESUME
```

Here is the program PAYABLE.BAS:

```
10 DIM CHECK.NUMBER$(1000)
20 DIM CHECK.PAYEE$(1000)
30 DIM CHECK.DATE$(1000)
40 DIM CHECK.AMOUNT(1000)
50 GOSUB 3900
60 PRINT
70 PRINT "THESE APPLICATIONS ARE CURRENTLY AVAILABLE:"
80 PRINT
90 PRINT TAB(15);"1.  POST CHECKS AND DEPOSITS TO FILE"
100 PRINT
110 PRINT TAB(15);"2.  DRAW A CURRENT BALANCE FROM THE FILE"
120 PRINT
130 PRINT TAB(15);"3.  MAINTAIN CHECK FILE"
140 PRINT
150 PRINT TAB(15);"4.  DISPLAY / PRINT CHECK FILE"
160 PRINT
170 PRINT TAB(15);"5.  BALANCE CHECKBOOK"
180 PRINT
190 PRINT TAB(15);"6.  EXIT THE PROGRAM"
200 PRINT
210 PRINT "SELECT: ";
220 Z$ = INKEY$:IF Z$ = "" THEN 220
230 IF Z$ = "1" THEN A = 1:PRINT "POST CHECKS AND DEPOSITS TO FILE":GOTO 310
240 IF Z$ = "2" THEN A = 2:PRINT "DRAW A CURRENT BALANCE":GOTO 310
250 IF Z$ = "3" THEN A = 3:PRINT "MAINTAIN CHECK FILE":GOTO 310
260 IF Z$ = "4" THEN A = 4:PRINT "DISPLAY / PRINT CHECK FILE":GOTO 310
270 IF Z$ = "5" THEN A = 5:PRINT "BALANCE CHECKBOOK":GOTO 310
280 IF Z$ = "6" THEN 3770
290 BEEP
300 GOTO 50
310 GOSUB 4400
320 ON A GOSUB 340,1710,1920,2710,3030,3770
330 GOTO 50
340 '********************************************************************
350 '* ROUTINE TO DEVELOP A FILE OF CHECKS WRITTEN *
360 '*********************************************************
370 GOSUB 3900
380 PRINT
```

```
390 PRINT "IS THIS THE FIRST TIME THE FILE HAS BEEN BUILT (Y/N)? ";
400 Z$ = INKEY$:IF Z$ = "" THEN 400
410 PRINT Z$
420 IF Z$ < > "Y" THEN 890
430 '*******************
440 '* FIRST BUILDING *
450 '*******************
460 FOR I = 1 TO 1000
470     GOSUB 3900
480     PRINT:PRINT "WHICH DO YOU WISH TO POST?":PRINT
490     PRINT TAB(15);"<C>HECKS":PRINT
500     PRINT TAB(15);"<D>EPOSITS":PRINT
510     PRINT "SELECT: ";
520     Z$ = INKEY$:IF Z$ = "" THEN 520
530     PRINT Z$;
540     IF Z$ = "C" THEN PRINT "HECKS":GOSUB 4400:GOTO 680
550     IF Z$ = "D" THEN PRINT "EPOSITS"
560     IF Z$ < > "D" THEN BEEP:GOTO 470
570     GOSUB 1590
580     IF SUBROUTINE.ERROR$ = "YES" THEN SUBROUTINE.ERROR$ = "NO":GOTO 470
590     IF Z$ < > "Y" THEN 470
600     PRINT:PRINT "IF TODAY'S DATE, JUST PRESS ENTER KEY":PRINT
610     LINE INPUT "ENTER DATE OF THE DEPOSIT: ";DEPOSIT.DATE$
620     IF DEPOSIT.DATE$ = "" THEN DEPOSIT.DATE$ = DATE$
630     PRINT "DATE USED: ";DEPOSIT.DATE$
640     GOSUB 4400
650     CHECK.DATE$(I) = DEPOSIT.DATE$
660     GOTO 800
670 '*******************
680     GOSUB 1260                    'OBTAIN THE CHECK NUMBER
690     CHECK.FILE.SIZE = I
700     TEMPORARY.CHECK.NUMBER$ = "C" + CHECK.NUMBER.ENTERED$
710     FOR J = 1 TO CHECK.FILE.SIZE
720         IF TEMPORARY.CHECK.NUMBER$ = CHECK.NUMBER$(J) THEN
                PRINT "THAT CHECK NUMBER IS ALREADY IN USE":GOSUB 4400:
                GOTO 680
730     NEXT J
740     GOSUB 1380                    'OBTAIN THE PAYEE, DATE, AND AMOUNT
750     IF SUBROUTINE.ERROR$ = "YES" THEN SUBROUTINE.ERROR$ = "NO":GOTO 470
760     CHECK.NUMBER$(I) = "C" + CHECK.NUMBER.ENTERED$
770     CHECK.PAYEE$(I) = PAYEE.ENTERED$
780     CHECK.DATE$(I) = DATE.ENTERED$
790     CHECK.AMOUNT(I) = AMOUNT.ENTERED
800     PRINT:PRINT "TERMINATE THE INPUT (Y/N)? ";
810     Z$ = INKEY$:IF Z$ = "" THEN 810
820     PRINT Z$
830     IF Z$ = "Y" THEN CHECK.FILE.SIZE = I:GOTO 860
840 NEXT I
850 CHECK.FILE.SIZE = I - 1
860 GOSUB 4260                        'WRITE THE CHECK FILE
870 RETURN
880 '*******************
890 GOSUB 4010                        'READ THE CHECK FILE
900 GOSUB 3900
910 PRINT:PRINT "WHICH DO YOU WISH TO POST?":PRINT
920 PRINT TAB(15);"<C>HECKS":PRINT
930 PRINT TAB(15);"<D>EPOSITS":PRINT
940 PRINT "SELECT: ";
950 Z$ = INKEY$:IF Z$ = "" THEN 950
960 PRINT Z$;
970 IF Z$ = "C" THEN PRINT "HECKS":GOSUB 4400:GOTO 1100
980 IF Z$ = "D" THEN PRINT "EPOSITS"
990 IF Z$ < > "D" THEN BEEP:GOTO 900
1000     GOSUB 1590
1010     IF SUBROUTINE.ERROR$ = "YES" THEN SUBROUTINE.ERROR$ = "NO":GOTO 900
1020     IF Z$ < > "Y" THEN 900
1030     PRINT:PRINT "IF TODAY'S DATE, JUST PRESS ENTER KEY":PRINT
1040     LINE INPUT "ENTER DATE OF THE DEPOSIT: ";DEPOSIT.DATE$
1050     IF DEPOSIT.DATE$ = "" THEN DEPOSIT.DATE$ = DATE$
```

```
1060      PRINT "DATE USED: ";DEPOSIT.DATE$
1070      GOSUB 4400
1080      CHECK.DATE$(I) = DEPOSIT.DATE$
1090      GOTO 1200
1100 GOSUB 1260                        'OBTAIN THE CHECK NUMBER
1110 TEMPORARY.CHECK.NUMBER$ = "C" + CHECK.NUMBER.ENTERED$
1120 FOR I = 1 TO CHECK.FILE.SIZE
1130      IF TEMPORARY.CHECK.NUMBER$ = CHECK.NUMBER$(J) THEN
             PRINT "THAT CHECK NUMBER IS ALREADY IN USE":GOSUB 4400:
             GOTO 900
1140 NEXT I
1150 PRINT
1160 PRINT "THE CHECK CAN BE ENTERED"
1170 CHECK.FILE.SIZE = I
1180 GOSUB 1380                        'OBTAIN THE PAYEE, DATE, AND AMOUNT
1190 IF SUBROUTINE.ERROR$ = "YES" THEN SUBROUTINE.ERROR$ = "NO":GOTO 900
1200 PRINT:PRINT "TERMINATE THE INPUT (Y/N)? ";
1210 Z$ = INKEY$:IF Z$ = "" THEN 1210
1220 PRINT Z$
1230 IF Z$ = "Y" THEN CHECK.FILE.SIZE = I:GOSUB 4260:GOTO 1250
1240 GOTO 900
1250 RETURN
1260 '********************
1270 '* GET CHECK NUMBER *
1280 '********************
1290 GOSUB 3900
1300 PRINT
1310 LINE INPUT "ENTER THE CHECK NUMBER: ",CHECK.NUMBER.ENTERED$
1320 PRINT
1330 PRINT "CORRECT (Y/N)? ";
1340 Z$ = INKEY$:IF Z$ = "" THEN 1340
1350 PRINT Z$
1360 IF Z$ < > "Y" THEN SUBROUTINE.ERROR$ = "YES"
1370 RETURN
1380 '********************************
1390 '* GET PAYEE, DATE, AND AMOUNT *
1400 '********************************
1410 PRINT
1420 LINE INPUT "ENTER PAYEE: ";PAYEE.ENTERED$
1430 PRINT
1440 PRINT "FOR TODAY'S DATE SIMPLY PRESS ENTER KEY"
1450 PRINT
1460 LINE INPUT "ENTER DATE:   ";DATE.ENTERED$
1470 IF DATE.ENTERED$ = "" THEN DATE.ENTERED$ = DATE$
1480 PRINT "DATE USED: ";DATE.ENTERED$
1490 PRINT
1500 INPUT "ENTER AMOUNT: $",AMOUNT.ENTERED
1510 PRINT
1520 PRINT "CORRECT (Y/N)? ";
1530 Z$ = INKEY$:IF Z$ = "" THEN 1530
1540 PRINT Z$
1550 IF Z$ = "Y" THEN 1580
1560 BEEP
1570 SUBROUTINE.ERROR$ = "YES"
1580 RETURN
1590 '*****************************
1600 '* GET DEPOSIT INFORMATION *
1610 '*****************************
1620 PRINT:INPUT "ENTER AMOUNT OF DEPOSIT: $",AMOUNT.OF.DEPOSIT
1630 PRINT:PRINT "CORRECT (Y/N)? ";
1640 Z$ = INKEY$:IF Z$ = "" THEN 1640
1650 PRINT Z$
1660 IF Z$ < > "Y" THEN SUBROUTINE.ERROR$ = "YES":GOTO 1700
1670 CHECK.NUMBER$(I) = "D"
1680 CHECK.PAYEE$(I) = ""
1690 CHECK.AMOUNT(I) = AMOUNT.OF.DEPOSIT
1700 RETURN
1710 '*******************************************************************************
1720 '* ROUTINE TO CALCULATE THE CURRENT BALANCE OF THE CHECKBOOK *
```

```
1730 '***************************************************************
1740 GOSUB 3900
1750 PRINT:PRINT "CHECKBOOK CURRENT BALANCE ACCORDING TO THE FILE"
1760 GOSUB 4010              'READ THE CHECK FILE
1770 CHECKS = 0:DEPOSITS = 0
1780 FOR I = 1 TO CHECK.FILE.SIZE
1790     IF LEFT$(CHECK.NUMBER$(I),1) = "C" THEN 1880
1800     IF LEFT$(CHECK.NUMBER$(I),1) = "D" THEN 1900
1810     PRINT:PRINT "RECORD";I;" HAS A TYPE PROBLEM"
1820 NEXT I
1830 PRINT:PRINT "CHECKBOOK BALANCE IS: ";
1840 PRINT USING "$$##,###.##";(DEPOSITS - CHECKS)
1850 PRINT:PRINT "PRESS ANY KEY TO RETURN TO MENU"
1860 Z$ = INKEY$:IF Z$ = "" THEN 1860
1870 RETURN
1880 CHECKS = CHECKS + CHECK.AMOUNT(I)
1890 GOTO 1820
1900 DEPOSITS = DEPOSITS + CHECK.AMOUNT(I)
1910 GOTO 1820
1920 '*****************************************
1930 '* ROUTINE TO MAINTAIN THE CHECK FILE *
1940 '*****************************************
1950 GOSUB 4010              'READ THE CHECK FILE
1960 GOSUB 3900
1970 PRINT:PRINT "CHECK FILE MAINTENANCE"
1980 PRINT:PRINT "DEPOSITS ARE ONLY AVAILABLE BY RECORD NUMBER"
1990 PRINT "CHECKS ARE AVAILABLE BY EITHER CHECK NUMBER OF RECORD NUMBER"
2000 PRINT:PRINT "WHICH WAY: RESPOND <R>ECORD, <C>HECK NUMBER, OR E<X>IT: ";
2010 Z$ = INKEY$:IF Z$ = "" THEN 2010
2020 PRINT Z$
2030 IF Z$ = "X" THEN 2590
2040 IF Z$ = "C" THEN 2080
2050 IF Z$ < > "R" THEN 1960
2060 PRINT:PRINT:INPUT "WHICH RECORD NUMBER DO YOU WISH TO SEE? ",I
2070 GOTO 2170
2080 PRINT:PRINT:INPUT "WHICH CHECK NUMBER DO YOU WISH TO SEE? ",WHICH.CHECK$
2090 WHICH.CHECK$ = "C" + WHICH.CHECK$
2100 FOR I = 1 TO CHECK.FILE.SIZE
2110     IF CHECK.NUMBER$(I) = WHICH.CHECK$ THEN 2170
2120 NEXT I
2130 PRINT:PRINT "THE REQUESTED CHECK IS NOT IN THE FILE"
2140 GOSUB 4400
2150 RETURN
2160 '********************
2170 GOSUB 3900
2180 PRINT:PRINT "THIS IS THE REQUESTED RECORD:"
2190 PRINT:PRINT "RECORD NUMBER: ";TAB(30);I
2200 PRINT "DEPOSIT/CHECK NUMBER:";TAB(30);
2210 IF CHECK.NUMBER$(I) = "DELETED" THEN PRINT "DELETED":GOTO 2240
2220 IF LEFT$(CHECK.NUMBER$(I),1) = "D" THEN PRINT "DEPOSIT"
2230 IF LEFT$(CHECK.NUMBER$(I),1) = "C" THEN PRINT
             RIGHT$(CHECK.NUMBER$(I),(LEN(CHECK.NUMBER$(I)) - 1))
2240 PRINT "DATE: ";TAB(30);CHECK.DATE$(I)
2250 PRINT "AMOUNT:";TAB(30);
2260 PRINT USING "$$##,###.##";CHECK.AMOUNT(I)
2270 PRINT:PRINT "YOU MAY:";TAB(20);"<D>ELETE THE ENTIRE RECORD"
2280 PRINT TAB(20);"<C>HANGE THE CONTENTS OF THE RECORD VIA RE-ENTRY"
2290 PRINT TAB(20);"<R>ETURN TO THIS SECTION'S MENU"
2300 PRINT"SELECT: ";
2310 Z$ = INKEY$:IF Z$ = "" THEN 2310
2320 IF Z$ = "R" THEN 1960
2330 IF Z$ = "D" THEN PRINT "DELETE":GOSUB 4400:GOTO 2530
2340 IF Z$ < > "C" THEN 1960
2350 PRINT "CHANGE"
2360 IF LEFT$(CHECK.NUMBER$(I),1) = "C" THEN 2440
2370 GOSUB 1590
2380 IF SUBROUTINE.ERROR$ < > "YES" THEN 1960
2390 SUBROUTINE.ERROR$ = "NO"
2400 BEEP:PRINT "RE-ENTER"
```

```
2410 GOSUB 4400
2420 GOTO 1960
2430 '********************
2440 GOSUB 1260
2450 GOSUB 1380
2460 IF SUBROUTINE.ERROR$ = "YES" THEN SUBROUTINE.ERROR$ = "NO":GOTO 1960
2470 CHECK.NUMBER$(I) = CHECK.NUMBER.ENTERED$
2480 CHECK.PAYEE$(I) = PAYEE.ENTERED$
2490 CHECK.DATE$(I) = DATE.ENTERED$
2500 CHECK.AMOUNT(I) = AMOUNT.ENTERED
2510 GOTO 1960
2520 '********************
2530 CHECK.NUMBER$(I) = "DELETED"
2540 CHECK.PAYEE$(I) = ""
2550 CHECK.DATE$(I) = ""
2560 CHECK.AMOUNT(I) = 0
2570 GOTO 1960
2580 '********************
2590 I = 1
2600 FOR J = 1 TO CHECK.FILE.SIZE
2610     IF CHECK.NUMBER$(J) = "DELETED" THEN 2670
2620     CHECK.NUMBER$(I) = CHECK.NUMBER$(J)
2630     CHECK.PAYEE$(I) = CHECK.PAYEE$(J)
2640     CHECK.DATE$(I) = CHECK.DATE$(J)
2650     CHECK.AMOUNT(I) = CHECK.AMOUNT(J)
2660     I = I + 1
2670 NEXT J
2680 CHECK.FILE.SIZE = I - 1
2690 GOSUB 4260                    'WRITE BACK THE COMPRESSED FILE
2700 RETURN
2710 '**********************************************
2720 '* ROUTINE TO DISPLAY / PRINT THE CHECK FILE *
2730 '**********************************************
2740 GOSUB 3900
2750 PRINT:PRINT "DISPLAY / PRINT THE CHECK FILE"
2760 GOSUB 4010             'READ THE CHECK FILE
2770 PRINT:PRINT "DO YOU WISH HARD COPY (Y/N)? ";
2780 Z$ = INKEY$:IF Z$ = "" THEN 2780
2790 PRINT Z$
2800 IF Z$ = "Y" THEN HARDCOPY$ = "YES":GOTO 2820
2810 HARDCOPY$ = "NO"
2820 FOR I = 1 TO CHECK.FILE.SIZE
2830     PRINT:PRINT "RECORD NUMBER: ";TAB(30);I
2840     PRINT "DEPOSIT/CHECK NUMBER";TAB(30);
2850     IF LEFT$(CHECK.NUMBER$(I),1) = "D" THEN PRINT "DEPOSIT"
2860     IF LEFT$(CHECK.NUMBER$(I),1) = "C"
             THEN PRINT RIGHT$(CHECK.NUMBER$(I),(LEN(CHECK.NUMBER$(I)) - 1))
2870     PRINT "DATE: ";TAB(30);CHECK.DATE$(I)
2880     PRINT "DEPOSIT/CHECK AMOUNT:";TAB(30)
2890     PRINT USING "$$##,###.##";CHECK.AMOUNT(I)
2900     IF HARDCOPY$ = "YES" THEN 2950
2910         GOSUB 4400
2920 NEXT I
2930 IF HARDCOPY$ = "YES" THEN LPRINT CHR$(12)
2940 RETURN
2950     LPRINT:LPRINT "RECORD NUMBER: ";TAB(30);I
2960     LPRINT "DEPOSIT/CHECK NUMBER";TAB(30);
2970     IF LEFT$(CHECK.NUMBER$(I),1) = "D" THEN LPRINT "DEPOSIT"
2980     IF LEFT$(CHECK.NUMBER$(I),1) = "C"
             THEN LPRINT RIGHT$(CHECK.NUMBER$(I),(LEN(CHECK.NUMBER$(I)) - 1))
2990     LPRINT "DATE: ";TAB(30);CHECK.DATE$(I)
3000     LPRINT "DEPOSIT/CHECK AMOUNT:";TAB(30)
3010     LPRINT USING "$$##,###.##";CHECK.AMOUNT(I)
3020         GOTO 2920
3030 '*************************************
3040 '* ROUTINE TO BALANCE THE CHECKBOOK *
3050 '*************************************
3060 GOSUB 3900
3070 PRINT:PRINT "HAVE YOU ENTERED ALL CHECKS WRITTEN AND DEPOSITS (Y/N)? ";
```

```
3080 Z$ = INKEY$:IF Z$ = "" THEN 3080
3090 PRINT Z$
3100 IF Z$ < > "Y" THEN PRINT "THAT MUST BE DONE FIRST":GOSUB 4400:RETURN
3110 GOSUB 3900
3120 GOSUB 4010                    'READ THE CHECK FILE
3130 PRINT:PRINT TAB(15);"C H E C K B O O K    R E C O N C I L I A T I O N"
3140 PRINT:PRINT "ENTER THE CHECKS YOU GOT BACK WITH YOUR STATEMENT"
3150 PRINT "ENTER 'X' WHEN YOU HAVE COMPLETED"
3160 PRINT:INPUT "ENTER CHECK NUMBER: ",RETURNED.CHECK.NUMBER$
3170 IF RETURNED.CHECK.NUMBER$ = "X" THEN 3300
3180 RETURNED.CHECK.NUMBER$ = "C" + RETURNED.CHECK.NUMBER$
3190 FOR I = 1 TO CHECK.FILE.SIZE
3200     IF RETURNED.CHECK.NUMBER$ = CHECK.NUMBER$(I) THEN 3260
3210 NEXT I
3220 PRINT "THAT CHECK IS NOT IN THE FILE - SET IT ASIDE"
3230 PRINT "IT MUST BE ENTERED AND THE RECONCILIATION REPEATED - CONTINUE";
3240 PRINT "TO POST CHECKS"
3250 GOTO 3140
3260 CHECK.NUMBER$(I) = "RETURNED " + CHECK.NUMBER$(I)
3270 PRINT "CHECK FOUND AND REMOVED"
3280 GOTO 3140
3290 '********************
3300 I = 1
3310 FOR J = 1 TO CHECK.FILE.SIZE
3320     IF CHECK.NUMBER$(J) = "DELETE" THEN 3390
3330     IF LEFT$(CHECK.NUMBER$(J),8) = "RETURNED" THEN 3390
3340     CHECK.NUMBER$(I) = CHECK.NUMBER$(J)
3350     CHECK.PAYEE$(I) = CHECK.PAYEE$(J)
3360     CHECK.DATE$(I) = CHECK.DATE$(J)
3370     CHECK.AMOUNT(I) = CHECK.AMOUNT(J)
3380     I = I + 1
3390 NEXT J
3400 CHECK.FILE.SIZE = I
3410 CHECKS = 0:DEPOSITS = 0
3420 PRINT:INPUT "ENTER THE TOTAL AMOUNT OF ANY CREDIT MEMO'S: ",CREDIT.MEMO
3430 PRINT:INPUT "ENTER THE TOTAL AMOUNT OF ANY DEBIT MEMO'S: ",DEBIT.MEMO
3440 PRINT:INPUT "ENTER SERVICE CHARGES: ",SERVICE.CHARGE
3450 GOSUB 4260                    'WRITE THE CHECK FILE
3460 FOR I = 1 TO CHECK.FILE.SIZE
3470     IF LEFT$(CHECK.NUMBER$(I),1) = "C" THEN 3540
3480     IF LEFT$(CHECK.NUMBER$(I),1) = "D" THEN 3560
3490     PRINT:PRINT "RECORD";I;" HAS A TYPE PROBLEM"
3500 NEXT I
3510 PRINT:PRINT "CHECKBOOK BALANCE IS: ";TAB(30);
3520 PRINT USING "$$###,###.##";(DEPOSITS - CHECKS)
3530 GOTO 3580
3540 CHECKS = CHECKS + CHECK.AMOUNT(I)
3550 GOTO 3500
3560 DEPOSITS = DEPOSITS + CHECK.AMOUNT(I)
3570 GOTO 3500
3580 PRINT "PLUS CREDIT MEMO'S:";TAB(32);
3590 PRINT USING "##,###.##";CREDIT.MEMO
3600 DEBIT.MEMO = (DEBIT.MEMO * -1)
3610 PRINT "LESS DEBIT MEMO'S:";TAB(32);
3620 PRINT USING "##,###.##";DEBIT.MEMO
3630 SERVICE.CHARGE = (SERVICE.CHARGE * -1)
3640 PRINT "LESS SERVICE CHARGES:";TAB(32);
3650 PRINT USING "##,###.##";SERVICE.CHARGE
3660 PRINT "RECONCILIATION:";TAB(30);
3670 RECONCILIATION = 0
3680 RECONCILIATION = RECONCILIATION + (DEPOSITS - CHECKS)
3690 RECONCILIATION = RECONCILIATION + CREDIT.MEMO
3700 RECONCILIATION = RECONCILIATION + DEBIT.MEMO
3710 RECONCILIATION = RECONCILIATION + SERVICE.CHARGE
3720 PRINT USING "$$###,###.##";RECONCILIATION
3730 PRINT:PRINT "YOUR CHECKBOOK TOTAL SHOULD MATCH THIS FIGURE"
3740 PRINT:PRINT "PRESS ANY KEY TO RESUME"
3750 Z$ = INKEY$:IF Z$ = "" THEN 3750
3760 RETURN
```

```
3770 '************************
3780 '* PROGRAM TERMINATION *
3790 '************************
3800 PRINT "DO YOU WISH TO REPEAT THE PROGRAM (Y/N)? ";
3810 Z$ = INKEY$:IF Z$ = "" THEN 3810
3820 PRINT Z$
3830 IF Z$ < > "Y" THEN 3890
3840 ERASE CHECK.NUMBER$
3850 ERASE CHECK.PAYEE$
3860 ERASE CHECK.DATE$
3870 ERASE CHECK.AMOUNT
3880 GOTO 10
3890 CHAIN "A:BUSINESS.BAS"
3900 '*********************************
3910 '* HEADING USED FOR THE DISPLAY *
3920 '*********************************
3930 CLS
3940 X = ((80 - LEN(COMPANY.NAME$)) / 2)
3950 LOCATE 2,X
3960 PRINT COMPANY.NAME$
3970 PRINT STRING$(79,220):PRINT
3980 PRINT TAB(25);"ACCOUNTS PAYABLE APPLICATIONS"
3990 PRINT STRING$(79,220)
4000 RETURN
4010 '*******************************
4020 '* OPEN AND INPUT CHECK FILE *
4030 '*******************************
4040 OPEN "I",1,"CHECK.DAT"
4050 PRINT:PRINT "READING THE CHECK FILE"
4060 INPUT #1,CHECK.FILE.SIZE      'OBTAIN THE RECORD COUNT
4070 '**********************************************************************
4080 '* THE DIMENSIONING IS ESTABLISHED ON THE BASIS OF THE FIRST RECORD *
4090 '**********************************************************************
4100 ERASE CHECK.NUMBER$
4110 ERASE CHECK.PAYEE$
4120 ERASE CHECK.DATE$
4130 ERASE CHECK.AMOUNT
4140 DIM CHECK.NUMBER$(CHECK.FILE.SIZE + 1000)
4150 DIM CHECK.PAYEE$(CHECK.FILE.SIZE + 1000)
4160 DIM CHECK.DATE$(CHECK.FILE.SIZE + 1000)
4170 DIM CHECK.AMOUNT(CHECK.FILE.SIZE + 1000)
4180 FOR I = 1 TO CHECK.FILE.SIZE
4190     LINE INPUT #1,CHECK.NUMBER$(I)
4200     LINE INPUT #1,CHECK.PAYEE$(I)
4210     LINE INPUT #1,CHECK.DATE$(I)
4220     INPUT #1,CHECK.AMOUNT(I)
4230 NEXT I
4240 CLOSE 1
4250 RETURN
4260 '*********************************
4270 '* OPEN AND OUTPUT CHECK FILE *
4280 '*********************************
4290 OPEN "O",1,"CHECK.DAT"
4300 PRINT:PRINT "WRITING THE CHECK FILE"
4310 PRINT #1,CHECK.FILE.SIZE      'PRODUCE THE RECORD COUNT
4320 FOR I = 1 TO CHECK.FILE.SIZE
4330     PRINT #1,CHECK.NUMBER$(I)
4340     PRINT #1,CHECK.PAYEE$(I)
4350     PRINT #1,CHECK.DATE$(I)
4360     PRINT #1,CHECK.AMOUNT(I)
4370 NEXT I
4380 CLOSE 1
4390 RETURN
4400 '***************
4410 '* TIMER LOOP *
4420 '***************
4430 FOR Z = 1 TO 1500:NEXT Z
4440 RETURN
```

INCOME.BAS

Recall that you had loaded figures (VALUE.BAS) for each income and each expense account established on the Chart of Accounts. Later, the receivables application ensured the existence of a Cash Account and an Interest Expense account. This particular income statement does not happen to reflect the interest expense, since it was drawn before the interest expense was posted, and the numbers have no specific relation to the figures that had gone before. But suffice it say that the data identified as INCOME and as EXPENSE is summarized in the following:

```
                    SMALL BUSINESS ENTERPRISE, INC.
                           INCOME STATEMENT
                        FOR PERIOD: MAY, 1982

  INCOME
        SALES INCOME            30,000.00
        RENTAL INCOME              473.00
        ROYALTY INCOME         20,000.00
                               ------------
  TOTAL INCOME                                     50,473.00

  EXPENSE
        RENT EXPENSE              600.00
        TELEPHONE EXPENSE         225.00
        TRAVEL EXPENSE            110.47
                               ------------
  TOTAL EXPENSE                                       935.47

                                                 ------------
  NET INCOME <LOSS>                              $49,537.53
                                                 ============
```

A block diagram of the preparation of the income statement is shown in Fig. 7-13. This program works with the Chart of Accounts (CHART.DAT) and with the Account File (*) for the period for which this income statement is to be drawn. The small business system is designed to deal with periods individually. If the system has to deal with an aggregate number of individual periods, it will be necessary to modify the program so that it can receive several independent inputs.

As you look at the program, you'll see that only those accounts whose codes are I or E are extracted from the selected account file. It's important to note that the program is structured to accept the Chart of Accounts (CHART.DAT) plus *one* account file, whose name you will specify in statement 120. Note also that the file counts for the two files are matched in statement 280 and that processing is halted if they do not match. Thus it becomes very important to ensure that the number of figures on the account file matches the number of accounts on the Chart file — and that means that you must set your accounts up properly in the first place — or you must be prepared to reload them when

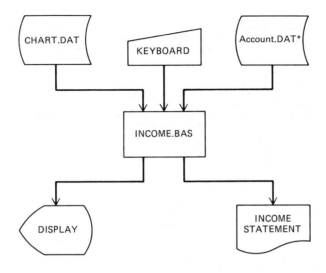

Fig. 7-13 Preparation of the Income Statement

the size of the file changes. Now, if it is your desire to consolidate data from several periods, you must incorporate the routines that will do so. Examine statements 330-360. It would be necessary to incorporate instructions for reading the specified number of files, beginning with INPUT #2. It should be remembered that there are three standard file buffer allocations (and more if needed), but that it's not necessary to use them if you'll remember to OPEN and CLOSE the files as they are used. Once you have begun the file load, it's a simple matter to go beyond the value of I. If you do *that*, however, you must make certain that the arrays are DIMensioned (statement 80) in a size large enough to accomodate everything to be entered.

Here is the program INCOME.BAS:

```
10 CLS
20 GOSUB 910
30 '*********************************************************************
40 '* T$ HOLDS THE ACCOUNT TYPE;  N$ HOLDS THE ACCOUNT NAME;  A HAS THE  *
50 '* BALANCE OF THE ACCOUNTS .  T1$ WILL HOLD IDENTIFIERS FOR INCOME AND *
60 '* AMD EXPENSES.                                                      *
70 '*********************************************************************
80 DIM T$(25),N$(25),A(25),T1$(2)
90 T1$(1) = "INCOME"
100 T1$(2) = "EXPENSE"
110 FILE.1$ = "CHART.DAT"
120 PRINT:INPUT "ENTER THE NAME OF THE ACCOUNT FILE (I'LL ADD .DAT): ",FILE.2$
130 FILE.2$ = FILE.2$ + ".DAT"
140 GOSUB 210               'OPEN AND READ THE FILES
150 GOSUB 380               'PREPARE THE STATEMENT
160 '*************************
170 '* PROGRAM TERMINATION *
180 '*************************
190 CLOSE 1,2
```

```
200 CHAIN "BUSINESS.BAS"
210 '***********************************************************************
220 '* OPEN AND READ THE TWO FILES (CHARTS AND THE SELECTED ACCOUNT FILE) *
230 '***********************************************************************
240 OPEN "I",1,FILE.1$
250 OPEN "I",2,FILE.2$
260 INPUT#1,FILE.1.COUNT
270 INPUT#2,FILE.2.COUNT
280 IF FILE.1.COUNT = FILE.2.COUNT THEN 330
290 PRINT "THE FILES DO NOT MATCH:"
300 PRINT TAB(5);FILE.1$;" RECORD COUNT IS: ";FILE.1.COUNT
310 PRINT TAB(5);FILE.2$;" RECORD COUNT IS: ";FILE.2.COUNT
320 GOTO 160
330 FOR I = 1 TO FILE.1.COUNT
340     INPUT#1,T$(I),N$(I)
350     INPUT#2,A(I)
360 NEXT I
370 RETURN
380 '********************************
390 '* PREPARE THE INCOME STATEMENT *
400 '********************************
410 '* REPORT HEADING *
420 '*****************
430 LINE INPUT "ENTER THE REPORT PERIOD: ",REPORT.PERIOD$
440 PRINT
450 PRINT "POSITION THE PAPER AND THEN PRESS ANY KEY"
460 Z$ = INKEY$:IF Z$ = "" THEN 460
470 X = ((80 - LEN(COMPANY.NAME$)) / 2)
480 LPRINT TAB(X);COMPANY.NAME$
490 INCOME.STATEMENT$ = "INCOME STATEMENT"
500 X = ((80 - LEN(INCOME.STATEMENT$)) / 2)
510 LPRINT TAB(X);INCOME.STATEMENT$
520 REPORT.PERIOD$ = "FOR PERIOD: " + REPORT.PERIOD$
530 X = ((80 - LEN(REPORT.PERIOD$)) / 2)
540 LPRINT TAB(X);REPORT.PERIOD$
550 LPRINT STRING$(79,220):PRINT
560 LPRINT:LPRINT
570 '********************************
580 FOR I = 1 TO FILE.1.COUNT
590     IF T$(I) = "I" THEN 630
600 NEXT I
610 PRINT:PRINT "THERE ARE NO INCOME ACCOUNTS ON THE FILE"
620 GOTO 190
630 SO.FAR = I
640 J = 1
650 LPRINT TAB(5);T1$(J)
660 FOR I = SO.FAR TO FILE.1.COUNT
670     IF (T$(I) = "E") AND (J = 1) THEN 720
680     LPRINT TAB(10);N$(I);TAB(40);
690     LPRINT USING "##,###.##";A(I)
700     CATEGORY.TOTAL = CATEGORY.TOTAL + A(I)
710 NEXT I
720 LPRINT TAB(36);"--------------"
730 LPRINT TAB(5);"TOTAL ";T1$(J);TAB(59);
740 LPRINT USING "##,###.##";CATEGORY.TOTAL
750 LPRINT
760 IF J = 1 THEN NET.INCOME = NET.INCOME + CATEGORY.TOTAL
770 IF J = 2 THEN NET.INCOME = NET.INCOME - CATEGORY.TOTAL
780 J = J + 1
790 CATEGORY.TOTAL = 0
800 SO.FAR = I
810 IF J < = 2 THEN 650
820 LPRINT TAB(55);"--------------"
830 IF NET.INCOME > 0 THEN LPRINT TAB(5);"NET INCOME <LOSS>";TAB(57);
840 IF NET.INCOME > 0 THEN LPRINT USING "$$###,###.##";NET.INCOME
850 IF NET.INCOME < 0 THEN LPRINT TAB(5);"NET INCOME <LOSS>";TAB(61);"<";
860 IF NET.INCOME < 0 THEN LPRINT USING "$$###,###.##";NET.INCOME;">"
870 IF NET.INCOME = 0 THEN LPRINT TAB(5);"NET INCOME <LOSS>;TAB(61);"- 0 -"
880 LPRINT TAB(55);"=============="
```

```
890 LPRINT CHR$(12)
900 RETURN
910 '*********************************
920 '* HEADING USED FOR THE DISPLAY *
930 '*********************************
940 CLS
950 X = ((80 - LEN(COMPANY.NAME$)) / 2)
960 LOCATE 2,X
970 PRINT COMPANY.NAME$
980 PRINT STRING$(79,220):PRINT
990 PRINT TAB(26);"INCOME STATEMENT PREPARATION"
1000 PRINT STRING$(79,220)
1010 RETURN
```

BALANCE.BAS

Like the Income Statement, the Balance Sheet program surveys the Chart of Accounts and account period files, extracting the data necessary for the report. Many of the very same remarks made about the Income Statement apply here, especially as they relate to the handling of multiple files. The Balance Sheet is as follows:

```
                  SMALL BUSINESS ENTERPRISE, INC.
                         BALANCE.SHEET
                       AS OF: MAY 31, 1982
```

```
                              ASSETS


ASSETS
      CASH                      101.23
      ACCOUNTS RECEIVABLE     1,000.47
      EQUIPMENT                 200.00
      PREPAID INSURANCE        400.00
      ROLLING STOCK          4,000.00
                             ----------------
TOTAL ASSETS                                    5,701.70
                                                ================


                    LIABILITIES AND CAPITAL

LIABILITIES
      ACCOUNTS PAYABLE          637.34
      NOTES PAYABLE           1,245.78
                             ----------------
TOTAL LIABILITIES                               1,883.12


CAPITAL
      NET INCOME/LOSS(-)      3,608.70
      SBE DRAW                 209.88
                             ----------------
TOTAL CAPITAL                                   3,818.58


                                                ----------------
TOTAL LIABILITIES AND CAPITAL                   5,701.70
                                                ================
```

A block diagram for the preparation of the Balance Sheet is shown in Fig. 7-14. This program works with the Chart of Accounts (CHART.DAT) and with the

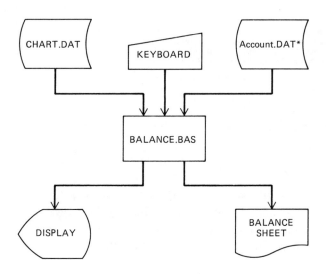

Fig. 7-14 Preparation of the Balance Sheet

Account File (*) for the period for which the Balance Sheet is to be drawn. The small business system is designed to deal with periods individually. If the system has to deal with an aggregate number of individual periods, it will be necessary to modify the program so that it can receive several independent inputs.

It should be mentioned that no tie was designed to effect a transition from the Income Statement to the Balance Sheet, even though the net income or loss is a required input. That procedure could be done easily enough by writing a one-record file in the Income Statement program and reading it in the present application. Because it would mean yet another file, however, and so small a file at that, it was felt that the single number required to satisfy the inquiry could just as easily be given from the keyboard. Otherwise, the approach to producing a Balance Sheet is precisely the same as that used for the Income Statement.

Here is the program BALANCE.BAS:

```
10 CLS
20 GOSUB 1020
30 '*******************************************************************************
40 '* T$ HOLDS THE ACCOUNT TYPE;   N$ HOLDS THE ACCOUNT NAME;   A HAS THE     *
50 '* BALANCE OF THE ACCOUNTS .   T1$ WILL HOLD IDENTIFIERS FOR BALANCE -     *
60 '* SHEET HEADINGS.                                                         *
70 '*******************************************************************************
80 DIM T$(25),N$(25),A(25),T1$(3)
90 T1$(1) = "ASSETS"
100 T1$(2) = "LIABILITIES"
```

```
110 T1$(3) = "CAPITAL"
120 FILE.1$ = "CHART.DAT"
130 PRINT:INPUT "ENTER THE NAME OF THE ACCOUNT FILE (I'LL ADD .DAT): ",FILE.2$
140 FILE.2$ = FILE.2$ + ".DAT"
150 PRINT:INPUT "ENTER THE NET INCOME OR LOSS (-) FOR THE PERIOD: ",NET.INCOME
160 GOSUB 230                'OPEN AND READ THE FILES
170 GOSUB 400                'PREPARE THE STATEMENT
180 '************************
190 '* PROGRAM TERMINATION *
200 '************************
210 CLOSE 1,2
220 CHAIN "BUSINESS.BAS"
230 '*****************************************************************************
240 '* OPEN AND READ THE TWO FILES (CHARTS AND THE SELECTED ACCOUNT FILE) *
250 '*****************************************************************************
260 OPEN "I",1,FILE.1$
270 OPEN "I",2,FILE.2$
280 INPUT#1,FILE.1.COUNT
290 INPUT#2,FILE.2.COUNT
300 IF FILE.1.COUNT = FILE.2.COUNT THEN 350
310 PRINT "THE FILES DO NOT MATCH:"
320 PRINT TAB(5);FILE.1$;" RECORD COUNT IS: ";FILE.1.COUNT
330 PRINT TAB(5);FILE.2$;" RECORD COUNT IS: ";FILE.2.COUNT
340 GOTO 180
350 FOR I = 1 TO FILE.1.COUNT
360      INPUT#1,T$(I),N$(I)
370      INPUT#2,A(I)
380 NEXT I
390 RETURN
400 '********************************
410 '* PREPARE THE BALANCE SHEET *
420 '********************************
430 '* REPORT HEADING *
440 '********************
450 PRINT:LINE INPUT "ENTER THE REPORT DATE: ",REPORT.DATE$
460 PRINT
470 PRINT "POSITION THE PAPER AND THEN PRESS ANY KEY"
480 Z$ = INKEY$:IF Z$ = "" THEN 480
490 X = ((80 - LEN(COMPANY.NAME$)) / 2)
500 LPRINT TAB(X);COMPANY.NAME$
510 BALANCE.SHEET$ = "BALANCE.SHEET"
520 X = ((80 - LEN(BALANCE.SHEET$)) / 2)
530 LPRINT TAB(X);BALANCE.SHEET$
540 REPORT.DATE$ = "AS OF: " + REPORT.DATE$
550 X = ((80 - LEN(REPORT.DATE$)) / 2)
560 LPRINT TAB(X);REPORT.DATE$
570 LPRINT STRING$(79,220):PRINT
580 LPRINT:LPRINT
590 '********************************
600 T = 50
610 SO.FAR = 1
620 T$(0) = T$(1)
630 FOR J = 1 TO 3
640      IF J = 1 THEN X = ((80 - LEN(T1$(1))) / 2)
650      IF J = 1 THEN LPRINT TAB(X);T1$(1)
660      IF J < > 2 THEN 720
670      T = 40
680      L.AND.C$ = "LIABILITIES AND CAPITAL"
690      X = ((80 - LEN(L.AND.C$)) / 2)
700      LPRINT TAB(X);L.AND.C$
710      LIABILITIES.AND.CAPITAL = 0
720      LPRINT
730      LPRINT TAB(5);T1$(J)
740      IF J < > 3 THEN 780
750      LPRINT TAB(10);"NET INCOME/LOSS(-)";TAB(T);
760      LPRINT USING "##,###.##";NET.INCOME
770      CATEGORY.TOTAL = CATEGORY.TOTAL + NET.INCOME
780      FOR I = SO.FAR TO FILE.1.COUNT
790           IF T$(I) < > T$(0) THEN 860
800           SUB.ITEM = A(I)
810           LPRINT TAB(10);N$(I);TAB(40);
```

```
820          LPRINT USING "##,###.##";SUB.ITEM
830          CATEGORY.TOTAL = CATEGORY.TOTAL + SUB.ITEM
840          SUB.ITEM = 0
850       NEXT I
860       LPRINT TAB(35);"----------------"
870       LPRINT TAB(5);"TOTAL ";T1$(J);TAB(55);
880       LPRINT USING "##,###.##";CATEGORY.TOTAL
890       IF J = 1 THEN LPRINT TAB(53);"================"
900       SO.FAR = I
910       LPRINT
920       LIABILITIES.AND.CAPITAL = LIABILITIES.AND.CAPITAL + CATEGORY
930       CATEGORY.TOTAL = 0
940       T$(0) = T$(I)
950  NEXT J
960  LPRINT TAB(53);"----------------"
970  LPRINT TAB(5);"TOTAL LIABILITIES AND CAPITAL";TAB(55);
980  LPRINT USING "##,###.##";LIABILITIES.AND.CAPITAL
990  LPRINT TAB(53);"================"
1000 LPRINT CHR$(12)
1010 RETURN
1020 '********************************
1030 '* HEADING USED FOR THE DISPLAY *
1040 '********************************
1050 CLS
1060 X = ((80 - LEN(COMPANY.NAME$)) / 2)
1070 LOCATE 2,X
1080 PRINT COMPANY.NAME$
1090 PRINT STRINGS$(79,220):PRINT
1100 PRINT TAB(28);"BALANCE SHEET PREPARATION"
1110 PRINT STRINGS$(79,220)
1120 RETURN
```

And that's it for the small business system. The system, remember, is a 64K system; only the Accounts Receivable program comes near that capacity and can be scaled back, if necessary, as previously discussed.

There is one thing you must learn about business applications. No matter how well tested they are, some combination of things will eventually occur and cause problems. Even the slightest change can cause unpredictable output. After the development of these applications, each was as exhaustively tested as the author could test them. They are useful applications, and although you may need to modify them to make them more appropriate for your specific needs, they will no doubt present a suitable place to start. Several hundred hours of keystroking are involved here. If you find problems needing correction and can offer a fix — or if you would like to obtain a copy of these applications on disk — write to the author at Winchendon, MA 01475, with details.

Epilogue

It would be unfair to bind up the book without some reference to Advanced BASIC and to color. Most of the features attributable to Advanced BASIC (BASICA) have been identified. Those which have not been are as follows:

PLAY These instructions have the capacity to play more complex music than we have developed in this book, including two-part harmony.

CIRCLE These instructions draw eliptical objects on the screen of a color monitor. Differences in shape can be achieved in accordance with what is known as *aspect* (the ratio of the width to the height of the screen) and by specifying the necessary formulae. CIRCLE may be used to contribute to the visual attractiveness of business data displays. Make reference to the PIECHART.BAS program that comes on your DOS disk.

PAINT This instruction is literally the brush with which you can color objects. The selection of colors is wide. If you are skilled in graphics, you will be able to present business data in a most palatable manner.

DRAW If you've ever played with the toy known as Etch-A-Sketch, you will have some idea how this command works. There are subinstructions for up, down, left, right, and diagonals.

GET
PUT Although these instructions are ordinarily used for random files, they can also be used as logical input/output instructions when the color screen is the source or the target. The reference manual refers to these instructions as *bit pumps*, and, indeed, they allow the skilled graphics programmer to indulge in such things as animation.

What has gone before is the result of three months of continual work. Throughout it all, there has been the joy of the hardware. It simply is a fine microcomputer — capable, reliable, rewarding, and a pleasure to use.

There were also a few frustrations — for example, the week spent on the game application that resisted attempt after attempt to make it work; it therefore wasn't meant to be included. And there was the intense anxiety when the book's largest application didn't seem to want to perform reliably. There was the recognition that it would have been nice to have the color features and the communications features to write about, but the publisher, in his wisdom, listened to the advice presented in this book and responded accordingly.

No warrantee is given that all the applications presented will work perfectly in every case. Since the intention of the book was not merely to offer complete applications, but also to walk you through the applications so that you could learn concepts as well, you should be more than up to creating many applications yourself — provided you have paid attention. You will still need the reference manuals, of course. If you don't, thanks for purchasing the book; it will keep part of your shelf from gathering dust. It's a book to use time and again, and we trust that you will do just that.

Most of what's in here is brand new. Some of it is an adaptation of other things the author has written; some of it is based upon things others have written. It is all, however, uniquely dovetailed to give you the best possible instruction.

We'll accept all suggestions for later inclusion. If you find an error we haven't found, we'd appreciate knowing about it. And if you decide that what's in here is useful but don't want to do all the work involved, we'll even sell you a disk with the programs on it. Just write for details.

Postscript

It has been said that a teacher ought to be one of his own best pupils. As a teacher by book, I became one of my own pupils after this manuscript was submitted.

Back in Chap. 3 we discussed the concept of an in-memory sort, concentrating upon a type of sort known as a *bubble sort*. Among all the available sorts, the bubble sort is the most easily explained. It can be clearly diagrammed, as well as programmed in any language with a minimum of effort. Furthermore, for systems without extensive input/output media, it can be most simply executed by the programmer himself. As mentioned in that chapter, however, the bubble sort tends to be slow.

I've been teaching the bubble sort for years — both in the classroom and in print — and have used it in many programs. But in both cases, it always involved only a small number of elements so that the amount of time required was relatively insignificant. If longer files of data were involved, I merely invoked a sort utility. On the larger machines, that's an easy thing to do, particularly when you have 50 million bytes of disk storage to work with.

Years ago, when it became necessary to index the second edition of the *CDP Review Manual*, the effort was staggering — requiring extensive hand writing upon file cards and their subsequent sorting and typing into a form usable by the publisher. No way was I going to do the same thing when it came time for the third edition to be indexed — this time I had an IBM PC. I proceeded to devise a system of data capture, maintenance, presentation, and organization that would eliminate all that drudgery. The sort module was duly written as an in-memory bubble sort. I extracted the letter "A" from my data disks and was off and running. *Fifty-three hours later*, the sort was complete. (The sort was begun at 5 P.M. one night and was not finished until two days and five hours later.) Then something happened and I couldn't get it written back to disk in the new sequence. I lost everything. Of itself, that wouldn't be astounding unless you were aware of the size of the file to be sorted on two fields: only 507 records. That amount of time was a bit much.

As a result, I did some digging and found an in-memory sort known as the *Shell-Metzner Sort*, which was reputed to be a bit faster. I should say so! The sort that had taken 53 hours to complete via the bubble route took 1 hour and 20 minutes with the Shell Sort. Obviously, you needed to be told about such a difference. That's what this postscript is all about.

I learned a few things about my PC and BASIC in the process. My machine is a 64K unit. That may seem like a lot of storage, but it fills up very rapidly when you load the available memory with 32-character records as I was doing. I learned that I could fit, at most, only slightly more than 800 records into the available memory. I could increase that figure somewhat by tightening up the program, removing comments, and so forth, but the additional capacity gained would be marginal. Since programming a multiple-disk input to a sort would be an extremely difficult task with limited media, it became necessary to find a way to break down my data into manageable portions. That took some planning, particularly when one of the alphabet letters exceeded the capacity of the sort *all by itself.*

Next, I learned something that I should have known before. It wasn't news that whenever you load a string variable, it occupies space in RAM. What was news was that it occupied *more* memory *with each loading* even though it was reduced to null after use. Thus, my 32-byte record occupied an additional 96 bytes for each iteration involving an exchange — first 96 bytes, then 192, then 288, 384, and so on — *without releasing the unused space.* The space was posted as being unused, but the available memory decreased in leaps and bounds, especially when the index entries were significantly out of order. The amount of time any sort will take is based on the condition of the initial file. A file already in sequence will require only the passing time. The most extreme case would be a file that is completely reversed. Anything in the middle requires a shorter amount of time, naturally, but the more out of sequence a file is, the more exchanges that will have to be made and the quicker the memory will be used up until there simply isn't any more available. At that time, the whole process comes to a screeching halt while BASIC cleans up its memory (the process can be enhanced I found, with one form of the FRE instruction, but not significantly). As soon as all the unused memory had been released, the sort would take off again.

By this logic, the smaller the input file is, the more memory that will be available before the cleanup process is required. I learned to sort smaller amounts of data whenever possible, and although the cleanup process took longer, there were fewer cleanups needed. We tend to think of a computer as a kind of magic that can do things quickly. Nevertheless, a file of 274 records still took 29 minutes to load and sort. I chose to include instructions to show available memory. Although displaying moving data on the screen took time and though the sort would certainly have worked faster had it not been, I wanted to see some of it while it was moving, simply as reassurance.

Enough general discussion. What follows is a "bare-bones" Shell-Metzner Sort. The basic approach is that the file is not examined in contiguous pairs — as is the case with the bubble sort — but rather in terms of halves of the file. The file is split in two, and those things that belong in the first (left) half are exchanged with those that belong in the second (right) half. Then each half is split into quarters — with the same process taking place within each new half — and then into eights and so forth. The work space continues to diminish until everything is in its proper sequence. This example assumes that you have already read from your disk file and stored the data in array A$. The process begins at this point, the variable LAST being the count of records. Variable M is used to develop the midpoint, and variable J is what we'll call the *left-pair, left-side marker.* Correspondingly, variable K is the *left-pair, right-side marker;* variable I is the *right-pair, left-side marker;* and variable L is the *right-pair, right-side marker.* If you can think of the left-side as being the first half of the array to be sorted and the right-side as being the second half, you should be able to figure the process out. The example follows:

```
10  '*****************************
20  '* THE ARRAY MUST BE LOADED  *
30  '* FROM DISK OR KEYBOARD TO  *
40  '* PREPARE FOR THIS ROUTINE  *
50  '*****************************
60  M = LAST
70  M = INT(M/2)
80  IF M = 0 THEN 300
90  J = 1:K = LAST - M
100 I = J
110 L = I + M
120 IF A$(I) < = A$(L) THEN 230
130 LOCATE 10,20:PRINT I,L,M,K
140 '*****************************
150 '* T$ IS A TEMPORARY HOLD    *
160 '* AREA.  OTHER VARIABLES    *
170 '* ARE EXPLAINED IN TEXT.    *
180 '*****************************
190 T$ = A$(I):A$(I) = A$(L):A$(L) = T$
200 I = I - M
210 IF I < 1 THEN 230
220 GOTO 110
230 J = J + 1
240 IF J > K THEN 70
250 GOTO 100
260 '*****************************
270 '* THE ARRAY IS NOW SORTED   *
280 '* AND IS READY TO BE USED.  *
290 '*****************************
300 ' INSTRUCTIONS BEGIN HERE
```

In my system, it was necessary to have two fields — one for the index entry and one for the page number. You will recall that on disk the data must be string data; it was therefore necessary to convert it. Furthermore, since the idea was to have the page number (minor sort) *within* the index entry (major sort), two uses of the Shell-Metzner Sort were required. Theoretically, sorting by page number first would ensure this result. Don't you believe it. It was supposed to do so, logically speaking, but computers are all too subject to Murphy's Laws. Thus, the second sort had to be modified to straighten out reversed sequences that I was never able to account for. Never mind; I now have something to work on for my next book. Here is the modified Shell-Metzner Sort in its entirety, and I can assure you that it works. One hour and 20 minutes instead of 53 hours shows an improvement of almost 4000 percent. It seemed more than worthwhile to add this postscript.

```
10 '**************
20 '* SRTIDX.BAS *
30 '**************
40 CLS
50 TIME$ = "00:00:00"
60 CLEAR 2000
70 KEY OFF
80 PRINT TAB(22);"I N D E X    S O R T I N G    P R O G R A M"
90 PRINT
100 PRINT "MOUNT DATA DISK IN DRIVE B - PRESS ANY KEY TO CONTINUE"
110 Z$ = INKEY$:IF Z$ = "" THEN 110
120 KEY OFF
130 CLS
140 '****************************
150 '* OPEN AND DEFINE THE FILE *
160 '****************************
170 OPEN "B:INDEX.DAT" AS #1 LEN = 32
180 FIELD #1,28 AS INDEX.ENTRY$,4 AS INDEX.PAGE$
190 FIELD #1,4 AS FLAG$,4 AS RECORD.COUNT$,24 AS SOMETHING.ELSE$
200 GET #1,1
210 PRINT "RECORD COUNT RECORD FLAG IS: ";CVI(FLAG$)
220 PRINT "NEXT RECORD NUMBER IS: ";CVI(RECORD.COUNT$)
230 PRINT "IDENTIFICATION IS: ";SOMETHING.ELSE$
240 HOLD.ID$ = SOMETHING.ELSE$
250 FOR Z = 1 TO 1000:NEXT Z
260 IF CVI(FLAG$) = 9999 THEN 280
270 PRINT "SOMETHING ISN'T RIGHT":END
280 NEXT.RECORD = CVI(RECORD.COUNT$)
290 PRINT
300 PRINT "HAVE YOU FLIPPED THE CAPITALS (Y/N)?"
310 Z$ = INKEY$:IF Z$ = "" THEN 310
320 IF Z$ = "Y" THEN 400
330 IF Z$ = "y" THEN 400
340 IF Z$ = "N" THEN 370
350 IF Z$ = "n" THEN 370
360 GOTO 310
370 PRINT "RETURNING TO MAIN MENU TO ALLOW YOU TO FLIP THE CAPITALS"
380 FOR Z = 1 TO 1000:NEXT Z
390 GOTO 1470
400 DIM TEXT.ENTRY$(NEXT.RECORD)
410 DIM TEXT.PAGE$(NEXT.RECORD)
420 '******************************
430 '* LOAD THE DISK FILE TO THE ARRAY *
440 '******************************
450 FOR I = 1 TO NEXT.RECORD-2
460     GET #1,I + 1
470     LOCATE 10,20:PRINT "READING RECORD: ";I
480     LOCATE 12,20:PRINT "    MEMORY FREE: ";FRE(0)
490     TEXT.ENTRY$(I) = INDEX.ENTRY$
500     TEXT.PAGE$(I) = INDEX.PAGE$
510 NEXT I
520 CLOSE
```

```
530 CLS
540 TEXT.ENTRY$(NEXT.RECORD) = STRING$(25,"Z")
550 TEXT.PAGE$(NEXT.RECORD) = STRING$(15,"Z")
560 '*******************************
570 '* EXCHANGE SORT ON THE ARRAY *
580 '*******************************
590 LOCATE 6,20:PRINT "SORTING BY PAGE NUMBER"
600 LAST = NEXT.RECORD -1
610 M = NEXT.RECORD -1
620 M = INT(M/2)
630 IF M = 0 THEN 860
640 J = 1:K = LAST - M
650 I = J
660 L = I + M
670 LOCATE 8,20:PRINT "MEMORY: ";FRE(0)
680 LOCATE 8,40:PRINT "LAPSED TIME: ";TIME$
690 LOCATE 10,20:PRINT I, L, M, K
700 LOCATE 12,20:PRINT VAL(TEXT.PAGE$(I)), VAL(TEXT.PAGE$(L)), "FILE LOCATION"
710 IF VAL(TEXT.PAGE$(I)) < = VAL(TEXT.PAGE$(L)) THEN 830
720 HOLD.PAGE$ = ""
730 HOLD.PAGE$ = TEXT.PAGE$(I):TEXT.PAGE$(I) = ""
740 TEXT.PAGE$(I) = TEXT.PAGE$(L):TEXT.PAGE$(L) = ""
750 TEXT.PAGE$(L) = HOLD.PAGE$
760 HOLD.ENTRY$ = ""
770 HOLD.ENTRY$ = TEXT.ENTRY$(I):TEXT.ENTRY$(I) = ""
780 TEXT.ENTRY$(I) = TEXT.ENTRY$(L):TEXT.ENTRY$(L) = ""
790 TEXT.ENTRY$(L) = HOLD.ENTRY$
800 I = I - M
810 IF I < 1 THEN 830
820 GOTO 660
830 J = J + 1
840 IF J > K THEN 620
850 GOTO 650
860 LOCATE 6,20:PRINT "SORTING BY INDEX ENTRY"
870 LAST = NEXT.RECORD -1
880 M = NEXT.RECORD -1
890 M = INT(M/2)
900 IF M = 0 THEN 1150
910 J = 1:K = LAST - M
920 I = J
930 L = I + M
940 LOCATE 8,20:PRINT "MEMORY: ";FRE(0)
950 LOCATE 8,40:PRINT "LAPSED TIME: ";TIME$
960 LOCATE 10,20:PRINT I, L, M, K
970 LOCATE 12,20:PRINT VAL(TEXT.PAGE$(I)), VAL(TEXT.PAGE$(L)), "FILE LOCATION"
980 IF TEXT.ENTRY$(I) > TEXT.ENTRY$(L) THEN 1010
990 IF TEXT.ENTRY$(I) < TEXT.ENTRY$(L) THEN 1120
1000 IF VAL(TEXT.PAGE$(I)) < = VAL(TEXT.PAGE$(L)) THEN 1120
1010 HOLD.PAGE$ = ""
1020 HOLD.PAGE$ = TEXT.PAGE$(I):TEXT.PAGE$(I) = ""
1030 TEXT.PAGE$(I) = TEXT.PAGE$(L):TEXT.PAGE$(L) = ""
1040 TEXT.PAGE$(L) = HOLD.PAGE$
1050 HOLD.ENTRY$ = ""
1060 HOLD.ENTRY$ = TEXT.ENTRY$(I):TEXT.ENTRY$(I) = ""
1070 TEXT.ENTRY$(I) = TEXT.ENTRY$(L):TEXT.ENTRY$(L) = ""
1080 TEXT.ENTRY$(L) = HOLD.ENTRY$
1090 I = I - M
1100 IF I < 1 THEN 1120
1110 GOTO 930
1120 J = J + 1
1130 IF J > K THEN 890
1140 GOTO 920
1150 '*********************
1160 '* SORT IS COMPLETE *
1170 '*********************
1180 CLS
1190 LOCATE 6,20
1200 PRINT "SORT IS COMPLETE - PREPARE DISKETTE TO RECEIVE NEW FILE";
1210 LOCATE 7,20
```

```
1220 PRINT "PRESS SPACE BAR WHEN READY";
1230 Z$ = INKEY$:IF Z$ = "" THEN 1230
1240 OPEN "B:INDEX.DAT" AS #1 LEN = 32
1250 FIELD #1,28 AS INDEX.ENTRY$,4 AS INDEX.PAGE$
1260 FIELD #1,4 AS FLAG$,4 AS RECORD.COUNT$,24 AS SOMETHING.ELSE$
1270 COUNT.FLAG = 9999
1280 LSET FLAG$ = MKI$(COUNT.FLAG)
1290 LSET RECORD.COUNT$ = MKI$(NEXT.RECORD)
1300 LSET SOMETHING.ELSE$ = HOLD.ID$
1310 PUT #1,1
1320 LOCATE 10,20
1330 PRINT "COUNT RECORD HAS BEEN LOADED - FILE LOAD FOLLOWS";
1340 LOCATE 14,20
1350 PRINT "LOADING RECORD: ";
1360 FOR I = 2 TO NEXT.RECORD
1370     LSET INDEX.ENTRY$ = TEXT.ENTRY$(I)
1380     LSET INDEX.PAGE$ = TEXT.PAGE$(I)
1390     PUT #1,I
1400     LOCATE 16,20
1410     PRINT TEXT.ENTRY$(I) + TEXT.PAGE$(I);
1420 NEXT I
1430 LOCATE 18,20
1440 PRINT "FILE LOAD COMPLETE";
1450 FOR Z = 1 TO 1000:NEXT Z
1460 CLOSE
1470 CHAIN "A:INDEX.BAS"
```

Index